Strategies of the Serengeti

Strategies of the Serengeti

Where Having the Right Strategy is a Matter of Life and Death

2nd edition

STEPHEN BERRY

a division of Neos Learning Limited

PUBLISHED BY
Neos Publishing: a division of Neos Learning Limited
2 Bulkeley Close, Englefield Green, Surrey, UK
www.neoslearning.com
www.stephenberry.com

© Stephen Berry 2010

The moral rights of the author have been asserted

ISBN 0–9553498–1–8
978–0–9553498–1–2

British Library Cataloguing in Publication Data
A catalogue record of this book is available from the British Library

Cover artist: Jeni Nash
Chapter artist: Stephen Mead

Typeset by Cambrian Typesetters
Camberley, Surrey
Printed and bound by MPG Books Group, UK

Acknowledgement and thanks

STEPHEN JARRETT – for starting the thought process with his zebra

STEVEN SONSINO – for giving me the kick to get started

PARTICK HARE (decd) – for his valuable insight into the habits of the dung beetle

IAN MASON – for organising the practicalities of producing the first edition

ALISON, AMELIA, VICTORIA and JOEL – for allowing me the space and time to write

RIOJA – for most of the good ideas (except strategies of the giraffe – Pinotage)

Everyone who purchased the first edition of the book in any of the three languages in which it was published and everyone who has invited me to make Strategies of the Serengeti conference speeches – in 25 countries on 4 continents

And some great customers who have tested the ideas, models and structures for me in their businesses. With many of you, the distinction between 'customer' and 'friend' is undoubtedly blurred.

Contents

Preface to the 2nd edition

The first edition of the book has taken me on a tremendous journey – addressing conferences in many cities; from New York to Colombo, from London to Lusaka, from Antwerp to Vienna, from Seville to Munich and many wonderful places in between. At the last count, copies of the book have been posted to just over 100 countries.

The first edition has almost sold out, ahead of schedule, and I now have the opportunity to make some changes. Edition 1 sought to have both the 'large chapters' with heavy content of new models and also the smaller chapters with more examples and easy reading style. My intention for edition 2 was originally to go for one or the other of these contrasting styles dependent on the feedback received. However, as many people seem to say that they prefer the more academic model approach as say they prefer the lighter stories and examples of the later chapters – so the second edition has kept the same format as the first edition – longer, heavier chapters at the start and shorter lighter ones after the half way point.

Some of the businesses used as examples have moved on – so they have been replaced with other examples. Others remain.

I am also indebted to the many people who have given such wonderful feedback and have suggested some minor alterations. I would like to particularly mention Paul Gillot of The Chartered Institute of Management Accountants (CIMA) for some helpful observations and Luud Berings for his encouragement.

Prologue: Strategies of the dung beetle

A lighthearted look at business life:

With in excess of 3 million animals on the Serengeti, most with herbivore diets, the grassland plains are dung beetle heaven. Dung beetles love nothing better than to burrow deep into a mound of dung, carve out their own unique piece of dung – a boli – and roll it away. This fulfils a whole range of purposes. For the Serengeti it provides a distribution of rich fertiliser. For the dung beetle it provides both extrinsic and intrinsic motivation, sustenance, evidence of a worthwhile life and the means by which it can impress and attract a mate. Dung for the dung beetle provides a similar function to that of work for many of the newer species known as homo sapiens.

Life for the dung beetle is a hard slog of locating, manipulating and eventually pushing dung. There is a degree of specialisation within dung beetles. Some dung beetles take a particular liking to wilderbeest dung. Others prefer the droppings of the zebra and others, looking for the more impressive profiles on the plains seek out the mountainous evidence of elephant presence. For them it is about ego, about posturing, about parading pretentiously

1

demonstrating the evidence of their social standing amongst dung beetles. One presumes that an elephant dung beetle is held in higher esteem than a zebra favouring dung beetle but one must also assume that the king of the pile is the dung beetle brave enough to seek out the consequences of a carnivore diet to become a lion specialist. Few and far between, of elevated status in society, these are the beetles to emulate. The social debates of whether a zebra pile is superior to a rhinoceros pile must occupy plenty of time at dung beetle social events and at the annual career tour of dung beetle universities, but every horned beetle head must turn when the lion beetle enters the room. In some homo sapiens circles these could be the politicians, in others the lawyers and barristers, others still, the wealthy or bizarrely they may occasionally even be the sportsmen, singers and actresses, but they exist to impress.

Rolling, pushing and shovelling dung is mostly about impressing others. The dung beetle quivers with delight as it sights a fresh mound of raw material. The beetle reacts rapidly as the opportunity presents itself – *carpe dungem* – seize the dung. It boldly dives head first into the pile and gorges itself on the contents. Having satisfied the lower levels of Maslow's hierarchy of needs, the astute beetle then turns to the upper hierarchy levels such as esteem and self actualisation. He considers why is he delving in dung? What are the benefits and potential for learning or advancement? There may be the possibility of transforming his pile into a wondrous bolus which will be the talk of the dung beetle community for generations – a dung beetle legend. If he could set new standards in bolus construction by creating the highest quality bolus ever seen he may achieve fame, fortune and the ability to further the dung beetle gene pool with whichever female dung beetle he chooses. The benefits of shovelling dung progress far beyond the mere functional and clearly justify the enormous effort required.

Having consequently immersed himself in dung, to the exclusion of all else, the beetle pauses to consider its work-life balance and seeks to leverage its advantageous position within the pile to its benefit. *"Dung is not just about survival"* the beetle tells itself, *"it is about prestige, getting what you want in life, about achievement and self satisfaction"*. The line of argument continues *"I don't want to be burrowing in dung all my life, but if I do it exceptionally well for a few more years I may be able to evolve into something else and take life easier in the future."* The rest of the animals on the Serengeti are not fooled. They have seen thousands of dung beetles with their hopes for the future buried neck deep in the very dung from which they are trying to escape. The avenue through which the beetle seeks to escape his mundane existence becomes the very cul-de-sac of ensnarement. They become so immersed in dung that they become dependent on it. Their very being seems tied to their workload and for some the challenge becomes lamentably fatal. The challenge of getting the freshest offerings of the pachyderm could result in the overpromotion into areas in which the dung beetle is ill equipped to survive – namely the unfinished article. The delight of the promotion into the freshest of elephant dung can soon become erased by the suffocation of the viscosity of the matter, or by the dumping of further dung workloads from above. Some beetles who have travelled in too deep, fall gracelessly into depression and even lifeless immersion in the over-viscous matter. Others, seeking elevation before due time may occupy a mound before the provider has left the vicinity only to be crushed underfoot as the elephants move on.

The more strategically astute beetles choose their time for engaging with the dung carefully. They ensure that they do not have the high risks associated with an overly new venture and its suffocating consequences, nor the dangers present from prematurely occupying a mound where the possibilities of being crushed underfoot exist. They bide their time. Too early and they have this dual risk. Too late and they miss the market opportunity as other beetles scurry into the raw material, carving their own market niches. At precisely the right time, the astute beetle advances and takes possession of the dung – neither too fresh, nor too market-weary and, as such, hard to penetrate. Having occupied the pile the challenge is now to extract a suitable amount to impress others. The greater the pile of dung one can carve out, the more impressive one is in dung beetle society. Carve out too little and you could be humiliated by those with greater dung-balls. Carve out too much and you could suffer the indignity of being unable to propel your dung-ball. This beetle then sits ignominiously beside its unfeasibly large bolus, exhausted, prematurely washed out and useless to any dung beetle mates. This is also the time of greatest vulnerability. An experienced savannah-wise beetle may take careful note of those with oversized boli and wait, predator fashion, for them to be overwhelmed by what they have taken on. At the point of exhaustion the predator beetle will pounce, attack the exhausted dung pusher and steal his bolus. These are some of the bloodiest corporate wars in the savannah – testosterone fuelled battles for domination and control of the largest bolus. An experienced combative beetle can throw another, judo style, up to two feet.

Using the refined sharp elbows of six legs, the cutting of the claws and the tearing of the mandibles, the beetle generates for itself a perfectly sized pile to impress. Once carved out, the pile must be manipulated into a perfect sphere and then pushed aimlessly across the plain. To increase the analogy to much human employment, the beetle graciously agrees to push the ball backwards so that it is not only pushing a pointless pile of poo, it is also doing so with no idea of where it is going. Seeing only the route already taken, like an Olympic rower, the beetle strains as he forges ahead into the unknown and unseen future of his chosen course. Occasionally the beetle will stop pushing its dung-ball, climb on it and survey the scene in its path ahead. This time of stopping all profitable activity to view its future direction gives the beetle renewed vigour to return to the pushing side of the bolus. It will then leverage its rear legs to generate momentum whilst exhaustingly using its front legs to push against the hard ground of the Serengeti floor. In business we often take longer and refer to it as an 'awayday'. The homo sapiens, as a social creature, often engages in this activity in small groups when the term becomes 'teambuild'.

The female dung beetles stare in amazement as the impressive males shovel greater and greater balls of dung past their appreciative gazes. The effort is palpable as the ball can be many times the size of the beetle. Gradients present problems. Pushing a pile uphill is, indeed, most impressive to the female beetle yet at some point the force of gravity will create an inevitable consequence. Either as gravity outweighs the strength of the individual beetle, or in the event of the beetle making a slight error in his pushing trajectory, the neat sphere stutters and then rolls backwards temporarily squashing the hapless beetle. The heavy workload of the beetle means that it is inevitable that there will be such setbacks, but few other creatures spend their lives pushing piles of dung only for the very dung which has been the object of their efforts and affections to become the item which rolls over them in a humiliating and painful saturation. With energy sapped, pride tarnished but determination undiminished, the more successful beetles rise from such a crushing experience to scurry back to their rogue dung-ball and recommence pushing despite the ground temporarily lost. With uncomplaining and enviable resolve the beetle heaves and pushes its dung to retread the path thinking only of the unknown route ahead rather than dwelling on the course already trodden which spans so visibly in front of him as he pushes. Being competitive, male beetles rarely work together but seek to push individually huge impossible piles which could enter the realm of the possible within a team environment. This trait is not unknown amongst the similarly competitive homo sapiens.

Despite pushing a pointless pile, backwards with no indication of direction, but a clear sense of where he has come from and alone as collaboration is seen as weakness, the male beetle perseveres. Eventually he may impress the female sufficiently for a brief copulation. At best this can be a brief moment of transient satisfaction as a reward for his effort and achievements, but at the worst it can make the dung beetle feel that he has pushed poo all his life with no idea of where he is going only for the object of his posturing to have fleetingly taken advantage of him to further her own procreational activity. Feeling used and abused, with nothing to show for his Herculean efforts, the beetle applies for voluntary redundancy and sits back to watch the Serengeti whilst the next generation of dung beetle avidly chase after the nearest elephant. He then sits in the gentlemen beetle clubs with other old-timers reminiscing and regaling junior beetles with the tales of the 'great bolus of '79', of heroic deeds and of female beetle affections won – but, as with most old timers tales, it's just a pile of dung.

Exhibiting a life of:

- Shovelling dung
- Push to impress
- No long term plans
- 'My pile is bigger than your pile'
- Focus on the past rather than where they are going

there is not much worthy of emulation in the strategies of the dung beetle – yet many companies and many individuals seem keen on doing so.

There is, of course another way. We can choose not to be a dung beetle in business but to observe the other residents of this edenic Serengeti paradise. We can choose to develop strategies with purpose, with drive, with track records of success – we can choose the strategies of the many and varied Serengeti residents. The success of the giraffe, the longevity of the elephant, the accomplishments of the wildebeest are all available to us – if only we would observe and emulate.

CHAPTER 1

Setting the scene

This book is about strategy – business and organisational strategy. It is not a wildlife book, and whilst it will give interesting insights into a variety of animals and their survival strategies, the intention is to learn from them in order to make our organisational strategy better. We can observe the breadth of strategies used by the animal residents of the savannah and seek to determine which of these strategies are appropriate for our organisations. This book is not about one strategic 'fad' which will fade as all others have, it is about the vast range of successful strategies available to us through observing the masters of one of the most exciting and awe inspiring landscapes in the world – the highly competitive environment we know as the Serengeti.

The strategies employed by the variety of animals in the book are all applicable to our organisations – profit focused and publicly owned, commercial and charitable, large and small, local and global, high tech and low tech, well established and newly started.

These strategies will be of considerable interest to executives and managers of large businesses, students at all levels and those who run small businesses. There is a very large extent to which the strategies we explore are applicable in non-organisational areas such as human behaviour and inter-personal relationships. This however, is not my field of expertise and so I will leave that to those more able in such an arena. My area of expertise is business strategy and my intention in this book is to make strategy accessible to a much wider range of individuals than currently consider strategy to be of interest.

'Strategies of the Serengeti' seeks to learn the art of business strategy from the masters – those who live in a competitive, deadly and threatening environment where the difference between success and failure to survive depends on having the correct strategy. These masters are the animals of the Serengeti, the worlds best known wildlife reserve. For centuries the zebra, the crocodile and the cheetah have used strategies to ensure their own prosperity and can now teach the business homo sapiens how to do the same in our complex deadly environment of the business marketplace. ➜

→
Different animals employ different strategies, each successful in their own way. Many businesses may aspire to be the lion – although the lion's strategies would fail for the wildebeest, or would render the giraffe extinct. *'Strategies of the Serengeti'* develops a wide range of business strategies, by exploring those employed by a variety of the larger, well known, species of the region. The reader is able to explore which are the most appropriate business strategies for their own organisation.

'Strategies of the Serengeti' gives the reader a wealth of strategic alternatives in an innovative, memorable and practical format. This book seeks to take the 'dark arts' of strategy and make them accessible to all. Readers will remember warthog, hyena and elephant strategies long after they have forgotten the more conventional 5 'S's of strategy, 7 steps to strategy or 10 rules of successful strategy. Whilst some organisations may not be flattered to be compared to a hippopotamus, the 'river horse' is supreme in its chosen domain and, in common with all the animals listed, offers strong, innovative and practical advice to business in the 21st century. Some organisations may be loathe to imitate the hyena, yet its strategies have made it the most abundant carnivore in the Serengeti. Many may overlook the aesthetically challenged warthog, yet her strategies have also led to abundance and prosperity. Each animal has a story to tell and a strategy to imitate.

Forget the fads, forget following the current market leaders, forget the business gurus, forget the business schools (even the one where I lecture!), look to the experts – the zebra, the giraffe, the lion. Look beyond the 'nice' animals – the threatening crocodile has much to teach us, as has the ungainly rhinoceros, the aesthetically challenged warthog, the much maligned hyena and the wallowing hippopotamus. They have each survived and thrived with their blends of strategies for centuries longer, and in a tougher environment, than have our businesses who follow the human experts. This book seeks to unlock the secrets of these, the real experts and help us to apply the vast range of strategies they undertake within our own organisations. These are not transitory strategies, they are the strategies which have passed the test of thousands of years of time. These are the real strategies of 'excellence', these are the strategies which have proven that they are 'built to last'.

However, before we examine the animals and their strategic responses to their environment, let us dismiss a few myths of strategy which have kept many people from getting involved in strategic thinking within organisations. These myths are blockages to increased accessibility and wider strategic thinking and must be removed.

Myths of strategy

Business strategists have perpetuated a variety of myths which discourage many people from examining the disciplines and concepts of business strategy. They are myths, and like most professional myths, they exist so that those on the outside of the discipline generate a 'rose tinted' impression of those on the inside.

Myth 1 – Strategy is high level

The first myth of strategy is that it is like elephants mating – something which is done at very high level, with a lot of grunting and groaning and takes a couple of years before you see any benefit (actually 22 months for an elephant gestation). In business, after the couple of years many of those who formulated the strategy have moved to other companies and the original driving concepts are forgotten!

Strategy must percolate into daily action. If it does not, it is not strategy, it is daydreaming. In the section on the strategy of the giraffe we will explore some of the mechanisms for this but conceptually, the ivory tower is not the place for strategy. Without a clear connection to terra firma the strategy is valueless, unable to be implemented and a waste of time seeking to formulate it.

This frequent inability to connect strategy to daily activity has not been helped by the strategy consulting industry. One large UK customer of mine used a very well known global strategy consultancy who produced a voluminous report after many days working with the customer and many thousands of pounds in invoices. Never has the traditional strategy consulting joke been so apt – the story of the hippopotamus and the butterfly.

One day, the hippopotamus was in the river enjoying the coolness of the water in the heat of the Serengeti sun. He spotted a butterfly tracing patterns in the sky as she danced on her way across the river and was mesmerised by her beautiful movement. The next day the hippopotamus spoke to the butterfly as she crossed the river. She perched on his nose and they passed the afternoon in frivolous conversation laughing like hyenas – it was the best afternoon the hippopotamus could remember. The same thing happed the next day, and the next and slowly the hippopotamus fell in love with the butterfly.

The hippopotamus realised that their relationship may be difficult and went to see the wise lion. *"What can I do?"* asked the hippopotamus.

➜

→

"I am in love with the butterfly, she is so beautiful, so delicate, so mesmerising, but if I do as much as lean forward to kiss her, I will squash her delicate wings with my bulk". The lion thought long and hard. He paced up and down considering the hippopotamus's problem. After deep thought the lion turned to the hippopotamus and said *"My advice would be for you to become a butterfly"*.

"But how do I do that?" replied the hippopotamus.

"Don't ask me" responded the lion *"I'm a strategist, that is an implementation question"*.

Concepts disconnected from implementation and action are not strategy, they are daydreams. Strategy is not a 'high level' exercise, it is an 'all level' discipline.

Myth 2 – Strategy requires remarkable intelligence

The perpetuation of the myth that strategy is excessively difficult makes others in an organisation gaze admiringly upward at those with the word 'strategy' in their business title. I sometimes refer to this as 'the Einstein myth' but have a preferred name for it – 'the Marvin myth'. In the tremendous book *'Hitch-hikers Guide to the Galaxy'* by the late Douglas Adams, there is a robot called Marvin. He is a perpetually depressed android who explains that he has a brain "the size of a planet". Despite his excessive cerebral equipment, his owners persist in instructing him to do menial tasks – like opening a door, picking up a piece of paper or parking a spaceship. Strategists frequently perpetuate the myth that one needs a brain the size of a planet to merely entertain strategic conversation. It's a myth.

I prefer the approach once played by one of my favourite actors Denzel Washington. Like John Wayne or Clint Eastwood, Denzel Washington frequently plays the same character regardless of whatever the film is. Fortunately I find the character engaging and will happily watch any film with him in it. One of the best is *Philadelphia*.

In the film *'Philadelphia'* Tom Hanks plays the character of high flying lawyer Andrew Beckett who is a practising homosexual. Beckett contracts aids, and when his employer, the top legal firm in Philadelphia find out, in a pique of homophobia, they fire him. The film was groundbreaking in its time. Released in 1993, AIDS was little understood and the only person touching victims was the late Diana, Princess of Wales. The rest of us were wondering whether you could catch AIDS from touching something previously touched by a sufferer – a door handle, a toilet seat, a coin.

In the film Andrew Beckett seeks to sue the company. No lawyer in their right mind would represent Beckett against the top legal firm in Philadelphia and so Beckett moves downwards through the 'food chain' of lawyers until, at the bottom, he asks a small time personal injuries lawyer Joe Miller (Denzel Washington) to represent him. Miller has his own prejudices and fears surrounding AIDS and does not want to take the case on. The drama unfolds as Miller, being black, understands the receiving end of prejudice but then has to confront his own prejudices. He accepts the case. The remainder of the film is the building of the case and the gradual challenging and reduction of Miller's homophobic prejudices.

In one scene Beckett (Tom Hanks) is talking through high flying issues which are going right over the head of Miller (Denzel Washington). Miller gesticulates for him to stop and says "No, no, no, talk to me like I'm a five year old." Beckett then re-explains the issue in a simpler format.

I am of the opinion that almost anything can be explained in five year old language. The mysteries of physics, biology, astronomy, finance or strategy can all be put into five year old language.

When we overcomplicate issues such as finance or strategy there can be several possibilities:

- We are trying to make it sound complicated to make ourselves appear intelligent.
- We are unable to fully explain it as we do not fully understand it.
- We have a communication inability.

Cumbersome financial reports in accountant's formats with difficult words and voluminous numbers do not assist communication. I am of the opinion that as a CFO you can run any company from one piece of A4 paper. What is on that paper will vary from company to company and from level to level within a company, but the principle of the financial report part of the board meetings being from one piece of paper is highly attractive to all board members except the CFO. It is '5 year old business communication'.

As a strategist I warmly recommend the 'strategy at five year old level'. If your business strategy cannot be explained at five year old level, which of the three excuses above is the most pertinent?

One of my favoured approaches to strategy in practice is also the simplest – the map analogy. Imagine a map to represent your business, market and industry. Strategy is about following the process of:

- Where am I? – a realistic analysis of current position considering internal, market and competitive factors – this book will provide tools for all of these.
- Where do I want to get to? – my business aim, my vision, my desired destination – the 'strategies of the giraffe' will give practical steps here.
- What are my options? How can I make the journey from where I am to where I want to be? Which routes? Which modes of transport? The host of examples in the book seek to illustrate a breadth of choices.
- On what basis do I make my choice of how to get to the destination? In the map analogy, is it the rapidity, scenery, cost or comfort which I value the most? There are a variety of guidelines for this process in *'Strategies of the Serengeti'*, particularly in the 'strategies of the elephant' chapter.
- Make a choice – the 'strategies of the zebra' will be invaluable to us here.
- Collate the required resources – follow the 'strategies of the lion' to co-ordinate the requirements for success.
- Plan staging posts – so that we can measure our progress and determine any required adjustments. Ongoing strategic review is a pre-requisite for successful strategy – the annual exercise of tediously collating written strategies to stand behind the annual financial budget has limited value. Ongoing strategic review has immense value.
- Take the first step – implementation means action. Too many senior executives and strategists feel that their job is planning the strategy and other people are to implement it. Unimplemented strategy is valueless, wastes time, wastes money and causes resources to be utilised fuelling the futile.
- Measure progress and refer back to the planned staging posts.

The map analogy falls down, as do most analogies. With the map, the terrain and destination are likely to remain constant through your journey. However, in business, the destination can change rapidly, as can the market terrain. A degree of alertness and fleetness to identify and respond to such changes are a welcome addition to the map analogy.

Myth 3 – Strategy is dry and dull

Many years ago, at school, I discovered that people were dry and dull, not subjects. Aged 15 I had to, against my will, study the history of architecture as a minor part of a history examination syllabus. Surely nothing can be as dull as that? Fortunately we had a history teacher called Bob Creighton. He brought a potentially mind numbing, coma inducing topic to life to the extent that our class of teenage boys even looked forward to visiting 17th century English country houses. To this day I can spot a fluted Corinthian column at 100 metres and differentiate it from a Doric column, although I struggle with my cornices after all this time.

Regrettably, much of business strategy is taught in a traditional pedagogic academic way. The subject matter is not dull, the method of communication frequently is. I usually start business strategy training events by open discussions of household name brands and the strategies we see every day – Coca-Cola, Virgin, Tesco, WalMart/ASDA, Levi Strauss, Mercedes, McDonalds, Budweiser and the likes. This creates a degree of tangibility.

With MBA students I draw a distinction between some parts of their syllabus which I see as having negligible worth in real life and those which I think can be applied. In business everything must pass the 'So what?' test. Every training course, every meeting, every idea. In academia this is not necessarily the case and many models remain on the syllabi of prestigious business schools despite their lack of ability to be applied practically. For the executive or the manager this is of no use, and regrettably many excellent strategic approaches get tainted due to the lack of application of some others.

So, the methods we have used to communicate or formulate strategy may not be good, some of the models we have had thrust upon us may not be perfect, but that doesn't make strategy dull, it just makes those communicators and those models dull. In *'Strategies of the Serengeti'* I aim to breathe new life into some well known and poorly used models and approaches. I also seek to develop a few new models and approaches. The test for inclusion is 'can this be used in real life? Will this be beneficial for people seeking to develop strategies for their own organisations?' If the answer is 'No', it doesn't make the cut.

For this reason, the chapters will be rich in examples. These illustrations are designed to explore points but also to generate ideas for your own organisation – if McDonalds or Coca-Cola chose an option, if it would work for you – copy it. If Levis or M&S made mistakes, put in place whatever is required to ensure that we can learn from their mistakes and not repeat them. I use a wide range of examples – from different industries, different countries and also some smaller companies in addition to the global giants. This is also designed to make the examples as accessible as possible for all. The strategies of a minnow are frequently just as relevant for a global company as vice versa.

Myth 4 – Strategy is military

Most basic strategy books point out that the origins of strategy are military, including the Greek derivation of the word 'strategy' ('leading an army'). These origins have hung like a millstone around the neck of the discipline of business strategy. Much of our business parlance uses military terminology as our Chief Financial and Executive "Officers" have "come through the ranks", "earned their stripes" to live in Corporate "Headquarters" gaining market "intelligence" before "mobilising our resources" and launching a media "salvo" as a "pre-emptive strike" against the competition. We wonder why the boardrooms of our corporations are male dominated and exceed the demographic averages for controlling/aggressive/red/alpha managers!

Whilst there are some helpful uses of the military analogy, I feel that it is generally more destructive than constructive. In business, who is our enemy? 'The competition' we loudly reply. So should all of our strategies be focussed on defeating the competition? Obviously not. Companies whose primary focus is the competitor rather than the customer have a life expectancy akin to that of the 7th cavalry setting out to Little Big Horn under the leadership of George Armstrong Custer.

Business is different from war. The objectives are more multi-faceted. We are not about defeating an enemy but instead aim to create competitive advantage, develop unique selling propositions, penetrate markets, make profits and generate longevity. Our motives are more complex than merely defeating a single enemy. We have long abandoned the simplistic myths of profit maximisation or shareholder value maximisation to embrace the realisation of executives 'satisficing' the multiple desires of the shareholders, employees, customers, governments and themselves. The multi-million dollar Directors tie in clauses, executive share schemes, executive pensions, obscene levels of bonus payment and 'golden handshakes' which are frequently in the news, elevate the desires of the executives above all other stakeholders. No further proof is required of the absence of the profit or value maximisation motives. Even if it were, consider the extravagant palatial offices our executives inhabit – fish and fountains in the atria are not a sensible use of shareholders monies. Yet the shareholders, who own the business, largely tolerate such practices provided that share price growth meets their expectations. Presently it is much more common for shareholders to vote against excessive executive pay than it was a few years ago. In 2005 United Business Media saw 87.2% of voting shareholders decide not to back a £250,000 'golden goodbye' to Lord Hollick; 60.5% of MFI shareholders chose not to back executive service contracts in excess of 12 months and 58.1% of Pendragon shareholders withdrew their support for changes to executive bonuses which they deemed to have insufficient disclosure. The misuse of executive powers and abuse of executive positions have started the flexing of shareholder muscle in ways not previously seen. This new, increased level of accountability and visibility does not help the single focus military analogy. Questioning a general and asking to see his receipts would surely land us in trouble. Getting sidetracked with peripheral issues could lose us a war.

It is not just the focus on the customer and the multi-faceted nature of business which make the military analogy virtually redundant. Business is about gaining and maintaining an edge in the market. There is not always an 'endgame', as in war or chess. An aim is continuity rather than a victory or an end.

Strategy – of critical importance

Having dismissed the myths, strategy as high level, requiring exceptional intelligence, dull and military, it should be underlined that strategy is absolutely essential for business success. Furthering the map analogy, strategy is the collective planned actions we undertake in order to take us to our desired destination. A pre-requisite, as we shall see in the strategies of the giraffe, is that we know where we want to get to. This is not earth shattering, yet I encounter organisations who have no idea where they are aiming to be – they are lost and directionless. The requirement for the knowledge of a destination as a pre-requisite for strategic direction is not new either. It is most ably exhibited by Lewis Carroll in *Alice's Adventures in Wonderland* when Alice first encountered the Cheshire cat:

> 'Cheshire Puss,' she began, rather timidly, as she did not at all know whether it would like the name: however, it only grinned a little wider. ... 'Would you tell me, please, which way I ought to go from here?'
> 'That depends a good deal on where you want to get to,' said the Cat.
> 'I don't much care where' said Alice.
> 'Then it doesn't matter which way you go,' said the Cat.   ➜

➔
'... so long as I get SOMEWHERE,' Alice added as an explanation. 'Oh, you're sure to do that,' said the Cat, 'if you only walk long enough.'

Lewis Carroll, *Alice's Adventures in Wonderland*

Strategic success is dependent on firstly knowing where we are aiming to go. The old adage is true in strategy as in any other area of life; 'Aim at nothing, and you're sure to hit it.' Another requirement for strategic success, as the strategies of the lion will show us, is that every part of the organisation must know where it fits in to this strategy and the part it is playing.

In their *Harvard Business Review* article (June 2003) Nohria, Joyce and Roberson concluded that success in business was the successful combination of only four management practices – strategy, execution, culture and structure. They state that it is essential to devise and maintain a clearly stated strategy. The article says "the key to achieving excellence in strategy ... is to be clear about what your strategy is and consistently communicate it to customers, employees and shareholders."

My encounters of different layers within organisations gives a frighteningly familiar pattern. The top team state that they have a clear knowledge of where they are seeking to take the company and a definite understanding of the strategies they are employing to get there. The next level down state that they have not been told the strategies nor the destination and are afraid to take initiatives in case they interfere with wherever the top team are thinking of taking the company. The next layer down say that the second layer is a barrier to communication of strategy and vision downwards and a hindrance to initiative and ideas upwards.

Strategy should be clear, in five year old terms, seeking to get to the chosen destination and communicated effectively. Fail to do this and the link between top level strategy and day to day action is broken – the company will fail to realise its aspirations.

One essential point to make is that many of the observations I make in this book are with 20/20 hindsight. I do not necessarily think that I, or anyone else, could have made better decisions than some of those I criticise within their time and context – with some exceptions. My criticisms of company decisions should not be taken as criticisms of the companies themselves nor necessarily the individuals who made the decisions, they are observations with the enormous benefit of hindsight. I am sure that if others viewed many of my past decisions they would be equally justified in appropriate criticism. I will give personal opinions, often strong ones, rather than produce a bland and uncontroversial series of statements. If some of these are offensive, I apologise in advance for any offence caused, but not for causing the offence

– opinions are what make debate and critique interesting, and the stronger the better. If critique challenges preconceptions, it has been valuable. The models I develop will also not be flawless and in due course will no doubt be criticised or built upon by others. This is a good and healthy way to develop improvements – so chop them up and cart away the pieces which are useful with my blessing.

My invitation to the reader is to use this book to change your thinking about strategy, about your organisation and about the alternatives available to you. It is intended to be practical – a book for action rather than debate. Different strategies will be appropriate at different times for a business – sometimes you may seek to be a crocodile and other times a zebra – so please do not seek to limit your organisation to the strategies of just one animal. The chapters are different lengths and are essentially independent – so there is no need to read them in the order in which they are printed – if you want to look at the ostrich before the zebra, that is perfectly acceptable. The chapters also have differing styles – you may warm to the writing style of the warthog chapter more than that of the cheetah. This is fine, different people like different approaches – some like the analytical nature of the zebra's 'fight' strategy, others will prefer the example laden approach to the zebra's 'freeze' strategy. Some will have large sections dedicated to examples, for those who attach better to these, other chapters will be more academic with fewer examples and more of a model structure – some will prefer those. My aim has been to generate a variety of approaches to give maximum access to strategic thinking to as many people as possible.

The book also has major chapters and minor chapters. This is a reflection of size rather than importance. The strategies of the ostrich are vital for its continued success. They are not any less important than the strategies of the giraffe, it is just that in the major chapters I have sought to develop aspects which need more time. All chapters could have been of 'major' length, but a book in excess of 1,000 pages becomes unwieldy! So I have had to make choices of where to condense and where to allow the expansion of a topic.

The key for using this book successfully is in establishing the nature of the strategies of each animal and in how to employ these strategies within your organisation. For example, in the 'strategies of the zebra', I focus on organisational response to threat. If your business is encountering threats, that is the chapter to read. Alternatively, in the 'strategies of the ostrich' I focus on seeking to 'punch above your weight' – for example, a small company such as mine regularly being in competition with top level universities and multimillion dollar consultancies with thousands of employees – how is that done? Ask the ostrich. The cheetah uses speed to get there first – 'first mover advantage'; the hippopotamus is supreme within its domain and weak outside it – knowing your niche; the warthog has some impressively sharp tusks but a weak vulnerable rear end – protecting your vulnerabilities; the hyena picks up on what others leaves behind – seeing value where others do not. But most of all, you will remember the strategies due to the Serengeti animal analogy. You will remember the warthog long after you have forgotten a dry dusty strategy book on protecting vulnerabilities. The zebra is more memorable than a book entitled 'five ways to deal with threats to your business'.

So please enjoy the book, enjoy the ideas, the models, the examples and the case studies, but most of all please use it – put it into practice.

Stephen Berry

Chapter summary

- This book is about organisational strategy.
- Too many people in this world work like the dung beetle.
- Strategy has a variety of myths attached to it including:
  - It is very high level – wrong – real strategy is at every level.
  - High intelligence is required – wrong – everyone must engage in strategy.
  - It is dry and dull – wrong – that is just how many people have presented strategy.
  - It is military – wrong – business is multi-faceted and more complex and aims for continuity not an end game of victory.
- Strategy is essential for business success – the alternative is to be directionless.
- Strategy seeks to deliver the business vision – it does not exist in a vacuum.
- Strategy should be simple to explain, and be communicated widely.
- The strategies of the animals give a wide repertoire for any business.
- Remember the various strategies of the animals and you will have a very wide range of strategic options at your disposal to face a very wide range of business situations.

CHAPTER 2

The Serengeti

In 1913 an American hunter/explorer Stewart Edward White headed south from Nairobi. His now famous record of the journey states *"we walked for miles over burnt out country. ... Then I saw the green trees of the river, walked two miles more and found myself in paradise"*. History, although it is disputed, records Stewart White as the first 'westerner' or white man to find the Serengeti. For many years the Maasai had lived, hunted and grazed their cattle within this 'paradise' and called it 'Siringittu' which means 'where the land is constantly moving', 'extended place' or 'where the land goes on forever' depending on which translation you trust.

It is one of the most fascinating and oldest ecosystems in the world covering in excess of 30,000 km^2 in the areas of our political maps called 'Kenya' and 'Tanzania'. Within the region of the Serengeti is the world famous Serengeti National Park approximately 75% of which is within Tanzania to the south and the remaining 25%, still a huge area, is in Kenya to the North. However, the Serengeti is bigger than just the National Park and the political divides of Kenya and Tanzania are the mere invention of modern man, a relative newcomer to the environment. For the real established residents, arbitrary human borders are an irrelevance. The Serengeti comprises of seemingly endless plains of grassland punctuated by ample but well spaced trees which provide shelter, food and habitation yet do not have the density and impenetrability of the jungles. The terrain varies from the open grass plains of the south, the savannah with its scattered acacia trees in the centre, to wooded grassland in the north, and west. Small rivers, lakes and swamps are scattered throughout.

My personal encounters with the Serengeti started with a honeymoon in 1994 when we only chose it as a destination because November was too wet in Sri Lanka. Since then, my wife, Alison and I have toured the Serengeti grasslands, trekked through Southern American jungles, dived in several enchanting oceans with countless glorious creatures and swam amongst the mangroves (beware of alligators!), all of these habitats have their charm but honeymoon is always special and the Serengeti is the probably the most enthralling place in the world. Its sheer size is awesome. Its independence and resilience is inspiring. The diversity of wildlife, the variety of the seasons and the way in which it makes us humans feel insignificant makes it a mesmerizing yet humbling environment. Over 90,000 tourists visit each year. Some stay in lodges, some less sane visit under canvas in organised camps protected by local guards – the words 'just say 'no'' spring to mind. We have trekked in vehicles and walked, frequently with armed guards. The guards are not there to protect us from other humans but from the ferocious predators of the region, particularly the lion and the crocodile. We, and the other 90,000, are also walking in human history. The Olduvai Gorge in the south east of the Serengeti was where Louis and Mary Leakey discovered some of the oldest human remains on the planet. These are allegedly 3.6m years old, but unless they are buried with a copy of that day's Times I retain the healthy scepticism of dating techniques which was drilled into me at school.

Despite the presence of potential ancestors, all 90,000 tourists are conscious that we are the visitors. This is the domain of the animals and we visit their domain with both a fascination and a mild fear – a fear that they are in control here. Were we to be left alone without our 4×4's, our protective AK47's and without our comfortable lodges, few of us would last a single night, as many found when the British used colonial labour to construct the Nairobi to Mombassa rail line. Lions even found their way into the railway carriages used as sleeping quarters. This caused some workers to spend the night sleeping in trees. Fortunately it was not leopard country otherwise that would have been a dangerous place to sleep too.

The animal masters of the Serengeti have adapted perfectly to this ecosystem, we humans have not. Even the Maasai, tribesman who have trod the plains for generations, tread the ground in reverence as human visitors in an animal dominated kingdom which includes 30 species of herbivores and over 500 species of birds. For my wife Alison, and I, our first guide to this wonderland was Ali. At first we thought that this portly, slightly cumbersome man was not the best of allocated guides. Within just a few days we noted that all other guides, without exception, would pay their respects to Ali. He knew everything – every flower, every bird, every habit of every animal. He also had eyes a hawk would be proud of. He would jerk our truck to a halt and declare 'hyena' whilst pointing at a seemingly blank landscape.

After much searching with binoculars, usually with Ali's guidance, someone would spot this speckled creature miles away. He was never wrong.

The spectacular geography and migration

The Serengeti has highlands to the south east, particularly the volcanic Ngorongoro crater which is the largest unbroken caldera in the world at 610m deep, 260km^2 in area and 14 miles (22.5km) at its widest point. The volcano has long been extinct but its sheer mass remains impressive. For budding volcanologists, the nearby Oldonyo Lenga volcano is still active. Safari lodges on the rim of the Ngorongoro crater provide views of the most exquisite proportions, especially as the sun sets. This is the best place in the world to see the black (pointed lip) rhinoceros (who are not black) and the unusual black maned lions whilst the nearby Lerai Forest is one of the best places in Africa to view leopards.

From here northward and southward runs the great African rift valley – a 6,000-mile crack (fissure) in the earth's crust, stretching from Lebanon to Mozambique and defining the eastern side of the Serengeti.

The western side is truncated by Lake Victoria which is the world's second largest freshwater lake covering an area of 67,850 km^2. This vast expanse, about the size of the Republic of Ireland, forms the headwaters of the River Nile.

The Serengeti's climate is usually warm and dry. The main rainy season is from March to May, with short rains falling from October to November. The amount of rainfall increases from about 500mm on the plains at the foot of the Ngorongoro highlands to about 1,200mm on the shores of Lake Victoria. All is lush and green after the rains, but a gradual drying up follows which restricts plant growth and encourages the herbivore animals to migrate in search of grasses and water. With altitudes ranging from 920 to 1,850 metres – higher than most of Europe – mean temperatures vary from 15 degrees to 25 degrees Celsius. It is coldest from June to October, particularly in the evenings.

From the south of the region, where the vast open grass plains stretch seemingly endlessly, the lower tip of the famous Serengeti National Park defines an area where the animals enjoy a degree of protection from the newcomer – humans. Dozens of tourist lodges now make this area and the animals within it, accessible to the affluent masses, and I would suggest that a visit to the Serengeti should be on everyone's 'must' list at some point in their lives.

The southern area has lush verdant grass during the rainy season of the spring where hundreds of thousands of wildebeest, zebra and gazelles graze in comfort. After May, the grasses begin to turn brown in response to the

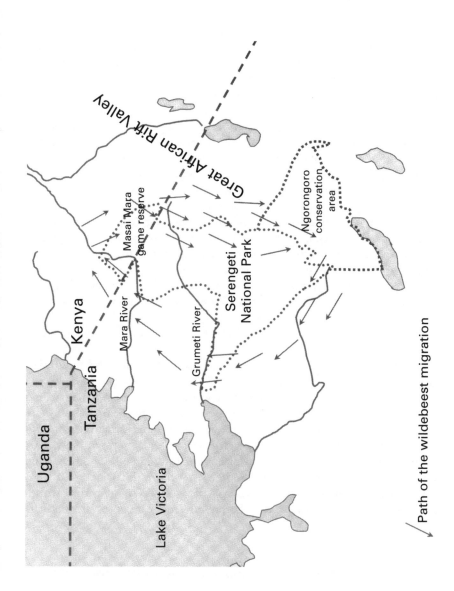

Uganda

Kenya

Tanzania

Lake Victoria

Mara River

Masai Mara game reserve

Grumeti River

Serengeti National Park

Ngorongoro conservation area

Great African Rift Valley

Path of the wildebeest migration

end of the rains, and the wildebeest mass for one of the most spectacular sights on this planet – the annual migration. This coincides with rutting season so the annual fight for survival is twofold – firstly for the short term by gaining sufficient grazing and water, and secondly for the long term by ensuring the survival of genes through successful mating.

The migration is the largest movement of wildlife on earth and involves up to 2 million herbivores travelling in enormous processions from the southern plains, through the western Serengeti, crossing the Grumeti and Mara Rivers, to the northern hills for the water sources there. Only the animals who do not need such regular water intake, or who are better able to extract plant moisture from the remaining vegetation stay in the south. As the migrating animals move northward, the grasses become longer and the geographical domains of the ostrich and warthog are invaded. Further north the landscape variety increases with granite outcrops, and small hills. This is where the acacia tree flourishes, and with it, the giraffe – one of the few animals able to cope with its spiky branches. Here the silence of night is punctuated by the 'cough' of the nocturnal leopard and the whimpering laugh of the hyena. Grazing becomes more perilous as predators increase. The less fit, the old and the sick are ruthlessly removed from the gene pool and in turn ensure the survival of the carnivores.

As the northern migration continues, the terrain becomes more hilly and woodland increases. Many of the trees show evidence of severe damage – a sign of elephant presence. To reach the higher leaves, the elephant will use its great strength and weight to bulldoze the trees and then strip the prone branches bare.

The herbivores reach the northern Serengeti and enjoy the months of August to October in the Kenyan part of the region. By late October the northern pastures are exhausted and the enormous procession starts heading south using a more easterly route, once again crossing the Mara river. By late November, or early December they return to the areas near Ngorongoro after the late autumn (fall) rains have regenerated the southern grasslands. The next May the pattern repeats, as it has been doing before humans were ever there to observe it, or possibly were ever even on the planet.

This interdependent ecosystem is one of the wonders of the natural world. It is finely balanced with grasses, herbivores and carnivores all mutually reliant.

The climate of the Serengeti, and of business

The analogy of the Serengeti climate to business climate has much value. The Serengeti migration is caused by the herbivores following the path of prosperity, in their case, for grass. The non-migrating animals inhabit their own areas 'rain or shine'. Some parts of the Serengeti may suffer a short term drought, or there may be a disease which impacts on one species or another. One year may bring favourable situations for one species which results in higher offspring survival percentages and an increase in numbers. Simultaneously, another species may have had a tough year. One would expect that if the lion has a tough year, the zebra may find itself on the menu less and therefore have a better year!

We do the same. Booms and recessions of varying heights and depths are part of global economics. Different growth rates in neighbouring nations are part of our complex interdependent yet highly competitive environment. The UK enjoyed higher growth rates and endured higher interest rates than continental Europe for the early part of the 21st century, prior to the banking system collapse and global recession of 2008–9. The last few years of the 20th century saw enormous growth rates in Eire particularly fuelled by a favourable tax regime for inward investment. Both the positive and negative consequences of this were seen in the Irish economy with growth rates of GNP and GDP in excess of 5%, yet manufacturing output declining in excess of 5%. Rates of employment increased, inflation began to decrease but house price inertia continued. Simultaneously, other parts of our business Serengeti were not enjoying this growth rate – Germany is the fifth largest economy in the world yet was one of the slowest growing in the early 21st century with several quarters of 'negative growth' or recession before it became a trend which almost all nations embraced. German economic growth 2001–3 was less than 1%. With an aging population profile, high unemployment and approximately \$70bn transferring from West to East Germany each year as part of the modernisation and transformation of the former communist state, there was little prospect for a rapid return to prosperity for a nation just a few hundred miles to the east of the buoyant Irish even before the 2008/9 collapses. The collapse saw the Irish economy plummet with the rest of us.

At macroeconomic, national and international level, we can see the Serengeti in action. Some parts in drought, some in plenty. Some animals benefiting, some suffering. A single species disease can have an effect, as can a single industry 'disease' in our world such as the international travel market, particularly trans-Atlantic, after the New York terrorist atrocities of 9/11. However, the primary focus of *'Strategies of the Serengeti'* is not the equally valid and equally fruitful macroeconomic analogy. The primary focus is for each of us to increase our awareness of the wide range of strategic options available to each of our organisations. It is the adaptations the animals make to ensure survival which create our lessons in successful strategy rather than the root causes of why these strategies are necessary. It is more important for our companies that we learn from the elephant how they survive drought than it is for us to understand what caused the drought. Whilst fascinating, the climate and all its variability, is part of the uncertain and challenging environment in which they live. We can sit in our companies bemoaning interest rate rises or consumer demand variations, or we can develop strategies to deal with these factors. The elephant doesn't trouble itself with debating the cause of a drought – it just goes and finds water!

Serengeti and business

The Serengeti offers enormous species diversity within an environment which is simultaneously interdependent and highly competitive, hence the analogy to our modern business environment. The Serengeti, like business, is 'red in tooth and claw'. The struggle to survive and flourish is lived out on a daily basis with casualties, survivors and a periodic thriving for one species. We are not dis-similar. At the beginning of the last century the heavy industries including vehicle manufacturing and chemical production dominated our industrial world. These gave way to more technologically based industries as computerisation swept the world. We saw the rise of the IT giants. More recently, the big winners are information companies, and in due course they will wane and another business species will thrive. The Serengeti has considerable advantages over our business environment – it has lasted centuries longer, they have seen it all before. Presently the rhinoceros is struggling, not long ago it was the lion and the elephant. Were the human invader to be removed from the equation, the probability is that the cycle would swing around and the rhinoceros would possibly recover. Ironically, with the influx of human interference, the best hope of the endangered rhinoceros is currently with protection by humans from other humans.

There are isolated pockets of collaboration within the Serengeti. Grazers like to be close to giraffes as their high viewing platform and excellent eyesight are one of the best early warning systems amongst mammals. Zebras join wilderbeest for the migration as safety in numbers assists their survival. Lions collaborate within a pride – the combination of their skills develops a greater good than any solitary lion would be capable of. Despite these examples, the overwhelming focus of the Serengeti environment is cut throat competition for scarce resources – the very essence of business.

As with business, there are niche focussed strategies and broad strategies. There are deliberate strategies and opportunist strategies. There are aggressive and defensive strategies. The one thing we do not observe in the Serengeti are failed strategies. These have long since become extinct in this harsh unforgiving climate. In our commercial world we continue to observe champions of previous decades becoming the carcasses of the current decade. In our business environment we see the continued use of strategies which were once successful but have now been rendered obsolete. Technologies change, markets change, perceptions change, managerial fashions change and all will only continue to do so at an ever increasing pace. The animals of the Serengeti, by the very longevity of the strategies they have perfected, and their ongoing successes, have the ability to demonstrate to us a series of strategies which transcend the dry seasons of recessions, the perilous river crossings of take over predators, the seasonal diversity of transient opportunities and the unequal economic rainfall of fluctuating consumer demand.

It is rare that we can have an advantage over these seasoned strategy experts, but we can have one. The cheetah has honed the variety of skills of its ancestors based around acceleration, short term speed, the ability to change direction without losing speed and the use of sharp claws and teeth. What it cannot do is become a warthog or an elephant or an ostrich when the strategies of those animals would be more appropriate. We can. Not only can we transform our businesses from using one animal's strategies to using another's, we can mix and match various strategies using some strategies of the crocodile whilst simultaneously operating other strategies of the rhinoceros or the giraffe.

Animal strategies in practice

The hippopotamus is a highly specialised creature. It may be bad tempered and responsible for many human deaths each year, but in its domain it reigns supreme. The 'hippo' spends most of the day in the water, sleeping in the morning, grazing on vegetation in the afternoon. Its thick hide and fat reserves prevent hypothermia which would otherwise result from spending so much time in the water. Simultaneously the coolness of the water prevents sunburn and blistering which would occur on land. Within the water the hippo is unchallenged. No lion would dare attack an adult or even adolescent hippo near the water and crocodiles know to keep well clear. The massive size of the hippo prevents croc attack, and the gigantic jaws combined with its habit of sitting on opponents, would inflict potentially fatal retribution were any croc sufficiently unwise to attack any hippo other than a very young and small one. The hippo is well aware of its territory, knows its niche and operates very effectively within that niche. Outside the niche the hippo becomes vulnerable. At night time the hippos leave the safety of the water and move onto dry land to graze. Here, outside of their niche they are able to be challenged. A young hippo could become a challenging but entirely feasible meal for a nocturnal lion hunting party. Having been attacked, if it is able to make it back to the river, the lions will break off their attack. However, on dry land, the very factors which make it so perfectly suited to river life – the cumbersome fat layers, bulk and resultant slowness, make it unwieldy and consequently vulnerable. Grazing is therefore usually close to the rivers edge. Crocodiles also inhabit the river's edge.

An adult croc would still not be a match for an adult or adolescent hippo as being sat on by up to three tonne of hippo does diminish any crocodile's ability for future participation in the survival of the species. However, a smaller hippo and a number of crocs would be a battle the crocs could win. The young hippo therefore has a dilemma – stay close to the river's edge and risk the crocodile, or stray a hundred yards from the river and risk the lion. Option three is to stay in its niche where it is king of the river.

Mercedes-Benz was once king of one river. This river being high quality executive motor vehicles. They could stretch as far upstream as the highest quality arena where they compete with Bentley and Rolls Royce brands, but the majority of the river in which they ruled was from the C-class, through to the more upmarket E-class and beyond into the executive S-class. For people who required high quality estate vehicles the choice used to be Mercedes or Volvo – apologies to other manufacturers but they were the 'also–rans'. Drivers of Audi's or lower series BMW's would aspire to drive the luxurious, prestigious, reliable, stylish Mercedes. Customer satisfaction tables almost always had Mercedes at the top. The river was theirs; the other manufacturers visited the river of the Mercedes domain but could not topple the niche leader. Competition intensified from the higher end of the Japanese brands, and in the UK from Jaguar, but Mercedes still held the European dominance of their niche. The strategy of the hippopotamus would have been to stay in the niche, magnify their dominance and seek to relegate the Volvo's and higher end Audi's and BMW's from their arena.

Perhaps driven by Chrysler, Mercedes-Benz opted for a different strategy. Rather than stay with the hippopotamus strategies of niche development, driving dominance and exclusivity within the niche, they embarked upon a 'something for everyone' strategy. They did have major penetration of further distinct and separate 'rivers' of commercial trucks and of sports cars with the SL range, but each of these were separate hippopotamus niche driving – there is little cross over from a truck to an executive sports car. A series of strategies aiming to develop and master these three niches would have been entirely in keeping with the strategies which built the success of the car over the decades, but this was not their choice.

The 'something for everyone' strategy will be explored with different examples in the 'strategies of the wildebeest' chapter, but for Mercedes it has meant a plethora of curious vehicles:

- The A-class which initially had a tendency to fall over in sharp cornering and was the butt of many jokes.
- The B-class, billed as a compact sports tourer, or multi-activity vehicle, isn't quite sure what it is. It merely sits along with a wide range of mass market mobile boxes.

- The M-class 4×4 simply replicated what everyone else did with 4×4's.
- The R-class which is billed as a grand sports tourer – another entry into a mass market area with negligible differentiation from other providers to that market.
- The Viano – was a van with seats in – and an attempt to take part of the people carrier market so beautifully created by Renault.
- The Vaneo proclaimed itself to be a compact multi-purpose vehicle and strikes me more as being a no-purpose vehicle.

The strangeness of the range is not its biggest crime. I was a satisfied Mercedes customer for about 10 years and they have enjoyed many thousands of pounds of my custom. When I first started driving a Mercedes it was viewed as 'upmarket', the quality was high and there was a degree of pride associated with owning one. Now, with the 'something for everyone' strategy that has evaporated and Mercedes is just another mass market producer seeking a few euros in any market in which it can launch a vehicle.

The niche has gone. Or rather the three niches of trucks, sports and quality executive have been smeared into a generalised vehicle manufacturing blur. The brand which used to stand for quality and a degree of exclusivity is now a mass market manufacturer like Ford – or Chrysler! The Mercedes brand is no longer associated with aspirational high value motors, but now also with lower level 'value' vehicles. The price of 'entry to the brand' (i.e. the cheapest available vehicle with the brand or badge) has halved – this does not aid quality brand building. All of the niche strategies of the hippopotamus which had generated an enviable platform for the success of the brand and the company have been absorbed into the mass market strategies of the wildebeest. Not only has this hippopotamus strayed from the water, it has joined the wildebeest on their annual migration!

One alternative could have been to realise that the hippopotamus strategies had driven success, retain them and enter other markets with another brand – as Mercedes have done with the Smart car, or Volkswagen group with its wide range stretching from Audi to Skoda. Other possibilities to protect rather than destroy the Mercedes customer perception may be gleaned from learning about the strategies of the warthog, or the elephant, or the lion.

However, the analogy is clear. Mercedes had successfully used the strategies of the hippopotamus, and had become one of the world's most successful brands in so doing. Had they studied the habits and lifestyle of the hippopotamus they would have realised that straying too far from the niche river courts disaster. If they want to seek pasture further afield, the hippo is not the animal to follow – they could have learnt to keep in the river, gain dominance in the river (or all 3 rivers) and sought a different approach with a different animal to seek advantage in the mass market.

Whilst Mercedes could have learnt from the hippopotamus, other companies and industries could have learnt from the cheetah, the ostrich or the giraffe.

The giraffe has the largest eyes of any mammal and operates them from a height of up to 6 metres. It has the ability to see further than any other land animal. Serial author and former London Business School Professor Charles Handy associates effective leadership behaviour with the ability to develop a vision. He states that it is essential for leaders to 'reframe the unknown scene, connect the previously unconnected, dream the dream.' This is the strategy of the giraffe – the strategy of looking further and clearer than anyone else. History yields us a highly amusing selection of people who have failed to employ the strategies of the giraffe and whose mentality was set in the immediate space in front of them. In the Serengeti of the business world they now stand as clear examples of poor vision, of failing to observe the giraffe.

"I think there is a world market for about five computers."
Thomas Watson Chairman IBM 1943

"Computers in the future may weigh no more than 1.5 tons"
Popular mechanics publication 1944

"Groups featuring guitars are on the way out."
Decca recording chief Dick Rowe, whilst turning down the Beatles for a recording contract in 1962 – they went on to be the world's first supergroup
George M Cohan fired a young actor as he decided that the young man had no romantic appeal – the actor – Clark Gable.

"People will soon get tired of staring at a box every night."
20th Century-Fox boss Darryl Zanuck decided that television would never become popular.

Isaac Newton's mother grew tired of her young boy's obsession with designing what she saw as irrelevant. As a young boy he designed and built a windmill, sundials, paper kites, paper kites with lanterns for night flying and a water clock. She declared that he should become a farmer as his father Isaac had been (Isaac was named after his late father who had died three months before his son was born) and did everything in her power to persuade him. Fortunately Isaac Newton (1643–1727) had the vision strategies of the giraffe. He ignored his mother and became possibly the greatest mathematician,

astronomer and scientist the world has ever known. The moral of this tale –
don't choose your children's careers for them!

Chapter summary

- The Serengeti is an old interdependent and highly competitive
  environment
- There is massive diversity of wildlife, each animal applying its own
  honed strategy
- It is a natural wonder of the world with its ecosystem and annual
  migration
- There are variations in the geography – from grass plains to woodland
  – animals need to adapt their strategies to fit with the environment
- The climate is challenging. Sometimes a situation will arise which
  favours one group of inhabitants and is to the detriment of others
- These strategies have proven their success by their longevity – unlike
  many of our management theories and business strategies

The major chapters

Incorporating a variety of models and analytical techniques

Ch 3 **Giraffe** **(keeping the vision)**
Ch 4 **Elephant** **(using knowledge)**
Ch 5 **Zebra** **(response to threat)**

Note: the chapters are distinct – please read them in any order you choose.

CHAPTER 3

Strategies of the giraffe – keeping the vision

The giraffe is one of the most impressive residents of the Serengeti plains. It is the tallest mammal on earth and can grow up to 6 metres in height (over 18 feet). This allows it to feed from tree foliage unavailable to others. It has a very keen sense of sight with large, well developed and effective eyes which are the largest of any mammal – only slightly smaller than tennis balls. The combination of such keen eyesight and height create an ability to see further than any other terrestrial animal. Whilst the giraffe uses its size, speed and camouflage as secondary defence strategies, its primary defence against predators is this immense sight advantage. The giraffe aims to see the potential predator and react appropriately long before the predator is within its striking range. The giraffe's response to threats is almost always by removing itself from the vicinity. It is thought that one reason why the giraffe is frequently seen in mixed herds is that other animals such as zebra and wildebeest rely on the giraffe to see predators and alert them.

Giraffe fact file:	
Height	Up to 6 metres
Mass	up to 1,350 kg
Life expectancy	30 years in captivity, nearer 20 years in the wild
Diet	Tree foliage from the wooded grasslands
Reproduction	15 month gestation producing a single calf (very occasionally twins)

The name 'giraffe' (*giraffe camelopardalis*) has an immediate history from Arabic dialects (*zirafa*) but probably has an earlier linguistic history from central Africa where travellers brought the local name and inserted it into Arabic.

The obvious feature of the giraffe is its exceptionally long neck. Nature has not duplicated this feature except to a smaller extent in the only relative of the giraffe – the Okapi of the central African rain forest. Amazingly, despite the length of the neck the giraffe has only seven neck vertebrae – the same as a human being. The difference being that each giraffe vertebra can be up to 10 inches high – longer than all 7 human vertebrae together. Neck muscles are connected to the dorsal spines which gives greater strength but hinders the lowering of the neck to ground level. For this reason, the giraffe drinks with its forelegs spread out as far as possible. This time of water intake is when the giraffe is temporarily without its great height and sight advantage. This, combined with the ungainly positioning of spread forelegs which dramatically reduce the ability to execute a hasty exit make water replenishment the time of greatest vulnerability to attack.

The neck is also used to express emotion. A lower position, often horizontal, would indicate anger. Such an animal should be avoided by human visitors as a large dent in a vehicle and smashed windscreen could easily result. The opposite emotion would be exhibited by an erect neck, with nose in the air, the human equivalent would be where we look aloof. For the giraffe, this stance signifies submission.

Bull giraffes combine their neck and horns when fighting. The two horns are short and are thicker in the male. One way of distinguishing between the sexes is to observe the horns – the female has tufts of hair at the tips of the horns whereas the male horns are bare. Some species of giraffe have developed additional horns as genetic mutations. When fighting the male giraffes will stand side by side and aim to hit each other with their necks or horns. Fatalities in such conflicts are almost unheard of and the fight usually finishes when one or both males are either too exhausted, or too concussed, to continue.

A running speed of 50km/hr can be maintained for up to 7km which makes the giraffe the long distance champion of the Serengeti. To facilitate this, an immensely strong heart approximately 2 feet in width, beats at a resting pulse of approximately 60 beats per minute – only marginally slower than an average human resting pulse rate. The giraffe's heart has to pump blood around its massive body and so is immensely strong. It can pump up to 16 gallons of blood per minute. Blood pressure is very high – in the region of 260/160 compared to a human ideal of 120/80. This is the highest known blood pressure amongst land animals. Neck arteries have developed valves, like those in veins, to prevent blood flowing back, away from the brain

Some of our knowledge of the giraffe is as patchy as its coat – tan with orange–brown, sometimes deep chestnut or even black, blotches which provide camouflage. It is thought, but not certain, that the giraffe can exist for long periods without water, bizarrely, even longer than a camel, yet there is no storage mechanism such as that exhibited by the camel. If water is available a giraffe will drink up to 50 litres, although a daily average is nearer 20 litres. Another area of controversy is that of smell. Some think that the giraffe has an acute sense of smell; others declare that it is unexceptional. The giraffe's sleep patterns are also not fully understood. It is believed that a giraffe will sleep for no more than half an hour each day, and that will be in a number of small 'power naps' rather than all at once.

The frequently stated comment of giraffes being mute is incorrect. They do have vocal chords, and do utter deep grunting or bellowing sounds. They can also moo like a cow, hiss like a crocodile or snake and even give a faint whistle. This mostly happens during times of stress and in more placid times the animals are silent – hence the mistaken belief in muteness.

Giraffes are social and inquisitive creatures, often stopping to stare at an unusual object (such as a 4×4 full of tourists and cameras) for a very long time. They will herd together in groups of up to 20, yet at other times are happy to be solitary. The herd structure is loose and this non-territorial giant may be part of a herd dispersed over several square miles.

A female produces a single calf after a 15 month gestation but the majority do not survive to adulthood. Estimates exist between 50%–75% for the number of calves killed. The main predators are lions and hyenas in the open and crocodiles whilst the giraffe replenishes its water supplies at rivers. Leopards and cheetahs will also occasionally treat themselves to a giraffe lunch. The giraffe does not take great care of her young, often being left alone for most of a day. Despite having the ability to stand within an hour of birth and to run after a few days, the calf will usually sit quietly by itself awaiting its mother's return. For those who survive the first few months, a 'nursery' often develops and the 'flock' strategy (see the 'strategies of the zebra') increases their protection. Those who have experienced *Strategies of the Serengeti* conference speeches, if I am using the example of the giraffe in 'talent development', or bringing up its young, will probably have seen a photograph of me demonstrating this poor parenting. On a horseback safari I came across a giraffe mother and calf. To demonstrate the maternal lack of concern for the young, I rode between the two. The mother was unconcerned. Had I attempted to do this with an elephant or hippopotamus who would aggressively tackle any perceived threat to their young, it is unlikely that I would be in a position to be writing this!

Unusual features of the giraffe would include the nostrils, tongue and tail. The nostrils are able to close completely, like those of a camel, the purpose of which must be to prevent dust inhalation. However, this is an almost worthless ability outside of sandy deserts, and certainly of no value in the Serengeti. The tongue is an exceptionally strong muscle, up to 30 inches long and blue. It is sufficiently robust to cope with the leaves and thorns of the acacia tree. The acacia thorns mean that few other animals are able to eat its leaves, but it is defenceless against the tongue of the giraffe. One reason why the giraffe may be able to survive extended periods without water could be that the acacia leaves have a high water content. A thought about the unique colour of the giraffe tongue is that it may be impervious to sunburn, and as the giraffe spends huge amounts of time eating up to 75kg of leaves a day, the tongue is perpetually extended in the hot equatorial sun.

And the tail – the longest of any land mammal – up to 8 feet in length.

Vision

The giraffe's combination of height and exceptional eyesight give an unequalled advantage when compared to other land animals. These two areas of competitive advantage create a situation where all other aspects, including its speed and lack of dependence on regular water intake, are subordinate to the giraffe's vision. The strategy of the giraffe is the strategy of vision.

One view of business is that it is 'vision driven'. In this view, the primary purpose of the Executive Board is to develop, communicate and drive a compelling vision which employees can enact with passion and commitment. This is the view of the giraffe. I seek to illustrate ways in which that can be considered practically but also to explore some of the complexities with this approach which I do not feel are adequately developed from the 'get a vision and everything will be alright' school of management.

I have read numerous business books which give an adamant definition of 'vision' and another equally adamant definition of 'mission'. The next book will be equally adamant, but the other way around! I have yet to find consensus amongst strategy or business writers as to the nature and definitions of mission and vision. What one says, another contradicts. The old adage of *"three strategists in a room will generate at least four opinions"* seems pertinent even at the most basic level of defining what a vision is. Consequently, I use the words 'mission' and 'vision' interchangeably, and add my 'five year old' definition.

Vision – where I am aiming for

Whether this is corporate or personal, it stands.

The primacy of vision as a pre-requisite for business success is nothing new. Charles Handy associated effective leadership with the ability to develop a vision and outlined 5 conditions for visionary leadership:

1. The vision has to be different – reframing the unknown, reconceptualising the obvious, connecting the previously unconnected, dream the dream.
2. The vision must make sense to others.
3. The vision must stick in people's minds – unlike most corporate vision statements.
4. The leader must exemplify the vision in their behaviour.
5. Sharing the vision is a pre-requisite of implementation.

Later, in 2002, Philip Sadler reinforced the primacy of vision from a different angle establishing his list of reasons for business success:

- A clear purpose.
- Shared values embedded in company culture.
- Sound corporate governance.
- Deep knowledge of the industry.
- Set challenging performance targets.
- Deliver value for money.
- Loyal employees.

Whether it is from Handy's angle of leadership, Sadler's angle of empirical research into success or any other business angle, vision is vital for business success. Some authors make great play on the achievability of the vision – I disagree. I can see no reason for not having a vision which states 100%. UK firm Brush Switchgear once had a statement of 'Right first time, on time, every time'. I am sure that they have periodically slipped from this 100% target, but it is an aim. A construction company where I was CFO required 'on time, on budget, snag free, every time' – 100% (a 'snag' is a building term for issues outstanding after the construction project is completed). Sometimes we failed, but the aim was clear. Having a 100% vision is sometimes frowned upon as the unattainable nature of it supposedly discourages. I disagree. I want 100% every time. When I have given a speech, or run a training course, I do not look for the feedback which tells me how good it was, I look for the feedback which shows me how to make an improvement – large or small. Satisfaction with the status quo is the first indication of complacency and the first step towards extinction.

Strategy is a subset of vision. Strategy is not a stand alone discipline. For success it must be inextricably linked to the organisational vision as the means by which this vision is achieved and it must, simultaneously be inextricably linked to the day to day actions of every member of the company. Stand alone strategy is not strategy – it is daydreaming.

Returning to the story of the hippopotamus and the butterfly, the strategy consulting industry does not seem particularly concerned by this – they seem to generate strong work streams without always establishing implementation success. Strategy which is not implemented has failed – withhold the consulting company's payment!

Strategic thought without a strong and tangible link to its day to day implementation will certainly not result in a solution and has certainly made millions in consulting. Strategy should be measured by successful implementation, not the impressiveness of the bound report.

Corboy and O'Corrbui (1999) highlight the detachment of strategy from the organisational vision and detachment of strategy from day to day activities as one of their *'Seven Deadly Sins of Strategy'*. They highlight over centralised planning, failure to recognise 'brick walls', lack of clarity, poor or non-existent communication, lack of individual responsibility and the senior team feeling that their job stops when implementation starts as examples of failure to link to the day to day activities. They illustrate failure to link with the organisational vision with issues such as employees not thinking that the strategy is worth implementing and failure of the employees to fully understand the strategy. In this latter case, communication clarity is always the responsibility of the communicator not the receptor – the senior management have probably failed to communicate the strategy at five year old level.

Linking vision, strategy and activity

In my observation from a variety of organisations, the most widespread tool for this purpose is the M.O.S.T. (Mission, Objectives, Strategies, Tactics) or P.O.S.T. (Purpose, … etc). Another variant on the same theme is V.A.S.T. where the 'V' is for Vision and the 'A' is Aims. This model and structure can become a bit simplistic, one-dimensional, academic, dry and detached, but before breathing new life into it, commenting on its existing widespread use would seem wise.

The M.O.S.T. starts at the top with a definition of the organisational mission – what is it that the organisation seeks to do? What is its purpose?

Objectives are then derived. In order to achieve this mission, what are the required critical success factors? What areas need to see success in order to achieve the mission? The 'acid test' is that if there is a proverbial tick in the box for each of the objective areas, would the mission automatically, without qualification, be achieved? If the answer to this is 'Yes', move on. If the answer is 'No' there is probably a missing objective yet to be defined. Too many objective areas make the model too cumbersome and conventional wisdom recommends that the 'O' has a single figure number of constituents.

The pyramidal nature of the tool then becomes evident. For each of the objective areas, what strategies are we engaging or developing to generate success in this objective? There can be a number of strategies for each objective and so the pyramid widens. Finally, for each strategy, what are we doing at tactical level to make this strategy happen? Strategists sometimes express a reluctance to get into the lower level detail of tactics. This is dangerous. As the first acclaimed strategist, albeit military, Sun Tzu said:

> "Strategy without tactics is the slowest route to victory. Tactics without strategy is the noise before defeat."

In our fast moving, and ever accelerating commercial world, we do not have the luxury afforded to previous generations of seeking slow routes to victory.

Key to this M.O.S.T. model is that it is driven from the mission (or purpose, or vision) which drives the objectives which then drive the strategies to fulfil them which then drive the tactics to achieve the strategies. Strategies do not emerge from the ether; they are developed specifically to achieve the objectives which are required for the fulfilment of the mission. I would add to Sun Tzu's comment

Strategy without objectives is directionless; strategy without a mission is purposeless.

Through its mechanical pyramidal formulation M.O.S.T. can sometimes present an inflexible approach to strategy. In our ever increasingly dynamic world, adaptation and the ability to react rapidly are survival pre-requisites – see the 'strategies of the cheetah'. Inflexibility in strategy formulation is as great a step towards extinction as not having a vision and strategies at all. Incredibly, some people are postulating the idea of not having strategies but using a more chaos based approach where they see planning as irrelevant in a rapidly adapting business environment. I would suggest that it is better to have a plan and be able to deviate from it than not to have a plan and be running around blindly with competitive predators lurking in your part of the business Serengeti.

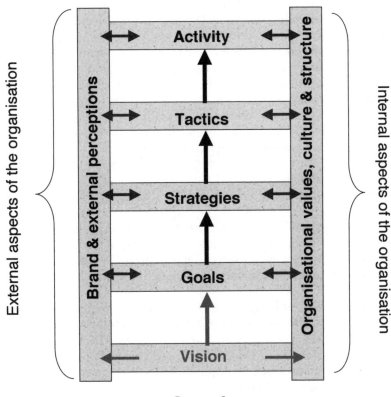

GIRAFFE 1

Whilst M.O.S.T. is designed to connect the vision, or mission, to the daily activity, I feel that stopping at 'tactics' level is one step short. The enacting of the tactics is the daily activity of the organisation's individuals – the daily 'do-list' or day job. There should therefore be another level after tactics which is about the actual performing of those tactics.

I also feel that there are omissions. The four factors of M.O.S.T. must not operate in a strategic vacuum; they are the lifeblood of any business. They should therefore have interaction with, be impacted by and have impact on, both internal and external aspects of the organisation. The internal factors would include organisational culture, values and structure. The external factors would include the brand and perspective of those outside the company – customers, potential customers, owner shareholders, potential employees and even governments.

In order to incorporate these missing factors and to move a fifth stage into activity I therefore suggest that for the strategy of the giraffe – the ability to use the competitive advantage of vision and to percolate it effectively into daily activity, the performance ladder of diagram 'giraffe 1' could be more useful.

The first four rungs of the ladder bear an uncanny resemblance to M.O.S.T. – there is no need to re-invent the proverbial wheel here – it is often wiser to take the good parts of a working structure and improve them rather than starting with a blank design sheet.

Vision

> The primary purpose of the Executive Board is to develop, communicate and drive a compelling vision which employees can enact with passion and commitment.

I find the word 'vision' more appealing than 'mission', but feel free to disagree and substitute it if you choose to use this model within your own organisation. Vision can be all sorts of things – a destination if the map analogy is used, a future scenario if the visualisation process is used, a utopia if the unattainable perfection concept is embraced or a generalisation if the non-specific approach to vision is used. By whatever method, it is the perception of a future state which is desirable and engaging.

> Many organisations appear to have 'visions' which are not visions. Many have uninspirational statements, others have cumbersome unmemorable
> ➜

→
paragraphs and some others have pithy but impractical platitudes. I would suggest that for a vision to achieve its role in the business – the core driver of everything the business does – it should have vowels – A,E,I,O,U. If it can tick all 5, it is likely to achieve its purpose.

A   Action oriented
Driving people on to making things happen. Visions are not passive dreams – they are active stimulation, motivation and encouragement.

E   Easy to remember
The ability to be simply memorised and retained in the mind. There in the mind the vision is explored, expanded and enacted. Powerful visions are always able to be recalled instantly, with no effort, from the heart.

I   Inspirational
Visions paint a picture of a future which is better than the present. They give us the incentive to leap out of bed every morning with the sole intent of furthering the goal of bringing the vision one step closer to being achieved.

O   Obvious
The meaning must be clear and unambiguous to those envisioned. Whether it is clear or esoteric to those outside the vision is immaterial – but to the envisioned it must be lucid and unequivocal.

U   Unique
Your vision is yours – no-one else's. It is exclusive and distinctive such that no other organisation can own it. We are not called to do what everyone else is doing – we are called to create a whole new pathway.

Goals

To get around the overlap and possible confusion with performance management, change the name from 'objectives' to 'goals'. This is the domicile of the Key Performance Indicators, Critical Success Factors or whatever else has become popular for the concept of what is required for success. If we succeed in these things, we will, *ipso facto*, achieve our vision. If that is not automatically true, there must be something wrong with either the vision or the goals and they should be revisited before progressing. My observation is that organisations frequently have five:

1. something about what they do
2. something about how they do it
3. something about money
4. something about their people
5. something about their customers

Strategies

Strategy exists to bridge the gap between where we want to go and what we are currently doing. Strategy is the process by which we consciously align our daily activities to ensure that they are mutually focused on taking us to our desired destination.

Tactics

These are the short term, often rapid combinations of actions which unite to achieve our strategies. I do not believe that there is value in spending time debating the nuances of the differences between strategies and tactics. One person's strategy could be another person's tactic depending on their level and role within a business. More importantly, any change of strategy is probably a major issue for a business. Strategies are meant to be robust, well thought out and long term. Good strategy does not knee jerk from one change to another. Tactics conversely, change rapidly, and especially rapidly if a company is moving fast. I would expect a successful company to be using its people's activities so effectively that the tactics are achieving their desires and are consequently revised and enhanced on a regular basis because they rapidly become obsolete through success. For example, Norwich Union (now Aviva) have continually pushed tactics to drive down their Combined Operating Ratio and as each success is achieved, they celebrate and then drive further tactics to achieve the next target. The strategy is the same – reduction of the C.O.R. The goal is the same 'cost control', but as each tactic yields its benefit, new ones are generated to take the company further – an example of continual improvement or *kaizen*, a Japanese term that means continuous improvement, taken from the words '*kai*' meaning continuous and '*zen*' meaning improvement.

Within the insurance industry, as with most industries, one key to success is to control costs. To focus on one isolated measure of this I will introduce the Combined Operating Ratio (C.O.R.). All Insurance companies take payments for insurance which are the primary income of the organisation. This income is spent on three key areas – the
→

→

payment of insurance claims, the payment of sales commissions and the meeting of the organisation's own expenses such as salaries, property, IT, marketing, administration and all the usual business running costs. A secondary income is available because customers generally pay in advance for insurance thus generating an immense cash surplus for the insurance company which it will invest, under a degree of regulation from authorities, such as the Financial Services Authority in the UK. These investment returns mean that an insurance company is able to operate successfully with a C.O.R. in excess of 100% – in other words, the claims, commissions and expenses can be more than the monies from insurance receipts because there is additional income from investment. Throughout the late 1990's and early part of the 21st century, for a number of reasons, investment returns were not at the envious levels of the preceding decade. This secondary income was therefore becoming smaller. In addition, the market was becoming more competitive, the consumer more aware and the internet gave the customer the ability to make easier comparisons, shopping around for the best price – margins therefore fell. Being squeezed on both insurance policy margins (primary income) and investment returns (secondary income), all insurance companies had to look aggressively at their costs in order to continue to be successful. As these primary and secondary income reduction factors started to bite, despite being amongst the lowest cost companies by the C.O.R. measurement, Norwich Union examined their own costs, implemented radical cost reduction as a strategy and aspired to a C.O.R. of 104%. Tactics were formulated to achieve this, but the strategy was not 'achieve 104%' the strategy was to continually lower C.O.R. Once 104% was achieved, 100% became the target and tactics were generated to achieve it – the strategies were unchanged. As at the end of 2003, they were operating at 99%. By 2005 it was 94%. The market leader in this measure is Direct Line at 90% and very few companies in the UK have achieved less than 100%. The 'under 100%' club was just Direct Line and Norwich Union in 2003, but as time and cost focus progress throughout the industry this exclusive club is gradually expanding.

I hasten to add that there are other measures of market leadership and success in the insurance industry, I have chosen C.O.R. as a stand alone example of a rapidly changing and highly variable combination of tactics established to achieve a focused unchanged strategy, in this case cost reduction.

Activity

The day to day – the 'do list'. This is the key to effective strategy implementation. Unless the purpose of strategy is to drive the organisational vision into the daily activity of each individual, it is valueless. Using the map analogy, the vision may be to travel to a certain destination, but the activity is each individual step. It is difficult to see any particular step having earth shattering impact on the vision, but the combination of all of the steps constitutes a journey.

Having briefly described the rungs of the ladder, let us consider the sides of the performance ladder. The right side is all the internal factors – values, culture and structure – internal factors over which the organisation has control. Control is not easy, as anyone who has ever been involved in a cultural change programme will testify, but nevertheless, you are in control of your own internal factors – including culture. The left side is the external factors – brand and perception. These, we seek to influence by employing marketing and public relations professionals but we are influencing not controlling. It cannot be guaranteed that our brand will have the 'personality' that we wish it to have.

I once participated in a focus group for a financial company who was seeking to launch into a wholly new, non-financial sector aimed at the domestic consumer. The financial company was seeking to promote itself as a caring, sensitive, soft provider of helpful services to the poor embattled consumer who would appreciate a helping hand from such a commercial giant. They had clearly put much effort and market research into the need and their ability to meet it. My feeling was that this, and presumably other focus groups, was one of the final stages to test public perception before a wider and more expensive market testing exercise in a more live environment, such as a localised or partial launch. The session did not go well for the company. My fellow focus group participants declared that the last type of organisation they would trust with their domestic issues was a finance company – they were perceived as greedy, profit focussed and cold – the complete opposite of the brand they were seeking to project. I genuinely felt sorry for the poor marketing graduate brand manager behind the one way glass – seeking to present their company as a helpful friend, developing an admirable needs focused product to then be told by the potential customer that they were about as friendly as a hungry crocodile on a Serengeti riverbank.

The initiative never launched.

The right side (internal) is within your control, the left side (external) you seek to influence.

The internal side of the performance ladder (right side)

Values, culture and structure play an integral part in the achievement of the organisational vision. I initially developed this model with one way arrows, but the more I experimented with it in real organisational situations, the more I realised that the relationship was two way. The difference in the nature of the direction of the influence indicated by the arrows was primarily that of the timescale involved. The values, culture and structure all have an impact at every level of the ladder – at every rung.

Culture is an all embracing umbrella which many differing academic definitions have struggled to explain. However, the most commonly used, most frequently quoted and most widely embracing definition is *"the way we do things around here"* for which I have discovered a number of claimed original sources but my best guess for the original is McKinsey's Marvin Bower in *'The Will to Manage'* published in 1966.

> "What really drives culture – its essence – is the learned, shared, tacit assumptions on which people base their daily behaviour. It results in what is popularly thought of as 'the way we do things around here' "
> Edgar H. Schein *The Corporate Culture Survival Guide* (1999)

If culture is the way we do things, it will obviously impact on every rung of the performance ladder. It will incorporate the type of vision we have, the goals we seek, the strategies we formulate, the tactics we employ and the activities we undertake. Whilst the Bower definition is all embracing, the vernacular use of it appears to me to be focussed primarily on behaviour, as illustrated by Schein's comments. "The way we do things" seems to have a disproportionate emphasis on what we do, what we observe and what we say rather than looking deeper at what is the cause behind our actions, observations and words. I think that there is a lot more to culture than behaviour, but behaviour is one integral part of culture. I will explore the others shortly.

Structure will also impact at every level. If the organisational culture is a militaristic hierarchical position, do not expect initiative and questioning of the status quo at 'activity level' behaviours. Do not expect challenges of ideas nor people feeling free to stick their head above the parapet with an idea. This will impact at strategic level. I recall the exact opposite with an excellent boss I once worked for, Rick Turnbull, then of Rank Hovis McDougal (subsequently Tomkins) and later of Golden West Foods, but now retired. We had an absolute 'humdinger' argument about some business issue which I cannot recall. The argument was professional, business orientated, intellectually challenging and we still did not agree at the end of it. We discussed as equals, both knowing that the other's primary concern was for the success of the business and respecting each others opinions. Rick actively encouraged people to put their head above the parapet and supported them accordingly. A boss such as Rick, who invited and encouraged challenge is the antithesis of the militaristic hierarchical approach.

Values, culture and structure therefore impact on each rung of the ladder in directing and shaping the vision, goals, strategies, tactics and activities we employ. As mentioned, I now draw the influencing arrows both ways as the vision, goals, strategies, tactics and activities also have an evolving and shaping influence on the values, culture and structure. I am not alone in evolving this two way inter-relationship. Sheshunoff (1991) observed that strategy will fail without a supportive culture – the two are inextricably linked. Saker and Speed (1992) commented that culture is dependent on objectives, strategy and structure. Not only are these factors linked, there is no simplistic direction of the causation of the linkage. One affects another, and is in turn affected by that other. Furthermore, these factors on the right side of the ladder are not immutable. As they both influence the items on the rungs of the ladder and are simultaneously themselves influenced by the items on the rungs of the ladder, they are in constant flux, adjusting as the organisation develops. An alteration to, or development of, a vision may have a significant impact on organisational culture in the same way that an organisational culture may have a significant impact on vision development, or goal establishment, or strategy creation – any or all of the ladder rungs. Generally in the short term the right side, or upright, of the ladder is an enabler or limiter for the fulfilment of the vision, but in the longer term the vision is an enabler or limiter of the values, culture and structure – the rungs affect the uprights and the uprights affect the rungs.

Values & beliefs

Virgin Holidays, at their UK Head Office in Crawley, Southern England have this definition displayed:

> Values are the beliefs that shape the way we work together, every day
> They help us see eye to eye
> They help us work together better
> They help us solve problems, take opportunities and sort out disputes.

I think it is priceless! Rather than relegating values to the 'warm and fluffy' department, they have elevated them to the fundamental drivers of what we do every day. Even better, the values of Virgin Holidays are:

> Red
> One more time
> Mrs Cunningham

To an outsider, at first sight, they are meaningless. However, after consideration – what does 'red' mean to you? Dynamic, just a little bit dangerous, alive, fun, vivacious, effervescent, bold, 'in your face'. With just three letters, they have captured an entire lifestyle – brilliant. And it is their corporate colour too.

If you want to try the same with the other two values, a little clue – Mrs Cunningham is Richie's mother in the US sitcom Happy Days.

Also on the wall at the Crawley office is one of the most interesting bits of publicly displayed advice I have ever come across "don't leave your knickers off to iron someone else's" – a tremendous and memorable statement. Perhaps it would have saved a Michigan company the embarrassment of being used in a strategy book as an illustration:

> The Allied Roofing Company of Grand Rapids, Michigan, US created an innovative solution to the slowdown of business caused by the exceptional snowfall in the winter of 1979. Using their roofing technology they worked to clear business premises roofs of snow and hence ensure that the excessive weight did not collapse the roofs. This was proving to be a lucrative venture as a small payment to have a roof cleared ensured continued trade for businesses otherwise at risk from many days loss of trade due to a collapsed roof. Regrettably the Allied Roofing Company did not clear one particular business roof in Grand Rapids – their own. Their lucrative initiative had to be halted when their business premises roof collapsed under the weight of snow! Don't leave your knickers off to iron someone else's!

Values are deeper than behaviours, they are some of the drivers of what we do and how we filter our observations to make conclusions. Psychologists will inevitably develop a semantic differentiation between values and beliefs, but, like strategists defining 'mission' or 'vision', I have not found consistency in definition. In his groundbreaking book *'Changing Belief Systems with NLP'* Robert Dilts used the term 'beliefs' and expounded their importance in driving our behaviours. More recently, he makes a definition of: "Beliefs are the foundation of everyone's personal outcomes".

> "A company will have to formulate its own standards and values to supplement the laws and regulations in the various countries. It will have to ensure that these are accepted internally and complied with."
> Morris Tabaksblud CEO Unilever NV 1997

Our personal and corporate values drive our behaviour and, more than that, are the most important driver of the culture of our organisations. Let me illustrate at national level. In the Southern USA pre-1960's and even in later decades in South Africa, there was a belief by some that 'white' was better then 'black'. This belief, or value, drove cataclysmic behaviours but also drove the culture of these respective regions with segregation, unequal wealth, a flawed legality and disproportionate opportunity. The values drove not only behaviours, or actions, but culture as well.

Further into history, with Nazi Germany in the 1930's and 1940's, the Nazi's developed and evolved a belief that the Jewish race was inferior and over time even relegated this inferiority to sub-human levels – hence the extermination programme.

Through history we can see values driving behaviour with, for example, religious martyrs and in more modern times with the evils of suicide bombers – their values and beliefs somehow seem to suspend what the rational majority would see as 'normal' and lead to almost incomprehensible acts.

Before any of us think that considering beliefs and values at national level is inappropriate for a consideration of business or organisational strategy, the colonial attitudes of British companies towards employees in former colonies is a matter of recent history rather than the distant past. I recall seeing a 1970's BBC documentary which was being shown to an international group of MBA students. In the programme the British colonial attitudes verged on being racist as viewed through our modern eyes. Times have changed, colonialism has moved on but our present enforcement of democracy and low regulation capitalism worldwide is also based on a series of values or beliefs which are driving behaviours. I wonder whether we will be judged in two or three generations time with the same disdain that we now hold for the way in which those colonial organisations operated – "the way they did things".

Values and beliefs are critical to our companies as well as to us as individuals. If we use the parallel of a company being a separate person, (which in law it is), the values of that individual will be the primary force in determining how the 'person' behaves.

Current leadership theories espouse values as critical, or as Ciulla wisely states, *"the question is not so much about what a leader values, but what a leader actually does to demonstrate his or her values"* – again the link of values and behaviour, this time with behaviour as a 'proof' or 'example' of values. Leadership theory has spent decades trying to define leadership, to the extent that Joseph Rost gathered 221 definitions of leadership! Most definitions since the work of James MacGregor Burn's 'Transforming leadership' theories of the 1970's have included elements of values as important aspects of leadership. The trouble with considering values in isolation is that, again quoting Ciulla *"Values are static concepts. You have to make a lot of assumptions to make a value do something ... while values change all the time, having a value does not mean that one has or will do something about it."* She gives examples such as a CEO having a value where he or she has a moral obligation to employees, yet still cuts jobs to ensure his or her obligations to shareholders – something most of us have had to face at some time in our career. For many this develops into a guilt as our behaviours are at odds with our values rather than being driven by our values. In a different scenario, I recall being voted down 7–1 in a board meeting on an issue where I viewed that the company behaviour decided by the majority of my fellow directors was to be at odds with my personal values. This was a fundamental stepping stone for me – within a year I had departed.

Values are therefore deep and complex. They *"change all the time"* (Ciulla), they largely determine our behaviour, they generate internal conflict if there is a gulf between behaviour and values, and more relevantly for this book, they have a massive impact on the culture of the organisation.

Culture – a new model

Having argued that the modern usage of Bowers "the way we do things" falls short, I need to provide a substitute. Some writers on culture focus on values, some on behaviour, some on formal statements and some on surface issues (what Schein termed 'artifacts'). These seem to have differing levels of impact on organisational culture and also a degree of influence over each other. My 'Culture Determinants' model seeks to draw these together and identify the inter-relating influences of one part on another. Again, rather than claiming to have invented something entirely new, I am merely seeking to draw together what many others have postulated.

The model allows us to explore:

- Values and beliefs – what we stand for
- Behaviours – what we do
- Written statements – what we publish
- Surface level – some of the seemingly trivial consequences which 'speak loudly'

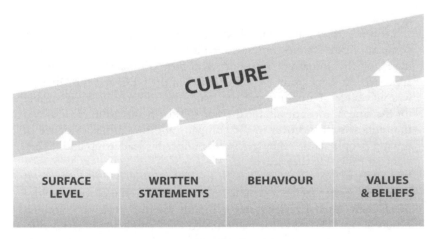

GIRAFFE 2

The essence is that culture is complex, dynamic and has multiple influences – some small and some large. The relative sizes of the sectors in the diagram are intended to visually reinforce the level of influence each one has. As discussed earlier, I surmise that the greatest influences on organisational culture are the organisational values. It is important here to note that these are not necessarily the contents of the organisational 'values statement' – those are contained within the 'formal statements' influencers. The values and beliefs here are the real, often unwritten, often unsaid, values of the organisation as driven by the behavioural examples of the leaders. These must be 'values in action' at the top of the organisation to be able to influence the culture by becoming the established values lower down in the organisation.

In 2005, the new CEO of a rapidly expanding European IT based company, which needs to remain anonymous, brought with him more modern, inclusive, leadership ideas focussing on employees' development, performance through people and the reduction of the 'command and control' approach which the organisation had grown from. These were value based – he believed that employees worked better when treated in his way rather than the way of 'command and control'. Most of the executives, including those who had been with the company in its infancy saw that this was the way ahead and supported the CEO's practical outworkings of these values – i.e. behaviours. He also ensured that this rapidly expanding organisation recruited senior people who shared his ideas.

➔

→

However, one long established director, who had helped grow the company from a minor enterprise to a large PLC, paid lip service to many of the initiatives but preferred the 'command and control' approach. At some point a conflict between the CEO and the Director was inevitable. To compound the issue, this director was responsible for the largest, most profitable division of the organisation. He also had the highest staff turnover in the company and saw this as evidence of driving people hard – they get results under his leadership and if they want an easier life they leave!

As part of his values revolution, the CEO instilled a fairly standard performance management programme. This involved employee development plans, annual reviews and 6 month informal reviews – nothing extraordinary. The CEO then announced that completion of the performance management for each individual would be a measurable issue which therefore partly determined bonuses for the top 3 levels of management – including the board. The amount of bonus attributable to this was 5%. At the beginning of the year when this was announced, the old established director said "you may as well take the 5% off me now as I won't do it". The long brewing conflict battle line had been drawn.

The CEO did not have many options:

1. Seek to persuade the director to comply
2. Remove the director from his post
3. Continue the 'values based revolution' excluding the board
4. Continue only with the other 3 business divisions
5. Abandon his values based approach until the board unanimously backed it.

Option 1 is obviously the preferred option – but if this fails, which of the others would be preferable?

Option 3 is regrettably a very common action, particularly in performance management. I will consider this more fully in a later chapter, but it does not work. This is a 'guaranteed fail' option.

Option 4 is effective unilateral declaration of independence – it is entirely feasible, would give the CEO more time to explore option 1, may well see an exodus from this division to others as bonuses are higher and may well therefore force the unwilling director into compliance, but would take a brave CEO as it is a high risk strategy. It will only succeed if the revolution is sufficiently positive in the other divisions to leave the major division lagging visibly behind.

The CEO chose option 4. He was willing to postpone success in one area in order to develop his vision in the majority of the company (the

→

> → other 3 divisions represented approximately 60% of the company). He decided that he would rather resign than take option 5 – it was a conflict with his personal values and his vision for the company. If option 4 did not have the desired effect within 18 months to 2 years, he still had option 2 as a fallback position.
>
> 2nd edition update: by 2007, the formerly dominant division was still successful but no longer dominant. The Divisional Director departed into early retirement as an alternative to changing his modus operandi. New Divisional Directors progressed the CEO's revolution.

As this model deals with 'real' values as well as the formal written value statements, it becomes more difficult to quantify. It is easy to tick a box which states that we have, or are committed to, a particular value. As soon as we start testing the extent to which we actually believe in the value, different reactions result from individuals – despite them all answering 'yes' to the question of whether they hold the value. Consider the following values test:

> Values test:
>
> Q1 Do you believe that stealing is wrong?
> Q2 Do you think that Robin Hood generally had a justified cause?
>
> Most people answer 'yes, yes' – but he was a thief! The value which outlaws stealing is modified by context, so measuring values cannot be done simply by asking questions such as 'do you believe that stealing is wrong?'
>
> A more difficult one:
>
> Q3 Do you believe it is wrong to kill civilians, women and children indiscriminately?
> Q4 Do you think that the US was right to drop the A-bomb on Hiroshima on 6 August 1945?
>
> Generally people say 'yes' to Q3 and then split between 'no' and 'yes' on Q4 with the majority 'yes' side stating it was right because it saved more lives by ending the war earlier. The answer is again modified by context. →

➜
Even more difficult:

Q5 Do you think people with a physical handicap should be allowed to live?
Q6 Do you think that abortion on the basis of physical handicap is justified?

This testing of a value is delving into very deep areas as some people on both sides of this argument can be driven to kill – one to kill the unborn baby and some, in the recent past, to risk killing doctors through the bombing of abortion clinics. Values are so strong they can lead us to kill.

How does this fit in with business strategy? If values directly affect all rungs of our performance ladder, and if values are the most significant influence on organisational culture, they have the greatest chance to influence our strategic success – ignore them and we have cut off a, possibly the, major influence on business performance success – from vision, through strategy to activity.

From the difficulties which would occur with incontextual values statements such as 'stealing is wrong' the only way in which we can have a view of values is how they work out into behaviours – hence the large, strong influence arrow in the diagram from values & beliefs to behaviours.

One business framework for this is a 'values quantification' or 'values barometer', such as demonstrated in diagram Giraffe 3, which asks for behavioural evidence of the values. I am indebted to Ian Mason of Neos Learning, who created the illustrated barometer, for permission to include it. In this real life example, the four values of the hosting organisation are: being positive, being helpful, being straightforward, being spirited. If these do not percolate into action they are not values, they are valueless, and so it is utterly reasonable to consider not whether an individual holds these organisational values, but on whether the individual is actively and consistently demonstrating these values. In the boxes to the right can be a score for self analysis or opinion of others. This can be numeric, letters, traffic lights or words. A full 360 degree approach would accumulate other's ideas and generate something such as that of diagram Giraffe 3.

Culture – organisational behaviour

The secondary influence according to the 'Culture Determinants' model is that of organisational behaviour. The organisational behaviour is a collaboration of

Value	Behaviours needed for value	All Respondants	Self	Manager	Peer	Direct Report	No Relation	Total Team	Total Company
Being positive *lets us get the best out of life, looking forward positively and passionately. We have confidence in ourselves, in each other, and believe there is always a solution.*	Shares ideas and knowledge, whilst seeking answers from others								
	Inspires others and influences innovative and creative solutions								
	Applies energy and enthusiasm to both challenging and routine tasks								
	Demonstrates empathy with others differences, coaching and leading where possible								
	Reinforces change by personally embracing it								
Being helpful *is working more closely together, to get closer to our customers. In this way we bring our customers closer to whom and to what they want.*	Identifies interdependent relationships on all tasks and projects								
	Strives to build bridges across locations and builds networks outside of immediate work environment								
	Consistently relates tasks and projects to the needs of internal and external customers								
	Has knowledge of competitors, and what impacts on our ability to acquire and retain customers by experiencing customer facing situations								
	Demonstrates the ability to influence others to find customer focused solutions.								
Being straight forward *means being clear and uncomplicated in all that we do. We will strive to make even complex things as accessible and easy to use as possible. We believe in brilliant basics.*	Considers overall objectives and strategy when undertaking or planning new tasks								
	Identifies and analyses causes/issues and generates and implements successful solutions/options								
	Ensures all oral and written communication is clear and straightforward								
	Clarifies and questions to ensure needs are understood								
	Attempts to understand others and not make assumptions or judge								
Being spirited *is having a constructive, open and can do attitude. We are determined to succeed.*	Strives to develop collaborate and supportive relationships								
	Demonstrates an open mind, seeks feedback and embraces a variety of methods to achieving goals and objectives								
	Strives to meet deadlines and maintain quality								
	Takes ownership and responsibility for completing tasks and understanding impact on others								
	Demonstrates resilience, determination, and commitment through professional behaviour								

GIRAFFE 3

the behaviour of its constituent parts – i.e. the people. The application of human behavioural diagnostics to an organisation is widely practiced and wholly applicable.

For almost 2,500 years we have considered human behaviour in 4 parts or preferences. Many individuals have published models and theories around the same basic pretext. Some like DISC and Myers Briggs are well known and well used today; others such as 'facial shapes'(Mar) and 'blood types' (Nomi/Besher) are now consigned to history. There are also new variants on the theme emerging every year with different organisations creating new words to give their variation of the basic 4 part behaviour preference understanding that has stood the test of time.

Some of the more foundational, mixed for amusement with some of the more curious are shown in the diagram 'giraffe 4'.

Each of us is unique. We all behave differently. Behaviour can be defined as merely a combination of our voice (pitch, tone and volume), our facial mask (how we are looking) and our body language. Behaviour then generates action. We each choose to use behaviours based on a variety of factors such as personality, experience, situation and role. The advent of Neuro-linguistic programming (NLP) has re-enforced individual behavioural studies by considering the values and personal identity behind our behaviour.

Each behaviour is in itself both good, when used appropriately, and bad when under or over used. One key to success is the ability to judge and choose the most appropriate behaviour at any one time.

My personal preference is to use SPECTRUM (from EvaluationStore.com) as it is able to be understood without having to pay expensive consultants. Myers Briggs (MBTI) is globally larger, although my personal opinion is that MBTI is both overly complex and does not have some of the nuances which make SPECTRUM so flexible and effective – I have to think hard what INTJ means when I meet one – it is too cumbersome for a person with a '5 year old' approach to life. I will therefore draw heavily on SPECTRUM terminology and framework.

The essence of explaining SPECTRUM or any Jungian influenced diagnostic, is in the graph on page 58.

The task-people dichotomy and the self-other dichotomy are interfaced graphically. All people, and all companies, can choose to use all types of behaviour – we are not programmed to behave in a certain way and a type-casting or labeling does not excuse bad behaviour – "I am an ENTJ therefore I can be abrupt when speaking to you" is nonsense. We are not, however, all equal in our preferences of using behaviours, nor do we use the same behaviours in different circumstances. We tend to favour some preferences and choose to use others less. We can use, underuse or overuse behaviour. We can be most adept, or find it difficult to use different behaviours when they are needed. An example in the history of UK politics would be

Models	Red	Yellow	Green	Blue
Hippocrates & Galen 370 BC & 190AD	Choleric - enthusiastic	Sanguine - cheerful	Melancholic - sombre	Phlegmatic - calm
Aristotle 325 BC	Warm	Moist	Dry	Cool
Jung Functions	Intuition	Sensing	Feeling	Thinking
Jung Attitudes	Perceiving/externally focused/subjective	Extrovert/externally focused/subjective	Judging/internally focused/subjective	Introvert/internally focused/objective
Katcher & Atkins	Controlling	Adapting	Supporting	Conserving
LIFO 1960's	Taking Over	Dealing Away	Giving in	Holding On
DISC	Dominance	Influence	Conscientiousness	Steadiness
SDI	Red	Mix of all 3	Blue	Green
Eric Fromm	Taking Exploitative	Exchanging Marketing	Accepting Receptive	Preserving Hoarding
Isabel Myers	Extrovert Thinking	Extrovert Feeling Sensitive	Introvert Feeling Sensing	Introvert Thinking Intuitive
MBTI 1950's	Intuitive Perceiving	Perceiving	Judging	Judging
Watson & Crick	Adrenine	Thymine	Cytosine	Goanine
Pavlov & Lykken	Energetic	Excitatory	Inhibitory	Steadfast
Plato 340BC	Intuitive	Artistic	Sensible	Reasoning
Mar - Facial Shapes	Oval	Triangular	Round	Square
Empedocles	Fire	Air	Earth	Water
Hippocrates	Blood	Yellow Bile	Phlegm	Black Bile
Eric Adickes	Doctrinaire	Innovative	Sceptical	Traditional
Eduard Spranger	Economic	Artistic	Religious	Theoretic
Ernst Kretschmer	Insensitive	Manic	Oversensitive	Depressive
Benziger	Results	Creativity	Empathy	Routine
Birkman Method	Authority, Challenge	Activity, Change,	Acceptance, Esteem	Structure, Thought
OPQ	Extrovert task focused	Extrovert people focused	Introvert people focused	Introvert task focused
Pavlov	Active Moderate	Active Extreme	Passive Moderate	Passive Extreme
Adler	Ruling	Social	Leaning	Avoiding
Marston	Dominance	Inducement	Submission	Compliance
Merrill	Driving	Expressive	Amiable	Analytical
CPI	In Charge	Get Things Going	Behind the Scenes	Chart the Course
Famous examples	Winston Churchill / Mao Tse Tung / Margaret Thatcher	Christopher Colombus / Walt Disney / Leonardo Da Vinci	Mother Theresa / Mahatma Ghandi / Florence Nightingale	Isaac Newton / William Shakespeare / Johan Sebastian Bach

GIRAFFE 4

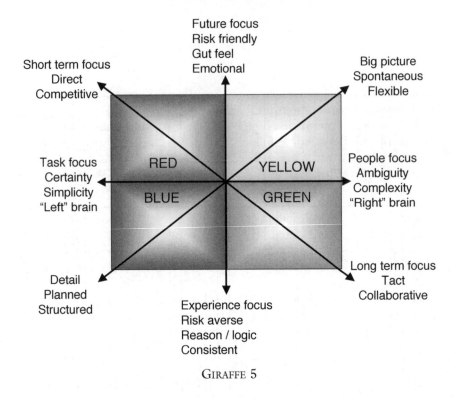

Future focus
Risk friendly
Gut feel
Emotional

Short term focus
Direct
Competitive

Big picture
Spontaneous
Flexible

Task focus
Certainty
Simplicity
"Left" brain

RED   YELLOW

BLUE   GREEN

People focus
Ambiguity
Complexity
"Right" brain

Detail
Planned
Structured

Long term focus
Tact
Collaborative

Experience focus
Risk averse
Reason / logic
Consistent

GIRAFFE 5

that of Margaret Thatcher. She used very 'red' behaviour which at the time was appropriate – it achieved the objective (task focus) and made most people sufficiently impressed by her aptitude that the voting public re-elected her (externally focused). When, later, this behaviour was no longer appropriate and a gentler more conciliatory approach would have been better, Margaret Thatcher was unable to adapt. The only behaviour she felt comfortable with was the 'red' behaviour and she chose to continue using it. As her problems with a situation-behaviour mismatch developed, she did the only thing she was comfortable with – used even more 'red' behaviour and thus increased the mis-match still further. In the end she was dramatically ousted from power and replaced by John Major – a man who exhibited extreme 'blue' behaviour, and even struggled to use 'red'.

To summarise

- We have preferences as to which of the four behaviours we use in any circumstance.
- We can use, overuse or underuse each one.
- We use different behaviour combinations in different situations.

- When faced with a situation-behaviour mismatch we can use a different combination, or increase the usage of the type of behaviour we are employing.

And remember, each behaviour can be good if used well, and almost always has a positive intention in its use.

This leads to summaries of the expected attributes and examples of overuse of each behaviour as follows.

Green	Red	Blue	Yellow
Productive use of each behaviour			
Attentive	Fast Reactions	Pragmatic	Adaptable
Visionary	Self-Assured	Cautious	Exploratory
Humble	Radical	Detached	Friendly
Faithful	Demanding	Steady	In tune with others
Reactive	Dynamic	Rigorous	Diplomatic
Exemplary	Ambitious	Systematic	Versatile
Critical	Resolute	Thrifty	Ingenious
Intuitive	Intense	Efficient	Witty & Funny
Unproductive (over) use of each behaviour			
Dreamer	Tactless	Obstinate	Insincere
Servile	Dictator	Pedestrian	Tricky
Soft	Combative	Private	Absurd or silly
Scathing	Over-bearing	Uninterested	False
Emotional	Takes-over	Analysis paralysis	Whimsical
Unproductive (under) use of each behaviour			
Thoughtless	Slow	Careless	Unsociable
Cynical	Uninspiring	Unstable	Unaware
Irresponsible	Apathetic	Shallow	Tactless
Intolerant	Indecisive	Extravagant	Unimaginative
Selfish	Conservative	Messy	Disagreeable

A full diagnostic at personal, team or company level will be available from EvaluationStore.com.

So far, the primary influence on culture is the organisational values and beliefs – for this we have explored a few areas and suggested the values barometer as a practical tool. The secondary influence in the model is organisational behaviour – where SPECTRUM has been very briefly explored and offered as a practical tool. The tertiary influence is what I have termed the 'written statements'.

Organisational written statements

Mission statements, vision statements, values statements and the like. Some are one sentence, memorable statements, others almost take the form of a religious creed. The most comprehensive 'creed' I have found is:

> We believe our first responsibility is to those who use our products and services. In meeting their needs everything we do must be of high quality. We must constantly strive to reduce our costs in order to maintain reasonable prices. Customers' orders must be serviced promptly and accurately. Our suppliers must have an opportunity to make a fair profit.
>
> We are responsible to our employees, the men and women who work throughout the business. Everyone must be considered as an individual. We must respect their dignity and recognise their merit. They must have a sense of security in their jobs. Compensation must be fair and adequate and working conditions clean, orderly and safe. Employees must feel free to make suggestions and complaints. There must be equal opportunity for employment, development and advancement for those qualified. We must provide competent management and their actions must be just and ethical.
>
> We are responsible to the communities in which we live and work. We must be good citizens – support good works and charities and bear our fair share of taxes. We must encourage civic improvements and better health and education. We must maintain in good order the property we are privileged to use, protecting the environment and natural resources.
>
> Our final responsibility is to our stockholders. Business must make a sound profit. We must experiment with new ideas. Research must be carried on, innovative programmes developed and mistakes paid for. New equipment must be purchased, new facilities provided and new products launched. Reserves must be created to provide for adverse times. When we operate according to these principles, the stockholders should realise a fair return.

By contrast, many companies produce short, pithy statements with the primary aim being memorability rather than to be comprehensive. Whether they call them mission, vision or any other form of strap line is immaterial – they are statements of what the company is seeking to do and in the context of 'the strategies of the giraffe' they are statements of vision, of something they want to be or do, of the future.

Microsoft
"We work to help people and businesses throughout the world realize their full potential"

Yamaha
"We will continue to create 'Kando' and enrich culture with technology and passion"

Google
"To organize the world's information and make it universally accessible and useful"

Levi Strauss
"We will clothe the world"

There is, of course, an infinite range from the few words to the comprehensive statement. Simon Webley conducted research into 'value words' used in UK company formal statements and generated a top 10 of:

1. Integrity
2. Highest ethical standard
3. Responsibility
4. Reputation
5. Honesty
6. Openness
7. Fair
8. Competitive
9. Trustworthy
10. Profitable

Whilst all of us would agree to probably all of them, the complexities of business life create grey areas. I recall, as an accountant in a property company I had one highly visible, highly contentious and highly political piece of land where I could have justified a value of anything from £5m to £50m depending on which valuation arguments I gave precedence. Whilst it is very unusual, possibly unique, to have such a huge range, where would integrity, highest ethical standard, honesty and fair come into my debate? As a famous First Century Roman Governor once said *"What is truth?"*

This ambiguity is true of almost all aspects of higher level corporate finance – we accountants live and work in 'grey areas' as Dyson explains:

"Accounting Profit is an estimate, based on highly questionable assumptions. Thus Companies can and do vary their results by changing their assumptions. It should be viewed only as a guide to decision-making."

Accounting for Non-Accountants J R Dyson (1994)

One of the problems with any of the corporate written statements is, like ethical audits, companies can 'play the game', providing some beautiful words for external consumption whereas their real, unwritten mission statement is more like:

> We want to make as much money as possible and are going to screw our workers and suppliers into the ground to do so. We will charge our customers as much as we think we can get away with and will provide a product that does the job – just. Quality will be the least we can get away with without annoying customers haranguing us. We will entertain whatever financial practices give us the right numbers, and by the way, don't think we care about the environment as we'll all be dead and buried by the time global warming wrecks the planet – the next generation can sort it out.

I argue that the formal mission or vision or values statement has very limited impact on a company culture but is more a statement of how they would like to be seen by others. It is a narrative of intended behaviour, intended action or intended purpose. It becomes valuable not only if the behaviour backs it up but more importantly, if there is accountability to uphold it and action is taken when it is not upheld. If such accountability is in place then the arrow of influence from 'written statements' to 'culture' in the Culture Determinants model is justified. Returning to the earlier values example of treating suppliers in a professional and businesslike manner – including paying them on time; occasionally a customer is late in paying me. Perhaps because they are aware of my intolerance of such practice, and previous choices not to repeat work for poor paying customers, one UK PLC followed up their late payment with a telephone call and an insistence that I invoiced them for the interest as per the terms and condition of our contract – something I could never be bothered to do. The amount of interest was minimal £18.34, but the principle of insistence on acting on the value gave credibility to their written statement, this time in the form of an agreement of how we will act together. A Canadian customer, with a similar written commitment to paying fairly tasked their Finance Director with a challenge after I had completed a training event for them. The challenge was to get the invoice paid, and the money into my company bank account before my plane landed at Heathrow. Regrettably, international date lines and banking hours meant that I beat the cash by a few hours – but the written statement, reinforced by the behaviour, created a very positive impression of a company whose culture includes what it has said it includes.

"Shell companies have as their core values honesty, integrity and respect for people. Shell companies also firmly believe in the fundamental importance of the promotion of trust, openness, teamwork and professionalism, and in pride in what they do. Our underlying corporate values determine our principles. These principles apply to all transactions, large or small, and describe the behaviour expected of every employee."

C.A.J. Herkstroter

"Greenpeace learned that the UK government had granted permission for Shell Oil to dump a huge, heavily contaminated oil installation, the 4,000 tonne Brent Spar, into the North Atlantic despite it being loaded with toxic and radioactive sludge. ... ... Ironically, the planned Shell dump came just one month before North Sea environment ministers were due to meet in Denmark in June to discuss measures to eliminate the discharge of hazardous substances from all sources into the North Sea and the marine environment. At the Oslo and Paris Commission (OSPARCOM) meeting, 11 out of 13 countries agreed a moratorium on the dumping of offshore installations, pending agreement on an outright ban".

Greenpeace web site on-line archives from May 1995.

On 20 June 1995, following a decision by Shell not to dump the Brent Spar, the oil installation was towed to Erfjord in Norway – it has been moored there ever since.

"A two-month long oil spill in the south-eastern part of the Niger delta in Nigeria is wrecking havoc on the local population and ecology. To date, the operating company, Royal Dutch Shell, has done nothing to stop the flow. Greenpeace says that this is yet another example of the malpractice of this giant petrochemical company which likes to masquerade as environmentally responsible."

Pip Hinman Greenpeace On-line archives

Creating a written statement does not ensure or generate a culture or a behaviour. It does not change a culture nor does it change behaviour. The statement is usually about describing public behavioural aspirations – albeit with a sense of 'rose tinted' spectacles. The written statements are the formal extrapolation of an idealised version of desired behaviours. Rather than driving current behaviour, the written statement is therefore itself driven by behaviour – desired or current – hence the horizontal arrow on the model.

The 'strategy of the giraffe' – keeping the vision foremost – should include some form of statement about what that desired future should be – in five year old terms. It could also include a statement about what sort of behaviour is best suited to achieving that vision. It could also include a statement of what sort of values would be required in order to bring that vision to reality. The combination of these will generate the culture which is best suited to achieving that vision. If the values, the behaviours and the written statements are all aligned to the delivery of the vision, only one factor could still mess up the generation of the ideal, vision supporting, corporate growth compost of the most appropriate culture. These are the 'surface level' items which illustrate culture.

Surface level issues

These are the issues described as 'artifacts' by Schein, and include the aspects combined by Johnson & Scholes in the 'culture web'. On their own they do not create a culture. My opinion is that their existence actually has very little influence on the culture. However they can be important as they assume a relevance far beyond their reality. There could be many examples of surface level issues, and many writers have compiled lists. The following list includes some by Schein, Lundberg and Johnson and Scholes, plus others, and is intended to be illustrative rather than exhaustive – so please add your own.

Status symbols – what are they and when do you get them? I know of one company where you know you have 'made it' when you get the pager to attach to your belt which indicates any significant share price movement. Most organisations have a variety – what are yours and what do they say about the company? My first job upon leaving university was in a bank. There were 3 sets of toilets – male, female and managers. I wondered whether surgical reconstruction was necessary when one became a manager.

I've been in organisations with executive dining rooms, companies where working on a certain floor of the building was the symbol, and another when your office window faced the beautiful view to the south. In one company we did the reverse. On an office move, the ground floor had the worst natural light. We, the executive board, located ourselves there.

Personal car parking space – which says 'I'm so important I must be nearer the door'. I prefer the communication of 'each of our contributions are equally useful' from having no reserved spaces. I think it is a healthy sign when the CEO's Jaguar is parked next to the cleaner's Skoda.

Car parking protocol – I commented to one customer that their habit of staff parking in visitor spaces and the disabled spaces made a very strong statement of what they thought was important. By my next visit two weeks later the visitor and disabled spaces were all available!

Heroes and villains – the corporate stories of the past – the success stories, the 'do this and you'll be sacked' stories, the maverick stories – who are they about and what do they say about the company? Type "Malden Mills fire 1995", or "Aaron Feuerstein" into a search engine and find his story. No-one could ever lead that business in the future unless they exhibited the same values.

Myths and legends – what other stories are told about the company and its actions? What are the things which have passed into folklore? I recall one story from one of my former companies where a 'grade 8' manager was replaced with a 'grade 7' manager for a job. The facilities team then came and removed the 'grade 8' manager's desk, chair, pictures and plant, replacing them with the marginally inferior 'grade 7' versions.

Offices and buildings – palaces or portacabins? I am aware of one premises built near sewage works in Birmingham UK, where only the executive suite has air-conditioning – the office and warehouse have to open the window if it is too hot. This can apparently be very unpleasant if the wind is in the wrong direction – what does this say about the company?

Handling bad news – in 2005 one UK PLC announced massive director pay rises in the same week that they announced largescale redundancies. That spoke very loudly to the staff about company culture. Another announced redundancies by texting employees.

One friend was appointed a CEO of an organisation, and chose an appropriate car. He arrived for work, parked his top of the range BMW in the CEO space and within his first week made decisions that would make many people redundant. The juxtaposition of his expensive car and his first large action prompted him never to get a top range car again, and certainly never to have a CEO parking space.

Power structure – who are the people who wield the real power, not just the formal power? I recall, as a fairly junior accountant asking my Divisional Finance Director what he actually did. His reply – "I am an oiler of wheels". Early on I was told that it was useful to always be on the right side of him.

To my knowledge, I always was and somehow my requests for capital expenditure were always turned around very quickly whereas some other sister companies had to wait months – I do not think the two parts of the story are disconnected.

Routines, systems and processes – what do they say about the company? I recall one company for whom I worked where the annual budget first draft was made about 4 months before the start of the year and countless revisions were laboriously debated until about the third month of the year – 7 months of non-value-added number crunching speaks of conservatism, losing focus, analysis paralysis. The Head Office employed a team of about 30 people to check and question these reports from our 90+ subsidiaries.

With one customer, the process which had to be endured in order to bring coffee into a training environment was tortuous. There were various levels of authorisation for such a simple request. We produced a flow chart of their decision making process, estimated a cost and, to further emphasise the point, brought our own flasks of coffee to a meeting stating that this saved them several hundred pounds. They changed their system.

Language, words, the vernacular – I believe that words are the outflow of the heart – listen carefully to what someone says and you can tell more about what goes on in their mind and heart than with a full diagnostic. What are the words and abbreviations in company common speech? How do we refer to superiors, staff, customers, suppliers, competitors, and what does this tell us about the heart and mind of our company? Staff of a global retailer told me that their colloquial term for potential shoplifters was TGB – Thieving G**** B****rds. So when you hear a member of staff's radio crackling '*Dave, please check TGB row 8*' it tends not to show respect for the customer.

Rewards and recognition – are they of high perceived value or just a short term cash bonus? Are they what the staff want? One year, in one factory where I worked, the Directors decided that it would be a good idea to buy every factory floor worker a turkey. It was not something they valued and many became 'rugby balls' ending up in bins rather than taken home.

In another, a food company, the senior chefs would cook a stupendous Christmas meal for all factory floor workers and it was served, black tie, by the senior managers in the lunch break. The night shift were always the most appreciative – we would come back to work in tuxedo and serve their meal at 2.30am. I have a saying for both home and business "small things are big things". I believe this to be particularly pertinent to rewards and recognition.

Technology – what does it say when people have to work with antiquated technology? What does it say when we expect their handheld to make them available 24/7? In our training company we do not have mobile e-mail. That could say 'antiquated' or it could say, when our trainers are running a course for a customer, that is their sole focus, they are not to be distracted by anyone else, even another customer. As all customers are in the same position, they all appreciate that and the feedback has always been positive.

One-off acts of management – what do the 'random acts of management' say about the company? A Belgian advertising agency I worked with had a dull grey breezeblock wall by the staircase. It became a symbol of dullness and oppressiveness, so late one Friday night, unannounced to the staff, the management donned their overalls and painted it. When the staff came to work the following Monday it was bright and vibrant. A month later they did it again, and again, and again, each time getting more creative. Later they even brought in a professional artist to help them. On one occasion it had zebra stripes, on another it was a country landscape, on yet another it was turned into a giant stone cigarette. Creative and a bit whacky works well in an Ad agency.

Expenses claims – the level of scrutiny in some companies appears disproportionate to the potential of misuse. Many companies rightly put a 'cap' on the cost of an overnight meal, have staff staying in low quality hotels and do not pay for their morning newspapers but then, elsewhere show gratuitous waste. Our company policy is that if we, as a company, have asked you to be away from your family overnight, we expect you to have a good bottle of wine – not the cheap 'house wine' – and ordering Chardonnay is bordering on a disciplinary offence!

Rituals and ceremonies – from the 'breakfast with the boss' to the 'employee of the month', they all have a cultural message. In one company where I was CFO, we started 8am–9am Monday with a Board members 'check in' where we had mostly informal 'catch ups'. Monday 9am–10am was always ruled through in my diary and I would wander around the building talking, mostly with direct reports and their direct reports, and mostly about football. I made sure I knew how the teams everyone supported had played – not just the results but the details – I had to ensure a knowledge of Arsenal, Tottenham, Millwall, Crystal Palace, Ipswich, Charlton, Chelsea, Aston Villa. Was that a good use of a CFO hour? What did that little ritual say about culture? 10am the cash forecast was on my screen – back to the numbers.

Working hours – what is the norm in your organisation and what does it say about "the way you do things around there"? In the UK we tend to work more hours than others in Europe. Much of this is by choice, but some is by guilt. I have been in offices where no-one leaves their desk until the boss goes home, in others were there is a mass exodus at 5pm prompt. In our company the policy is that we do whatever is required, with no formal times. One colleague tends to wake very early with the early sunrise in the summer and it is not uncommon to get e-mails from him at 5am. His wife works some weekends and so it is not uncommon for him to be working at weekends and taking time off during the week as his diary allows. In the same company, another prefers the structure of as close to a 9–5 as he is able to do. Both approaches are fine.

The essential nature of these surface issues is that they are relatively meaningless, yet can assume a meaning. Changing them will not change a company culture, yet if the culture is shifting and these do not change, they can become stumbling blocks and fuel for discontent. The alteration of them is therefore more about avoiding a negative rather than generating a positive. Either way, they have an influence, admittedly a small one, on organisational culture. Disproportionate focus on them, I feel, is a mistake. To use a medical analogy, they are the symptoms, not the disease, and no-one would recommend treating measles by merely covering the spots.

Culture summary

The culture determinants model illustrates the influences on the nebulous, contentious but vital concept of company culture.

- Organisational values and beliefs
- Organisational behaviour
- Written statements – mission, vision, culture, values etc
- Surface level issues

These do not have equal influence over company culture, and in turn have influences over each other generating a complex structure for the practical exploration of organisational culture.

In the short term the culture will be able to facilitate or enable a particular vision or strategy. It also has the ability to inhibit or hinder any particular vision or strategy.

In the longer term, the vision, if driven and reinforced, will generate a culture which is appropriate for the fulfilment of the vision and so the vision will be the influencer rather than the influenced.

In practice, the culture determinants model can be used to describe and explore the current organisational culture and then used again to describe the most appropriate future culture for the fulfilment of the vision. The gap between the two can then be bridged with active, vision inspired, strategies for cultural change. The circular and two-way nature of the influence of culture, vision and strategy is then apparent.

Culture change in practice

Culture change processes are exceptionally difficult, with numerous complexities and possibly fatal hurdles. One reason why I believe so many cultural change programmes do not achieve their intended objectives is that we have not learnt from the giraffe. Vision is everything. The giraffe builds and uses other strategies, always using vision as the central competitive advantage.

Due to the complexity and two way nature of the interactions between values & beliefs, culture, strategy and vision which we have explored, I am not surprised that cultural change programmes are so frequently unsuccessful. It is intellectually difficult, and it is also concerned with one of the most irrational and complex elements in the universe – human behaviour.

I struggle to understand the purpose of an attempted culture change without vision as the fundamental driver. To entertain any other driver would be to establish a cultural direction out of harmony with the performance ladder and consequently fail to develop continuity between strategy, vision and culture. The integration of vision, strategy and culture provides a platform for achieving the vision.

Structure

Having considered the complex issues of the values and culture on the internal (right) side of the performance ladder, by comparison, consideration of structure is simple. The purpose of an organisational structure is to facilitate the successful implementation of the strategies which are in place to achieve the company vision.

Structure follows strategy	Alfred Chandler (1962)
Strategy follows vision	The giraffe

Structure, like culture, can have a short term facilitating or inhibiting influence on the rungs of the performance ladder, but, even more so than culture, is within the control of the executives and so can be adapted to ensure enabling rather than hindering.

Structural change without reference to the need to use it as a tool to enable organisational vision is not the strategy of the giraffe – it is the pointless 'frolic' which will be outlined in the strategy of the zebra chapter.

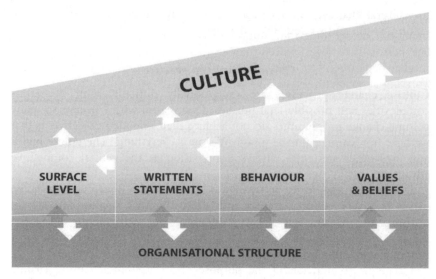

GIRAFFE 6

By itself, structure does not impact on culture – people do. How people respond to an organisational structure and how the structure interfaces with the four determinants of culture is an issue for exploration, but to think that an alteration of structure will automatically result in any alteration of culture is delusion.

Diagram 'giraffe 6' illustrates how structure can be added to the culture determinants model.

The addition to the model demonstrates:

- Values and beliefs – what we stand for
- Behaviours – what we do
- Written statements – what we publish
- Surface level – some of the seemingly trivial consequences which 'speak loudly'
- Structure – how we are organised to work

Structural change can be a powerful part of an organisational culture change programme, but only if there is integration to the organisational vision.

Representing structure

The diagrammatic representation of a company structure can be a source of more ego battles and power posturing than is evident during the entire Serengeti rutting season. Who is higher up than whom? Which lines connect whom and where a dotted line should go. I have heard tales of managers falling out over a dotted line and permanent umbrage being taken because one person is a 'layer' lower than someone else doing the same job in another department. Surely there must be more to running a business than worrying about getting a load of boxes in order?

Traditional 'organograms' are good for illustrating human reporting structures but have limitations for the consideration of overall organisational structure. A tip I find useful for structural demonstration is to focus on the function the individuals are fulfilling rather than the individuals themselves. This sounds suspiciously like an 'ignore the people' recommendation, which I do not mean it to be, I merely reiterate that the purpose of the structure is to enable the implementation of business strategy which in turn is there to bring into being the company vision.

One structure diagram I assisted with was for a UK construction company which was then small but with a meteoric growth rate. It needed a structure representation which could flex as the business grows, which showed strategy as the purpose, dealt with a multiplicity of titles for similar functions and could also enable a little bit of demonstrating some part of company vision. That sounded a 'tall order', but we did our best, as shown in 'giraffe 7' on page 72.

The positive points are:

- **It shows function not role** – Project Management covers project managers, senior project managers, sector project managers and any other title – their function is project management whatever their business card says. The UK construction industry has more of an obsession with job titles than any other industry I am aware of. I recall once almost facing a riot when suggesting the title of 'Divisional Director' rather than 'Director' for one group of senior managers!
- **It demonstrates vision** – the company, at the time of the diagram conception, has three sectors with plans for a fourth. The blank quadrant shows something of the future – a structure fitting in with organisational vision
- **It allows flexibility** – the sectors need slightly different structures due to the differing nature of their roles. There is no need for 'roll out' to have any similarity to 'offices' in its structure – both are to formulate the best structure to enable successful implementation of their sector strategies. In one part of the 'hotels' sector surveying is nearer the centre than project management, in another part of the same sector this is reversed. The structure diagram represents what actually happens rather than trying to force uniformity
- **It negates egos** – people don't have to consider whether they are nearer the centre than someone else, as there are different numbers of

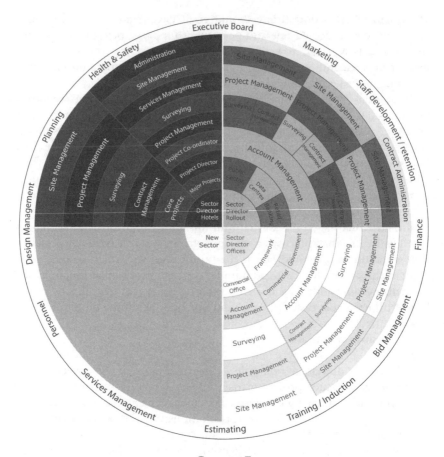

GIRAFFE 7

bands in each sector the position relative to the centre is not so relevant. Of course a hierarchy still exists, but it is less relevant that a project manager in the 'Offices' sector is not the same number of centimetres from the centre or edge than a project manager in the 'hotels' sector – and anyone who gets a ruler out to measure it needs to get a life!

- **Support functions are shown as supporting** – peripheral ring – including the CEO and the Board – their role is to support and facilitate the company achieving its vision. Being on the outer ring rather than at the head or centre is a strong message from the CEO.
- **It can be changed at any time**. With the rate of growth being experienced this will probably change several times during the year – change is easy to accommodate.

- **Other factors can be accommodated**. On the internal version, there is a further outer circle which relates to annual workload completed, booked, expected and still required.
- **It is comprehensive** – the entire company can be shown on one diagram and all employees are able to position themselves on it – even if they were to move between sectors

The internal side of the performance ladder (right side) summary

- Values, culture and structure all impact on every rung of the ladder – vision, goals, strategies, tactics and activity.
- These internal factors of the right upright of the ladder are within the control of the company management – some are easy to control (e.g. structure), some are difficult (e.g. culture).
- In the short term they can be positive facilitators or negative hindrances to the rungs of the ladder – they affect the rungs.
- In the longer term driving the organisational vision will make adjustments to the values, culture and structure – the rungs will affect the factors on the upright.
- Values are deep and complex – they are observed in our behaviour. What we describe as our values may not be what we act out as our values.
- Culture has a multiplicity of influences – its purpose is to enable the organisational vision by assisting the implementation of company strategies.
- Structure follows strategy, which follows vision. The organisation is to seek the best structure to enable the furtherance of the organisational vision.

The external side of the performance ladder (left side)

The left upright of the performance ladder incorporates the organisation brands and the perception of the organisation by those outside it – customers, potential customers, suppliers, communities etc. Whereas the right side of the performance ladder is within the control of management, the left side is not. We spend millions of dollars/euros/pounds seeking to influence these external factors but we cannot control them. These external factors are all able to influence organisational vision, goals, strategies, tactics and activities.

Brand

There is no universal definition of a brand – like vision, strategy, culture, values – we all have perceptions of what we mean by a brand, but these may differ from someone else's definition. This does not aid effective communication.

What is a brand?
Brand is ...

- an identification mark on skin, made by burning
- an owner's identification mark applied to a specific area of an animal's body
- a fictional character from J. R. R. Tolkien's Middle-earth
- the name of a beer produced in Wijlre, Netherlands.
- a play by the Norwegian playwright Henrik Ibsen.
- A cooking oil – 'olean brand olestra' is a no-fat cooking oil manufactured by Procter & Gamble.
- a verb – to accuse or condemn, openly or formally e.g. to 'brand' as disgraceful
- a type of sword: a cutting or thrusting weapon with a long blade
- the name of 31 separate villages throughout Germany and Austria
- a trade name: a name given to a product or service
- the sum of all the characteristics, tangible and intangible, that make the offer unique
- the immediate image, emotion or message people experience when they think of a company or product

---

If we take the definition of "a trade name and all associated factors, attributes and messages of a product or offering", we can use a more widely embracing definition incorporating 'perceptions' thus including the characteristics of the product or offering and the less tangible 'what people think of' the offering. It may be helpful to focus the 'brand' more towards distinctive company products and 'perceptions' more towards people's actions and reactions to the wider company – an example where a strong distinction between brands and perceptions would be useful is that of Swiss giant Nestlé.

Nestlé has a plethora of brands, such as Shreddies and Shredded Wheat breakfast cereals, KitKat chocolate, Coffee Mate milk substitute, Perrier bottled water, Felix and Purina cat foods, Buitoni and Maggi prepared

➔

→

foods to name but a few. One area where it has international dominance is that of the baby milk industry where its products have been
used as a substitute for mother's milk. Nestlé has approximately 50% of
the global market.

From the very beginning, Nestlé's product was never intended as a
competitor for mother's milk. In 1869, Henri Nestlé wrote: *"During
the first months, the mother's milk will always be the most natural nutri-
ent, and every mother able to do so should herself suckle her children."* The
World Health Organization (WHO) recognizes that there is a legiti-
mate market for infant formula, when a mother cannot, or chooses not
to, breast feed her child and the very first milk substitute used by Henri
Nestlé resulted in saving the life of a baby who was refusing his
mother's milk. I declare a personal interest as I would probably not be
here were it not for the existence of milk substitutes such as those
manufactured by Nestlé.

Without breast feeding babies don't get the benefit of passive immunity normally passed on in the mother's milk. The risk of contracting
serious diseases from inadequate immunity is therefore high, but the
risk of disease is further compounded by the fact that, in the
Developing World, many people do not have access to a clean water
supply with which to make up the milk formula. Waterborne diseases
are therefore fed straight to vulnerable babies and causes illnesses
including – diarrhoea, vomiting, respiratory infections, malnutrition,
dehydration and commonly death – known as Bottle-Baby disease.
Additionally, poverty can lead to mothers over-diluting the formula to
make it go further and hence giving inadequate nutrition to their child.
Protestor groups estimate that every 30 seconds a baby dies, somewhere in the world, from Bottle-Baby disease.

Pressure groups in the 1970's and 1980's accused Nestlé of aggressive promotional activities and seeking to persuade mothers that its
substitute milk was superior to mother's natural milk. From 1977 they
organised a boycott of Nestlé products. This highlighting of the issue
led to the drawing up of the WHO/UNICEF International Code of
Marketing of Breast Milk Substitutes in 1981. The protestors argued
that Nestlé did not fully embrace this policy in practice and continued
the boycott of all Nestlé brands. Nestlé subsequently agreed to abide
by the code and the boycott was called off in 1984, but by this time
the company's name had been tarnished with the association of the
alleged practices.

However reports have continued to come in from around the world
that the code is still being violated by baby milk companies.

→

➜ *"I saw mother after mother in the paediatric wards, head in hands, crying beside the cribs where their babies lay, malnourished, dehydrated, sick from Bottle Baby Disease. It doesn't need to happen. A decade ago we knew the truth about irresponsible marketing of infant formula. Allowing the companies to continue these practices is an inexcusable outrage of humanity, if not outright criminality."*
Janice Mantell, Action for Corporate Accountability (USA)

The boycott campaign of Nestlé products was re-launched in 1988, and is still active in over 80 countries. The International Baby Food Action Network (IBFAN) groups continue to lobby for world-wide adoption of the code, and to monitor all companies producing breast milk substitutes.

This example illustrates the distinction between brand and perception. The breast milk substitute brand is not currently relevant to me personally, nor to my family, and so whatever the brand communication, whatever the brand attributes, whatever the marketing effort, it will pass me by. However, the impression many people have as a result of the protesters' campaign, whether true or not, is an impression not of the milk brand but of Nestlé. I recall the boycott of the 1980's and recall actively choosing to avoid a totally unrelated Nestlé brand (I love Shreddies for breakfast!) as my perception of the company had been altered by the message of the protestor groups. The brand of 'Shreddies' had one message and list of attributes, but the perception of Nestlé dictated that I chose not to buy it.

The performance ladder 'external' upright (left) is all about the messages and impression of the product or company in the wider community. Brands are immensely powerful and valuable possessions – the top ten global brands in 2009 were:

1.	Coca-Cola	$68.7bn
2.	IBM	$60.2bn
3.	Microsoft	$56.6bn
4.	GE	$47.8bn
5.	Nokia	$34.9bn
6.	McDonalds	$32.3bn
7.	Google	$31.9bn
8.	Toyota	$31.3bn
9.	Intel	$30.6bn
10.	Disney	$28.4bn

The dominance of the US is awesome with only Finland's Nokia and Japan's Toyota (6th in 2008, now 8th) making the top 10. Germany's Mercedes-Benz is in 12th place and BMW in 15th. 51 of the top 100 global brands, by value, are from the US (down from 53 in 2005, edition 1 of *Strategies of the Serengeti*). (Source *Interbrand* 2009)

A brand is much more than a product. Many analogies have been used, but I like the brand as a personality. The brand creates a separate personality and, if that is a personality an individual warms to, they are more likely to purchase the product. Nike supports its brand with successful top athletes who are attractive and 'trendy' role models. It would be inappropriate for the Nike 'personality' to sponsor sports people who do not fit the 'aspirationally trendy' part of the Nike brand message. Nor could they sponsor a lower league football team – the brand personality is all about winning and being at the top level. Instead, Nike sponsors people such as Lance Armstrong (conqueror of cancer and serial winner of the Tour de France), prior to his misdemeanours, Tiger Woods (golf), Serena Williams (tennis) and Ronaldo, possibly, at his peak, the best footballer in the world.

The number one global brand has a personality of being young, refreshing, cheerful, alive, vibrant – and all advertising reinforces this. Advertisements always feature the young and beautiful having a good time assisted by the sipping of cola.

The number 6 brand, McDonalds has had to make some changes to its 'personality'. It has always been about consistency, cost, children, coverage and speed.

- Consistency – a Big Mac is a Big Mac whether you buy it in London, New York, Tokyo or Jakarta.
- Cost – McDonalds seek a price leadership strategy – with national variations
- Children – from the Ronald McDonald clown to 'Happy Meals', there is a bias to the young. Much of the marketing is aimed at children.
- Coverage – you are never far away from a McDonalds
- Speed – McDonalds emphasise the 'fast' in fast food

The company, along with its competitors have been the target of consumer groups concerned about rising rates of adult and child obesity. The precedent in the US of smokers suing tobacco companies for their smoking related illnesses is concerning the fast food industry as there may be a possibility of such lawsuits from the obese – "It's not my fault I ate 3 Big Mac's a day – it's McDonalds fault!" Whilst the argument is weaker than that against the tobacco companies on the basis of the latter's alleged use of addictive additives, there is sufficient cause for concern for the fast food industry to take action. McDonalds, and others are seeking to alter the brand personality before it becomes irrevocably associated with obesity and poor health. Presently we see the inclusion of healthy options on the menu and additional recommendations within the child focussed advertising reminding children that they need to exercise and drink juice, water or milk. It would be too much of a leap for the brand message to be 'health', but if the brand can shake off the 'junk' attachment, that would have been a major marketing coup on the same scale of tremendous success achieved by Volkswagen as they have managed the Skoda brand. It would also be the avoidance of a threat on the same scale as Nike achieved when they survived the 'sweatshop' and child labour scandals of a decade ago.

From the perspective of strategy formulation, and in the context of the primacy of vision as illustrated by the strategies of the giraffe, the aspect for consideration is less about brand extension, brand development or brand protection and more about consistency. Extension, development and protection are all vitally important, but in this context we need to focus on the message linkages to other aspects of the performance ladder. The consistency we seek is not necessarily consistency of the ongoing brand message or personality over time or over geographical boundaries, but consistency with the rungs of the performance ladder and consistency with the right (internal) upright of the ladder. Inconsistency, where the left upright of the ladder is going in one direction and the right upright in another direction does not make for a useable ladder. For the performance ladder to be effective, the brand personality on the left of the ladder should be the external reflection of the attributes amplified by the internal aspects of the right upright.

Consider the provision of tap water. As a consumer I require attributes such as consistency, safety, supply continuity, no risk. I want safe, clean water whenever I turn my tap on. This is not exciting. In fact it is a very dull vision, but as a qualified banker and also qualified accountant I probably have at least a masters degree in 'dull' (apologies to my fellow finance professionals, but we do have a 'brand image' to live up to). Dull is good for water supply. So, if a water company, with all the dull attributes I desire seeks to develop a 'water is sexy' brand image, the lack of uniformity with the internal attributes of the values, culture and structure will become a source of conflict. The right upright of the ladder will not be supportive of the left upright and the rungs will not have the foundations for success.

The brand image of UK low cost retailer Matalan is reinforced by its consistent internal upright of a cost-conscious culture; head office in Skelmersdale where land and labour is much cheaper than, say, central London; by its off High Street retail locations; its 'warehouse' feel to the stores and relatively low staffing levels – everything internally is consistent with the brand. By contrast, for example, Barclays Bank has splendid premises in London's fashionable Docklands, near to London City airport, thus near the financial heart of London with an international flavour. Were

Matalan and Barclays to swap places it would be a disaster for both as the internal–external, left–right ladder uprights, consistency would be shattered. Both companies are successful in their own rights and both have consistency within their own performance ladders. Swapping one upright would kill both of them – although I am sure that the staff at Skelmersdale would appreciate the splendid lunches at Canary Warf!

I always think it amusing that the world's most famous retail store, Harrods of Knightsbridge, London, has a sale. For a few days only Harrods becomes accessible to the masses. The sale has become an institution and something which at face value is the antithesis of the brand, generates more publicity and TV airtime than would be justified with any other store anywhere else in the world. In the end it reinforces the brand – people queuing outside for days before as the chance to get something valuable at a cheap price. What at first sight is a brand inconsistency becomes a brand reinforcement in line with the internal factors and company vision.

Conversely, imagine the vehicle equivalent to Harrods – the Rolls-Royce. An urban myth is that Rolls-Royce dealers say that if you have to ask the price, you cannot afford it. The Rolls-Royce brand is the pinnacle of luxury. Even in the vernacular we refer to the 'Rolls-Royce' solution to an I.T. or consultancy or training issue as the ultimate, no financial limitations, solution. With a brand such as Rolls-Royce, it would be ridiculous for a Rolls-Royce motor dealer to set up in downtown Skelmersdale, to have a strategy of an end of season sale, for the head office of the dealership to be in a portakabin. The lack of internal-external harmony would damage the brand.

My wife drives a Toyota. She was very pleased with it and has had years of happy motoring. I have driven Mercedes and Jaguar for many years. My wife takes her car to the dealer for servicing; I have someone collect my car. Her dealer phones her with what needs to be done on the car whilst servicing, mine just does it and charges me 'through the nose' for the privilege. Her car returns clean, mine fully valeted. Her conversation with the salesman has a major focus on price, mine on quality and function. Each of the companies brilliantly reinforce their brands with the internal aspects of the business and the approach of the staff. The companies have consistency of brand, internal issues, vision, strategies and actions, and a performance ladder which works.

Perceptions

- Nestlé lost my custom for a box of Shreddies due to the 1980's baby milk protest.
- Shell endured a petrol forecourt boycott over the 1995 Brent Spar issue.
- Nike endured criticism of poor Developing World working conditions and child labour.

- McDonalds had a long running legal case in the UK which became known as the McLibel trial. It was between McDonald's and a former postman and a gardener from London (Helen Steel and Dave Morris). It ran for two and a half years and became the longest ever English trial after which Mr Justice Bell delivered his verdict in June 1997. As a result of the court case, an anti-McDonald's campaign mushroomed, the press coverage increased exponentially, and a feature length documentary was filmed and broadcast around the world.
- Perhaps the most powerful consumer action of all was the student initiated boycott of Barclays Bank which started in 1971 as a protest against the South African apartheid regime. It saw the bank have sub-branches at UK universities forced out. Ultimately it led to a change of company policy and an increased awareness of the South African situation.

The external perception of the company is to be guarded as jealously and as carefully as the brand. Lack of congruity with the remainder of the ladder will hinder the furtherance of the vision. Returning to our earlier definition of organisational external perception – "the immediate image, emotion or message people experience when they think of a company or product" – this need not be rational. It needs no logic, nor explanation from each individual as we human beings are not always logical people. My perception of a brand or company will affect my behaviour and so it is vital that the companies seek to ensure that this is positive.

One of the most concerning aspects of perceptions is their longevity. Many years on, and despite changes to company policy some people, of my age and older, still look back to the 1970's whenever they think of Barclays. The tarnish is still there, in perceptions if not in reality.

The tactic of seeking to give a positive perception through charitable work is now fairly commonplace, usually within their own company 'foundations' to ensure control and the achievement of corporate objectives rather than just donating money. My favourite business in this area is Hasbro Inc. At a local level UK they run reading clubs in primary schools, painted a mural in a children's ward of a hospital, run drama and basketball clubs in schools, have an employee volunteer scheme to mentor children who are seen as 'problematic' and liable to remove themselves from the education system and Hasbro UK have even reached a different continent by transforming a South African school doing everything from painting it to supplying teaching equipment. This is no surprise for Hasbro. It is the same company, who in Rhode Island US, built the Hasbro Children's Hospital (HCH) in 1994, which cares for some 7,000 inpatients and 60,000 outpatients annually and has the area's only paediatric intensive care unit and paediatric oncology and cardiac programs. That is a serious commitment to social involvement and a huge message for perception.

Another perception rising aspect is media coverage. UK retailer Tesco seek to have some form of coverage every day – whether it is TV, national papers or local news – at some point, every day, there is something about Tesco retaining it in the forefront of people's minds. Richard Branson spends approximately 20% of his time on perception influencing activity. Whether it is crossing the Atlantic for the Blue Ribband Trophy or failed attempts to circumnavigate the globe in a balloon, he generates massive media coverage and as all such activities are audacious, challenging, enterprising actions, they reinforce the dynamic, adventurous, risk taking Virgin image. If he chose conventional advertising, it would cost possibly billions to get the prime time coverage that he achieves through a boat or a balloon. He is therefore possibly the smartest perception worker in current global business.

The external side of the performance ladder (left side) summary

- 'Brand' means different things to different people
- The brand is much more than the product
- Brands have messages or attributes, such as an associated lifestyle
- Perceptions reach beyond brands – they impact on our thoughts about an entire company
- Perceptions can last a very long time
- Strategies for perception raising can vary – from Hasbro's philanthropy to Virgin's adventure

Developing vision

The strategy of the giraffe is a strategy of the primacy of vision. The message is 'keep the vision'. In the strategy of the giraffe, everything follows from the vision – the goals and strategies, the internal factors of values, culture and structure, the external factors of brand and perception. The ability to develop a vision is therefore a pre-requisite for success.

> Vision is about the future. The present is only our starting point, and when considering strategy, the present is history already.

So the first part of developing an organisational vision is to envisage the future. There are a variety of errors we can make when seeking to describe the future. We can look briefly at three – too short, too long and too insular.

Too short: we make minor extrapolations of the present, and our vision of the future takes what is currently developing and develops it just a few stages further. This is more evolution than envisioning. Vision sees what is presently unknown. First Direct Bank (HSBC) revolutionised the domestic banking world with telephone banking and subsequently internet banking when most other banks were stuck in the myopic branch mentality debating whether or not to close loss making rural branches.

Too long: we can tend to dream too far whereby our view of the future is more like Star Trek. I think that the motor industry can probably resist the temptation to worry about Scottie in the transporter room for a few centuries. However, as the essence of vision is the future, I believe that this is a lesser error than thinking too short. I struggle to imagine how we would now conduct business without e-mail, yet I remember receiving sales orders by telex! Presumably soon Alexander Graham Bell's telephonic communication machine will be relegated to the museums and I will have faces on my PC when I am talking to them. My mobile phone will have the power and capacity of my desktop and would have made my 8 megapixel camera redundant. I think we will still read books – although every book will have the option of book, pdf for self print and podcast.

Too insular: the world does not revolve around your organisation. The area of focus should be the wider market and the challenge of vision is to adjust the shape of your company, through the mechanism of the performance ladder, to best fit the shape of this future. In 1986 Fahey and Narayanan first offered P.E.S.T. and over the years it has extended to S.T.E.E.P., P.E.S.T.L.E. and now S.T.E.E.P.L.E. Consideration of each of these factors to explore what the world would be like in 3, 5 or 10 years time may well be a useful exercise as a start of vision development. The factors are:

- Social/cultural – the human dynamics, demographics, social trends, population growth,
- Technological – moving ever faster, the vinyl record was replaced by the cassette tape which was replaced by the compact disc which is now being replaced by the iPod or MP3. Each had a shorter period of dominance than the last, the iPod will probably be shorter still – what's next?
- Economic – national and international factors, if our market is dollar dominated, how do you see the dollar moving? The current Indian economy growth, will it fizzle or become a major trade area? How will the Chinese market develop? Which areas will boom and which will see recession?
- Environmental – as the US is the world's second largest polluter and is reluctant to sign up to environmental protection which would add cost to its traditional industries and lifestyle. President Bush told the BBC

"The Kyoto treaty would have wrecked our economy" (BBC web site July 2005). One day it will have to deal with the issues, as will China, now the world's greatest polluter. What happens beyond petroleum? When do other limited resources expire?

- Political – how will political influence change? Interventionalism, protectionism, trade barriers and free trade agreements. Farm subsidies are large in the US and France, but seen as boosting inefficient trade by the UK – how will this develop, and how will the development affect world trade with cheaper LDC produced food? How will the Middle East situation progress and what will be the effects?
- Legal – how will the law change? How will corporate governance legislation affect the way we do business?
- Ethical – fairly traded products, public protests and lobbying, green audits. How will corporate values change?

The telecommunications industry requires the ability to have a perception of future trends technology and habits. In the 1990's BT surmised that most internet users would need to download more from the net than they uploaded to it. By sending two non-synchronised signals of different frequency through the same piece of copper wire they could create the ability to have data and voice simultaneously through the same wire. Asynchronous Digital Subscription Lines (ADSL) were therefore developed and 'broadband' was born. Their vision of the future was sufficiently robust to drive their development and whilst cable companies were spending a fortune burying cables under our pavements, BT developed the technology which has forced the competition to struggle.

In corporate vision workshops, the two examples of envisioning the future most frequently used are the speeches by Dr Martin Luther King 'I have a dream' and president J.F. Kennedy's commitment to put a man on the moon. Both of these are widely available in video format on the internet.

Dr King paints a picture of the future in an exceptionally eloquent format. His picture is about the removal of prejudice and a vision of a situation in the future (the speech was 1963) where "one day the state of Alabama ... will be transformed into a situation where little black boys and black girls will be able to join hands with little white boys and white girls and walk together as sisters and brothers".

Kennedy's vision is equally far sighted. In May 1961 he said "I believe this nation should commit itself to achieving the goal, before this decade is out, of landing a man on the moon and returning him safely to the earth". On

July 20th 1969, 4.17 EDT the lunar module touched down on the moon in the area known as the Sea of Tranquillity.

We may not be as eloquent as Dr King, nor have the resources of the world's richest nation to fulfil our vision of the future as JFK did – but we can articulate it. From the output of the S.T.E.E.P.L.E. we can make a statement of the future as we see it. Having developed a picture of the future, how will it affect your market and your organisation?

Finally, for the vision formulation part of your leadership role – describe and define the vision for your organisation. You have analysed and recorded your ideas of the future. You have articulated them. You have considered the market in which you operate. You have examined how you see your organisation fitting in to it. The following stages are then, having created the first rung, to build your performance ladder.

Chapter summary

- The giraffe has exceptional eyesight from the largest mammalian eyes on the planet. These are mounted on the viewing platform of the tallest animal on the planet.
- Vision is everything.
- The strategy of the giraffe is for vision to drive everything it does.
- A tool for exploring this is the performance ladder.
- The rungs are not new – only a minor adaption of a standard business tool:
  - Activity
  - Tactics
  - Strategies
  - Goals
  - Vision
- The ladder has two sides, internal and external.
- The internal side deals with values, culture and structure. In the short term they can inhibit or enable the vision. In the longer term they are changed to adapt to the vision. The relationship is two way.
- The external side deals with brand and perception outside of the organisation.
- Key aim is for the whole ladder to be pointing in the same direction – for the two sides and the rungs to be heading the same way, each seeking to drive the vision.

CHAPTER 4

Strategies of the elephant – using knowledge

The African elephant is the largest land animal on the planet and can weigh as much as four cars. It differs from the Asian (or Indian) elephant in that in addition to being taller it has larger ears and tusks, a more sloping forehead and the end of the trunk has two small protrusions for grasping small items whereas the Asian elephant only has one. These protrusions enable the gargantuan herbivore to manipulate small seeds and nuts with impressive dexterity. In contrast to this genteel micro level manipulation, the elephant can use its enormous bulk to push down fully grown trees in search of food. The elephant is undoubtedly the Serengeti's worst vandal, ruining trees and leaving a trail of devastation akin to a hurricane as each adult seeks to consume in excess of 225kg of leaves and plant matter each day. Further south than the Serengeti, in South Africa's Kruger National Park, it has tragically become necessary to instigate an elephant cull in order to preserve other species, including trees, some of which are estimated to be 4,000 years old.

Elephant fact file:	
Height	Up to 3 metres
Mass	up to 6,000 kg
Life expectancy	up to 70 years in captivity, nearer 60 years in the wild
Diet	Tree foliage, grass and fruit from a wide range of habitats
Reproduction	22 month gestation producing a single calf

The name 'elephant' has changed little from the Latin *elephantus* or Greek *elephas.*

Elephants live in herds from single figure small herds to large scale herds approaching thirty. Each herd can include several family groups and is led by the matriarch, or oldest female, although, most commonly the herd is comprised of the matriarch's daughters and their young. The society is female dominated and male offspring leave the herd once reaching puberty at the age of about twelve or thirteen. They then roam alone or form bachelor herds. In the mating season, during the seasonal rains, herds mass together forming 'superherds' of up to 200 animals. A strict hierarchy exists within each herd generally based on age, but it is always the matriarch who decides when to move, when to stop and eat, and where to go.

They have the ability to thrive in a variety of environments and can be found throughout the Serengeti, and further afield – savannah grasslands, swamplands, woodland or thin forests, and even far away to the south west, in the open wastelands bordering the Namibian desert. It is to our enormous shame that we humans once hunted these majestic creatures to the brink of extinction to fuel our appetite for ivory piano keys, billiard balls and ivory carvings in the late 19th century. In both sexes, two incisor teeth in the upper jaw grow to become tusks and continue growing throughout the elephant's life. These tusks form a formidable weapon but make the elephant commercially attractive to mankind. Fortunately we now have modern synthetic substitutes to ivory. However, matters were not that much better in the late 20th century when the price of ivory again soared fuelled by ivory trinkets and artefacts for decorating windowsills and mantelpieces in the rich world. Poaching increased and the Serengeti National Park estimated that as few as 500 elephants were left within the boundaries of the park by 1990. Many herds migrated north to Kenya. After the ivory trade was officially banned the animals returned from the north and it is estimated that the Serengeti National Park is now home to over 2,000 elephants. This is still a microscopic number and the animal is in serious decline throughout the continent. For example, 30 years ago it was estimated that there were 130,000 elephants in Sudan alone. Drought and people have now driven this figure to about 20. Kenya had up to 65,000 elephants in the late 1970s, according to IUCN – The World Conservation Union, but poachers and other threats reduced the herds to about 20,000 animals by 2004. Poaching continues in many areas and the Born Free Trust web site estimates that 3,600 elephants were killed for their tusks by humans in 2003–4.

The requirement to fuel a body with such a massive bulk, combined with the fact that as a herbivore greater quantities of food are required than would be for the higher calorific foods of the carnivore, means that the elephant spends up to sixteen hours a day feeding. Of the remaining eight hours, probably five are spent sleeping and the remaining three travelling. Sleeping can be standing, leaning against a tree or lying down. Whilst they have the capacity to live for many days without water, elephants will drink every day if water is available and will travel extraordinary distances to locate water when it is scarce. This is where the matriarch is often the deciding factor, the difference between finding water and not finding it, the difference between life and death. As the sole decision maker of journeys (or safaris – Swahili), she decides where to seek water. It may be that the main reason why the matriarch dominates the herd long after she has exceeded breeding age is her memory. We jest about elephants having long memories, and there appears to be no study which will verify this undisputedly, but a matriarch may take a herd to a watering hole, or underground water source which she has not visited for decades. Somehow, an intimate knowledge of the terrain leads her to recall the location of water and use this knowledge to ensure the wellbeing of the herd. The herd will follow, usually in single file, and no terrain is too difficult for them. Whilst the elephant is the only mammal who cannot jump, they can climb excessively steep inclines or navigate hard surfaces with angular sharp stones. Despite their great weight, sharp stones are no obstacle for their hardened soles. The only terrain they avoid if given the option is slippery mud where the young are particularly vulnerable to falling and failing to be able to rise.

Once located, a water source can become a source of drink and a bath. Via the trunk an elephant can drink up to 100 litres at a time. They are often seen near to water sources digging with their front feet. This is because they prefer sweeter tasting water, ideally with a high sodium content, and will dig to reveal it.

Elephants have no natural predators – their only enemy is man. A very small calf could feasibly become prey to lions or hyenas, but as it is an extreme rarity for a calf to be separated form its mother, this seldom occurs. Even a fairly young elephant has the bulk and strength to see off any attacker foolish enough to approach. When threatened, elephants crowd closer to the matriarch and take aggressive postures. These involve pulling themselves to their full impressive height, spreading the ears to emphasise size and often moving the head up and down as if threatening to charge. If they do charge, often it is a 'bluff' charge where the elephant will run past the threat. If however, this is not successful, a full impact charge can result. The elephant may try to throw its smaller opponent using its tusks or to trample or kneel on it crushing it to death. A more mild weapon is the trunk which can swing and beat most other creatures away.

Elephants are able communicators. They can be heard several miles away with long deep rumbles – many so low in tone that they are inaudible to the human ear. Their hearing, like their sense of smell, is exceptional, but their sense of sight is only moderate. There is strong evidence of learning behaviour in herds with the elder members teaching the younger ones aspects of behaviour and communication. Modern research has surprised many with findings that elephants are able to imitate not only each other but other species or objects too. Joyce Poole of the Amboseli Elephant Research project in Kenya believes that the vocalisations often imitate others in the herd and cement bonds between herd members. A 2005 National Geographic article focussed on a ten year old female orphan elephant named Mlaika who lived in a sanctuary two miles from the Nairobi-Mombassa highway. She was able to perform a convincing imitation of a truck. Another African elephant, twenty three year old male Calimero, has spent eighteen years living in a Swiss Zoo (Basel) with Asian elephants. He now communicates with the clicking and chirping noise of the Asian elephant rather than the deep rumblings of the African elephant. The elephant can now join the list of creatures able to imitate others – a select club which includes the dolphin, parrot, some songbirds, some apes and, of course, humans. Dr Poole says "it will be very interesting to see whether African elephant groups have different dialects".

Corporate knowledge

There are many aspects of the elephant which we could learn from, many of which are covered as we consider the strategies of other animals. The elephant will continue travelling huge distances in search of water – moving on and on without giving up – but the rhinoceros will teach us some of the strategies of continuing. The enhancement of size when threatened by spreading the ears is impressive, but the elephant is big already – the ostrich uses the same tactic despite not having the initial size advantage and we will explore it there. But there is one strategy which appears to be unique to the elephant – the way they use their incredible knowledge. Firstly there is the existence of the knowledge which enables a matriarch to lead a herd for days to a water hole which none of the other younger elephants would know even existed and secondly there is the ability to pass on knowledge, not only of water holes but also of behaviour, skills and other aspects such as communication. There is even some evidence that knowledge may have an element of being passed on genetically such that a matriarch can lead the herd to a waterhole she has never visited. This is unproven and is beyond our current understanding of knowledge transfer, but as the world's animals have a habit of surprising us, do not be alarmed if future research proves this presently vague and weak hypothesis. The elephant's brain is four times the size of the human brain and their ability to use it effectively has meant that they have survived and thrived in the harsh climes of the Serengeti. Were it not for human encroachment on their territory and the penchant of some humans for ivory trinkets, they would be far from the endangered list.

Part of the long list of requirements for business success is knowledge. The collection, filtering, storage, retrieval and application of corporate knowledge can create organisational competitive advantage. There are obviously many areas where knowledge is vital for any business, and I would suggest that there are some areas where many firms have good knowledge but some areas where we often fall short. Our businesses often have excellent knowledge of our products. We can wax lyrical about the technical specifications, functionality and aesthetics as anyone who has met a car salesman can vouch. We sometimes accumulate an in depth understanding of our customers but other times history shows us that we can make erroneous assumptions with the false impression that we have a good understanding of our customers. I propose that there are six core areas of knowledge in which, to learn from the elephant's application of knowledge, our organisations must be able to excel.

1. Knowledge of our product or market offering (including processes) – the 'internal' side – what our organisation does.
2. Knowledge of our customers and potential customers – why they choose to buy from us rather than someone else or vice versa.
3. Knowledge of our supply chain – suppliers can be a scarce resource and can cripple an organisation as both Land Rover and British Airways found out in the summer of 2005.
4. Knowledge of our corporate history – the adage "history repeats itself – it has to, no-one listens the first time" is just as real in business where

we can observe companies making mistakes they, or others made 20 or 30 years ago.

5. Knowledge of our competition – as with our knowledge of the customer, we probably think we are more aware of the competition than we actually are.

6. Knowledge of the wider market – myopic or narrow visioned business will not survive. With the ever increasing pace of market change we need to look beyond the immediate market in which our organisations operate. The present is only the starting place, business is about the future.

We will deal with some of these briefly and then major on the ones where I feel I can bring something new to the debate rather than just repeating what others have written – particularly the area of knowledge of our competition and competitive advantage tactics. The analytical tools I am suggesting have evolved and been explored in a wide range of organisations, industries and national cultures, but they will inevitably need to evolve further – feel free to adjust them, develop them and apply them to your own organisation.

Using knowledge

Having knowledge is one thing, using it is another. Having knowledge is one thing, having useful knowledge is another. Having knowledge is one thing, having presently unapplied knowledge which will have a future use is another. Much of the present trend in management thinking is in the area of knowledge management. We originally termed it 'Information Technology'. This term was then broadened to encompass everything to do with computers! 'Knowledge Management' then became the latest management trend and panacea. The phrase is now becoming a little passé and 'Business Intelligence' is taking over. The concept of all of the terms are similar – we explore the technical ways to store and retrieve information, we find electronic means to make connections between different aspects of stored knowledge and we find new ways to present the knowledge with clarity. These are all vital, but there are many more able than I to consider the technical aspects and techniques of knowledge management or business intelligence. The elephant does not know how it knows what it knows – it just uses the knowledge to survive. A combination of zoologist and psychologist may be able to expound how the elephant knows what it knows but that will not add any value to the elephant, so as a strategist observing the Serengeti experts, I am less concerned about the process or mechanics of knowledge management. From my perspective, from observing the elephant, there are three aspects of using corporate knowledge to focus on – use, useful and future use.

Use of knowledge

Unused knowledge is worse that valueless – it is value destroying and demoralising when it emerges too late. It is not just the cost and resource for storing knowledge that is wasted with unused knowledge. Of greater destruction is the realisation of what could have happened had the knowledge been used. Have you ever been in a business situation where a piece of information existed somewhere in the organisation, yet you proceeded unaware of that knowledge? Possibly it resulted in a lost contract or just in large amounts of your time being used when the hidden knowledge would have negated the requirement for the use of this time. What was your reaction when you found out that the knowledge which was the key to your issue emerged?

I can recount several examples from my working life, maybe the most common, as a CFO, is subsidiary companies or divisions not fully disclosing potential downsides. They give the 'everything is OK' message, and then start flagging a potential problem which they had been aware of for some months but had hoped would be waved away by the magic wand of the 'rescue fairy'. I recall having to make some very hurried property sales to compensate for a development which had been 'on track' for over a year but the divisional Directors suddenly alerted me to a possibility that it may not be able to be sold until month 1 or 2 of the subsequent financial year. This development had been slipping for over 6 months but the Directors responsible chose to keep the 'everything is OK' message until just under a month from the year end. Not only did we have to perform some rapid juggling to compensate, I don't think I ever trusted those Directors again and always wanted onerous proof for any comments they subsequently made. Were that knowledge of slippage been available to the Board when it was known by the divisional Directors, we could have had a more measured and controlled response.

In the toy industry, Hasbro regularly seek to extend brands by the launch of new characters. This has included some in the 'My Little Pony' range and some in the 'Weebles' range. Amongst the character names were 'Morning Glory' for a 'My Little Pony' (1999) and 'Major Wedgie' for the 'Weebles' range (2003). Any American readers will now be thinking "is there a problem with that?" whilst UK readers, particularly those with children will be wiping away tears of laughter. I have heard the story of a UK product manager having to explain to her US counterparts in explicit and specific words the precise nature of a 'wedgie'. I don't know whether the Brits went into detail on the 'Morning Glory'. In this case it is an example of correct and appropriate use of local corporate knowledge as these names were never used in the UK, and so the ridicule and subsequent expensive product launch closely followed by a humiliating recall never had to happen. But it would have done if the UK team did not communicate their knowledge to the US merchandisers. For US readers, I won't expound the British use of these words – but there are some hilarious sites you could find with a web search!

For amusement, here are a list of reasonably well known errors made within the automobile industry when all the appropriate knowledge was available through simple translators, local offices and employees, yet somehow, for some manufacturers, the knowledge was never used. Others did use the knowledge and were able to make changes before making embarrassing errors.

- Fiat, the Italian manufacturer, had to rename their "Uno" when selling it in Finland. "Uno" means garbage/trash/rubbish in Finnish.
- Rolls Royce intended to expand their successful Silver Cloud product line, with a car called "Silver Mist." Product planning developed well until the Germans pointed out that in German "mist" means manure.
- Toyota released their MR2 sports car in France, they encountered a similar problem to that of Rolls Royce. MR2 was pronounced as "m-er-deux,", frighteningly similar to "merde" – which is less polite than "manure".
- Mitsubishi of Japan tried marketing their Pajero car in the Spanish market but were perplexed by their failure to get a grip on the market. The reason? Pajero is apparently slang in some areas of Spain for "masturbation".

Not a car, but in a related industry, Standard Oil decided that it sounded too much like a U.S. company, so they changed the corporate name to "Esso." Unfortunately this has some negative connotations in Japanese as phonetically it translates as "stalled car." Having learnt from this, Esso spent large amounts of money studying language to generate an inoffensive name suitable for an international market. A carefully checked list of words resulted in the choice of "Exxon" which unfortunately is allegedly similar to an obscure obscenity in Aluet Eskimo. Never having met an Aluet Eskimo, this remains second hand information.

A few others from other industries, purely for further entertainment:

Pepsi made a few errors with the marketing slogan "Come Alive with Pepsi" it was translated into the Chinese as "Pepsi brings your dead ancestors back to life," and in German as "Come out of the grave with Pepsi."

➜

> ➜
>
> We hope that adequate corporate knowledge is procured and used if the following Japanese brands ever seek exposure to the UK or US markets – a soft drink called "Calpis", a lawn fertilizer called "Green Piles", a brand of shampoo called "Cow", a coffee creamer "Creap", and from the fashion clothing industry "Trim Pecker" trousers (pants US).
>
> And going the other way, if you wish to set up a "Taverna" in Japan it may be wise to change the name as "taverna" translates, approximately, to "Do not eat."

Usefulness of knowledge

The academic will delight in knowledge for its own sake. The pragmatist will only delight if they can perceive an application for the knowledge.

The accumulation of data is costly. Modern high capacity computers and effective knowledge management software mean that the knowledge is cheap to store. What is not cheap is the human aspect of initial storage and classification. Any system is only as good as the data input and so if we witness insufficient or blinkered effort at the time of storage categorisation, we are probably wasting time effort and resource in storage because retrieval will be difficult. Much of the responsibility for such categorisation is left to very low levels in many organisations – whilst such work may not be rivetingly interesting, I feel that we often relegate work on the basis of 'interest' rather than 'importance'. This may be very costly in lost opportunities and unmade linkages. Stored knowledge may not be as valuable as it could potentially be due to inadequate coding or linking at the time of storage – long live the 'knowledge management industry'.

Future use of knowledge

This is the most difficult call to make. What do we know, which does not have an application presently, but may in the future? Perhaps one approach to this is to take the vision considerations from the strategies of the giraffe and then ask 'if this is how we see the future what will be the driving pieces of information? What will be needed to know? What knowledge could enable this vision sooner?' The earlier vision examples used, King and Kennedy, had a grasp of a future beyond their current experience. What would they need to enable it? For King it was national attitudinal change and a reinforcement that the constitution was equally for all, for Kennedy it was financial resource to kickstart the technological advancement needed to make it happen.

Most Insurance or Financial Services companies have products which parents or grandparents take out for children. The children then encash the product upon reaching adulthood. One UK Financial Services company had such a product which sold well throughout the late 1960's and the 1970's. It's phraseology was such that it equated adulthood with being 18. This was challenged by a Jewish boy, in whose culture adulthood was after the Bar Mitzvah at 13. With family backing, legal proceedings were commenced and there was enormous potential for negative publicity for the company. All of the company's instincts were to defend the case as the consequences of early release of funds for all such policies could have been dramatic.

One advisor to the board was Jewish. He was asked to consider the issue from the Jewish perspective to assist the board in understanding the other side of the debate. He did so with such eloquence and clarity that the board decided to capitulate, pay the 13 year old policy beneficiary and to change the wording of all future policies.

This is an example of the future use of knowledge. The Financial Services company did not employ the advisor because he was Jewish – they employed him for his business acumen. However, due to his faith, he had some critical knowledge which no-one else on the board had and which became useful by saving the company the embarrassment of an emotive legal case.

The usefulness of non-Executive Directors is well documented and recommended as an integral part of corporate governance. The experience from other areas and the inability to get involved in detailed operation give them the position to offer the wisdom of years, the experience of other industries and the impartiality of remaining at strategic level. There is the implicit assumption in their appointment that they will offer similar 'future knowledge' and thus they should be essential to the operation of every business.

Knowledge of our product or market offering

This is the area where most of us are experts. We know our businesses, we know our products, we understand our offering to the marketplace with unrivalled intimacy. We understand the features and benefits of our offering and cannot understand why customers are not queuing at our door every morning. Sometimes we are very good at our own product knowledge but utterly fail to understand it from the consumer's perspective.

The Sinclair C5 was ahead of its time. A battery powered car which could be energy efficient, reduce road congestion and was affordable. Sir Clive Sinclair was a very rich, but eccentric British genius who had previously accumulated a significant fortune in developing and selling revolutionary, arguably visionary, electronic products. These included calculators, watches, pocket TV's, and micro computers.

The idea of producing an electric vehicle was a personal obsession for Sir Clive, fuelled by the higher profile of 'green' or environmental issues in the 1970's and 1980's. He produced the C5 with the chassis designed by Lotus, the motor by Philips Electric, and the polypropylene body was the largest one-piece injection moulding at that time. Each aspect was cutting edge in design and technology for its day. After negotiations to use the former DeLorean car plant in Northern Ireland failed, the C5 was built in a Hoover factory in Wales.

The high profile launch was a total disaster and the press ridiculed the product. It was launched in the middle of the British winter. The C5 had no roof – so any driver would be soaked in rain and in icy conditions the vehicle was unable to gain traction and so steering control was lost. Safety and Advertising Standards organisations became active in their criticism especially as the vehicle involved driving on roads at a height of about one foot with buses and articulated lorries thundering over the drivers right shoulder. The press seized upon the location of the production and likened the product to a mobile vacuum cleaner. Manufacturing at the desired location of the hi-tech DeLorian sports car would have given a different message and marketing angle, but alas, the parallel to vacuum cleaners was unavoidable. Sales and production nosedived, and the company was wound up in October 1985 after less than one year, with Sir Clive Sinclair having personally lost in excess of £8.6 million.

Sir Clive Sinclair was ahead of his time in many ways. With increased numbers of cycle tracks and greater resistance to gratuitous carbon emission, I wonder how the vehicle would have fared if launched 15 or 20 years later – and in the summer, and not manufactured in a vacuum cleaner factory. What he did very well was to have an excellent knowledge of his products, their operations and the ideas behind them. What he did not do was sufficient market research and testing, and it is a great shame that for many, their strongest recollection of Sir Clive is the disastrous C5 rather than the successes of calculators and computers.

Knowledge of our customers and potential customers

The key to understanding our customers is in understanding the nature of 'competitive advantage'. There are a myriad of books on the subject – some brilliant and some considerably less so. My 5 year old definition of competitive advantage is 'whatever it is that causes your customer to choose you rather than anyone else.'

To compliment knowledge of competitive advantage, a strong knowledge of the customer base, of customer perceptions and of brand loyalty is an essential asset. BBDO (part of Omnicom Inc), using research by Campbell's, estimate that 50% of profits come from 10% of customers. Their summary table below shows that in this research, by retaining its top 10% (by number) of customers (first two categories), a company would retain 24% of its volume, but 50% of its profit.

Customer type	Return per marketing $	% customers	% volume bought by these customers
Most profitable	3.38	4%	15%
Profitable	1.80	6%	9%
Borderline	1.00	25%	25%
Unprofitable	0.38	65%	51%

Source note: BBDO quote Campbell's as the source, but Campbell's are unable to confirm or deny details of the original research – they do not appear to have the access or retrieval ability for this corporate knowledge! I am working from the BBDO versions.

This data estimates that 65% of customers are unprofitable, and they account for over half of their volume. If this is true, halving the customer base and increasing the profits as a result would be a tempting effort – less work, more money.

The same BBDO report illustrates the point with:

- Coca-Cola   most profitable 10% of customers = 46% of profits
- Kraft cheese   most profitable 8% of customers = 54% of profits
- Pepsi-Cola   most profitable 12% of customers = 63% of profits

In February 2006 Telecoms group Cable & Wireless announced that it was to cut 3,000 jobs in the UK within 5 years (over half its workforce). This was to be part of a strategy to decimate the customer base from 30,000 customers to 3,000. In doing so it expected to focus on the most profitable customers, with a lower cost base and enhance both its customer service and financial performance.

For me there is an even more interesting part to the BBDO report where it splits customers into four segments:

- Category buyers
- Shortlist buyers
- Preference buyers
- Brand enthusiasts

Category buyers have no preference for any particular brand and will usually make a purchasing choice based on price. They have no brand loyalty and the effort to attract them will be not only be by having cost/price advantage over the competition but also communicating this through the media. Supermarkets create high profile loss leader products in order to attract these customers. They also loudly proclaim that, for example, they have *"cut 2,000 prices since the beginning of the year"*. This is a direct appeal to the category buyer. They tend not to add "but we've increased 2,000 elsewhere so that we'll still get your money". In the UK in early 2005 there was a media report which indicated that supermarkets did exactly this 'up and down' tactic, but in 2005 the 'up's' were heavily biased towards staple goods and so average shopping baskets increased in price. Category buyers primarily make purchase decisions based on price, and if your product is not the cheapest, they will purchase from a competitor without hesitation.

Shortlist buyers are prepared to purchase within a range of brands, probably choosing from amongst a range of 4–8 brands. They are still cost conscious but will buy usually the lowest cost option from amongst their short-list. The information which would be most use to us would be, to know the price difference required to enact a change of purchasing from one product in their short list to another, and the price difference required by them to buy outside their short list. The paper states that a negligible price difference, even less than 1%, will cause a change from one short-listed product to another, but in order to move to product not on their shortlist, the change would need to be in the 5% range.

Preference buyers have a very limited shortlist – typically 2, but can be 3. They are a more narrowed option version of the shortlist buyer. In their case it would take in excess of 5% of a price differential for them to move from their chosen brands to another outside their preference. The range of this required price difference to ensure buying elsewhere varied enormously from 5% to over 20% with different products and different customers.

Brand enthusiasts love their chosen brand. They are the cola drinkers who would only drink Coke, the beer drinkers who will only drink Budweiser, the bikers who would not be seen astride anything other than a Harley-Davidson. This segment of purchaser, according to the BBDO paper would take a massive 25% price premium before considering moving to another competitive product.

The four customer segments approach yields a structure of different price sensitivities amongst different customer groupings. It may be that one product, or company, has all four customer price sensitivity segments, or it may be that one product, or company specifically appeals to customers in one segment.

For example, Harley Davidson is more likely to sell to people searching for a Harley rather than a customer who is indifferent between a Harley, Yamaha, BMW or Moto Guzzi. I am told by those insane enough to ride bikes that there is no such thing as indifference between these brands – you are either a Harley buyer, or a Motto Guzzi enthusiast or you settle for the mass market Japanese brands. As hurtling between fast moving cars with minimal self protection is not on my list of suicidal tendencies, I am unable to add personal comment. So Harley Davidson customers will probably show an exceptionally high proportion of 'brand enthusiasts' for whom only a Harley will do.

In 1901, 21 year old William S Harley completed a drawing of a plan to attach an engine to his bicycle. The plan turned into a dream, the dream into a company and the company into a legend. In 1903, with his friend Arthur Davidson, William produced a motorised bicycle in a 10 foot by 15 foot wooden shed. The wooden shed based manufacturing continued and more motorbikes were produced. A kindly retailer exhibited them and the first Harley Davidson dealership was born. In 1905 a Harley Davidson won a 15 mile race in Chicago with a breathtaking average speed of just over 47 miles per hour. Design and manufacturing expertise flourished and by 1908 a Harley Davidson scored a perfect 1,000 in the 7th Annual Federation of American Motorcycles Endurance and Reliability contest. The spotlight was then on this fledgling speed machine as this created widespread interest throughout America. As part of the fruit from this achievement the police bought their first Harley Davidson and thus started one of the longest and most celebrated customer relationships of all time.

In 1910, 7 US national races were won by Harley Davidsons. In 1917 the US had belatedly entered World War I and required motorcycles for communication riders on a vast scale. By the end of WWI 20,000 motorcycles were in use in the US military – the overwhelming majority of which were Harley Davidsons. By 1920, Harley Davidson

➡

→

had become the largest motorcycle manufacturer in the world and in 1922 won a clean sweep of all 8 US national motorcycle racing events.

The US again missed the start of a world war in 1939 but made up for lost time after Pearl Harbor ordering 90,000 motorcycles, predominantly Harleys, by the end of WWII. Many GI's rode Harley's for the first time during the war and sought them upon return to civilian occupations. Further custom was achieved with the publicity from the film *Easy Rider*, the 1960's quest for individual freedom and even from the formation of the Hells Angels who, in the US, have Harley Davidsons as their vehicle of choice. Unpaid publicity was the hallmark of the company – they could generate strong levels of brand awareness from events and supporters which would take other companies many millions of dollars to achieve.

In 1981 13 Executives completed a Management Buy Out from AMF who had previously acquired Harley Davidson. Their slogan was 'the eagle soars alone' which fed the free spirit exemplified by motorcycling, and particularly by the Harley rider. This was an enormous boost to the gelling of customer and company – sharing the same dreams and values – freedom – whether it was corporate freedom or freedom of the roads.

The new company lobbied the US Government and were successful in persuading the granting of trade protection policies in their favour. A tariff was placed on all Japanese bikes over 700cc for 5 years from April 1983. This gave Harley Davidson a huge opportunity to develop market penetration strategies fuelled partially by the creation of a political competitive advantage of the tariff and partly by the aligning of corporate and customer ethos.

The company wasted no time and formed Harley Owner Groups (known as HOG's). This almost instantly became the largest factory sponsored motorcycle club in the world encompassing thousands of individuals, including those from opposite ends of the legal framework – two of the most celebrated groups of Harley Davidson enthusiasts: the police and the Hell's Angels. The HOG's are organised in 'chapters' with the mission statement 'to ride and have fun'. One of the benefits of ownership is the chance to purchase copious Harley paraphernalia, and receiving the '*Enthusiast*' magazine. Started in 1916, the magazine has become a vital part of the company's marketing armoury, but especially since its revival after the MBO.

The 90th anniversary of the brand formation was celebrated in 1993 when 100,000 riders paraded through Milwaukee. The 95th anniversary in 1998 saw 140,000 riders. By 2000 HOG's had 500,000

→

→

members. By late 2005 the number was approaching 1,000,000. As an example of effective marketing driving customers further and further towards the brand enthusiast segment, Harley, in my opinion, is unrivalled. According to almost all non-Harley bikers I have met, the machines do not live up to their glorious technical past. Descriptions vary, but my favourite was hearing this iconic brand, a symbol of motorcycling, being called 'agricultural'. To the Harley enthusiast it is not just a bike, it is a way of life. What Harley Davidson have so cleverly accomplished is to match the lifestyle aspirations of its customers at attitudinal level rather than product or functional level. This deeper level creates a stronger emotional tie and hence generates stronger customer loyalty, ultimately brand enthusiasts. The benefits do not end there. These enthusiasts are then unpaid brand evangelists spreading the good news of Harley Davidson to motor cycle riders everywhere. The tremendous advantage of this is that these enthusiasts will now spend considerable sums of money on repeat and ancillary purchases, despite the premium price of the product, and would not even consider buying a cheaper and technically superior competitor product – because Harley means more than the bike. As a strategy that is absolutely brilliant and has generated enthusiastic brand evangelists with the lowest price sensitivity possible.

Conversely, consider some of the players in the UK supermarket industry. The lower end of the market actively competes on price and seeks the category buyer. A range of 'value retailers' has developed whose constant and consistent message is 'cheap'.

Lidl, the German company which opened its first UK store in 1994 and now has in excess of 300 stores. Its competitive focus is clear – on the web site, the banner states 'Lidl is cheap'. The site further states "Lidl takes pride in providing top quality products at the lowest possible prices"

Netto, the Danish grocery retailer commenced trading in the UK in 1990 and is now approaching 150 stores. They state "Just as low-cost airline carriers take the smart travellers to where they want to go, Netto provides a crucial service to today's smart shopper".

Aldi is another low cost grocer specialising in own label goods and no frills – very low staff levels and a 'low-cost airline mentality' – if you

→

➜
want a plastic bag you pay for it! It states that Aldi "offers you a wide choice of carefully selected products, all of which match the quality of leading brands, while being significantly cheaper".

ASDA, now owned by US giant Wal Mart perpetually promotes itself with one message – that they are the cheapest place to buy groceries. In the UK in 2005 ASDA used a survey by the trade magazine '*The Grocer*' to justify the strap line "officially Britain's lowest priced supermarket". The survey was based on only 33 products from only 8 supermarkets, none of which were the 'low cost' supermarkets. Competitors, particularly Tesco, complained to the Advertising Standards Authority and ASDA was forced to withdraw the strap line, but the intention is clear – an appeal to the low brand loyalty category buyer.

These 4 supermarket competitors make price the basis of their competition. Their customer base is therefore likely to have a strong skew towards the category buyer. Customers shop at each because they are cheap. If a cheaper source were to be located nearby, the customers would probably change their loyalty without compunction. The low price end of the supermarket fraternity therefore operates extensively with the category buyer customer.

Some products may have a more diverse customer category population. As an example, beer drinkers often have preferences for which beverage they consume, but the level of preference varies. Most beers, particularly the higher quality beers, will find that they are marketing to several of these customer segments. Some beer drinkers will only drink Budweiser, or Stella Artois, or Marsden's Pedigree Bitter unless it is unavailable – the enthusiast, usually defined by their beards and ample waistline as evidence of copious consumption.

The second category of preference buyer may be indifferent between Marston's Pedigree and Everard's Old Original. At a push they may also condescend to a Theakstone's Old Peculiar.

Others will drink from a shortlist – mine would include Marsden's Pedigree, Black Sheep, Waggledance, Old Speckled Hen and Old Hooky, or maybe an occasional Hobgobin or Bishop's Finger. Readers from outside the UK – do make sure you try these if you visit our shores. I am undoubtedly a shortlist beer drinker.

Marston's Pedigree features in all three higher categories – the only area in which they will not compete is on price as it is a premium bitter and there will always be the category beers in both bitter and larger formats – the Heineken's, Carling's and mass produced tied house bitters.

Harley therefore has a bias to enthusiasts, Aldi to category buyers and Marsden's Pedigree stretches three of the customer segments. Supermarkets such as Tesco are seeking to capture sections of all segments by having a product range from the cheap to the exclusive.

If we explore the concept of our customer price sensitivity we can make some interesting observations. The following graph shows the four customer segments on the price sensitivity format from the BBDO information, on the upright (Y) axis, and adds what I will term 'competitive differential' on the horizontal (X) axis. Price sensitivity can be determined by aspects other than the brand loyalty considered in the quoted report and so the four customer segment titles – enthusiast, shortlist, preference and commodity – are inserted to identify their position, and to mark the level of sensitivity – the 1%–2%, 2%–5%, 5%–25% and 25% levels. It must be recognised that there may be other reasons for price sensitivity and so a customer grouping towards the bottom may not necessarily be a grouping of brand enthusiasts. In other words, brand enthusiasts are at the bottom of the graph, but there are other customers there too. Category purchasers will be at the top of the graph, but there are other reasons for being at the top – other non-category purchasing customers will be there too.

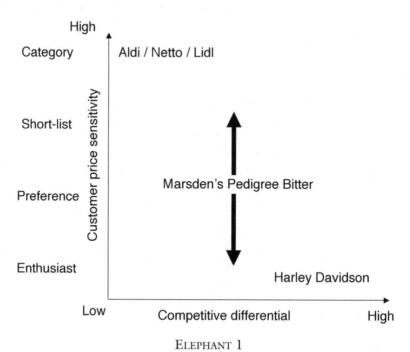

ELEPHANT 1

Competitive differential

Recall my 5 year old definition of competitive advantage – 'whatever it is that causes your customer to choose you rather than anyone else.' There could be a multiplicity of factors. A few of the most obvious examples, with personal rather than general examples, are:

Price – your product is cheaper and customers are making a decision based on price, as we have just explored with the customer segmentation approach.

Value – a slight variation from the price reason for purchase is the offsetting of price and quality to generate 'value'. The traditional, price-value trade-off is depicted in the graph 'elephant 2'.

Product 'A' is low price, low quality, product 'B' is high price high quality. The diagonal, measures 'value' as the trade-off between the two. As products 'A' an 'B' are on the same diagonal, they are at the same perceived value – i.e. with 'B' the customer is getting better quality but paying more money for it, hence the value remains the same. Competitors will crowd into the middle zone and generally seek to persuade the customers that they are of a higher quality than their price suggests, i.e. seek to persuade you that they

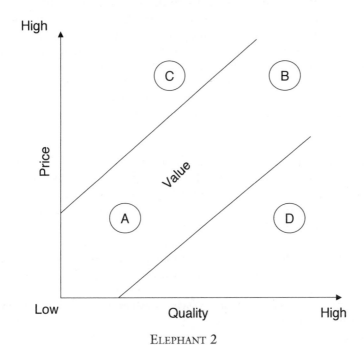

ELEPHANT 2

are lower and to the right. Product 'C' is of marginally higher quality than product 'A' but at a significantly greater price. The quality enhancement does not justify such a price difference, and so, even though it is of a higher quality, it is of lower value. Conversely, product 'D', the one we would all like to purchase, has higher value because it has higher quality than product 'A' but is at the same price.

This gives three areas for customers to focus. Some will focus on price, some on quality and some on value. The category purchaser generally focuses on price. There are some simple ways to enhance value by manipulating the price axis using special offer pricing techniques such as BOGOF (buy one get one free), 25% extra free, etc, and some simple ways to enhance value by making an addition to perceived quality by making enhancements to the offering such as upgrading (pay for a 17" PC screen and get a 19"), additional loyalty card points for certain products, linked discounts (buy more than 30 litres of petrol and get a mapbook for only £2.99) or free additional product – for example, my sales catalogue for Viking office suppliers has free additional unrelated products. With various quantities of purchases of office paper products I can get a picnic hamper, an emergency road kit or with 30 reams of premier paper – a mountain bike!

The 1990's obsession of 'value engineering' has mostly focussed on price reduction – i.e. moving vertically downwards in the diagram by retaining the quality level whilst reducing the price to the customer. I will tell the Schlitz beer (US) story later, but the summary is that they destroyed the brand and ruined the company by 'value engineering' making the product cheaper. UK retailer Matalan has embarked on a deliberate value engineering strategy where they seek to hold their prices steady, already one of the lowest price clothing retailers, then gradually, specifically and deliberately make incremental increases to quality. This is the same 'value engineering tactic' that many have worked with but the alternative dimension – seeking to move further right on the diagram.

Habit – customers buy something because they have always bought it. At home, we enjoyed Sainsbury's Duck and Wild Cherry pate. We purchased it regularly, often weekly, despite many other available alternatives. Its competitive advantage was that we did not seek an alternative, each week we bought our favourite and usually one other at random. Alas, we must have been in the minority as Sainsbury's ceased selling the product and we then became indifferent to whether we purchased a random pate from the 'deli counter' of Tesco or from Sainsbury. It's also a great example of how a very small thing (one minor product) created our habit of shopping at Sainsbury's rather than Tesco. The cost of removing a small, presumably loss making, product had been the loss for Sainsbury's of about half of our main weekly shopping.

I say 'had' because our home grocery shopping habits have subsequently changed, which in turn affects our reasons for purchasing. We now shop on-line and get the majority of our shopping delivered to our home. This makes us even more indifferent between Sainsbury's and Tesco as all the physical competitive advantages and disadvantages have been removed. As Jeff Bezos of Amazon observed – the ease of transferability between competitors in an on-line environment reduces habitual purchasing, reduces loyalty through habit and enhances the need for stronger branding than in the physical shopping environment.

Convenience – prior to its closure, I had the slowest Post Office in the world in my particular part of Surrey UK, but it was more convenient to walk to it and wait in a queue than to get in the car and drive to the nearest town, park the car, use the larger, quicker Post Office and then come home. Their competitive advantage was their physical location – walking distance from my house.

I recall another example of where convenience led to habit. I once worked in London, near Great Marlborough Street, and would frequent the nearby Coffee Republic outlet far too many times a day for my health. When we moved offices, the convenience was no longer appropriate. However, due to the previous convenience, I had formed a habit and was a Coffee Republic preference buyer. If I had the choice between Coffee Republic and another coffee house, I would choose the Republic. Whereas if my choice is between Starbucks, Café Nero and Costa, I choose the one with the smallest queue or the one with a comfortable chair available. I am aware that there is probably no difference in the coffees of each brand, but what was convenience had become habit. Regrettably Coffee Republic went into administration in 2009, so despite a few outlets remaining open, I now seldom have that choice.

Product performance (real or perceived) – the product does something. It can be a real performance – such as my wife's brand enthusiast approach to Diet-Coke and preference buyer approach to Pampers or Huggies nappies (diapers US). She is insistent that no other cola tastes the same and no other nappy delivers the high qualities of these brands.

A perceived performance reason for purchase often include those with a high emotional attachment – for example a cleaning product or a cosmetic product. The perception that brand 'Mr Muscle' cleans the kitchen better than brand 'Flash' (or vice versa) has fuelled countless commercials.

Product features – purchasing because there is one, or a number of, key features. There could be hundreds of examples, but in this section I am deliberately using personal examples. Some years ago I changed cars. Having driven Mercedes for many years, I considered a change. Due to the amount of equipment I often have to carry with me, an estate (US stationwagon) is essential and Jaguar had brought out an estate version with a larger internal capacity than the Mercedes. It seemed good to investigate it.

Whilst the following was not the deciding factor, it was a serious factor – one feature. As I carry kit around, sometimes piled to the roof, there is the possibility that in an 'emergency stop' the kit will lurch forward. This is not a problem in the Mercedes as the netting separating luggage space from seating space can be in either of two positions – for when the back seats are up or down. When I travel with kit, the seats are down; the netting is secured behind my head, and were I to be in an accident, or have to stop suddenly, none of it would spill into the driving compartment, nor fall over the top of the head-rest and hit me on the head. This feature probably cost about £20, yet the real-isation that I wasn't going to get a broken neck if I had to stop suddenly or someone shunted my rear was an excellent reassurance which the Jaguar could not offer – their netting was only workable in the 'seats up' position.

Availability – in our instant gratification society, if I can't have it now, I'll have something else. It is not just the availability of the product, the support-ing infrastructure and processes can combine to maximise availability. I work with customers in the fashion retail industry. For them, ensuring that the shelves are full and the stock rooms are meticulously ordered is vital. I worked with the manager of one leading UK store who took the initiative of adding further staff after store closing time just to restock and have every-thing in the stock room checked into product code order and size order every night. His store is now one of the best performing stores in the company – because his systems and staff rosters maximise product availabil-ity. For many years UK retailer Marks & Spencer refused to take credit cards. That was a barrier to purchase for many. Ikea have started making an addi-tional charge to credit card customers. This creates a barrier and negative image for some – their problem is with the excessive charges of the credit card companies – don't blame the customer! The Marks & Spencer and Ikea decisions have therefore reduced availability from the perspective of a customer, even though the shelves are well stacked – that gives a wider view of the concept of 'availability'. Marks & Spencer changed their policy many years ago and have accepted credit cards for some time.

Direct image – customers enhance their own image through having or using your product, such as a customer buying aftershave or cosmetics – people purchase the product to make themselves smell or look pleasant. It is not vital that others know which brand of eye shadow is being worn. The image based on the features of the product alone – the colour, aroma – and the image it creates of the user.

Imputed image – customers buy the product due to the image of your brand or company. By creating an association of themselves to your brand they are making a statement that they are like your brand personality. For example, a Rolex watch or Nike trainers – the statement of "he has a Rolex, the type of people who have Rolex watches are smart fashionable and wealthy, therefore he is smart, fashionable and wealthy". Or "He's wearing Nike trainers – he must be like Lance Armstrong or Ronaldo". Current trends or fashions usually come into this arena of purchasing decisions fuelled by image, and mostly imputed image.

Ethical – not long ago, 'fairly traded products' were the preserve of the fringe and the health food shops. Now 'fairly traded' coffee is available in most supermarkets. For us, if it does not have the 'Fair Trade' label, we don't buy the coffee. The Nestle and Shell boycotts, covered earlier in the chapter on the strategies of the giraffe, are examples of negative ethical responses. Whether or not products are tested on animals is becoming an issue influencing the decision to purchase and I can envisage widescale boycotts of Japanese and Norwegian products if the anti-whaling groups were ever to realise the powers of ethical awareness marketing as an influencer of buying decisions.

Personal relationship – we make a purchase decision based on the people we know. Today I have visited my dentist – a personal friend. I have had a note from my financial advisor – a personal friend. The cover design of this book could have been configured by any one of hundreds of agencies, but we chose personal friends.

All of these reasons why purchasers choose your product are aspects of competitive advantage, by my definition. By the term competitive differential I am trying to separate the choice based on price from the other factors, yet retain as many of the other factors as I can in order to make analysis straightforward. Were I to separate them into a large number of points, graphical representation becomes difficult after the third – and even with three, a three dimensional graph is always unclear on two dimensional paper. Competitive differential is the combination of all those factors which make you different from your competition. Your offering may be unique, but is it totally unique or is it a case of minor nuances between your offering and that of competitors? High competitive differentiation is where your market offering is unique, unrivalled and distinct from anything on the market. Low competitive differential is where you are essentially offering the same product as your competitors as perceived by your customers or potential customers.

This analysis is deliberately in the section about knowledge of our customers. Whether your product is different or similar to that of the competitor is not your decision. All that matters is the perception of the customer.

My reason for considering price sensitivity as the purchasing motivation and offsetting it with other areas of competitive advantage which I have termed 'competitive differential' is to generate possible real life strategies from the analysis. If we are able to consider our own competitive position, a 'generic strategies' approach may lead us to the preferred or better option strategies for our situation. I am generally dissatisfied with the small range of generic strategies which appear in academic and executive material on the basis that I do not find them able to be widely applied practically. This generic strategy approach based on competitive advantage will not be the cure for all known strategic dilemmas but it has been useful during development to explore the most appropriate strategies for several companies and situations. It has illustrated the actions of other companies and guided customer companies in the development of possible approaches to the marketplace.

Consider again the market for motor vehicles. Using the graph of diagram 'elephant 3' (following) we can position a variety of vehicles.

Land Rover – consider the Land Rover Defender. This vehicle deals with the harshest of terrain and is the favoured purchase of two distinct groups for whom harsh terrain is part of their environment – the military and farmers, particularly hill grazing livestock farmers. The Defender is also robust. They can endure extremely harsh treatment and are a favourite for off-road leisure activities. The Defender is durable – it is not unusual to see examples which are decades old and still in use.

To position it on the graph (see 'elephant 1' earlier) consider the price sensitivity of the purchaser and the competitive differential of the product through the eyes of the consumer.

The military and farmers are notorious for their price sensitivity – they will move as high as possible on the price sensitivity axis. However, it is not low price at any cost – they need a vehicle that will do the job. They cannot afford to get bogged down in mud, or fall over on an incline, so it is price for achieving that specific functionality which needs to be considered.

The Defender has some qualities which give it competitive differential. There may be a degree of habit, there are certainly advantages of function – product performance and product features. The Land Rover in the UK has strong availability. The Hummer would be an excellent alternative to the Defender, the lower level options can compete on price with the Defender, but the company web site only lists one dealer in the UK. It has a competitive disadvantage of unavailability.

In summary, there are a number of reasons why customers purchase the defender which combine to give it a high competitive differential – it is able to demonstrate a significant series of points of difference between itself and other motor vehicles as perceived by the purchasers. High price sensitivity and high competitive differential is therefore top right on the diagram.

Range Rover is also manufactured by the Land Rover company. The company emerged in the post-WWII economy and rapidly became a market leader in the 4×4 market. In the 1960's the company developed a more luxurious 4×4, unveiled to the press and public in June 1970 – the Range Rover. This is not for the cost conscious farmer. Current specifications can include a supercharged 4.2 litre 396bhp V8, naturally aspirated 4.4 litre 306bhp V8, or the technically advanced 177bhp in-line turbodiesel engine. It has 4-channel ABS, electronic traction control and dynamic stability control, a new 6-speed automatic for petrol derivatives, a colour touch-screen control for satellite navigation, personal telephone integration with Bluetooth™, rear DVD entertainment, a full 4×4 information system, harman/kardon LOGIC7® premium sound system with 14 speakers and MP3 capability. This is luxury in the guise of a 4×4. The fact that it can climb seemingly impossible gradients is irrelevant as it is more likely to be seen on the streets of fashionable London's Chelsea than on a mountain. The price of the most basic model is approximately that of two Land Rover Defenders, and a more expensive top of the range version approximates to the cost of four Defenders.

Does it have strong differential to other vehicles in the market? Absolutely – in terms of product features, product performance (mostly perceived rather than actual, but it is comforting to know that you could still get to the office if global tectonic movements generated a mountain in Chelsea one evening), and most certainly in terms of imputed image. A Range Rover stands for status, success, even opulence. So position it far to the right.

Are those who purchase the Range Rover cost conscious? Probably not – they could buy a much cheaper vehicle, if they chose to, but their choice is based on the competitive differential aspects of the prestigious vehicle. There may be some element of price consideration, particularly at the lower levels of the range, and so it would be unfair to suggest that money was not a concern for a Range Rover buyer – just that money, or value, was one of many contributing factors. The Range Rover cannot therefore move into the very lowest part of the graph inhabited by brand enthusiasts and would sit slightly higher. So position the Range Rover towards the extreme right, and towards the bottom but not at the very bottom.

Family saloons are the mainstay of the traditional vehicle industry. Each manufacturer tries desperately to convince us that their offering in this market is better than another and all mainstream manufacturers now have something in this range. Whilst we could work through the specification

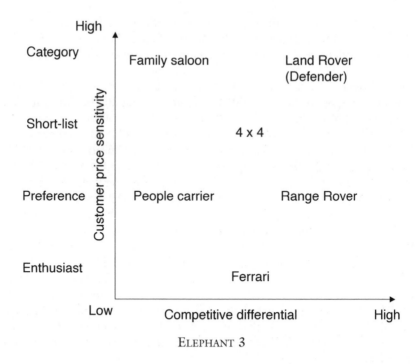

ELEPHANT 3

differences of the Renault Laguna and compare them with those of the Ford Mondeo, despite minor nuances, the essential characteristics and functions are the same. It is fiercely price competitive with the Mondeo LX having a list price of £15,800 and the Laguna Expression list price being £15,780. High price sensitivity and the product in essence very similar – top left.

People carriers (MPVs) were the innovation of Renault, but now most major vehicle manufacturers offer something in this area. In essence they have 'van' characteristics with the internal comforts of the car. The differences between them are more in the eyes of the salesmen than the consumers. Simultaneously, some friends and my wife separately considered people carriers for our then almost identical family needs. Between us about a dozen alternatives were derived, most of the products were similar and we made different decisions based on minor minutiae. We ended with a Toyota, they had a Citroen. The competitive differential is minimal – to the left. Cars are cheaper than people carriers – so the people carrier buyers are not as price sensitive as the family saloon buyers. Like the Range Rover buyers, they consider price amongst a number of other issues. Having decided to buy a people carrier they move into the short-list or preference buyer category and so probably sit to the left (minimal difference between the products) and below half way down but not at the very bottom (price is a factor but equal to other factors – perhaps comfort, economy, safety, number of seats).

4×4 vehicles from mainstream manufacturers are not as prestigious as the Range Rover. The Mitsubishis, Chryslers, Hondas, Fords, Vauxhalls and now even 4×4 BMW's crowd the market. I would argue that there is greater differential between 4×4's than there is between people carriers as the range seems greater, the market offering is wider and the performance, functions, features, imputed image and availability differences generate the opportunity for the creation and exploitation of competitive differentials. Greater than people carriers, but nowhere near the level of differentiation of the Range Rover or the Land Rover Defender. 4×4's therefore have a middle positioning on competitive differential and a price sensitivity probably greater than people carriers due to the plethora available on the market. The similarity of price bandings for 4×4's is evidence that the motor industry agrees.

Ferrari do not compete on price. The price of some are equivalent to purchasing a small house. The customer price sensitivity should therefore be rock bottom. Regarding competitive differential, Ferrari would say that they are at the extreme right, and their brand enthusiasts would agree. However, I am not convinced that the difference between the Ferrari and other high value, high performance sports cars such as a Lamborghini is sufficiently wide to position Ferrari far right, I have therefore suggested on diagram 'elephant 3' that Ferrari has a similar differential to the 4×4 – the middle.

Generic strategies based on differential

The positioning on the axes of consumer/customer price sensitivity and competitive differential can assist us to consider the types of strategies available to the companies or products illustrated.

Top right – lowest cost

If a product is perceived as of negligible difference to its competitors and the customer has high price sensitivity, it does not take a neurosurgeon to work out the basis of competition. Either move from that position or compete on price. In that position, the cheapest will win. The decision to make is either be the cheapest or choose to move. In the UK grocery market, Aldi, Netto and Lidl have all chosen to stay top left and make price the primary competitive issue.

Bottom left – increase differential

Low price sensitivity with products which do not appear to have high competitive differential could result in inefficient sluggish markets. The US book industry was loitering unambitiously here before the advent of Amazon. Staying here is comfortable, fairly unchallenging but can also create vulnerability if an entrant to the market creates a movement – either to the right or upward (Amazon moved in both directions, but majored on the upward movement by aggressively creating price differences). One possible example of a product in this area is the premier resort holiday market. One 5*, 6* or 7* hotel is much like another regardless of its global geographical positioning – great service, tropical climate, luxurious pools, an adjacent ocean, sumptuous rooms and fine dining. Whether it is in the Far East, Caribbean, East Africa or South Africa or elsewhere the recipe for success is the same. Despite the almost ubiquitous offering, many customers generate brand loyalty based on good holiday experience. Pre-children, my wife and I toured the Serengeti, toured the world's jungles, dived in the oceans provided that they were warm and relatively shark free, and would often move to a premier location for a final beach week before flying home. We always went with the same company – we trusted their customer care, their staff and their decisions (including a change of hotel once). Price was a very minor consideration.

In a stable market, this would be a fine place for the company to inhabit. However, were a new entrant to offer something different (move to the right) or be significantly cheaper (move upwards), our holiday company would be vulnerable. They would need the strategies of the cheetah to survive – see the later chapter.

In order to negate such a potential threat the strategies which could be beneficially implemented by a company positioned towards the lower left part of the graph would include deliberate attempts to move to the right. The bottom left is so attractive that it is unlikely that the competitive space will remain unchallenged for too long. Strategies would therefore include the building of differentials. By seeking to identify and amplify differentials the company is actively building competitive advantages. This is exactly what the holiday company is doing. It is emphasising its longevity, experience, customer satisfaction ratings – all seeking to make it a perceived cut above others in the sector.

Bottom right – build

The companies in the bottom right have low customer price sensitivity and are perceived as being very different from their competitors – this is Harley Davidson territory. This competitive space is also envious and strategies should encompass seeking to build either positively by further penetration of the market or negatively by seeking to build barriers to entry – either for new competitors or for those in the bottom left sector seeking to move towards the bottom right.

In this case, particularly towards the bottom right extreme, market penetration cannot be achieved by price as this is not a major customer motivation. The factors mentioned earlier such as performance, features, availability, image etc are all relevant aspects to build on.

Top right – exploit niche

The customer is highly price sensitive and the competitive differential is high – so the customers view the company or product as being significantly different from that of the competition. Apple PC's live here. Used by designers and 'creatives', Apple have carved a niche within the hardware and software markets. The exploitation of the niche means further specialising and further emphasising the aspects which the consumer already sees as differentiators. In Apple's case, the introduction of colours to the hardware is a classic niche development strategy. They are marketing essentially to professionals who do not do 'grey' for anything in their lives – so their PC's should reflect that.

Quadrant diagrams are abundant in strategy literature. Whichever box your company or product fits into, there is a strategy for the box. As diagrams 'elephant 2, 3 and 4' show, this is not a quadrant model. Above, I have described the generic strategies of the extremes but many companies and products, like the 4×4's, Range Rovers, People Carriers and Ferraris are not positioned at the extremes. They therefore have strategic choices available to them. Ferrari's choice is most obvious – there is no reason to seek to move left or upwards – so Ferrari should be building competitive barriers to prevent Lamborghini and others being perceived as product substitutes and further penetrating the market by tactics such as greater commercial exposure. Sponsoring a winning Formula 1 vehicle fits perfectly into the aims of moving further to the right.

Range Rover's choice is more of a decision based on their perception of the future market (see S.T.E.E.P.L.E.). If they are able to decrease customer price sensitivity by emphasising the luxury of their product and taking the Stella Artois approach – 'reassuringly expensive' – they can make market penetration strategies. Alternatively, if they do not feel that their position is able to generate the decreased price sensitivity this requires, they will be forced into niche marketing where they will have to make specific targeting of specific customer types.

4×4's could potentially move in any of the 4 directions indicated in diagram 'elephant 4'. They could drive cost and compete on price, they

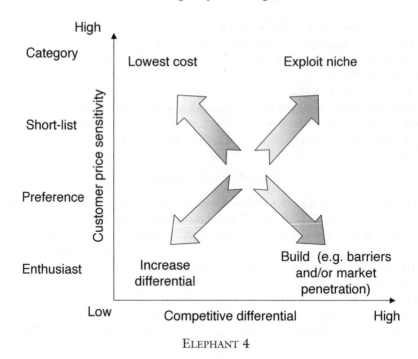

ELEPHANT 4

could develop the 4×4 niche, they could increase differentials between different 4×4's or between 4×4's and other vehicles or they could seek to generate non-price based market penetration by, for example, emphasising radical functionality, features or imputed image. The emphasis of radical imputed image is currently the tactic of the Land Rover Freelander where the advertising emphasises the rugged nature and adventurous style of the product – and then by association of the owner. On one radio advert a gloating father talks about how proud he is of his son who can endure excessive desert heat and survive winds which would whip the hide off a rhinoceros – just because he owns a Freelander. Another advert has a mock Freelander telephone helpline "for information about rescuing old ladies from burning buildings press 2, for information on venomous snake bites press 3" et cetera. However, the Freelander driver in the advert wants information on what to do when being attacked by grizzly bears – because all these things are the sort of thing Freelander drivers do!

Knowledge of our supply chain

We can perform our function brilliantly, but without our suppliers we are hamstrung. The elephant's position as king of the Serengeti is unchallenged, and its supply chain is gloriously simple – it needs trees (or rather the leaves on the trees), and water. As we saw in the opening pages of this chapter, the elephant has an immaculate knowledge of its supply chain – where to find the trees, then once located, how to get the leaves, and where to find the water – including if they have to dig for it as not just any water will do – given a choice they want the sweeter sodium enriched water often available with a bit of digging.

In business many organisations frequently treat customers like kings and suppliers like slaves – despite clichéd rhetoric about 'partnership'. In doing so we fail to realise the importance of our supply chain and this lack of knowledge creates a vast strategic vulnerability. In the summer of 2005 two British companies struggled with their supply chains. After the demise of UK car manufacturer Rover, the previously related manufacturer Land Rover found that mutual suppliers, without the volume of work required for survival, were going out of business. The collapse of Rover had a high impact on Land Rover. Knowledge of the supply chain and effective contingency planning may have averted some of the crisis if Land Rover had acted much earlier – perhaps years earlier as the warning signs of Rover's inability to compete were evident for many years.

British Airways (BA) extricated itself from the process of preparing in-flight meals and the former BA meal preparation division became the separate company Gate Gourmet. An industrial dispute at Gate Gourmet Heathrow created a employee walk-out and complete cessation of production. BA flights were then without meals and they were forced to having to resort to handing customers vouchers to buy their own sandwiches in the airport terminal before taking off. This was not the premium service associated with BA and the resultant premium prices are then not justified – on the price/quality/value graph BA dived heavily due to the action of its supplier Gate Gourmet.

I would suggest that knowledge of suppliers is a huge development opportunity for our businesses and may, in many cases, also need a huge attitude change. I recall in the construction industry many occasions of sub-contractor abuse where they would correctly put in a bill for, say £20,000 and the contractor would find some reason to seek to pay them less. This is not a way to generate sub-contractor loyalty and is a reason why some large construction organisations have historically found difficulty getting a consistent quality of sub-contractors.

Many of us collect data and press cuttings about customers, but only the companies with a keen awareness of their supply chain as a source of competitive advantage generate the same level of collation to news about their suppliers.

Getting independent facilitators to meet with a group of suppliers is an excellent way of gaining an insight to improve supply chain relationships and seek to turn this to a competitive advantage. I once facilitated a group of nine

European suppliers to one multinational company. The company paid for their representatives to attend and ensured that the representatives were from the right levels within the supplier organisations. My brief was to conduct open forum discussions about where the customer company was good, where it needed attention and to generate ideas on how they could enhance their supplier relationships. The trust required to have an open discussion, rather than conducting separate interviews, was laudable. The output from the day was transformational.

Conversely I have twice experienced a customer phoning to renegotiate the price of some work. My answer is usually curt – if the work is not worth the agreed charge, cancel the work and don't do it. If it is, we agreed a fee. Conversely, I am pleased to say that many customers treat me as a valued supplier. On one occasion I was arguing with a customer over who should pay for lunch – "I should pay – I'm the supplier and you're the customer" was responded to by "I'm the customer, and so I must be right – I'll pay!". This dispute was only solved when the female customer pointed out that she was bigger than me and would get violent unless I let her pay! Whilst that is a trifling example, I can give copious examples of customers giving various gifts just to say thank you, of them being interested in me and my family life, of them readjusting schedules to make my life easier (particularly the travelling) and also entertaining me in the way most companies entertain customers. This creates supplier loyalty and enhances the supply chain.

Knowledge of our supply chain means knowing our suppliers and taking a commercial decision to treat them like kings rather than slaves. As a supplier, I reciprocate by giving the best – on one occasion I had the usual sleepless overnight plane from Toronto to London, got home, 1 hour sleep and then washed, changed and off to do a keynote speech fuelled by adrenaline and caffeine. I wasn't going to let down the keynote customer who treats me well – even though my diary said I was unavailable! For another customer who treats me exceptionally well, I have conducted specialist sessions at a school where they are a governor – a service which would be well beyond a school budget was conducted for free. One colleague has gone a step further. He did a similar thing, and as the school was local to him, eventually became a governor himself. (Note for non-UK readers: UK schools have unpaid governors who are responsible for, and provide advice for the effective running of schools).

Knowledge of our corporate history

Understanding our own business is relatively easy in the present, but more difficult in the past. With the enthusiastic embracing of downsizing, right-sizing, outsourcing and offshoring, many companies have made large scale redundancies. Seeking voluntary redundancy as a preference, those closer to retirement and those who are confident of gaining employment elsewhere have been disproportionately removed from large companies at middle manager levels. There is a danger of corporate amnesia where the leavers take with them knowledge of both the present and the past. Few organisations engage in full effective departure sessions and so even the parts of this knowledge which could be retained are usually lost.

I recall one multinational reducing the role of the UK community affairs post to the point where it was financially unsustainable for the two incumbents. The incumbents took the voluntary redundancy option, negligible departure information was gleaned and the organisation sought to recruit for the new lesser role. This post requires extensive knowledge of the company, an understanding of what it has done and an understanding of the community and charity work in which it has engaged in order to represent the company to third parties (often mayors, the press, politicians, celebrities etc). It is not a post which could be filled externally. No internal candidate wanted the reduced hours and so the company sought external recruitment. This external recruitment failed as no candidate would like to be in a situation where they are asked a simple question at a charity function, and be unable to answer it due to lack of organisational knowledge.

In researching for some of the information of this book, I have been in contact with archivists from various companies. Some display an encyclopaedic knowledge of the company they have served for decades. I am not confident that there are newcomers ready to take over when these company brand enthusiasts retire as it is less frequent to have such loyalty to one company in this generation. A huge amount of corporate knowledge will be lost in the next 10–20 years unless we address this. Areas such as Community Affairs and Archives are often seen as non-productive and therefore under the spotlight for financial savings. I feel that this is short termism as the use of knowledge generates value. The question for these functions is how to ensure value generation, and how to communicate it internally.

Knowledge of our competition

The elephant does not have direct animal competition in the Serengeti other than mankind. With a number of escalating tactics to deal with threats, the elephant is rarely troubled. The first level of dealing with threats is that of warning: making noises, emphasising their size by flapping ears to maximize the visual mass directed towards the threat and even, in an extreme, 'false charges' where the elephant will run at a threat and then run past it or stop short. In the event of physical conflict, there are four options, also escalating. Firstly a slap with the trunk which would have sufficient force to send hyenas and smaller lions hurtling through the air. Secondly, using the trunk and tusks to lift and throw the threat judo-style would deal with a most determined offensive animal. The third level is to use the tusks to gore a victim although this is rarely used deliberately. The final, universally fatal ultimate deterrent is for the elephant, having restrained the threat with the trunk, to kneel on its victim. As an elephant weighs up to six tonnes, no creature could survive this. The lion is often stated as the king of the jungle, despite the fact that it rarely lives in jungle. However, no lion would dare attack a fit elephant. An entire lion hunting party would be required to tackle even an isolated young elephant, but the family nature of elephants mean that the young are never abandoned. The isolated, usually due to being either old or sick can be vulnerable, but otherwise the elephant is undoubtedly the king of the Serengeti. The only threats to the elephant are human and climatic. In this and the last century these two threats have become inextricably intertwined with our industrialisation affecting global climate changes.

With such a variety of tactics available, an entire book could be made of those elephant behaviours, and I was tempted to do so but the purpose of *Strategies of the Serengeti* was to produce the greatest variety of possible strategies for businesses and so the depth of considering only the elephant was sacrificed to enable the consideration of the breadth of the range of animals in the book. From the perspective of competition, the elephant's knowledge is that it is king of the Serengeti and is more than equipped to deal with animal competition through the combination of trunk, tusk, knees and pure mass. The elephant therefore has made a competitive assessment and has the ability to respond accordingly.

I was once conducting a four day exercise with the senior team of a European company on 'The competition'. We ran through a few issues and analytical tools, then came the time to start applying them to real competitors. Despite this being a very successful company, the envy of many in the market, they knew negligible amounts about their competition. We abandoned the set programme and spent about two hours surfing the web sites of competitors, and whilst that is not the best information, it still increased their knowledge of the competition several times over. I am sure that they are not alone as I believe that for many of us, our knowledge of the competition is at best 'patchy'.

In World War II, British Field Marshall Montgomery, the man who beat the Nazis out of Africa, kept in his mobile command caravan a picture of his rival Field Marshall Rommel. He was focused on his competition. Whilst the military analogy often breaks down and is sometimes counterproductive, the illustration is clear; 'Monty' knew his enemy and never made a move without considering him in detail.

We have explored our competitive advantage when we considered knowledge of our customers – but what are the relative competitive advantages of our competitors? Why do our potential customers buy from them?

I will suggest a new model for considering our position relative to the competition – to make sure that the competition is 'on our radar' – R.A.D.A.R. analysis.

R.A.D.A.R. analysis

The analysis has several stages:

1. Positioning ourselves and competitor(s)
2. Challenging our choice of positions
3. Considering all available options
4 Choosing options

The framework for R.A.D.A.R. is shown in diagram 'elephant 5'. Set to look like a radar pattern, we are to measure ourselves and the competition against the 5 criteria R, A, D, A, and R. The stronger we are in a criteria, the further we are from the centre and the more towards the extreme of the diagram.

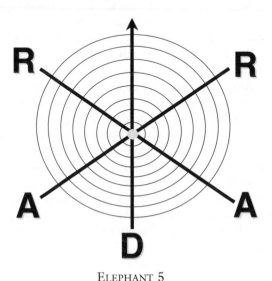

ELEPHANT 5

The model is best used for a 'one on one' or 'one on two' situation where an organisation is making a direct competitive analysis of itself against one or two other specific companies. It has been used profitably with six competitors, although it became a little cumbersome, and it has been used with a 'general market' as a comparison. I would seldom recommend the 'general market' comparison in addition to a specific competitor comparison as the more general the analysis, the less specific and practical the resultant developed strategies become.

Stage 1 – Positioning ourselves and competitor(s)

R – reputation

What is the reputation of the company and its products with the end users? The higher and greater the reputation, the further out on the first 'R' spoke the company, product or brand can sit. I have regularly used a number competing brands as examples when using R.A.D.A.R. and so could choose from a wide range. One which often engages strong emotion is the premium beer market comparison between Budweiser and Stella Artois. As Anheuser-Busche was taken over by InBev in 2008, the example is a now little false, but if we set the clock as 2007 or before, the learning will be evident. In 2007 the beers had markedly different approaches. Subsequently, many the differences appear to have eroded post-acquisition.

Belgium's InBev had (2005) a global market share of approximately 14% and deposed Anheuser-Busch as the world's largest brewer (by volume). To illustrate the R.A.D.A.R. model, we will use the Budweiser-Stella competitive scenario with the emotive, unquantified data of the opinions from delegates of about 100 training courses where we have considered this market conflict to explore the R.A.D.A.R. model before moving on to considering delegate's own competitive situations. One reason I choose the Bud-Stella competition as an example is that the emotive reactions and comments appear similar regardless of the gender, age or seniority of the delegates. For this illustration, we will consider the competition between the two in the UK market only – the more specific the parameters, the more specific the outcome. Whilst this comparison is imperfect compared with an example of direct competitors with similar products seeking to occupy the same market space (e.g. Renault and Ford with the Laguna and Mondeo), I prefer it as the benefits of gender age and seniority agreement outweigh the negatives of a divergent and interlocking competitive scenario, even with our 'clock' artificially set in 2007.

Premium beer in the UK is defined as Class III beer with ABV (alcohol by volume) of 4.3%–7.5%. Anheuser-Busch's Budweiser and InBev's Stella

Artois were both major players in this market. Stella is still the UK market leader. Budweiser is still the US market leader who has been actively seeking to increase its foothold in the UK for over a decade.

Budweiser – the question 'who has ever had a Bud?' will always generate a forest of hands on any strategy development session or strategy training course. We then proceed to extract individuals' comments on the drink. The follow-up question of 'Who is a regular Bud drinker?' occasionally gets a few hands, often gets none and usually gets just one or two. We've all tried Bud, we just don't like it. It is not beer in the British taste of beer. Despite millions of pounds/dollars in advertising, some of which is brilliantly creative, the beer has only recently broken through the barrier to achieve in excess of 5% of the UK premium beer market. The advertising has elevated awareness so that almost everyone other than a hermit would be aware of Bud, but it has not elevated reputation. The pre-2008 takeover advertising campaigns all related to attempting to reframe the reasons for purchase. The 'fresh beer tastes better' strap line sought to capitalise on the competitive advantage of 'freshness' with each beer's manufacturing date stated as 'born on dd/mm/yy'. The drinker will still maintain that duration between manufacture and consumption has little bearing on taste, up to the obvious point of product dilapidation, but if Anheuser-Busch continued to promote the strap line, my guess is that it would become a positive reputational aspect – we will believe that fresh beer is better even if it is not. This attitudinal change may take a decade, and if it does occur, other beers will be able to follow by stating their manufacture date. Conversely, other beers, such as Grolsch from the Netherlands, pushed the opposite message. Grolsch advertising informs us that beer needs time to ferment and mature. For the best product to be achieved it must not be rushed.

The summary of positioning for Budweiser on the 'R' for reputation (end user) axis is therefore at best mid-way. Generally, we don't like it and the 5% marketshare despite almost all of us having tried the product is testimony to a midway reputation perhaps even being a generous assessment.

Stella – generally a very high reputation, except amongst some women. The strength of Stella has earned it the unpleasant nickname of 'wifebeater' in some quarters and this is reflected in some reactions on training courses when exploring the R.A.D.A.R. model. However, many other women and a substantial number of male delegates are regular Stella drinkers. Using the terminology from the customer knowledge section, Stella will have a number of brand enthusiasts, many preference buyers and it is on almost everyone's shortlist. The end user reputation is therefore very high and so can be positioned towards the extremity of the first 'R' for reputation.

Competitive advantage
Budweiser / Stella Artois (pre-2008 takeover)
UK premium beer market
Subjective delegate opinion basis only

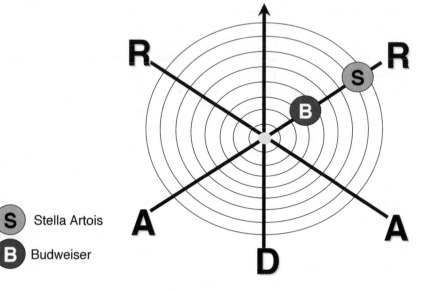

ELEPHANT 6

A – awareness

From the target market of potential customers, what proportion have heard of the product? Awareness from outside the target market is an irrelevance – we are only concerned here with those who are actively likely to buy the product. The usual test I ask is to consider whether we were to walk outside whatever venue we are using the model in, and ask the first 100 people of the legal drinking age whom we meet whether they have heard of Budweiser and Stella. Probably all 100 would say that they have – that is prompted awareness. For unprompted awareness, ask 100 people to make a list of premium beers – if you did this you would not use the phrase 'premium beer' which is a marketer's and strategist's term for market segmentation, you would ask them for a list of good beers of which they are aware, or maybe stipulate bottled beers. I would venture to suggest that even an unprompted awareness would yield in excess of 90% for both products due to their vast outlet coverage and exceptionally good, and frequent, TV commercial communications. Both Budweiser and Stella would therefore be almost at the top of the spoke for awareness. In using this example,

I do not believe I have even encountered a teetotaller who has not heard of both products.

D – development

To what extent is the company or brand able to do something new? To what level can they create what currently does not exist? Are they innovation leaders or followers? Cutting edge or trailing in the wake? Development, creating the new, is the domain of the creative entrepreneur. We think of Dyson, Branson and even Sir Clive Sinclair! This can create competitive leaps – or what others call first mover advantage, blue oceans or uncontested space. However, it is also a risky strategy. First mover advantage is the trailblazer who is able to explore bold new frontiers, find cul-de-sacs and make mistakes. The second entrant can follow, avoiding these costly mistakes. I recall one very conservative business colleague reminding me that *'the only thing trailblazers get is an arrow up the backside'*. Many businesses achieve great success by following others' innovations. In the male grooming industry, Gillette trades on innovation and cutting edge technology (excuse the pun) whilst Wilkinson Sword trades on tradition, history and reliability. The products are virtually identical, perform an absolutely identical function yet Gillette would score high on the development spoke and Wilkinson Sword would score low. This does not mean that Wilkinson Sword, as a company, is inferior to Gillette – it just has different strategies regarding development and innovation. Many 'follower' non-innovative businesses are successful. Utility, financial and consulting companies are generally non-innovative, yet many perform well. Development ability per se is not a recipe for success – it is how this ability is harnessed, leveraged and driven to derive competitive advantage that is the key to success.

Budweiser – in the history of the company they have been very innovative. During US prohibition they ensured survival by diverse non-beer production activity such as hotels, restaurants, ice cream manufacture, refrigerated cabinet manufacture and even the manufacture of vehicle bodies. A small sample of their innovations in the US:

1903 – capping bottles
1916 – launch of Bevo – a non-alcoholic drink
1920 – 'near beer' launched to deal with prohibition
1921 – ice cream manufacture started, launch of ginger ale, malt syrup, extra dry ginger ale and Old Devon Root Beer – the last two ceased in 1942
1951 – became the first US brewer to build a plant outside their home city with the development of the Newark brewery

1953 – purchased the St Louis Cardinals baseball team – sold in 1995
1959 – first Busch Gardens opened
1962 – plastic can carrier developed
1964 – innovation with using non-returnable bottles
1976 – further bottling innovations with the 7oz non-returnable bottles
1978 – Chelsea soft drink launched (withdrawn 1979)
1981 – Bud Light introduced (named Budweiser Light until 1984)
1990 – Bud Dry and Bud Cold Filtered Draft introduced (CFD ceased 1992)
1995 – Bud Ice and Anheuser Light launched
1997 – O'Doul's Amber, Meridian Blonde and Michelob Specialities all launched
2001 – Kilarney's Red Lager launched, Bud Light becomes the best selling beer in the US

This list could easily be doubled with innovations and new products launching. Some succeed, many fail – but most are innovative.

On the R.A.D.A.R. analysis, whilst we are considering the UK market, the company has a very innovative past and so a high positioning seems utterly reasonable. Their award winning advertising is famously innovative and creative – from frogs and chameleons to 'Wassup?'. Unfortunately the in-house 'fresh beer' and 'born on' approach, isn't as innovative, but the creative ads raised awareness to saturation levels, yet did not give us a reason to purchase. 'Fresh beer' does give a reason, the issue is whether we agree or not that fresh beer tastes better and whether over time the strap line will convince us that it does. Current market share is starting to increase.

Stella – in 1366, in the Den Hoorn Brewery in Leuven, Netherlands, a wonderous golden brew was first concocted. It wasn't the Stella we know today but if the marketing department of InBev had their way they would seek to convince us that it was and that the product hasn't changed since then. This is clearly impossible as the original brewery was destroyed in WWI artillery fire, but the site has iconic status in Belgium. However, the words Den Hoorn, Leuven and 1366 appear on the labels as does the horn symbol of the Den Hoorn brewery. Obviously from the development of processes and hygiene emphasis, beer has changed enormously since 1366 – the drink is produced at state of the art premises to exacting standards. The name Stella Artois is a combination of Sebastian Artois who was appointed master brewer in 1708, and later bought the brewery, and 'Stella' being Greek for star. The brew was originally a Christmas special brew, hence the star representing the one which led the magi to Jesus. Due to customer demand, the Christmas brew became an all year round brew but, to this day, a star adorns the label as a reminder of the beer's heritage. Considering innovation and brand extensions, we don't see Stella light, Stella dark, Stella ice, low alcohol Stella or other derivatives. Bottles, cans or draught, but don't expect packaging innovation. The message is clear – Stella doesn't change. The advertising even tells us this with television adverts which are as innovative as Budweiser yet wholly different. Most notable is the historic period in which each of the adverts are set. They seek to explain how people would give up anything for a Stella – a priceless painting, an escaped WWI allied airman, – or even spend time in the punishment area of a WWI prisoner ship. The most recent settings I can recall are the WWI adverts (1914–1918). The image is to project that Stella has longevity and is so valuable that people will do extraordinary things to acquire it. The strapline 'reassuringly expensive', used extensively since its introduction in 1982, perpetually reinforces this.

From a development perspective, the most that we consumers will see is different sizes of bottle – but still the same shape bottle! The brand Stella Artois deliberately sites itself at the 'no development' end of the 'D' in R.A.D.A.R.

An interesting aside, whilst we are setting the date for this example as 2007 or before, Stella are now abandoning this 'no change' strategy which has brought them such success and are developing Stella 4, a 4% (weaker) beer to offset the negative impressions of their strong traditional brew.

A – assets

From the R.A.D.A.R. analysis perspective, all assets can be considered – tangible and intangible. Tangible assets could include manufacturing facilities and distribution networks, finance or even aspects such as geographical location. I recall using this for an injection moulding business near the UK South Coast. Its products were low value and, in essence, consisted of low value plastic surrounding a large space of air. Major costs for the business were therefore storage and transport. With customers throughout the UK it had a competitive disadvantage from the asset of geographical location. Storage was no cheaper than in the UK Midlands, but transport was expensive. Distances to London and Bristol were similar to those of a competitor in the Midlands, but its deliveries to Birmingham, Leeds, Manchester, Liverpool, Glasgow and Edinburgh all incurred greater transport cost and time than its competitor. Unless it could find compensating competitive advantages, it would not be able to match the prices or profits of the competitor. The key to effective use of R.A.D.A.R. is identifying which are the most important assets to measure. As the R.A.D.A.R. structure looks at a directly competitive situation, the answer is probably most often the assets which enable the business to get one step ahead, or fall one step behind the competitor being measured. This is true for our consideration of both tangible and intangible assets.

Intangible assets can include a wide range of possible aspects such as human knowledge, aspects of the brand or copyrights and patents. One observation is that we often overstate our human assets. Our opinion of our staff's superiority over that of the competition would need to be proven in order to make it onto the R.A.D.A.R. analysis. So in all cases a 'reality check' would be useful. As we are considering a competitive situation with this analysis, the person best placed to give that reality check is the customer. In one company where I was CFO we always conducted a Client Satisfaction Questionaire (CSQ), face to face, Director to Director and a second one face to face with our project manager and the client project manager. We did not count the job as complete until this was fulfilled, and therefore bonuses were not paid until it was done. Completion of the two CSQ's had to be within one month of the job completion. On every CSQ we asked specific questions of how the client perceived us compared to whoever they considered our closest competitor. This obsession with gathering customer driven competitive data was an important driver for our business success.

For the illustrative, admittedly informal and subjective, Budweiser and Stella competitive situation we are considering, we need to establish the most relevant assets for this scenario. Both brands rely on strong marketing advertising. This is not cheap, particularly television advertising which both rely on extensively. Finance must be a factor.

The ability of the brand to mean more than just a product could be a consideration. In the same way that Rolex has an inextricable link with 'expensive', Mercedes means 'quality', McDonald's creates, for me, and instant image of the 'McLibel case' and Marlboro can't shake off a link to lung cancer. What do the brands of Bud and Stella mean? Both mean a quality drink. Bud has a more trendy appeal, it is American, it seeks to project the similar 'party' image that has been successful for Coca-Cola over the decades. So the Bud brand stands for trendy, American and party. Stella is about being traditional, reassuringly expensive, the best, consistent and strong. Both are targeting male traits, yet the 'party' image is the probable reason why I now see more women drinking Bud. In both cases, Bud and Stella brands transcend being mere beers. They are images of their respective styles. If we measure brand strength, from a UK perspective, they will both score well in their different areas. Budweiser becoming the official sponsor of the English Football Association Premier League (2005) enhanced their image to their target market, Stella sponsoring television feature films and having their logo at every advertising break enhances their image in their target market who are more likely to watch feature films. Stella's sporting appeal is more appropriately targeted by sponsoring the Stella Artois Queen's Club tennis event which is the annual pre-cursor to the world famous Wimbledon tournament. For illustrative purposes, we can therefore consider brand strength which would encompass all these factors, and perhaps others such as brand transferability, brand extension and brand longevity.

Another asset for consideration may be the respective manufacturing facilities. Each beer is manufactured under licence in the UK – it is far too expensive to transport heavy liquid very far – even worse than plastic injection moulding products.

So, on this illustration, we have three assets to consider. The R.A.D.A.R. analysis only has one spoke for 'Assets'. In order to cope with this the R.A.D.A.R. model can be split with extensions to the spokes. Diagram 'elephant 7' shows the 'Asset' spoke of the model as worked by a major, market leading, specialist holiday company. They were encountering strong competition from a small niche player and used the R.A.D.A.R. model to seek strategic suggestions.

The holiday market leader identified that overall its assets were much greater than the niche player but that in two specific areas it had a competitive disadvantage. The niche company staff were more knowledgeable and the quality of the accommodation offered was superior. Overall, the accommodation would be a competitive advantage to the market leader as they could offer a wide variety of well located premises. The niche player could

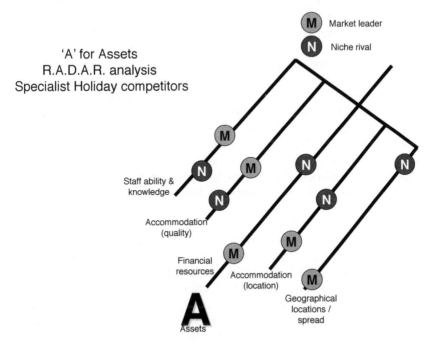

ELEPHANT 7

offer just a few premises in inferior locations but they were of higher quality. The analysis had a major impact on the action the business took and the competitor was out manoeuvred by the market leader placing huge marketing emphasis on its areas of R.A.D.A.R. strength. Half a day spent completing a R.A.D.A.R. analysis has now, over the years of implementation of that day's work, resulted in dominance in their geographical area and significant financial advantage from customers choosing them over the competitor who pre-R.A.D.A.R. was seen as a dangerous threat.

This multiple spoke adaptation of R.A.D.A.R. can be used on any of the five spokes. Over time I have seen it used on all. The only caveat is that it can become cumbersome on one diagram and so when several multiple spokes are being considered, we break the diagram into sections. I have used the diagram on A1 paper, on walls, on pinboards, but my favourite is using it on the floor with duct tape.

With the Bud – Stella example, for illustrative purposes, we will therefore have three spokes to 'Assets' – finance, brand strength and manufacturing facilities.

Budweiser – finance must be strong. As the second largest brewer in the world (2007), after a long spell as the largest, but with higher than sector average margins on its core products, and with just under 50% of the market in the US, the second biggest beer market in the world (was previously the first, overtaken by China in 2004) it has money to spend. Brand strength is immense – the link to UK football (US explanation – proper football, i.e. the round/spherical ball kicked with the foot, played by the 204 nations who are members of FIFA) enhances the brand image and strength, bringing it more into the public mainstream rather than the more fashionable bottled beer drinking market. Bud must therefore score high on brand strength. Regarding manufacturing facilities, the head office functions are based at Richmond in Surrey and brewing is carried out by Anheuser-Busch brewmasters at the Budweiser Stag Brewery in Mortlake, London. The facilities, albeit owned by InBev, are modern and of an exceptional standard. Again, Bud must score high in the facilities aspect of assets in R.A.D.A.R.

Stella – with the UK head office in Luton, North of London. InBev manufacture 30% of the beer consumed in the UK in a variety of locations. The global market of InBev is more widely spread than the American dominated Anheuser-Busch and it would be logical to assume that distribution, procurement and administrative costs are therefore higher. Consequently, I would guess that finance available for Stella is good, but not as good as that available for Anheuser-Busch's flagship Budweiser. Stella will therefore be further from the peripheral of the R.A.D.A.R. model.

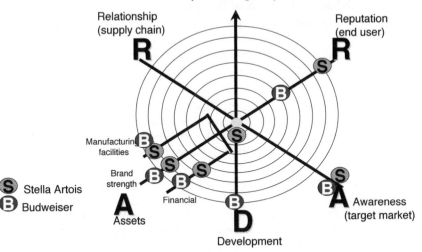

ELEPHANT 8

The brand is strong and recognisable. It is moving to a specific appeal to the more well off, film watching tennis watching public who like to buy something which is 'reassuringly expensive' whereas Bud was (2007) moving into the more mainstream football watching fraternity. The brand strength I would suggest is again good, but not as good as Bud.

Subsequent to the 2008 takeover, both positions have changed slightly, but for this example, we remain with the 2007 position.

Facilities, for the sake of this illustration, will both be excellent, meeting the stringent requirements of UK health and hygiene regulations. Let us assume they are equal.

The diagram 'elephant 8' shows us the R.A.D.A.R. position so far.

R – relationship

This is relationship throughout the supply chain. Backwards to suppliers and forwards to distributors and retailers. In training courses we have diligently put our observations to the test by frequenting noble hostelries to consider our observations. We conclude that Budweiser is always available in almost every pub we encounter. It is always in the refrigerated cabinet behind the bar and usually on the top shelf maximising visibility to the customer at the bar. Stella is available in most bars, but often lower in the cabinet and less prominent than Bud. For the comparison to be direct, we temporarily ignore draught availability. Bud is therefore more prominent in more bars. Our observational conclusion is that there must be reasons for this. They have persuaded publicans, by financial measures and ancillary provisions (such as refrigeration equipment), to put Bud first. Stella is still high on the R.A.D.A.R. as it is still widely available and prominent, but not as prominent as Bud who, on the limited example of the observation, must be near the R.A.D.A.R. extremity.

Your business

Constructing a R.A.D.A.R. for your business will require a few areas to ponder before the active positioning of yourself and the competitor(s).

- How will you quantify your, and your competitors', reputations with the end users?
- What is the objective measure of awareness you will use?
- Do you have sufficient knowledge of your competitors' development activities as much will not reach the public domain?
- Which are the tangible and intangible assets you wish to include for analysis?
- How are you seeking to explore 'relationship' in the supply chain – do you need different spokes for forward and backward in the chain – i.e. suppliers and distributors/retailers?

Stage 2 – Challenging our choice of positions

Having made our own R.A.D.A.R. we should challenge our data. 'Gut feel' data is, by definition, subjective and frequently merely reinforces organisational myths. I recall a conversation with Marks & Spencer where they were adamant that a large number of their food customers were 'LOL's' (little old ladies). I believed that this was not true and that the LOL's made purchasing decisions primarily on price due to their limited income. I saw them as category buyers who would occasionally venture into M&S food aisles for a 'treat'. The M&S employee with whom I was discussing the issue saw them as core. Now some 15 years on, she may have changed her views, but at the time, her opinions were the mere reinforcement of an organisational myth which had been transported from their clothing division where LOL's were mainstay customers.

The purpose of stage 2 is to ensure that there is some objective empirical aspect to the positioning. The more consideration given to the choices made before starting the R.A.D.A.R. (above) the easier it is to create objectivity.

Stage 3 – Considering all available options

Once the competitive scenario is mapped out a variety of options emerge:

1. continue doing what we are doing
2. catch up in an area where the competitor is ahead
3. choose not to catch up where the competitor is ahead and seek to shift any market focus away from this area
4. actively seek to forge ahead – this option can be enacted where we are ahead, level or behind a competitor
5. build barriers where the competitor is behind
6. seek to aggressively target the competitor by dragging them backwards – this can be where they are ahead, level or behind
7. choose to do nothing except keeping a watchful eye on the competitor and re-evaluate if their R.A.D.A.R. position changes.

Again, an entire book could be devoted to R.A.D.A.R. or to these options, but the aim of this book is breadth and variety rather than depth. However, a short comment on the seven options is warranted. Where appropriate I will relate this to the illustrative Budweiser-Stella R.A.D.A.R., the full R.A.D.A.R. positioning is as in diagram 'elephant 9'.

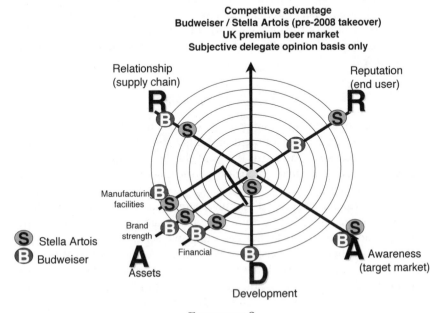

ELEPHANT 9

First reaction to the R.A.D.A.R. for Budweiser-Stella is that Budweiser is ahead in four areas, one of which Bud is hugely ahead. The two beer brands are equal in two areas and Stella's sole area of competitive advantage or positive competitive differential is that of the reputation with the end user. The scales therefore appear to tilt towards Budweiser. This is not necessarily the case. It is not the static position on the R.A.D.A.R. which will win any competitive battle – it is how the relative positions are leveraged to greatest effect. Stella make a massive positive statement about being very low on the development spoke – the position is not a negative, using it is the difference between success and failure. The output of the R.A.D.A.R. analysis is to identify the areas and aspect for competitive strategic action.

Option 1 – continue

If the analysis shows that success is being generated by existing strategies, and if the organisation does not perceive future market changes, this is a viable option. On the R.A.D.A.R. spoke of Awareness, both brands have awareness within their target market at saturation level. In order to gain this they have spent vast sums on television advertising, and it has worked. From that perspective, the strategy will be to continue the television advertising which has put both brands in the forefront of the minds of the UK consumers. Budweiser's recent change in advertising tactics from the creative frogs, chameleons and 'Wassup' to the 'fresh beer' is because the awareness has not generated repeat purchase. The strategy of high profile advertising is working, the tactics of the message is what is changing. If either reduce their advertising, they will slip in the unprompted awareness and move backwards on R.A.D.A.R.

Option 2 – catch up

The catch up option is possible if the gulf is not too wide to bridge. Stella catching up on Bud's development and innovation would be too much to ask except in the very long term. It would also be a complete reversal of the strategy of making a virtue of being at the lowest point of the 'D' for Development spoke.

In the areas of Relationship (supply chain) and Assets (financial), Stella trails by a bridgeable gulf according to our diagram. If the finance gulf was massive, Budweiser could launch an expensive series of campaigns which Stella would either have to match or fall behind. As our analysis shows that this is not the case, Bud would be ill advised to attempt this tactic – the gap is simply not large enough to damage the competitor without incurring serious financial damage to Bud. This is the observable position of the UK supermarkets. Tesco is the largest, WalMart's ASDA is probably their largest threat. Neither wants to start an all-out total price war because the gap between the two is insufficient to fatally injure just one party leaving the other to mop up the market. In a price war, both Tesco and ASDA would lose. Stella's InBev is seeking to close the financial gulf by global diversification and the saturation of a number of national markets. It must be aiming to increase margins above the market average by procurement and administrative efficiencies. It could also generate below the line marketing synergies in its working with distributors and retailers – for example, using the leverage of one best selling brand to persuade pubs to incorporate another brand. As we are considering the UK market, the 30% of UK production is an asset of market dominance to leverage but to watch unless anti-trust, restrictive competition agencies start getting concerned. I do not think that the UK would willingly embrace the near 50% dominance of Anheuser-Busch exhibited in the US.

The other area where Stella could 'catch up' is that of 'R for supply chain relationship'. Bud is higher in the fridge. Stella could seek to persuade the supply chain to give greater exposure – for example, having a greater emphasis on draught beer, price incentives to increase retailers' margins or greater advertising wall space in pubs. As much bottled beer is purchased in supermarkets, much of the supply chain relationship work is supermarket based rather than pub based. From a consumer's perspective, just keeping my eyes open as I use pubs and supermarkets, I observe these tactics being used by InBev.

Option 3 – choose not to catch up

As explored, Stella would not seek to catch up Bud's advantage on development, in the same way that Burger King should never try to match McDonalds in their areas of strength – price and speed. Both Stella and Burger King need to avoid the competitor's areas of strength.

Stella have turned this potential weakness into a strength and are an excellent example of the 'choose not to catch up' option being turned on its head into a strength. Burger King have tried to turn McDonalds ubiquitous product, which is a component of their speed, by the 'have it your way' message emphasising the ability to tailor-make burgers.

Option 4 – forge ahead

This is a deliberate decision to place a strategic emphasis on one aspect of the R.A.D.A.R. with the intention of pressing further towards the extremity of the diagram. The most obvious ones in the Stella-Bud example would be for Bud to press home its 'Relationship' advantage with the supply chain seeking to create a position where it cannot be caught by Stella. Similarly,

Stella could pursue the 'Reputation' with the end user to create an insurmountable gap for Bud to bridge. Once the R.A.D.A.R. gap is expanded, there is the strong possibility of other tactics coming into play. For example, if Stella became demand led it could neutralise Bud's 'Relationship' advantage. Demand led is where the drinkers are demanding Stella. The retail outlets either have to comply or lose sales regardless of the Bud advantage in the 'R for Relationship'. This could involve Stella seeking to build on its high awareness by actively seeking to move people from short-list buyers to preference buyers, and from preference buyers to brand enthusiasts.

Option 5 – build barriers

If ahead on an aspect of R.A.D.A.R., a company or brand can seek to raise the proverbial drawbridge such that others are unable to follow. What could be placed in the way, between your company and the rival to make it impossible for the rival to reach your position?

One example could be using Stella's Western European connections. This is a bit far fetched but as an example works well. In Germany beer must contain water, yeast, hops, and malted barley – nothing else. This purity law or '*reinheitsgebot*' dates back to 1516 and is believed to be Germany's oldest law. A recent challenge has been made (ruling date February 2005) which slightly bent the old rule so that Helmut Fritsche's Klosterbrauerei Neuzelle brewery can continue adding sugar syrup to its dark brew and still call it 'beer', provided it is termed 'special beer'. Other than that, the law has stood. Beer with additional ingredients – such as rice – cannot be called 'beer'.

If German purity laws were enacted throughout Europe, Budweiser would not be able to call itself a 'beer'. That could be a body blow to the product which gives itself the strap line 'king of beers'. It would be a barrier which would be instantly insurmountable, Budweiser could be knocked out in one move. More realistically, what barriers are there which could be raised by either Stella or Bud to prevent the other catching up? Bud's brand strength will increase enormously in the UK with its link to football. Not insurmountable, but Stella would find it difficult to compete and the move to the more sophisticated drinker, with film and tennis was already underway before the Bud-football link.

With your businesses:

- Where are you ahead?
- How did you get ahead?
- What would make it easy or difficult for a rival to catch up?
- How can you influence this and prevent catch up?

Option 6 – drag them back

This is the domain of the dirty tricks and the dark arts of strategy. What can be done to have a negative impact on the opposition? Probably the most famous 'dirty tricks campaign' in living memory was that of BA and Virgin Atlantic Airways.

The traditional rivalry between BA and Virgin Atlantic intensified from July 1991 when Virgin moved the centre of its operations to London Gatwick. By October 1991 Mr Branson (now Sir Richard Branson) had accumulated evidence of BA employees poaching Virgin customers and tampering with confidential company files. He also claimed that BA's PR consultant, Brian Basham, had been undermining him and his company's reputation in the City and the press. Mr Branson confronted BA's non-executive directors about these "sharp business practises" in an open letter. They dismissed the allegations and said he was simply seeking publicity.

In February 1992, after an investigative report by Thames Television, BA bosses, including the then chairman Lord King, repeated their claims that Virgin was "securing publicity" in an internal magazine and various letters.

These written statements formed the basis of Mr Branson's libel case. BA and Lord King then counter-sued over Mr Branson's original allegations.

British Airways then ended one of the most bitter and protracted libel actions in aviation history in a humiliating climb-down in January 1993.

At the High Court Christopher Clarke QC, counsel for BA, apologised "unreservedly" for an alleged "dirty tricks" campaign against Virgin Atlantic.

BA also agreed to pay damages of £500,000 to Virgin boss Richard Branson and £110,000 to his airline, as well as incurring legal costs of up to £3m.

Source: BBC news reports January 1993

In the BA – Virgin example the dirty tricks backfired and BA, the aggressor, lost both financially and more importantly, lost reputation. Just short of six years later another 'dirty trick' was exposed in the humble on-line greetings card industry:

On November 18, 1998 the digital greeting card company Blue Mountain Arts discovered that beta versions of Microsoft's Outlook Express (which comes free with Internet Explorer) were automatically filing Blue Mountain's e-mail greeting cards into the "junk" folder rather than the "inbox." Shortly afterwards, Blue Mountain Arts discovered that Microsoft's WebTV service was blocking their e-mail greeting cards as well.

Why would Microsoft want to prevent electronic greeting cards from being delivered? It turns out that after an unsuccessful attempt to purchase Blue Mountain Arts, Microsoft started its own electronic greeting card service. The "bug" in Outlook Express appeared at about the same time that Microsoft's greeting card service began.

Coincidence? The Honorable Robert A. Baines didn't think so, and granted a preliminary injunction against Microsoft to protect the delivery of Blue Mountain Arts greeting cards. Microsoft reacted to this injunction by removing the e-mail filter from Outlook Express.

Source: various including Blue Mountain and 'anti-Microsoft' websites

ASDA's *"officially Britain's lowest priced supermarket"* claim mentioned earlier in this chapter and based on a negligible sample is a 'drag them back' tactic as the implicit accusation is that all of the others are more expensive.

Renault's emphasis as the only vehicle with a 5* safety rating is another – amplifying its differential and setting a hurdle for others to vault. This time the research is more robust. It is more than just a 'barrier' tactic, it is a claim of superiority and therefore implicitly, a statement of inferiority of the competition. The barrier is so strong that it forces the competition to lose ground on the R.A.D.A.R.

The 'drag them back' tactic is not therefore always the dark or illegal, it can be a strong emphasis on your organisational strengths which cannot be matched by the opposition. HSBC is advertising based on its global size. The message is that a bank without such global knowledge would be an unwise choice by comparison. It can just be a contentious but perfectly legal suggestion. For years the Carlsberg's 'probably the best lager in the world' strapline has made the implicit suggestion that others are inferior.

Option 7 – choose to watch only

Action is not mandatory, as the zebra will teach us in his chapter. Watch and wait can be wholly appropriate. The ability to pause in order to collect more information, observe how the market is moving or to await the consequences of the competitor's actions are all valid responses. Watch, wait and prepare a response for immediate and rapid implementation when the time is right is part of the 'stealth and ambush' strategy of the crocodile and will be dealt with in that later chapter. The only part of the 'watch only' strategy which would be an error would be to cease watching by taking the eye off the competitor.

Stage 4 – Choosing options

Having examined the 7 options, what is the basis on which one chooses? Keeping with the 'five year old approach', one method is considering how F.A.S.T. the options are.

Feasible – can they be done? What are their chances of success? Are they within budgetary and risk tolerances? Are there sufficient resources to achieve this option?

Acceptable – not whether it can be done but whether it should be done. In business there are several shades of grey and several lines which different organisations would become uncomfortable crossing. This may be particularly relevant to the aspects of the 'dragging them back' tactics but certainly not exclusively. McDonalds were struggling in France as they did not sell beer. The subsequent debate of whether or not a child focussed outlet should sell beer had to be seen in the cultural context of the local French national market rather than the cultural context of the American parent company. In the US the answer would have probably been that beer was an unacceptable addition to the menu, in France it was wholly acceptable. It is interesting to see petrol (US gas) filling stations in the UK now selling beers and wines despite the obvious drink driving associations. A decade ago that would have been unacceptable, now the 'supermarket' feel of the forecourt has changed the boundaries of acceptability.

Sustainable – will the option provide a solution which lasts or will it be a temporary fix? There is no point in using a band aid solution for a surgical problem. The definition of the length required to satisfy the condition of sustainability will be determined by the circumstances and the issue in question. It is not a specific period of time. For one competitive scenario, six months may be classed as sufficient time and hence sustainable, for most it will probably not be.

Timely – can the solution be implemented in time? Given wide time parameters we can accomplish most things. However, wide time parameters are rarely the remit of the competitive environment.

The R.A.D.A.R. analysis provides a format through which competitive positioning can be assessed and from which competitive strategies can be developed. It is by no means exhaustive but provides a framework within the area of competitive strategy where frameworks are few and far between. Empirically, it has been used with a variety of organisations and has often resulted in the development of competitive insights previously unexplored and unconsidered. I recall one particular use where it provided the solitary ray of competitive hope in what had previously been seen as an insurmountable problem. In that instance, like Stella-Budweiser, the company had a solitary spoke of advantage. R.A.D.A.R. resulted in the identification of that previously unrecognised advantage and the generation of strategies to use it to the advantage of the business.

Knowledge of the wider market

R.A.D.A.R. has a focus of companies in direct competition. In order to widen this and provide an additional competitive strategic model, I suggest we return to the higher perspective of the overall market and the consumers' attitudes and needs within that market. By taking the consumers' market wide focus rather than the firm's focus we can frequently come to a similar point of strategic decision making from the opposite direction. The use of both directions – the firm and the market – gives greater perspective than the solitary use of either. The model I suggest for a market-wide competitive analysis, I have termed 'competitive mapping'. This, too, has been developed and tested initially in a training course environment before moving on to real life situations. Like R.A.D.A.R. it has also become useful in the identification of specific and practical action for the real world rather than the mere discussion of ethereal academic concepts.

Competitive mapping

The model has several stages of use:

1. Identification of the consumer's issues of importance (i.o.i.s)
2. Ranking of the i.o.i.s
3. Measuring of self and competitor(s) by the i.o.i.s
4. Estimating the market average i.o.i.s (optional stage)
5. Consider future i.o.i. positioning
6. Assessing anomalies
7. Considering all available options (as per R.A.D.A.R. step 3)
8. Choosing options (as per R.A.D.A.R. step 4)

Stage 1 – Identification of the consumer's issues of importance (i.o.i.s)

What is it that influences a consumer's decision to purchase? From the consumer's perspective what are the most important features? Our organisational focus combined with a penchant for reinforcing organisational myths often causes us to misunderstand the customer. The consequences are C5s and reliance on folklore such as LOL's. I have produced a template for consideration of i.o.i.s. It is not meant to be exhaustive, but to be a thought springboard. There may, in your industry, be different categories – please use them. With each i.o.i. area I have made five suggestions of what the specific i.o.i. is. For the competitive mapping process there is no limit to the number of i.o.i.s which can be used and it is wholly allowable to use several of the suggestions within each category. It will be necessary to make strong definitions of the customer to generate the best output from the competitive mapping process. For example, were Renault to use this process, the buyers of the Laguna will have different i.o.i.s to buyers of the Espace, Mercedes SL drivers will have a different range of i.o.i.s to those who seek to buy the 'A' class. With these four vehicle models we can easily understand that there is no such thing as the 'average' car buyer. The SL driver wants speed (functionality) and aesthetics whilst the Espace driver wants practicality and possibly safety. Probably both of the Espace i.o.i.,'s would come under the category of 'features', so it is wholly acceptable to delve down a layer lower than my suggestions – 'Product' has a subset of 'Features' which can have components including 'Practicality' and 'Safety' as separate i.o.i.s.

Suggested i.o.i.s

Identify the critical i.o.i.s for your **customers** – they may include:

Product – functionality, features, ease of use, performance, aesthetics.
Price/cost – initial purchase, maintenance, operating, disaster scenario, replacement.
Availability – distribution, convenience, location, speed, information.
People – relationship, ability, reputation, customer knowledge, service.
Technology – ease of use, interface ability, flexibility, systems/ processes, longevity.
Speed – of service, delivery, use, time savings, productivity.
Accuracy – reliability, consistency, error free, right first time, timeliness.
Image – quality, brand, association, imputed image, perception.
Aftersales service/support – speed, attitude, knowledge, function, problem solving.　　　　　　　　　　　　　　　　　　　　➜

> → **Additional offerings** – extra service, range, compatability, offers, complementarity.
> **Environmental & ethical** – political, pollution, workforce, conservation, practices.
> **Risk** – consistency, downside, variability, security, exposure.
> **Flexibility** – adaptability, expandability, variability, reactivity, speed of change.
> **Ability** – scope, geography, skills, experience, resources.

This list has been developed by use with a number of customers over time, but each organisation will have its own combination of customer i.o.i.s. In using this, please do not merely pick from the list – choose carefully from your knowledge of the customer and then perhaps use the suggested list as a checklist to explore areas which may have been omitted.

Stage 2 – Ranking of the i.o.i.s

Having decided the most important i.o.i.s for your business it is necessary to rank them in order of importance from the consumer's point of view. The ranking assists the clarification of our minds to focus on the most important aspects rather than becoming obsessed with relatively unimportant i.o.i.s.

For example, if we were to consider a competitive mapping for the business driver or salesman customers of motorway (US freeway) food outlets. We spend our time hurtling up and down the UK motorway network and occasionally the pangs of hunger force us to pull in for some hot food. We don't want to spend a long time off the road, and just want a simple quick burger with some fries and a traditional English cup of tea. We may be a small group, nationally unrepresentative and statistically numerically too small to be the basis for major corporate strategy, but I see fellow members of this group most weeks. Our i.o.i.s would probably include the following:

- **Cost** – fast food is highly price sensitive.
- **Speed of service** – it is not called 'fast' food for nothing.
- **Taste** – a pre-requisite of food!
- **Consistency** – that what I receive was the same as when I last had it.
- **Choice** – some varieties or peripherals would be nice, e.g. onion rings with my burger.
- **Location** – I won't go far to buy – if it is not close my trade will go elsewhere.
- **Health** – low saturated fats and few E numbers would be good.

- **Aesthetics** – in food, the nose eats first, then the eyes, then the mouth – if it doesn't look good, my brain will draw conclusions before I taste the food.
- **Surroundings** – the premises in which I will eat my burger.

Note how, in this specific food example, some are drawn from the example list and some are not.

It is clear from this list of i.o.i.s why McDonalds have been so successful – they deliberately target excellence in many of the i.o.i.s and few would challenge the suggestion that they are undisputed champions in the areas of cost, speed of service, consistency and location.

Stage 3 – Measuring of self and competitor(s) by the i.o.i.s

If we set up the i.o.i.s in ranked order and make an assessment of our organisation against that of the competitors in question, we can generate some information on which we can start making strategic decisions based on our knowledge of our relative positions in the marketplace.

The example of the Motorway food outlets is shown in diagram 'elephant 10'.

Competitive mapping – UK motorway fast food

Source: purely subjective – based on the opinion of a few of us drivers who seem to spend half of our lives on the motorway (US Freeway). Please do not read objective reality into these subjective examples.

ELEPHANT 10

On the left, in priority order are the i.o.i.s. Across the top is a scale from 'poor' to 'good'. As with earlier models in this book, challenging the data and the provision of evidential back-up could assist clarity of thought. For each i.o.i. a marker is made and, each company's markers are joined to show a mapping pattern. As the i.o.i.s are prioritised, the mapping generates some meaning. Were one company to show greater advantage in the higher ranked aspects, we would expect their competitive position to be superior.

Stage 4 – Estimating the market average i.o.i.s (optional stage)

Generally I am not an enthusiast for comparing an organisation with the perception of the market average. However, some people have found the inclusion of a line to represent their perception, quantified wherever possible, of the market average as a help in assessing the position of their company within the market and hence generating the requirement for specific strategic actions to address shortfalls. My lack of enthusiasm for this stage stems from the belief that organisations should aim for the top of their chosen market, not to look back at the 'average'. However, as some have found it useful, feel free to include this stage.

Stage 5 – Consider future i.o.i. positioning

The i.o.i.s are prioritised as at today's date. Static strategic models are of limited value in our dynamic business world and so considering the future importance of each i.o.i. is just as important as considering its present importance. Rather than create a cumbersome and complicated structure for considering the future I suggest simple arrows. If an i.o.i. is in ascendancy and you expect it to be higher in the prioritised list in the next 3,5,10 years, as appropriate, add a vertical upward arrow near the i.o.i. description. If you expect its importance to wane, add a vertical downward arrow. The length, width or colour of the arrow can be proportionate to the movement you see each i.o.i. making. In the diagram 'elephant 10' I have suggested that 'health' will become of increasing importance and that 'consistency' will reduce its level in i.o.i. terms. Clearly then, having a poor competitive position in an i.o.i. which is in ascendancy needs addressing whereas a poor position in a declining i.o.i. is of less concern. Focussing strategic activity on ascending, or static i.o.i.s is obviously of greater importance than focussing strategies on declining i.o.i.s.

Stage 6 – Assessing anomalies

In the diagram 'elephant 10', McDonalds as the global fast food superbrand would be expected to score high in most areas – and it does in the most important i.o.i.s at the top of the page. However, the shape of the competitive mapping is more erratic than that of Burger King. McDonalds suffers a little on 'taste' and a huge amount on 'health'. Bear in mind that the driver for all this is consumer opinion. It need not be fact – consumer perception is reality – if Budweiser can persuade us that fresh beer tastes better, that will become reality. If the McLibel case and surrounding publicity or competitive advertising persuades us that McDonalds is of poor taste and unhealthy – that is the reality regardless of any scientific, nutritional or quantifiable research to the contrary. The identification of anomalies generates areas for the development of strategies – just as McDonalds have done with healthy options, fruit, carrot sticks and exercise recommendations within the child-focussed advertising.

Stage 7 – Considering all available options (as per R.A.D.A.R. stage 3)

Once the competitive scenario is mapped out a variety of options emerge:

1. continue doing what we are doing.
2. catch up in an area where the competitor is ahead.
3. choose not to catch up where the competitor is ahead and seek to shift any market focus away from this area.
4. actively seek to forge ahead – this option can be enacted where we are ahead, level or behind a competitor.
5. build barriers where the competitor is behind.
6. seek to aggressively target the competitor by dragging them backwards – this can be where they are ahead, level or behind.
7. choose to do nothing except keeping a watchful eye on the competitor and re-evaluate if their Competitive Mapping position changes.

The details of each of these are discussed earlier within the R.A.D.A.R. analysis. For Competitive mapping I would add an eighth option – perhaps suggesting it as mandatory rather than optional:

8. keep an eye on the market i.o.i.s, establish which ones are moving up and down. Keep an eye on your competitors and continually evaluate which i.o.i.s they are directing their strategies towards.

Stage 8 – Choosing options (as per R.A.D.A.R. stage 4)

- F
- A
- S
- T

Challenge for action

The most important challenge would be to complete the suggestions of this chapter for your own organisation. The elephant spends its life gathering knowledge and the survival of this terrestrial giant is testimony to the competitive advantage generated through this knowledge. Without it, elephants would lose their supply chain of trees and water with the slightest seasonal climatic variation. The major part of the challenge is to gather the knowledge, process it using the tools illustrated in this chapter and finally to ensure that they generate strategic action rather than just good ideas.

For students, or readers without competitive scenarios, revisit diagram 'elephant 10'. If you were appointed to have strategic responsibility for any one of the businesses, what would you do?

Chapter summary

- The elephant uses knowledge to survive.
- We need business knowledge in several critical areas:
  - our product or market offering.
  - our customers and potential customers.
  - our supply chain.
  - our corporate history.
  - our competition.
  - the wider market.
- Knowledge is for use – but we may be currently unaware of a future use of some knowledge.
- There are 4 segments of consumers with different price sensitivities:
  - Category buyers.
  - Shortlist buyers.
  - Preference buyers.
  - Brand enthusiasts.
- There are many reasons other than price which can give consumers a reason to choose a product – these generate 'competitive differential'.
- The plotting of competitive differential against customer price sensitivity can show us 4 generic strategies:
  - Lowest cost.
  - Increase differential.
  - Build (positive e.g. penetration, or negative, e.g. barriers).
  - Exploit niche.
- We can conduct more than one of these generic strategies simultaneously dependent on our positioning on the graph.

→

→
- R.A.D.A.R. – a new tool for making a direct competitive comparison between companies focussing on the perspective from the companies.
- Competitive mapping – a new tool for making a direct competitive comparison between companies focussing on the perspective of the marketplace and the consumer issues of importance (i.o.i.s).

CHAPTER 5

Strategies of the zebra – responses to threats

The zebra is probably the most distinct and easily recognisable of the mammals from the *'equus'* (horse) genus. Named from an Italian word of old Portuguese origin *zevro* or *zevra*, which means wild ass, the zebra is the only wild equine found in large numbers in the world today. Its distinct patterns of stripes are predominantly black but can be brown or occasionally grey. No two zebras have the same stripe pattern as their stripes are as individual as the human face or fingerprint. These stripes tend to be narrower towards the head, broadening towards the rump and are thought to be part of the method by which zebras recognise other family members. Adult zebras stay in family groups and even if dispersed by predators, over a few days the family group will reunite.

The zebra is non-territorial and nomadic. Generally gregarious, fairly inquisitive and sociable, zebras will mix freely with other species. This, combined with their significant numbers, means that most major tourist Serengeti photo opportunities will have zebra somewhere in sight. Family groups generally consist of a dominant male, a harem of adult females and a number of foals yet to reach sexual maturity. Upon reaching sexual maturity at 3–4 years the mares will move to other groups and the stallions will form temporary bachelor herds until they are able to assume the leadership of a family – often the one from which they have come.

As with all herbivores, the savannah grass provides a plentiful supply of food for most of the year. Most herbivores use their tongue to tear up grass, including roots, but the zebra uses the front teeth cutting the grass right down to soil level. This savannah mowing machine consequently leaves the roots when grass is in abundance and this aids regrowth and sustainability of the food source. In times of drought the zebra is less environmentally friendly and will consume the roots. A requirement for approximately 14 litres of water a day generates a degree of dependence on a regular intake of water and if this vital resource is in short supply the herd will travel many kilometres to locate a source.

Zebra fact file:

Height	1.3m to the shoulder
Mass	227kg – 325 kg
Life expectancy	30 years
Diet	savannah grass
Reproduction	1 year gestation producing 1 foal. Breeding and birth are throughout the year but peak in August/September

---

Zebras possess very good eyesight, a keen sense of smell and, like most equines, have excellent running speed with good initial acceleration. This combination provides them with an enviable armoury of defensive strategies. The sharp hooves, strong kicking actions and honed teeth are formidable weapons against predators such as wild dogs and small numbers of hyenas. The dominant stallion will provide the first line of defence, but the females are similarly equipped and are equally able to render canine predators with at least a deterrent and at worst a fatal injury. To cope with larger groups of wild dogs or hyenas, the zebra will move closer together emphasising their collective mass and defensive solidarity. Any solitary dog attacking such a group is putting its life at serious risk. However, a co-ordinated attack by lionesses (see 'strategies of the lion' for details) or large groups of hyenas will overwhelm these aggressive defence strategies and the zebra will revert to other strategies, such as its speed, as an escape route.

A study of the strategies of the zebra could include a vast array of inter-dependent approaches the animal has to living, including their sociability, the way they ensure sustainability of resources, the leadership structure, the protection and development of the young, their 'travel light' ability which gives flexibility yet requires regular water intake or even the consideration of the longevity of the herd as it is not unusual for some mares and stallions to be associated for life. All of these are valid strategies and have parallels to business life where we can learn from these survival experts. However, the area we will focus on is that of the zebra's approach to threat. In our competitive environment, we may have the competitive advantages of good commercial eyesight (see 'strategies of the giraffe'), the ability to accelerate or change direction rapidly (see 'strategies of the cheetah'), the ability to 'herd' or join forces where appropriate (see 'strategies of the lion' and of the wildebeest), but in our commercial Serengeti we will always need to be alert for predators. We will always need an array of possible strategies to deal with a threat – actual or potential. We will always need the ability to choose the most appropriate defence strategy and implement it thoroughly. Failure to do so could lead to the extinction of our organisation as it is consumed by other co-habitants of our business savannah.

To consider organisational approaches to threat, imagine a zebra on the Serengeti. Create an image in your mind of the zebra. Imagine the background of the Serengeti scenery with miles and miles of grass covered plain and with perhaps a distant mountain on the horizon. Trees are present, but infrequent. The intense heat causes ripples of heat waves which make the horizon flicker. Perhaps there are other animals present, maybe a few distant elephants or giraffes, perhaps there are a few gazelles equally enjoying the savannah's green menu. Certainly there will be other zebras nearby because the savannah horse is such a social animal, seldom far from its family. Perhaps there are a dozen or so within eyesight. Listen in your mind and imagine the sounds. Far away from our cluttered lives of trains and planes, from the aural detritus of compact human civilization, from the consequential sounds as carbon monoxide emerges from every moving item. The sounds of the Serengeti move in waves. Sometimes there are long periods of near silence, then a gradual crescendo builds and fades before the near silence is further interrupted by someone announcing their arrival, calling to a potential mate or just posturing – not too dissimilar to most offices! The Serengeti sound patterns are more random and more varied than the constant hum of the city. The zebra in your imagination is grazing. The razor sharp teeth cut with surgical accuracy through the tough, wiry savannah grass as it moves slowly but relentlessly forward to the next mouthful. In your imagination, draw very close to the zebra. Listen to the sound as the incisor teeth slice through the grass before the tongue passes the nutritious mouthful to the molars at the rear so that this highly efficient grass fuelled machine can process the energy source. Your zebra is content but always alert.

Suddenly, the alert and highly developed nostrils pick up a familiar, but threatening scent. The zebra has to discern the nature of the threat and its direction. It raises its head and the nostrils flare as sharp short intakes of air and the airborne scent it carries are taken into the nasal laboratory for processing. Ears, eyes and nose harmonise as eating is suspended to give priority to the high urgent, high important task of potential threat analysis. Your zebra moves its head from side to side adjusting the input variables of the sound and scent received in an attempt to give greater accuracy to the direction from which they come. It may also give a short whine of a noise to alert others in the vicinity. Instantly over a dozen zebras are processing information about the perceived threat. The nature of the threat is critical as a solitary wild dog will require a different strategy from a co-ordinated hunting party of lionesses. Fail to identify the precise nature of the threat and the consequences can be infinitely more deadly than merely misinterpreting a business threat in the city. There is a big difference between losing your job and losing your life. The array of strategies available to the zebra must be applied correctly – the right choice must be made. Applying a defensive strategy appropriate to the solitary wild dog in a situation involving even a couple of lionesses and it will have an almost inevitable result of the diminishing of the zebra gene pool as the lionesses' hunger is assuaged. Correctly discerning the direction of the threat is critical because the choice of the wrong direction could mean running into a lion ambush rather than away from a combination of flesh tearing teeth and claws. The strategies are not just survival of the fittest but also survival of those best able to apply their strategic options correctly.

The zebra is likely to choose from six key strategic responses to a threat – the same six used by organisations and by individuals to almost all threats. Fight, Flight, Flock, Freeze, Fragment and Frolic. The critical decision is when to choose which one. The correct choice may mean survival and market advantage. The incorrect choice may result in the zebra becoming lunch, or the company becoming another statistic of national tables of corporate failure. Similarly with individuals, we have six basic options and survival of the smartest is about choosing the most appropriate one each time. Far too many people revert to their one favourite strategy rather than having at their disposal this range of six with equal ability to apply them. This is the message of survival, this is what we should have been taught at school. Had we skipped declining our Latin verbs and, instead, studied the zebra, we would have been more able and more prepared for life in the carnivorous savannahs of our cities and marketplaces.

Returning to your zebra on the Serengeti – what should he do? Fight, Flight, Flock, Freeze, Fragment or Frolic?

Zebra strategy 1 – Fight

The zebra's array of teeth, accustomed to acting with the precision cutting of a savannah lawnmower, combined with sharp hooves powered by muscular hind legs create weapons which only the foolish predator would underestimate. The zebra has a realistic assessment of its weaponry and a strong appreciation of when it is appropriate and when it is not. In business, alas, we often do not possess either such a clear understanding of our defensive strengths, nor the discernment to know when 'fight' is the most appropriate defensive action. In the alpha-male dominated board rooms of the corporate world 'fight' is frequently our first reaction and our default. The majority of practical business strategy books focus on 'fight'. Recalling the various strategy conferences and seminars I have attended over the years, the overwhelming majority of time and focus has been on aggressive, expansive strategies, forcing the competition onto 'the back foot'. We focus on gaining and maintaining competitive advantage to exploit a market or destroy competition. Much of this is useful. However, this may not be the best solution.

The success of the zebra over millennia is drawn from the ability to use their 'fight' strategy when appropriate and use other strategies when they are appropriate. Were we to be able to emulate this ability, perhaps our corporate longevity may be enhanced rather than finding ourselves 'bogged down' in the commercial equivalent of First World War European trench warfare.

As we explore the strategies of the zebra, we will focus on a simple practical tool to consider whether we are in a position to fight, thus whether this is a viable strategic option for a given situation and also how the fight should ensue – the focus is on whether we are in a position to fight and which weapons to use rather than actually how we should use them to conduct the fight. With the level of detail we have available in just one chapter, to keep the zebra analogy going, the process we shall explore is more likely to confirm or exclude the 'fight' option and to give a good indication of whether using the hooves or the teeth would be the better approach but space does not permit specific instructions on the implementation of the biting or kicking strategies.

The tool I suggest is nothing new. It has been around for decades and has been used by almost every organisation and individual I have met in business. However, I have never once met an organisation nor an individual using it well. Whilst training executives in strategic thinking, the most common reaction faced when unveiling the tool is the look on the face which says "Oh no, not again" yet after a couple of hours of driving the strategic tool to its conclusion the reaction is more as if I have explained a major mystery of the universe. The tool is S.W.O.T.

My view of S.W.O.T. is simple: use it well and it can be a valid practical tool for strategic decision making. Use it poorly and it is an utter waste of time.

Most companies appear to produce some form of annual strategic appraisal. It often includes a set of 4 disjointed lists under the title of S.W.O.T. This then happily gathers dust for the remainder of the year until it is replaced with the subsequent year's dust collecting mechanism. These disjointed lists appear to generate few, if any, conclusions and little, if any, action results. If we could capture the time wasted globally by executives and managers producing their four lists and rechannel it, we would probably have the collective brain power to have transformed a small nation. If S.W.O.T. wastes your time – don't do it! Or, do it properly.

To do it properly, I would suggest a series of stages:

Stage 1 – generate the data

This is the stage everyone does – the collection of an assessment of an organisation's Strengths, Weaknesses, Opportunities and Threats.

Frequently it is stated that Strengths and Weaknesses are 'internal' to the organisation and that Opportunities and Threats are 'external' to the organisation. I do not believe this. Whilst the predominance is true, huge internal areas can be missed if we limit the Opportunities and Threats to the external marketplace. In the strategy of the giraffe, we examined the intrinsic link between the 'internal' factors and the 'external' factors for the development of business success. Similarly, if we are purely introspective when considering our Strengths and Weaknesses, we fail to appreciate our interface with the market, with competitors, with customers and with movements made in any of those three areas. I would also add an appropriate and specific time perspective to any S.W.O.T. analysis. Strengths and Weaknesses are generally the current state of the organisation and its interface to its market. This is therefore a representation of the present situation. Opportunities and Threats may be ones which already exist, but may be ones on the horizon. It is critical to define this horizon appropriately. Define it too long and the organisation is gazing into distant unattainable space – thus wasting its time. Define it too short and the organisation will be seeking to develop myopic strategies. At departmental level, I suggest that Opportunities and Threats are generally those which people can envisage being real within the next 3 years. For larger company wide or organisational wide aspects this is far too short and the time horizon needs appropriate definition before commencement. For some 5 years is sufficient, for others a generation is more appropriate.

An example of an appropriate time horizon could be from the oil and petroleum industry, or as the company would argue, from the energy industry.

> BP changed its branding perspective from 'British Petroleum' to 'BP Amoco' in 1998, dropping the 'Amoco' to become 'BP' in 2000. Along with the 2000 brand change came the emphasis on 'Beyond Petroleum' rather than 'British Petroleum'. As part of this strategy the
>
> ➡

➜

logo changed to the green and yellow 'helios' – based on the symbol of the Ancient Greek sun god. This was a rebrand with three key facets:

- Firstly, the issue was to reflect the global nature of the brand rather than merely the emphasis on 'British'.
- Secondly it reflected the breadth of the organisation which had a public perception of being a petroleum company – not surprisingly as that is what the name stated and that was the origin of the organisation. However, the company had, for many years, been involved in multi-faceted energy provision and development. For example, it is currently the world's largest producer of solar panels.
- The third part of the rebrand is the realisation that our children will probably enjoy the benefits of the fossil fuel industries, but that by the time our grandchildren are adults, fossil fuels will be almost exhausted and in terminal decline. BP, Beyond Petroleum, also looks beyond the immediate technology and immediate resource to that which our grandchildren are passing on to our great-grandchildren. The third facet of the rebrand was also therefore a time horizon in excess of a generation. With that background, a 3 year focus an organisational level would be nonsense!

Having established a time horizon which is appropriate to the level of the organisation and the nature of the issues being considered, the generation of the lists can begin. 'Brainstorming' is now seen as a politically incorrect term as it is apparently offensive to those suffering from epilepsy. We are currently encouraged to use the term 'thought shower' although I do question whether this is offensive to the incontinent. By whatever name, it is a valid tool for a structured method of considering S.W.O.T. constituents for each organisational product, or department, or market, or sector.

The output of phase 1 is four lists S.W.O. and T. as most of us have done many times before, but hopefully with the time horizon they will be more relevant and with a more structured consideration the lists will be more complete.

Stage 2 – challenge the data

The challenge is 'Prove it'. For example, what empirical evidence is available to support the hypothesis that 'our people' are a strength? Nearly every organisation includes some form of stating that their employees are a tremendous strength and usually that their leadership team are a weakness – unless it is the leadership team who are conducting the S.W.O.T. when they naturally consider their leadership exemplary. However, few are able to justify the assertion when challenged.

- What evidence is there that your skillbase or knowledge is greater than that of your competitors?
- What level of innovation can be proven?
- How have your people changed the business and the marketplace in a way in which the competition haven't?
- How does your staff turnover rate compare with your marketplace?
- What are the main three reasons for people leaving according to your exit interviews?
- Why do you not do exit interviews with every employee?
- How long does it take to fill vacancies and how many applicants are there per available job?
- What is the perception of your organisation derived from your entrance interviews of new joiners?
- Why do you not formally collect the information from new employee entrance interviews (if you conduct these at all)?

It is a constant source of amazement to me that companies try to spend as little time as possible on an induction for new employees, trying to force feed them company information and processes with all the subtlety of Dordogne farmers force feeding their geese for the production of *fois gras*. The most important information is that which the new joiners can bring to the new organisation – particularly if they have joined from a competitor. The extraction of information is probably much more use to an organisation than the injection of processes. Furthermore, the content of inductions are usually biased towards facts, information and processes. These are fairly low level aspects of business. The exploration of organisational values and the nature of the brands cannot be completed with one list of bullet point words on a powerpoint slide. For example if the values include 'honesty' that will impact on every employee's interaction with every point of contact – internal and external. This would need the consequences exploring and majoring rather than being merely described and considered minor. So after a day of considering the company values and brands, half a day (or more depending on the role of the new joiner) drawing all that can be learnt from the external perspective and the former employer, the induction may then be ready to indulge in some input. If an organisation considers that too long a time for an induction and is in a hurry to get the new entrant to start earning business revenue, I would question the level of thinking involved. Short term tactical approaches to induction are more akin to the employment of people who will not 'live' the brand and values but will consider work as merely a means of earning a living. A longer term, neurologically deeper approach to understanding what makes the company 'tick' and how that impacts on their role and interaction with others is more akin to encouraging people to bring their brain, personal values and enthusiasm into work rather than leaving them in the car when they park in the company car park each morning. Induction at 'skill' and 'capability' level is appropriate for some manual, non-cerebral roles but induction at 'values' and 'attitudes' level is appropriate for all roles. The former will allow individuals to perform their function, the latter will allow individuals to engage with work.

One of the best induction programmes I have come across was from Guinness UK when the London Park Royal brewery was in operation. It was run by a refreshingly innovative and creative training professional, Steve Rhodes. In a separate building, undoubtedly commandeered from a former use, new entrants would 'experience' the Diageo brands in a series of rooms. The 'Guinness room' was mostly black with creamy white parts, and the new entrants would sit on black beanbags watching a highly informative and engaging video of the history and modern production of the beverage. The aim was not to inject data but for people to feel as if they 'knew' the product and the brand with its key messages and brand personality. My personal favourite room was the 'Gordon's Gin room' which, like the bottle, was predominantly green. The room was dominated by a large ceiling to floor Perspex fishtank containing green liquid with a constant stream of bubbles flowing to the top. The emphasis was on the branding use of the colour green and the refreshing qualities of a good gin and tonic – certainly not on the cost of juniper berries and the margins or market penetration of the product – that could come later. To this day, I associate gin and tonic as being refreshing due partially to seeing this induction room, despite the fact that I have never worked for Diageo nor even seen the induction day in its full detail. So, deep within my mind is an image which has been created so that when I am relaxing in my hammock at one end of my garden with a gin and tonic, enjoying the sun, the garden and refereeing the children, I am thinking of the brand messages of a company in which I have only a passing interest – even when the gin I am drinking is not even a Gordon's but a more expensive Bombay Sapphire – that is a powerful induction!

Whilst I have chosen to illustrate stage 2 considering 'our people', the challenging of data should be on all aspects of all four lists. Does each contribution pass the 'prove it' test and thereby justify inclusion in the S.W.O.T.? How many of the strengths are delusion or wishful thinking? How many of the weaknesses are self perpetuating criticisms of others?

Stage 3 – prioritise each sector – by impact/effect

Having challenged each of the four lists and refined them to include only that which is provable or, if intangible, is widely accepted, stage three asks us to make prioritisation decisions. The basis on which I ask groups to prioritise their list constituents is that of 'the impact and effect on the organisation'. The most effective way I have found is to use spatial prioritisation. This involves placing each individual item from each of the four lists on a small card (or post-it note) and then moving the position of the cards on a large blank space in order to make its physical position reflect its importance. Trying to contain all the information in writing on one sheet of paper does not give the flexibility or portability to adjust the positioning of the various aspects. One additional advantage is that, having completed the S.W.O.T. in the card or post it note format, taking notes and minutes are irrelevant because all can be captured by digital photograph and e-mailed to whoever is relevant within seconds of the session finishing – thus cutting out the non-value added activity of writing, checking and re-writing notes.

For reasons which will become clear later, the order I place them is a 4 sector box. Strengths top left, Weaknesses bottom left, Opportunities top right, Threats bottom left. Practically, this can be done on a blank wall, on a large floorspace, or on boards (such as those from www.pinpoint-facilitation.com). The really strong strengths which do have, or can have, a major impact on the organisation are positioned towards the top of the board or graph. The strengths which have a lesser effect stay within the top left quadrant but are towards the bottom of that quadrant. An array spread from top to bottom will usually result. There is no need to rank 1–10 or 1–20, as it is perfectly acceptable for several to be very high, several high, more quite high etc occupying equal heights on the board or graph. The same is true for W, O and T.

For the weaknesses, the really big weaknesses which have, or could have, a significant impact on the organisation within the time frame being considered, move towards the bottom of the lower left quadrant, the weaknesses with minimal impact are towards the top of the lower left quadrant (i.e. immediately below the lesser impact strengths). Diagram 'zebra 1' illustrates this.

For Opportunities – the huge opportunities which can be massive for the organisation are towards the top of the top right quadrant, lesser opportunities towards the bottom of this quadrant and each opportunity ranked to give a range in between.

For Threats – the really nasty, threats which can have immense negative consequences for the organisation are towards the bottom of the lower right quadrant and the minor threats towards the top of that quadrant, i.e. just below the minor opportunities.

For effect, I often colour code the 4 factors – Strengths as yellow (bright, summer, perceived as very positive), Weaknesses as blue (because they make you feel blue!), Opportunities as orange (because the future is bright, the future is orange, as the mobile telephone company strapline used to tell us before it was taken over by France Telecom), and Threats as Red (for danger). Some individuals may consider colour unnecessary, but the visual effect is very positive and more stimulating than a monochrome world.

Stage 4 – prioritise – by ease/difficulty

Having made a vertical prioritisation for each quadrant, we can now make a horizontal prioritisation. At the extreme left and right of the whole board or diagram, I place the items which are difficult. There will be strengths or weaknesses which are difficult for the organisation to change or difficult for it to affect. As these will mostly be internal factors within the organisation's control they will all be able to be changed or to be affected in the longer run. However, some may be more difficult than others. For Strengths and Weaknesses, aspects which are difficult to change go towards the edge of the board or diagram, to the left, whilst easy to change factors go towards the middle of the diagram, to the right of the Strength or Weakness quadrant. As before, there will be several of equal ease or difficulty, this is fine.

For Opportunities and Threats, the pattern is the mirror image. Many of these will be issues where the organisation can have little impact or effect and so the parameters of horizontal spacing are changed slightly. They can be positioned as easy or difficult (and every space in between) to have an impact on or to plan and prepare for. So, Opportunities or Threats on which it is easy for the organisation to have an impact move to the centre of the diagram (left of the O and T quadrants). Opportunities and Threats which are easy to plan and prepare for also move towards the left. Opportunities and Threats which are difficult for the organisation to have an impact on or plan for go to the right, or edge of the diagram.

By the end of stage 4 we have a distributed matrix of S.W.O. and T all prioritised by two factors – impact and ease. This is exhibited in diagram 'zebra 1'.

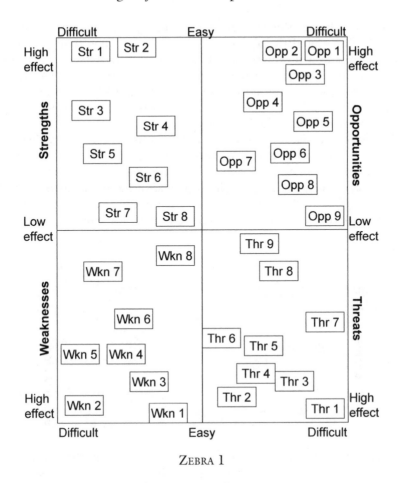

ZEBRA 1

Stage 5 – determine present direction

All business situations are dynamic. Regrettably many, if not most, business models are static. Unless we build the current momentum into our use of S.W.O.T. our analysis will be out of date as soon as we finish it.

There are a series of more complex ways to do this, but I, as always, prefer the simplest method. In this case, I suggest the attachment of small vertical arrows to any Strength, Weakness, Opportunity or Threat to show how it is becoming more or less influential in the organisation at present. The key is to establish the current direction of each aspect on the S.W.O.T. Is it currently increasing or decreasing? Where is it now compared with where it was six months ago, and more importantly, where do we consider it will be in six months time? A Weakness which is getting worse and becoming more likely to impact on the business will therefore have a downward arrow, a

Strength which is getting stronger and having a greater impact will have an upward arrow. Similarly, an upward arrow on an opportunity shows its ascendance, and a downward arrow demonstrates its reduction in importance. In short, upward arrows are good signs for the immediate future, downward arrows are bad signs. In the spirit of 'stage 2' and in the interests of being as practical as possible it may also be wise to record the evidence for the arrow rather than 'I think' as the reason.

It may also be that we wish to record how some aspects are moving horizontally. Perhaps some aspects are becoming easier to influence and change or others are becoming more difficult. Recording this, again subject to suitable proof, can be with the aid of horizontal arrows as on diagram 'zebra 2'. Arrows pointing to the centre of the diagram will generally be positive and beneficial for the business, arrows pointing to the outside of the diagram will

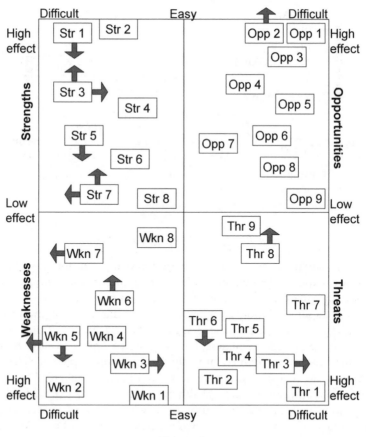

ZEBRA 2

be causes for concern as the issues to which they relate are becoming less tangible and less able to be influenced or changed.

Many aspects are likely to be static. Others will be moving both horizontally and vertically. In diagram 'zebra 2' there are many which we do not perceive to be changing position – for example, Strengths 2, 4, 6 and 8. They therefore have no arrow attached. Others, such as Strengths 3 and 7 are moving in both directions. Strength 3 is gaining in importance in its impact on the business, and is also becoming easier to influence and change. As it is in ascendancy, it may be appropriate to establish deliberate targeted strategies to draw it further to the right more rapidly and thus get further towards that ideal top right corner of the Strengths quadrant – very important and influential strengths which are easy to change, adapt, control or influence. The starting point of Strength 3 is dangerous – of significant importance but with minimal organisational control over it. It will therefore need some monitoring, but I would raise more concern about Strength 1.

The top left corner of the Strengths quadrant is dangerous, and Strength 1 is very influential in the business, but we have little influence over changing it. Our theoretical organisation, in this example, would be in danger of becoming dependent on Strength 1, but it could become a monster beyond our control exhibited by its far left positioning. I recall one manufacturing business in which I worked where this nearly became a reality.

I was the Chief Accountant of a UK manufacturing company in the early 1990's. We implemented a 'state of the art' computer based manufacturing, processing and ordering system. It was hugely successful, automatically determining future raw material requirements based on our product mix forecasts, recommending what we should order from the suppliers and when to place the order based on each supplier's lead time. It established our stockholding of every raw material and how long that stock would last with the current order book plus forecasts. It was powerful, it was better than anything any of our competitors had and it helped eliminate large sums of money wasted in inefficient stockholding. However, we were very conscious that this monster needed cautious guarding. If we did not pay exquisite attention to product mix variations, order changes, to manufacturing everything precisely to specification and to manually checking all the system's ordering recommendations we could have been in serious trouble with the machine controlling the production plant – more reminiscent of the Terminator films than of a strongly run business. I recall one management meeting where this dawned on us and the Factory General Manager raised his hands to his head and exclaimed

➜

> →
> "What is this monster we have created?" It would have been placed towards the top of our Strength quadrant, and our emphasis on it was to make certain that we established the checks and routines to ensure that it was kept to the right of the quadrant. Lackadaisical control processes would have seen it creeping gradually further to the left of the quadrant. I only once recall us making a serious error – the consequence was a huge container of butterfly shaped pasta which took us months to get rid of!

Conversely, Strength 7 is becoming more important but more difficult to change or influence. This would initially look to be a negative issue. However, its current position is sufficiently low to mean that it is an influence on the business but not a massive influence. The judgement to be made is whether, as its starting point is so low, it is of sufficiently high priority to seek to draw to the right, or are we going to allow it to get a few steps closer to that highly dangerous top left of the Strengths quadrant? It may be that we keep it under review but not prioritise the allocation of resources to dealing with it until we feel it gets as high as, say, where Strength 5 currently resides.

Stage 6 – make connections

Some of the Strengths and Weaknesses will have an influence on, or be influenced by some of the Opportunities and Threats. By using the board, graph or floor we are able to physically connect them using tape or ribbon. Not only is this visually effective, it adds flexibility and is a lot more interesting than sitting around a board table discussing sheets of paper.

The reasons why the quadrants are set out as they are is to maximise the visual impact of this method and have consistency in the movements of the differing constituents of the S.W.O.T. It may be that some Strengths and Weaknesses can be used to influence or take advantage of some Opportunities or to influence or neutralise some Threats. Here the direction of connection is from items on the left two quadrants to items on the right two quadrants. In diagram 'zebra 3' Strength 2, Strength 6 and Weakness 3 all have a bearing on Opportunity 4. I would also make a different type of connection (usually different coloured tape) if the connection is from a causation from Opportunity or Threat having an impact on a Strength or a Weakness. For example, in diagram 'zebra 3', this same Opportunity (Opportunity 4) has an impact on Strength 3. This impact may be positive or negative. At this stage that is usually self-evident, but should have attention paid to it, particularly in this case where Strength 3 is in the ascendancy

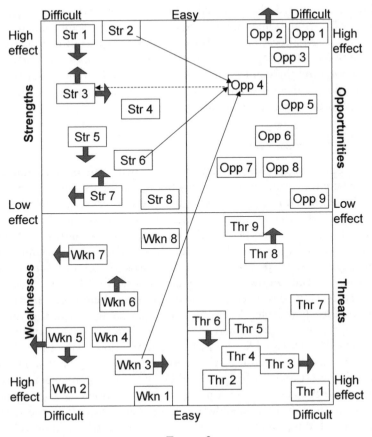

ZEBRA 3

and becoming more business critical. We would need to establish how Opportunity 4 affects it and what would be the organisational consequences of succeeding or failing to take advantage of Opportunity 4.

The connections are from left to right and from right to left. Connections from Strength to Weakness or vice versa sometimes, but seldom, develop into fruitful strategic decisions and so I tend to avoid these at this stage, bringing them in later if appropriate – see stage 7. Connections between Opportunities and Threats can also be of use, but, for simplicity I avoid these at this stage and again bring them in later if appropriate.

Some groups like to quantify the relative strength of the connection by considering the degree to which one factor influences or impacts on another. Some form of subjective numbering of a connection to add weight to it has occasionally been useful, but in most cases the strategies we develop from this approach do not need this.

Having completed the connection stage we generate a four quadrant diagram with enough lines across it to bear a passing resemblance to a map of the New York subway system. The connections give us some indication of the organisational strategic direction by considering the overall pattern but more importantly the connections can give us an indication of our strategic position and the type of strategy which would be most useful to meet each of the Opportunities and the Threats.

Strength to Opportunity connections

Here we can consider how the aspects which make our business good, the aspects where we are ahead of the competition, the things which others external to the organisation envy about us, become the very things which can be leveraged in order to take advantage of a specific opportunity. The strategies required for these connections are bold, aggressive, progressive strategies leveraging our strengths to make the opportunity a reality. In diagram 'zebra 3', Strengths 2 and 6 are the ones to focus on in order to develop Opportunity 4. Both of these strengths are fairly close to the 'easy' side of the graph and so strategies to engage them and focus them on Opportunity 4 should be entirely feasible. Where such strengths are further to the 'difficult' side (left), the organisation could actively seek strategies to drag them to the right, towards the 'easy' side. Even where they are, close to the easy side, they are not on the extreme right 'easy' boundary and so it may be that a focus to make them even easier to change would be beneficial. Simultaneously, wherever the strategy sits on the vertical axis, the organisation could choose active strategies to amplify them and hence move them upwards in the diagram towards the ideal top right corner of the Strengths quadrant. In order to take advantage of Opportunity 4 the company could therefore be working on:

1. Leveraging Strengths 2 and 6 directly focusing on Opportunity 4.
2. Seeking active strategies to increase the influence and impact of Strength 6, thus moving it higher up in the diagram.
3. Reinforcing Strength 2. It is already at the point of highest impact on the organisation. Active strategies to ensure that it remains there and is not undermined or diminished can be developed and implemented.
4. Seeking active strategies which will increase the organisation's ability to affect and influence Strengths 2 and 6 , hence seeking to move them to the right.

Were we only to focus on the Opportunity and not the strengths which can have an impact on this opportunity, we would only be working on one of these four areas of development. The linkage system gives an organisation or individual the ability to open up multiple strategies to develop the opportunity.

In the strategies of the zebra, the fight option is wholly appropriate if strong and multiple Strength to Opportunity links exist. This is an aggressive fight to make gains and seize the opportunity.

Strength to Threat connections

The organisational strengths have a link to the 'red for danger' elements which are seeking to bite us in the timescale considered. In diagram 'zebra 4' Threat 5 has Strengths 1 and 7 generating an impact on it. With connections in this direction, the expected strategies would be defensive, retrenchment, siege mentality approaches utilising and leveraging the organisational strengths to neutralise the threat. It doesn't take a Master's Degree in Business Strategy to establish that one of the organisation's core strengths (Strength 1) is the key defence to the attack by Threat 5. Strength 7 will

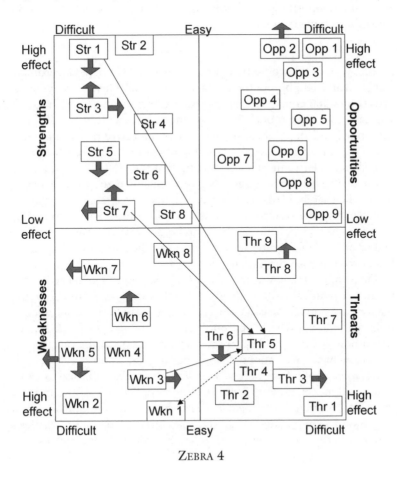

ZEBRA 4

inevitably play a key supporting role. However, one difficulty is that both strengths are shown well to the left of the diagram. This means that they are difficult to change and influence and therefore the organisation will find difficulty leveraging them to muster the defence of Threat 5. Unless it does so, Threat 5 will make an attack. The focus for this scenario is therefore:

- How to utilise Strengths 1 and 7 to neutralise Threat 5
- How to ensure that the business can leverage the strengths – in '5 year old terms' 'how can we move Strengths 1 and 7 to the right?'

With strong, applicable connections in this area the strategy of the zebra is to fight. The organisation is well armed to defend itself from these threats and can focus on combining the strengths to chase the threat away – in zebra terminology, a Threat with multiple connections to Strengths is no pride of lions – just an opportunist wild dog who needs a sharp kick to send it howling into the Serengeti sunset.

In 2005 CNOOC, whose parent company is the Chinese Government, launched an $18.5bn bid for US oil firm Unocal. This was a significant threat. Simultaneously US oil company Chevron offered $17.3bn for Unocal. In conventional business the CNOOC bid would have triumphed and the Unocal shareholders would have received an additional $1.2bn of revenue. For the board on Unocal, there was more than shareholder value at stake. Stating that the CNOOC deal posed a threat to US national security they recommended the lower Chevron bid to the shareholders. The board of Unocal were still not confident of generating the result they wanted. Their primary role is to run the company to the benefit of the shareholder owners, and clearly the higher offer was of greater financial benefit. Their strengths were insufficient to deal with this threat.

Their 'fight' tactic was to seek political support. The takeover then became a political issue with greater stakes than mere money rather than a commercial decision where the higher bidder should win and thus generate greater shareholder return. In July 2005, the Republican-led House of Representatives voted to obstruct the US Government's tacit support for the higher, more commercially favourable, more free-market CNOOC bid. The political pressure intensified and in August 2005, CNOOC pulled out of the bid stating that *"unprecedented political opposition"* was the reason for its withdrawal. They added *"CNOOC has given active consideration to further improving the terms of its offer, and would have done so but for*

→

> → *the political environment in the US."* Unocal had therefore assessed the strengths it was able to mobilise against this threat, found them insufficient and generated the additional strength of US political support to achieve its objectives – a well thought out, well planned and well executed analysis and generation of a winning 'fight' strategy of the zebra against what would have been a superior foe.

Weakness to Opportunity connections

There are a number of beautifully tempting and desirable opportunities in our business Serengeti. They would be tremendous for our organisation to be able to take advantage of. However, the links are to weaknesses. All the factors which would assist us to press home the opening and development of the opportunity are the things which other organisations do better than us. The opportunity may be the development of new products to fit a gaping hole in the market – yet if others are infinitely better than us at product development, bringing the product to the market, marketing and distribution channel control – the opportunity will sweep majestically past us into the hands of our competitors.

Or, they will do so if we continue with our current set of Strengths and Weaknesses. If however, we seek to redesign and redefine our organisational strengths, if we seek to re-engineer our business in order to amplify those aspects needed to take advantage of that opportunity, we have a chance. Look no further than the obvious, and overutilised, example of the Japanese electronics industry.

> After the Second World War, Japanese goods were considered to be of poor quality, shoddy, unreliable and the sort of products which would be purchased by people who could not afford quality. With a concerted effort, with a driven culture and with the not inconsiderable financial assistance of a combination of government support, low borrowing rates and trade protection policies, Japan has transformed itself from a maker of low quality to being at the cutting edge in both technology and quality for electronic goods – national transformation in only one generation!

The transformation is equally, if not more impressive with the Japanese automobile industry.

When I was very young, Japanese cars were a source of ridicule and a relative rarity on our streets. Now they are at the pinnacle of the trade to the extent that their onslaught on the American market has been rapid and all conquering. Toyota has overtaken Daimler Chrysler in the US car hierarchy by volume. This advance and potential dominance is perceived as being more serious in the US than in most of Europe because America has a more emotional attachment to their car manufacturers due to their long running dependence on and obsession with transporting themselves via the internal combustion engine (invented by Frenchman Rudolf Diesel 1858–1913). The American automotive industry is currently reeling in crisis with its antiquated infrastructure, archaic labour agreements and excessive cost structure. Famously General Motors stock was, in 2005, relegated below 'investment grade' stock, colloquially known as 'junk bonds' and in 2009 the industry was 'bailed out' by the US government at an enormous cost to the US taxpayer. Meanwhile, Nissan and Honda had been registering profits, albeit at reduced levels. The extent of the Japanese advance into the American market has been so intense that some Japanese firms, remembering the unpleasant Japanese-American trade and political conflicts of the 1980's, fear a resultant economic backlash from the United States. This prompted Toyota Motors Chairman Hiroshi Okuda to state in 2005 that *"we need to give time for some American companies to take a breath"*. He should have no worries as President George W Bush clearly had a fondness for harmonious relations with Japan. In a visit to Japan in 2002 he stated *"for a century and a half now, America and Japan have formed one of the great and enduring alliances of modern times"*. Perhaps President Bush should have concentrated more whist studying history at school, particularly the period 1941–1945.

In Europe, Japanese automobile manufacturers have even toppled the German giants from their prestigious plinths at the top of customer satisfaction ratings. Having held the high ground of being the volume manufacturers of prestigious, aspirational, high quality vehicles for so long, the German manufacturers are now actively having to combat aggressive 'strength to opportunity' tactics by a number of Japanese manufacturers. The tremendous success of the Japanese has been that the earlier weaknesses have been worked on, eliminated and in turn further worked on and turned into strengths. Thirty to forty years ago their connections were mostly 'weakness to opportunity'. Staying in that position would have been untenable for an ongoing business and the very aspects which were weaknesses one generation ago have been gradually and deliberately worked on to move upwards in our diagram.

→

→
Now many of them, such as customer satisfaction and reliability, are nestling at the very top.

Fortunately not all is negative for the German automotive industry. Look at the Skoda motor car brand purchased by the German Volkswagen Group. Dubbed 'the brand from hell', just a few short years ago, were a marketing manager to be appointed as the Skoda brand manager it would be a sure sign that their career had hit the buffers. Volkswagen purchased this Eastern European 'Weakness' – and a Weakness right at the bottom of the diagram – and started to transform it. With millions of euros of design, development and advertising plus a helpful amount of common parts with more reputable brands, it has become almost socially acceptable to confess to owning a Skoda. I say 'almost', but whilst working with a European part of a global super-bank, I encountered one very senior executive who was a Skoda enthusiast and owned seven of them.

In diagram 'zebra 3' Weakness 3 impacts on Opportunity 4, and despite the other strengths linking to the Opportunity, it may have the ability to prevent the organisation securing Opportunity 4. A series of strategies to minimise the impact of Weakness 3, or eliminate it completely could be implemented. The direct or indirect consequence would be the furthering of our objective to secure Opportunity 4. The good news is that it is well to the right of its quadrant and so relatively easy to influence or control. Further good news is that we perceive it to be increasing in ease. However, the bad news is that it is towards the bottom of the sector and therefore of major influence. If it remains in its current position, or even moves to the right as we expect (stage 5 arrow) it will still be a major issue for us unless we can:

- Eliminate Weakness 3
- Break the link of Weakness 3 to Opportunity 4
- Create compensating strengths to outweigh Weakness 3's negative impact
- Move Weakness 3 to a position of being less influential thus further up the diagram

The message of these linkages is that the zebra is not presently positioned to 'fight'. Stay where we are and at best, the opportunities will pass us by. At worst, we will commit ourselves to a fight to grab an opportunity which is unattainable, and a fight which we cannot win. The focus is therefore more on establishing where we want to be and driving towards that. The Japanese transformation took years and a co-ordinated effort built by multi-billion

Yen (and Dollar) backing. The Skoda transformation took redesign, re-engineering, an organisational shift and a brand shift of gargantuan proportions. So it can happen, but it takes time. With Weakness to Opportunity links dominating, the time would not be 'now'. Try to take advantage of the opportunities fuelled by strategies of our weaknesses and we will inevitably fail.

Weakness to Threat connections

Major connections from Weaknesses to Threats are a problem. All the 'red for danger' threats are circling like vultures and ready to attack us in our areas of greatest vulnerability – our weaknesses. If we stay where we are and let the present position persist, we are in trouble.

In diagram 'zebra 4' Threat 5 is impacted on by Strengths 1 and 7 as previously discussed. It is also impacted on by Weakness 3 and it has an effect on the influential, bottom of the quadrant Weakness 1. With the low quadrant positioning of Weaknesses 1 and 3, this is probably a serious threat. It is beyond half way down the Threats quadrant, any further down and it could be immensely serious. The strategies for the weakness are the same as discussed in the previous weakness to opportunity section, namely eliminate, break the link, compensate with strengths and/or seek to move the weaknesses upwards and to the right. The 'do nothing' strategy is probably not an option, but should the zebra fight?

Fight or not depends on the extent to which the Strengths 1 and 7 can outweigh the effect of Weakness 3. Using strengths 1 and 7 is almost compulsory in this situation but having Weakness 3 on the Serengeti plain is like the zebra trying to use its strengths whilst being handicapped by a physical impediment – blind or lame zebras do not grow to adulthood except in zoos. If we do not deal with Threat 5, the consequences will be seen in its impact on Weakness 1 which is already at the zenith of hampering our organisational development.

The answer to whether the zebra can fight this threat therefore lies in its ability to overcome the weakness, eliminate it or render it obsolete or irrelevant. However, fight is only one of its options.

Stage 7 – Vertical connections

Whilst the overwhelming majority of useful connections will be S/W to or from O/T, there is occasional use in making the S–W or O–T connections. I would not recommend spending much time on this stage but it may be that there is a strength which can be leveraged or utilised to negate a weakness, or a future threat that reduces the attractiveness of an otherwise desirable opportunity.

Stage 8 – action planning

Having explored a vast range of possibilities, there are a number of options:

- Strengths to seek to increase their impact – moving upwards
- Strengths to protect, so that they will not slip downwards
- Strengths which require more control and ability to leverage – to move right
- Strengths to leverage to seek to gain a particular opportunity
- Strengths to leverage to seek to defend against a threat
- Weaknesses to move, upwards or right
- Weaknesses which are hampering opportunity development and so need dealing with
- Weaknesses which are vulnerable to threats and so need strategic attention
- Strengths and weaknesses to ignore – if they are not relevant cease any organisational effort working on them
- Opportunities to attack – how to leverage strengths, neutralise weaknesses or how to create new strengths which will make gaining the opportunity more achievable

Effective use of S.W.O.T.

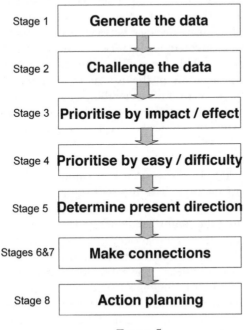

Stage 1	**Generate the data**
Stage 2	**Challenge the data**
Stage 3	**Prioritise by impact / effect**
Stage 4	**Prioritise by easy / difficulty**
Stage 5	**Determine present direction**
Stages 6&7	**Make connections**
Stage 8	**Action planning**

ZEBRA 5

- Threats to protect against – leveraging strengths, creating new strengths and eliminating weaknesses of the links to weaknesses

Suddenly, the humble and frequently used list of disjointed Strengths, Weaknesses, Opportunities and Threats has become a major driver for business strategies.

Remember your zebra on the Serengeti? It had smelled danger and was seeking sight, sound and smell information as a basis for making a decision about how to counter this threat. Your zebra had six options – fight, flight, flock, freeze, fragment or frolic. So far we have only considered 'fight'. Your zebra could choose an alternative strategy.

Zebra strategy 2 – Flight

The zebra's second option is to flee. Equipped with powerful legs and its equine running ability, the zebra has both speed and the ability to keep that speed for some distance. It is not the sprint, nor the long distance running champion of the Serengeti but it does possess the ability to compete reasonably in both competitions. The cheetah is the obvious winner in the sprint competition, and we have already seen that the long distance running champion is the giraffe. The zebra is well equipped to use acceleration to remove itself from a situation with instantaneous effect and equally equipped to maintain good speed to create distance between itself and a threat.

The ability to exit a threatening situation is a key to the zebra's survival and a key to organisational survival. In the chapter 'strategy of the warthog' we will explore some of the aspects to consider when making a strategic exit and the protection of vulnerabilities which could be damaged by an unplanned and inappropriate exit. In this chapter, the zebra, our consideration is making the choice to exit rather than how to implement the decision.

The 'flight' decision is frequently the option which managers and executives find most difficult. In our psyche it is often associated with having failed. Frequently organisations have invested significant sums of money in the market, have tried several alternative tactics to secure success in the market and finally used the 'flight' strategy as a last resort. The more alternative strategies used, and the more money invested to seek to force them to succeed, the more difficult it becomes to make the 'flight' decision subsequently. The zebra does not delay. The zebra does not attempt a number of alternatives, then finds itself fleeing as a last resort. For the zebra, 'flight' is a bona fide, lifesaving strategy when faced with certain types of threats. For our businesses we often find that it is a final conclusion of failed strategies and becomes a case of cutting the losses and abandoning the market due to significant trouble or due to failure to penetrate the market adequately. There are many examples, including:

C&A exiting the UK market
M&S exiting the non-UK markets (and subsequently having a partial re-entry)
BA with low cost 'no frills' airlines
AIB exiting internet banking in Eire

Carrefour, the largest retailer in Europe, is not afraid to exit when it feel that this is the most appropriate strategy. One distant example is in the 1970's when the French giant sought to gain a foothold in the UK market. Its multiple product offering, so popular in France, was new to the British retailing industry on this scale. The idea of purchasing food, clothes, stationery and barbeque equipment at the same store was a novelty in Britain. It was rapidly partially duplicated by the then 'up and coming' British grocer Tesco who launched a homeware addition to many stores which included some clothing. The British did not warm to the idea. At that time they still had butchers shops specialising in meat, fishmongers specialising in fish and, whilst the supermarket concept was well advanced, the British had not fully embraced it. The existence of specialist shops in the UK would not have been a concern for Carrefour during their strategic considerations of entering the market as the French did have, and still have, a plethora of *boulongerie, boucherie, choclatiers* etc. The idea was ahead of its time for Britain despite its firm establishment in France. Carrefour realised that the British shopper was not warming to their model and made an exit from the UK market as rapidly and as silently as they arrived. Tesco closed its homeware parts of the stores and reverted to being a grocer.

Now, some 40 years later, the concept has returned. It is being implemented by most supermarkets and embraced by the British public. Tesco are at the forefront of this retail trend as are ASDA, owned by the US giant WalMart. Carrefour have not re-entered the UK market which is dominated by the then 'up and coming' now seemingly omnipotent Tesco.

Carrefour remain adept at generating a good and clean market exit when they deem it an appropriate strategy. In 2005 Carrefour sold its retail interests in Mexico and in Japan to indigenous companies and no longer have a presence in these countries.

One of my favourite examples of the 'flight' decision is that of GE as told by former CEO Jack Welch in his imaginatively titled autobiography '*Jack*'. In 1981 he was appointed CEO and later in the year released a vision which was that GE was to be either number 1 or number 2 in all markets in which they compete. If they were not presently 1 or 2 the strategy was either to get there very quickly, or exit. The philosophy was built on a question asked by Peter Drucker *"If you weren't already in the business, would you enter it today?"* If the answer was *"No"*, the follow up question was *"What are you going to do about it?"* This fits in with my drive for simplicity – strategy for 5 year olds. It is a simple, honest and unavoidable pair of questions. It also fits in with the requirement for action rather than being satisfied with the status quo. Jack Welch instigated a 'fix, sell or close' strategy for all those businesses owned by GE who failed the first question. 71 businesses and product lines were sold for a relatively negligible sum of approximately $500m.

If the zebra is not in a winning position it does not waste time considering its options further. It does not try to engage in a fight where the odds are against it. 'Flight' is a bona fide and often brave strategic option. Regrettably many executives are not as brave as Jack Welch and perpetuate mediocre businesses with mediocre positioning in mediocre markets with mediocre business performance. The zebra does not do 'mediocre' – he is highly refined, tuned by years of evolution, adapted perfectly to the life of a Serengeti grazer and is a most adept animal at the 'flight' strategy when it is his best option.

In August 2005, the now defunct British retailer Woolworths finally sold its music retailing subsidiary MVC. The price raised was £5.5m ($9.7m) and this generated a one off (exceptional) loss in the accounts of Woolworths for the year of £34m. Woolworths Chief Executive Trevor Bish-Jones said *"the disposal of MVC removes a loss making business from the group and allows us to be solely focussed on our retail business in Woolworths"*. The key issue is that MVC had been loss making for some considerable time and had been rumoured to be the reason why Apax partners pulled out of a bid for the Woolworths group some months earlier. Had the disposal been made earlier, even at a greater paper transaction than a £34m loss, the Woolworths shareholders may have benefited from the acquisitive interest of Apax – the Woolworths board simply did not execute the strategy of flight with sufficient haste and the opportunity was lost. By January 2009, Woolworths had collapsed and ceased trading.

'Flight' is a brave decision which goes against the mantra of continual expansion, but as we shall see in the strategies of the hippopotamus, focussing and not overexpanding a business territory can be an exceptionally effective strategy over time.

The toy industry has witnessed a couple of interesting 'flight' strategies.

In 1999 Mattel, the world's largest toys and games manufacturer, purchased The Learning Company for $3.8bn. The company specialised in software which ensures that learning is fun. On paper this looked to be a wise and potentially fruitful acquisition. The world's knowledge of learning has changed and the pedagogic approach to education is slowly diminishing. A more modern approach to learning is exhibited in one of my favourite quotes:

"Learning is the greatest game in life and the most fun. All children are born believing this and will continue to believe this until we convince them that learning is very hard work and unpleasant.

Some kids never really learn this lesson and go through life believing that learning is fun and the only game worth playing.

We have a name for such people.

We call them geniuses."

Glenn Doman Founder The Institute for the Achievement of Human Potential

The blending of 'play' and 'learning', via computer based technology would score high on any strategic diagnostic and so Mattel's strategy seemed utterly logical. For reasons we do not have the space to consider, the acquisition did not work. Mattel could have taken the decision to push greater resource into this area or to develop the concept in a different way. They chose 'flight'. One year later Mattel left the market with $0. A brave 'flight' as many would have sought to recoup the $3.8bn before exiting ignominiously.

Mattel's great rival, Hasbro, for whom I have immense respect, unfortunately took a longer, more expensive and more painful series of strategies with the 'Sindy' brand.

In the 1960's in the UK, Sindy was the dominant doll and was owned by Pedigree Dolls and Toys. Almost every British little girl played with their Sindy whilst their brother was playing with Palitoy's Action Man – the UK equivalent of GI Joe. Sindy was developed for the UK as a response to the US success of Barbie, owned by Mattel, who was born in 1959. As Sindy reached enviable UK dominance, Mattel made a major push in the UK market with Barbie boasting significant marketing revenue behind her. Whilst Barbie was the world's first for this type of doll, Sindy was the UK's first and enjoyed initial market acceptance having achieved what strategists term 'first mover advantage' – i.e. Sindy got to the UK market first. Despite this, after a very short period of time, with Mattel's millions against them, Pedigree soon found themselves playing 'catch-up'. Barbie got longer legs, Sindy had to copy. Barbie got a boyfriend (Ken), Sindy had to find one (Paul). Barbie got an unfeasibly large chest, Sindy underwent similar surgery. Barbie had one advantage which is better understood now than in the 1960's. She associated herself with the colour pink. Many parents are in denial about a gender disposition towards pink by a large proportion of little girls, but modern behavioural studies seem to confirm a preference.

Barbie marched relentlessly through the UK market share statistics to overtake Sindy and in due course become the dominant doll amongst British children.

In 1986/7 the use of the Sindy brand was acquired by the world's second largest toys and games manufacturer, Hasbro. At this point, Sindy was in decline and Barbie was in the ascendancy. However, with the resources of Hasbro behind the Sindy brand the previous weakness of 'lack of financial resource' had become a strength of 'Hasbro's millions'. Add to this the strength of Hasbro's greater marketing experience and expertise, their greater exposure in the toys market and better relationship with suppliers, many of the items on the left side of the S.W.O.T. had shifted upwards.

They could have looked at the strategies of the zebra, determined their S.W.O.T. profile and determined whether they were in a position to 'fight'. This would have required the addressing or elimination of other weaknesses, the leveraging of different strengths, and other aspects discussed earlier in this chapter. Regrettably they did not make such incisive analysis. Hasbro chose to 'fight' when they were not adequately equipped to do so. Over the years, millions of pounds were spent supporting the brand with innovation and development, creating and distributing point of sale marketing material and exorbitant above the line advertising. Sindy was starting to become a loss making liability who, despite her impossibly slim waistline, was consuming huge quantities of company resource.

Much of this expenditure may have slowed the decline of Sindy, but the decline was inevitable. Eventually in 1999, after a twelve year relationship with Sindy, Hasbro 'pulled the plug' and released the monies previously earmarked for Sindy advertising to support other more profitable brands.

In the strategies of the zebra, 'flight' is rapidly decided, instantly executed and potentially huge quantities of money saved by not seeking a number of alternatives first. One of the barriers to executives making 'flight' decisions is previous success. We often believe that we can bring success where others have failed, and sometimes we do. However, some of the wisest words on the subject come from one of the most successful business people ever:

> "Success is a lousy teacher. It seduces smart people into thinking that they can't lose"
>
> Bill Gates

When our strategic analysis is dominated by Weakness – Threat links, unless there is a clear way to deal with this, as the Japanese automotive industry did, the wisest move may be to follow the examples of Carrefour and Mattel rather than try and try again as Pedigree and Hasbro did at great cost to themselves. In the case of the zebra, 'flight' gives you another area in which to graze; staying too long risks you being eaten.

Zebra strategy 3 – Flock

The zebra's most distinctive feature is, of course, its stripes. They are as distinctive as human faces and are thought to be a way in which zebras recognise each other. They also have another purpose which is part of the zebra's response to threats. Some animals, such as the tiger, use stripes as camouflage. The tiger's stripes break up its shape as it moves through the long grasslands of its terrain, the gold and black pattern fitting in with the shadow and light on long grasses. This cannot be the case for the zebra – they are too tall to hide in most of the Serengeti grass and the background is bright, clear, 'here I am' white.

However, camouflage is one major purpose of the stripes. When zebras herd together, a potential predator sees a visual cacophony of white and black (or brown, or grey) stripes. With the zebras huddled together the predator, from low ground level, can have difficulty discerning one zebra from the mass of zebras. As all predators will focus on a single animal to attack, flocking together confuses them by breaking up the shape whilst creating a mix of shadings.

The strategy of 'flock' is therefore about increasing the chances of survival by drawing together.

The most obvious form of the 'flock' strategy is seen in acquisitions. Companies acquire others for a number of reasons, but the success rate of acquisitions actually achieving their business or financial objectives is lamentable. Business fashion dictates to some extent the drive for and the type of acquisition. I recall when 'conglomerates' were fashionable as companies who spread market risk by holding a wide portfolio of businesses. They became 'diversified industrials' and fell out of fashion resulting in the partial dismantling of the likes of Hanson and Tomkins.

In early 2006, German sports equipment company Adidas-Salomon purchased US company Reebok for $3.8bn. The 'flock' strategy by acquisition creates a company with the ability to challenge the dominant Nike in the US sports footwear market. The US market is almost 50% of global sports footwear and Nike has a 36% of this market. Separately Adidas and Reebok are comparatively small players, but with the combined brands accounting for 20% of the US market they generate a position to challenge Nike. The 'flock' strategy provides the platform for this challenge, but a subsequent analysis to develop appropriate 'fight' strategies would be an imperative. A market 'number two' should always seek to attack the market leader by leveraging its own strengths and avoiding the strengths of the leader. The nature of the fight should be interesting to observe as Adidas, the former market leader was ousted from that spot by Reebok in 1987, who subsequently gave way to Nike in 1988. Nike have led the market ever since. The fourth largest, now elevated to third by the 'flock' of Adidas-Reebok is Puma with a 6.8% market share. The two dominant player 'oligopoly' scenario has been played out in other markets – most notably cola and burgers. So far, number one usually wins.

Acquisition is often an expensive option as investors seeking the best deal will naturally resist the offer to sell until they feel that the price is as high as it will go. Acquisition premiums must then be recouped in savings. Cheaper than the acquisition route is that of merger. Merger is another bona fide flock strategy. One example of a proposed merger 'flock' strategy which has been ongoing for over a decade is that of the accountancy institutes of Great Britain.

The UK has six accountancy bodies which have grown through a variety of historical factors. Many years ago, there was some differentiation, but in modern business most financial roles could be filled by an associate of any of the institutes. The players in this drama are:

- ICAEW (Institute of Chartered Accountants in England and Wales) which is suffering from slightly dwindling membership but still has a qualified membership of over 100,000 in the UK

→

and is therefore the UK's largest accountancy body. It has the lowest female level of membership (20%) and its traditional make-up no longer reflects the diversity of the British population, nor the population of accountants. 20 or 30 years ago it was considered by many to be superior to the other bodies.

- ACCA (Association of Chartered and Certified Accountants) has the fastest growth rate (almost 8% p.a.) and a strong international presence but declined to state their number of actual qualified members, only referring to their total number including students – obviously a much larger number!
- CIMA (Chartered Institute of Management Accountants) has a fast growth rate (over 5% p.a.) and an international presence based from nations which were former British colonies. Membership is approximately 50,000 qualified accountants in the UK and just under 20,000 overseas.
- CIPFA (Chartered Institute of Public Finance and Accountancy) specialises in public sector finance and is growing at less than 0.5% p.a. It has approximately 13,500 qualified members of whom less than 300 are registered outside the UK.
- AAT is a professional body whose qualifications are at a lower level of technical expertise than the major bodies but are often seen as a stepping stone to CIMA in particular.
- ICAS is the Scottish equivalent of ICAEW (S standing for Scotland, E and W standing for England and Wales respectively)

In 1969 a proposal to merge 5 bodies was rejected. Further partial mergers were proposed in 1988 and 1990. In 1995 ICAEW rejected a possible merger with CIMA. In 1998 ACCA, CIMA and CIPFA discussed merger possibilities with members but enthusiasm was patchy. In 2003 Accountancy Age magazine and Reed Accountancy surveyed a large number of accountants who overwhelmingly stated that a single body would be better for clarity and best able to serve members. It would also reduce duplication and the resultant waste of costs – borne by the accountants as annual fees. The UK Government also intimated that the six bodies created an unnecessary confusion. In 2004 formal merger talks and member consultation by ICAEW, CIMA and CIPFA were initiated.

The concept of the 'flock' strategy is that a larger body, reflecting a more diverse population would have greater influence and greater reputation than a number of bodies who appear to be squabbling over minutiae. With the transferability of accountancy jobs, the existence of

➜
the six is an anachronism with no observable benefit. The fall out from the Enron scandal and others in the US mean that the UK is keen to ensure that it is best placed to perpetually generate best practice. It is perceived that this would be easier with a larger and wider dominant professional accountancy body.

Take-overs are not appropriate as there is not a 'buy out' situation, merely a drawing together to create a better position in the market-place. The latest version of this 'flock' strategy was therefore three size-able and respectable organisations with huge areas of overlap within their functionality coming together to provide a larger and hopefully even more respected dominant organisation – probably the authority and 'final word' on all accounting related issues. Its dominance could also threaten the independent future of the smaller two institutes and were it to have progressed I could foresee a near future with two institutes – ACCA and the new entity.

As with any merger, there are egos involved, and the ACCA actively targeted ICAEW members opposed to the merger to seek to swell their ranks. In 2005 CIMA withdrew due to a disagreement and ICAEW failed to get sufficient backing for the merger from members and so yet again this most obvious of flock strategies is back to the same position it was in prior to the initial 1969 proposal.

Mergers still keep armies of lawyers in employment and, whilst cheaper than acquisitions, still have associated costs. They also have a degree of permanence about them – a merger is a marriage and any divorce can be costly with ungainly squabbling over assets. A more temporary, less formal arrangement, still with lawyers involvement, is also possible – the alliance. The lack of permanence of an alliance when compared to a formal merger gives both sides the comfort and flexibility to dismantle the partnership with less pain and cost if aims are not being met. Several forms exist, such as the pure 'alliance' which is an agreement between two firms but does not have large scale or structural implications, and the joint-venture which usually includes the establishment of a separate joint ownership company as a vehicle through which the joint activities are undertaken.

The power of the 'flock' by a less formal alliance was evident in the late 1990's when American Airways (AA) announced an intention to join forces with British Airways (BA) in 1997. Richard Branson's competitor Virgin Atlantic Airways (VAA) started in 1984 with the purchase of a very small airline British Atlantic Airways. By 1991 the UK Civil Aviation Authority had permitted VAA to operate from London Heathrow airport and consequently the new arrival was posing a threat to the major Atlantic carriers. They had to respond to this threat or it would increase in size and potency. The chosen strategy was 'flock' by alliance. This would not have involved the formal merger of the two companies but the two airlines would 'codeshare' various flights and routes over the Atlantic and between the US and the Middle East. Negotiations on the further opening of UK take off and landing slots did not progress sufficiently to allow the agreement to proceed.

In 2001 a similar proposal was made at a similar time to when further 'codesharing' arrangements were being made – for example, Delta, Air France, Czech Airlines and Alitalia in August 2001 and United Airlines and British Midland in September 2001. BA and AA between them controlled 52% of the air traffic between US gateway airports and London's Heathrow and Gatwick. BA and AA's dominance at Heathrow was exceptional controlling 61% of the US–Heathrow flights. The resultant US Department of Transportation (DOT) and the UK Office of Fair Trading (OFT) reports illustrated their concern that such an alliance would create the ability for these dominant airlines to create market advantage and in due course to raise prices if they so chose. The DOT and OFT estimated that approximately 200 additional take off slots for other airline competitors would be required to ensure adequate competition from other carriers. Some of the conclusions of the DOT report were:

- Without some regulatory remedy, AA/BA would likely exercise considerable control over routes between major US cities and London
- Gains from the alliance ... may not offset the harms from reduced competition

Whilst this is hardly a stinging rebuke and whilst the verbose report does its best to sit on any fence possible, the conclusion is that the 'flock' strategy would have resulted in decreased competition, increased power for the alliance members and the probability of increased profits. AA and BA are commercial organisations – that is exactly what the shareholders want, so congratulations for trying. Consumer protection thwarted a successful 'flock' strategy which sought to give alliance members a competitive advantage.

One successful informal alliance which has stood the test of several years is the global alliance of the UK's BP and Australia's Lend Lease. This alliance is mutually beneficial and whilst both parties have a degree of interdependence, they are both operating successfully in their chosen fields of activity with only the area of petrol retail station design, build

➡

→

and maintenance as the overlap. The alliance started in 1996. Covering 20,000 petrol retail sites in 14 countries, the alliance was initially a search by BP to secure a long term partner for its ongoing regeneration programme. Bovis Lend Lease (BLL) won the initial short term contract and after multiple extensions it is now a long lasting positive relationship. Annual build costs are approximately US$500m and so it has become BLL's largest ever contract. BLL are now the global experts at retail petrol station design and build, BP have some of the lowest cost and quickest site builds in the industry – everyone wins.

By 2000 the average cost of a petrol retail site build had fallen by almost 50% due to the combining of expertise and a variety of factors such as procurement savings (approximately US$130m), supply chain re-engineering, duplication eradication, build modularity, economies of scale and administration slimlining. The administration efficiencies have been estimated, in the first four years to have saved 12,500 admin hours, 9,000 materials requisitions and approximately 13,000 pieces of paper. In addition to this, the long term relationship has resulted in changes to petrol station design to increase site longevity and thus decrease the time between refurbishments.

The benefits from the alliance were most evident when BP acquired Amoco in the US and had to re-image 10,000 gas stations. Approximately 50 stations a week for 4 years starting in 2001. Probably no other construction company could have completed this operation at anywhere near the cost. The experience and supply relationships built up 1996–2001 by the alliance 'flock' strategy enabled BLL to achieve the re-imaging for BP in a mere 4 years.

The 'flock' strategy can therefore be by acquisition, merger, formal joint venture or informal alliance but it must be long lasting to achieve success. It must also have a commitment to mutual success without duplicitous self serving approaches. I am aware of a London based construction company, a competitor to BLL, where a small partnership agreement was instigated with a major player in the Financial Services market. It was very much smaller then the BP/BLL alliance, but the principle was similar. The contract stipulated the sharing of derived cost savings but the construction company allegedly chose the short term benefit route of not fully declaring the savings, in effect it kept two sets of books – one of the profits made and one which it showed its alleged partner. As the discrepancy became larger the consciences became more strained. At the point of a £2m discrepancy it was becoming difficult to conceal the deceit and the Divisional Managing Director was taking accounting records home to ensure that they were not left in the office and thereby found were he to be absent. To my knowledge the discrepancy was never discovered but the 'partnership' was not renewed beyond the first major job. The short term 'profits today' approach is not the strategy of 'flock'. It is the strategy of self interest. The consequences for the organisation were a solitary boost for the profits for one year and the destruction of a relationship which could have yielded profits for many years to come throughout Europe.

In the UK, the Ministry of Defence (MOD) needed to consider the building and long term operation of its residential accommodation. Thousands of service families rely on the MOD for their accommodation needs. The MOD split its geography into five parts and requested tenders for these areas for building and running the sites for the next 10 years. Few companies could encompass the entirety of the requirements – there was a building requirement, a project management expertise and an ongoing facilities management ability. A combination of construction companies and facilities management companies formed joint ventures to bid for the contracts. These 'flock' JV's were usually 'stand alone' companies comprising of staff from both the construction and facilities management organisations. Production of the tender document was so intense that it took several months for a team of over a dozen but the benefits for the winner would be an income stream of reasonable certainty for up to 10 years. Babcock plc was the only company to be awarded two of the five regional contracts – each time with different partners. In a classic 'flock' strategy Babcock joined with appropriate partners to bid for a number of the contracts. I had the privilege of a modest involvement with one successful team where the partner was an experienced provider of solutions to the US military who had provided support in Bosnia, Afganistan and Iraq. They made an ideal partner for Babcock. Both companies win. Babcock gain a programme of building and exposure to a new market and the US company gain a foothold in the UK which has been previously unattainable. They are mutually interdependent and the gain is beneficial to both – that is the strategy of 'flock'.

A variety of other 'flock' strategies in limited areas of operation are possible. A few examples drawn from a 1994 article by Pekar and Allio are a little dated, some no longer operative but are good illustrations of limited 'flock' strategies:

- Distribution alliance – Volkswagen and Nissan who distribute each other's vehicles – Volkswagen distributing both companies products in Europe and Nisaan doing the same in Japan.
- Collaborative advertising – American Express and Toys R Us co-operating in joint television advertising.
- Research collaboration – Cytel and Sumitomo Chemicals working together to develop the next generation of biotechnology products.
- Transference of technology – IBM and Apple making an arrangement develop software and operating systems together.
- Sharing manufacturing – Ford and Mazda designing and building cars using the same assembly line.

The zebra's stripes create the ability to engage the strategy of 'flock'. This is replicated in a variety of ways in business. To learn when the strategy should succeed and when it should not perhaps we should ask the expert – the zebra. Zebra 'flock' strategies are for the mutual benefit. The common good, mutual survival, a co-ordinated response to a threat, a classic 'win–win' are the aims. Many of our business 'flock' strategies are not mutual, they can be focus on MY win rather than ensuring OUR win. True 'flock' generates equal concern for gain. If the BP/BLL alliance benefited one organisation disproportionately to the other it would have failed many years ago. The Babcock alliances were a 'heart and soul' alliance with people from both organisations working at the same site and seeing themselves not as employees of their original companies but as people working for the same joint entity.

'Flock' means commitment, 'flock' means equal concern for the gain of all parties, 'flock' means enhanced chances of survival and the ability to secure opportunities not available by other strategies.

Even fiercely competitive rivals can 'flock' for mutual benefit. GE is the largest global provider of military aero engines. Rolls Royce is number 2. The project to develop the engine for the $116bn F35 Joint Strike Fighter to replace the F16, F18, A10, A18, Harrier and Sea Harrier has been jointly developed, jointly researched and will be jointly manufactured by these two aeronautical giants. The contract has been awarded and full production should ensue by 2013. The decision by GE and RR to pool resources and share the benefits has ensured beneficial business for both companies for the foreseeable future as the F35 is likely to be the main fighter aircraft for the US and UK from 2014 to beyond 2030.

Zebra strategy 4 – Freeze

On the Serengeti plain our zebra sensed danger. The scent and sound of a predator was evident. Our zebra's first task was to assimilate all the sensory information, process it and make a decisive response to the threat. Making a premature response could be fatal. For example, the choice of a 'fight' response when faced with a hunting party of lions would be about as good an idea as that of Mrs Lincoln when she said *"Hey, Abe, let's go to the theatre tonight"*. Making a premature 'flight' response without clear discernment of the direction of flight could be equally suicidal. Continuing the lion example, as we shall see in 'strategies of the lion', lionesses have a carefully orchestrated strategy for attack. Very seldom will the zebra's threat be only from one direction if lions are involved. If the sensed threat is from the north and the zebra chooses 'flight' to the east before appropriate consideration, east could be where the main hunting party is. Our zebra would be running straight into them.

Strategy 4 – 'freeze' is sometimes a wholly appropriate strategy for the zebra and for us in business. However, it is a strategy with a message – and the message is 'get the timing right'. Take the 'freeze' option for too short a period of time and premature action on partial information increases the risk to the organisation and decreases your survival chances. Take the 'freeze' option for too long and the zebra becomes a vulnerable static target dithering in indecision. 'Freeze' is never a long term option, but it is a vital option to prevent executive knee-jerking. Lurching from one action to another is a sign of panic, not of strategic implementation. I can recall one major airline lurching from strategies of 'added service at a price', to 'no frills' to 'business market only' to 'cut costs' to 'something for everyone' within the space of a few years. The most appropriate strategy would have been 'freeze' until they can make an appropriate strategic response to the threat they faced rather than spend vast quantities of shareholders money knee-jerking from one half-thought-out partial strategy to another.

One part of an industry which did get a 'freeze' right is that of the photograph processing services such as Bonusprint and Truprint.

In the old fashioned days we used to buy a reel of film, put it in our cameras, take the photographs, carefully extract the reel, send it to a processing service and a few days later beautifully pristine prints would drop through our letterbox. Digital cameras changed all that. Now we can snap, delete if we wish, store the images on our PC's and print them at will. On the S.W.O.T. for the processing companies, this new technology would have been in the far bottom right corner – the biggest, least controllable threat possible. Possible strategies could have

→

➔

been close down ('flight'), panic, or update the CV and circulate it to recruitment consultants. Bonusprint and Truprint chose 'freeze'. They waited to establish what would happen with this new technology and how the consumer would use it.

They soon found that many people would store the images on their PC's but not print them. Part of this was due to many not having photographic quality print capability, part due to not getting into the habit of buying photo quality print paper and part due to getting the sizing of photo prints correct. None of these are insurmountable, but many people were not overcoming these relatively small obstacles.

Bonusprint, Truprint and others then saw the potential in the market by utilising their core strengths built up over the years with the previous technology to connect on their S.W.O.T. with an opportunity of high quality professional printing of digital images. E-mail the images to the processing companies, pay by credit card and receive pristine prints through the letterbox just as you did previously. The advantage over the previous technology is that you only send the images you want printing – so when you've messed up the photo and omitted someone's head, or caught them whilst blinking, those are not sent, hence not paid for. What seemed like an insurmountable, undefendable threat had a side to it which has become a great opportunity. By applying the 'freeze' strategy, the companies could gauge the market direction, let the opportunity open up and due to the clear linkage to one of their core strengths, exploit it offering a superior customer service.

Zebra strategy 5 – Fragment

The first four possible strategic responses to a threat – fight, flight, flock and freeze will give a first reaction. It may be the only strategy needed. However, the zebra has a back-up plan. If any or some of strategies 1–4 have been used, but the lions are now amongst the zebra herd, the purpose of reactions 1–4 is now over. 1–4 are about preventing or seeing off a potential attack. If the attack actually becomes reality, the zebra still has a further strategy to play. As a herd on the plain, the lions are amongst you. Someone is going to get eaten, but if you use strategy 5 – fragment – it may not be you. In this strategy, with the lions amongst the zebra, the prey split up and head in different directions. Someone will be unfortunate, but 360 degree fragmentation will minimise the risk to the herd as a whole. After an attack and a 'fragment response', the zebra families regroup over the next few days, often some distance from where the attack took place and we are not certain how they manage this communication feat of regrouping at a certain time and place without the aid of cell phones.

One group I was in used the fragment response to prevent a hostile take-over. The hostile approach was made and we split the business into 3 parts to make it more difficult to the hostile party. That particular hunting party went away and a 'friendly' or 'white knight' takeover was proposed. We 'magically' sewed the group back together again and proceeded with the friendly party. The fragment strategy is used by the large accountancy part-nerships to seek to persuade people that there is no cross over between their audit function and their consultancy function.

The use of market fragmentation in the motor industry, e.g. Toyota/Lexus and Merecedes/SmartCar is not a zebra fragmentation in response to threat. This is seeking to have different offerings in different areas of the market, building niches, as will be explored when considering the hippopotamus, the niche market expert. As a threat response strategy it is a valid response and has served the zebra very well for countless generations.

Zebra strategy 6 – Frolic

There is a 6th response to a predator threat. Our zebra on the Serengeti may be faced with a number of threats and may not be able to process the infor-mation appropriately. He may be overwhelmed by the situation. In this circumstance, the reaction is to prance around in a panic mode. If there are a number of zebras they will run no-where in particular, often bumping into each other in the chaos. There is movement, noise, action but no discernable direction and no active strategy. Nothing worthwhile is being achieved, just action and movement for its own sake. This is the strategy of 'frolic'.

Organisational frolicking can take many forms – the most common is that of, in the face of a real threat, instigating an organisational review or re-organisation of the structure. Managers and Executives swap seats, organograms get redrawn, employees have new bosses to get used to, bosses have new areas of responsibility to get used to, but nothing actually changes. Nothing actually gets done.

This is not a new phenomenon:

"We trained hard ... but it seemed that every time we were beginning to form up into teams we would be reorganized. I was to learn later in life that we tend to meet any new situation by reorganizing; and a wonderful method it can be for creating the illusion of progress while producing confusion, inef-ficiency, and demoralization."

Widely attributed to Caius Petronius Arbiter, Roman Governor
at the time of Nero 1st Century AD

Actually this is a 20th century quote wrongly attributed to Petronius. There are references to it originating among disgruntled British occupying forces in post-1945 Germany (*Petronian Society Newsletter*, May 1981). The true author is unknown.

Other examples of the 'frolic' strategy would include Executives deciding that the problem is with the brand image rather than with more fundamental aspects of the business under their leadership. A few hundred thousand pounds/dollars/euros are then spent changing the name or the logo. The British Royal Mail postal service changed part of its brand to 'Consignia' for seemingly no reason. It was shortly abandoned and reverted to Royal Mail – 'frolic'.

Over about a decade, one UK business had discovered a competency in the efficient sourcing of signage throughout Europe. Their first foray into this was in the area of petrol forecourt signage and vast sums were saved for their clients. They naturally sought to apply this expertise to other opportunities in other industries and gained similar successes. As part of their multi-industry expansion of this expertise, discussions proceeded with a household name global, highly litigious, fast food outlet. The food outlet's signage throughout Europe differs – slightly different fonts to the logo, slightly different sizes – there must be room for consolidation, sourcing advantages and savings.

The British company undertook the job and provided a low cost solution with a single supplier in Turkey. The savings to the fast food company were allegedly approximately 40% of total signage costs. A meeting was convened with the various fast food company national heads in Western Europe to sign this cost saving initiative and commit to the Turkish supplier. The cost-driven British indicated a willingness to sign most enthusiastically, as did a number of other nations. Then it was the time for the French to pass verdict. *"I would not consider buying any signage which was not made in France"* was the narrow nationalistic response. Curious for a founding member of the European Union. The Head of Germany was next to contribute. *"I have no objection to manufacturing within Europe, or Eastern Europe – but not Turkey"*. The level of immigration from Turkey to Germany is high due to historical factors. With Turkish labour taking German jobs during a time of unemployment, there is a degree of scapegoating from the Germans aimed at the Turks. With two of the largest nations refusing the deal, it collapsed and the 40% savings were never made. Not only were the savings not made, the fast food company incurred the cost of the consultancy establishing the savings – they

➡

→

would have been better off doing nothing – zebras frolicking on the Serengeti.

> (*source* – informal from individuals involved,
> anonymity preserved on legal advice).

Another example of the strategies of frolic could be many aspects of the late 1990's and early 21st century demise of the once great Marks & Spencer stores of the UK, and formerly of Europe. There are so many areas where we could consider 'frolic' at that time in its history, but I will restrict to one – from where the company sources its products.

Marks and Spencer (M&S) was proudly pro-British. It sourced the vast majority of its products from the UK and saw that as a patriotic statement which would gain favour with the High Street shopper. An American equivalent would be Levi Strauss who were one of the last to manufacture outside the U.S.A. We shall discuss Levis later.

In 1997/8 M&S sourced 75% of its products from the UK. UK labour is well paid. Goods are therefore expensive. The attitude of the High Street shopper is that such a patriotic effort is most laudable – until the point where they are asked to pay more. At that point we consider value for money and buy elsewhere. For this, and a number of other reasons, M&S lost market share, failed to attract the British shopper and their treasured reputation was gradually tarnished. M&S tried a range of other strategies – new clothing ranges, new approaches, dealing with some of the other anomalies, changing the leadership – much of it was frolicking in the Serengeti. It was failing to address the real issues and playing on the periphery.

After the fashion retail giant Philip Green failed in his bid to buy M&S, Stuart Rose was appointed to recover M&S's fortunes. Stuart Rose had led Arcadia Group from the brink of disaster to fairly good success until Philip Green had bought the group. He had previously been with M&S and so had a combination of being an 'M&S man' and having turned around a failing company – possibly a unique combination. By 2004/5 M&S was only sourcing 5% of its goods from the UK with 49% elsewhere in Europe (especially the East where labour is cheaper – in 1997/8 that was 15%), 29% from the Far East (formerly 7%), and 17% from India (formerly 5%). The core issue of being overpriced was partially addressed through reviewing sourcing and doing what most other clothing retailers had done years ago.

→

➔
> It appears that Stuart Rose developed a real strategy to replace
> frolicking. Under his leadership there appears to be more direction and
> less of the frolic in the strategies of the M&S zebra.

The strategy of 'frolic' can take many forms, but the essence is that the
company wastes time and effort dealing with symptoms rather than the
causes of their problems. The focus is frequently internal or if it does have an
external perspective it is based on misguided or antiquated perceptions of the
market. Whilst restructures are the most visible and frequent example of
'frolic', I add a word of caution. The strategy of 'frolic' is as a response to a
threat. I am certainly not advocating maintaining an irrelevant structure or
market approach. I am certainly not 'anti-restructure'. What I mean by the
'strategy of frolic' is that these are undertaken as a response to a threat or as
a response to poor performance. They are often reactive changes based on
historical events. Restructuring to better fit the shape of the future market is
proactive and positive. The focus of these types of restructure is forward
looking and externally biased – that is not 'frolic'. 'Frolic' is internally
focussed and historic. Hamel and Prahalad in their 1994 book 'Competing
for the future' make a tremendously valid comment – "far from being a tribute to senior management's steely resolve or far-sightedness, a large restructuring and reengineering change is simply the penalty that a company must
pay for not having anticipated the future."

Zebra conclusions

The zebra has an array of strategies at its disposal for dealing with threats.
The fact that zebras have survived in such abundance for so long in the
Serengeti is partially a tribute to their ability to respond appropriately to any
threat. Their typical six responses are identical to ones psychologists would
argue humans invoke when faced with threats. As organisations are run by
people, it is not a surprise that these are also therefore organisational
responses. The challenge from the zebra, is that without management training and without reading books on strategy, sufficient numbers of them have
been making the right strategic choice for sufficient time to ensure their
abundance. Our task as leaders and managers is partially to learn from those
who know best, those who have proven their expertise in life and death
competitive environments – to learn from the zebra.

Chapter summary

The zebra responds to threats by a choice from the 6 'F's

- Fight – if you are in a position to do so and the odds of success are favourable
- Flight – if the odds of winning a fight are unfavourable, discretion is the better part of valour, flight gives the ability to survive rather than embarking on an unwinnable fight
- Flock – joining together, even with possible competitors, can give strength and depth. It can spread the risk in the market and two together are stronger than two separately
- Freeze – don't kneejerk into wasteful action – press the pause button. Fail to press it and you could fail to realise the full situation, press it for too long and you could become vulnerable through dithering or inactivity
- Fragment – breaking up into numerous factions – a bona fide response to threat
- Frolic – when faced with a real problem, why not do an internal re-organisation? It achieves almost nothing but gives the impression of activity as the last throw of the dice for desperate management

The minor chapters

Examples of Serengeti strategies

With a variety of styles and examples, several using some of the themes and structures developed in the major chapters – giraffe, elephant and zebra, all with copious examples:

Ch 6	Hippopotamus	(being in the right place)
Ch 7	Cheetah	(getting there first)
Ch 8	Warthog	(protecting vulnerabilities)
Ch 9	Lion	(co-ordinating resources)
Ch 10	Rhinoceros	(keep on going)
Ch 11	Wildebeest	(safety in numbers)
Ch 12	Hyena	(benefiting from others)
Ch 13	Crocodile	(stealth and ambush)
Ch 14	Ostrich	(looking big)

These strategies are equally valid and equally successful. Each of them could have been a major chapter, but I sought to produce a book, not an multi-volume encyclopaedia. The chapters are distinct – please read them in any order you choose.

CHAPTER 6

Strategies of the hippopotamus – being in the right place

A largely aquatic herbivorous mammal, the hippopotamus is a bad tempered river resident who will aggressively defend territory. They have thick dark skin which is almost hairless and this barrel shaped giant is supported by short but stout legs with four toes encased in rounded hooves. The name is Latin, derived from the Greek, '*hippos*' meaning horse and '*potamos*' meaning river – hence river horse.

The hairless skin is such that prolonged exposure to equatorial sun would cause blistering, and thus the hippo spends all day in the water. They have learnt to mate and give birth in water. At night the hippos leave the waters in search of grass to eat. Needing 100kg per night, this is a time consuming activity and it is when the hippo is at its most vulnerable. Predators are crocodiles and lions but neither will tackle a fully grown hippo. The hippo's mouth has an extended wide mussel with large teeth and exceptional jaw strength. A fully grown hippo is able to kill a crocodile by biting or by crushing it by sitting on it. A younger, lone and unprotected hippo could become an opportunistic feast for a crocodile, especially if a number of crocodiles attack en masse. Similarly, lions use their hunting skills of combined attack to deal with a young hippo, but the hippo is usually safe if it is able to fight its way to the water.

Hippopotamus fact file:

Height	Up to 1.5m
Mass	up to 3,200 kg but more commonly nearer 1,200–1,500kg
Life expectancy	40–50 years
Diet	grass and riverside vegetation
Reproduction	210 day gestation producing a single calf or very rarely twins

Hippos have large teeth with molars for masticating and large canine teeth which grow throughout the animal's life. At night grass is uprooted by the strong lips and passed to the molars for grinding. Their nocturnal eating habits are clumsy and destructive to foliage as the hippo usually crushes and destroys almost as much grass as it eats. This means that the hippo is less environmentally friendly and less able to sustain its food source than many other grazers.

Within the confines of the river, the hippo is unchallenged by predators – the lions will never venture into water and the crocodiles know to steer well clear. Large fat reserves around the hippo midriff protect them from hypothermia whilst spending the day in water and the fat also generates a specific gravity such that the hippo can submerge itself completely and walk on the riverbed. The ability to hold breath for long periods of time facilitates this curious habit of submarine perambulation.

The animal is one of contrasts – within the water the fat insulates, the bulk gives buoyancy, the specific gravity generates almost graceful underwater movement and the mouth provides a formidable defensive weapon. The body is cooled and the skin is protected by water. The river resident is then a gregarious social animal with some interesting habits when showing respect to others higher in the social structure. However, on the riverbank or inland, the fat and bulk make the animal slow, unwieldy, clumsy and vulnerable. The body overheats rapidly in the sun and the skin blisters with prolonged exposure – hence excursions onto the grasslands are usually nocturnal, or late afternoon when the sun is cooler. On land the animal feels vulnerable, becomes fiercely territorial and is responsible for several hundred human deaths each year as it defends its territory from human invaders in the same way as it would from other animals or from other hippos.

Graceful and unchallenged in the water, cumbersome and vulnerable on land. The hippo is an evolutionary conundrum as, were it to have evolved to eat river borne food such as river vegetation, or become a carnivore and eat small crocodiles or fish, it would reign supreme in its watery domain and never have to leave for the land where its weaknesses are evident. Alas, it has not done so and remains a nocturnal land grazer. It is a niche player. King of its river domain, weak beyond it. From the perspective of our business analogies, the hippo knows its supremacy in water and its vulnerability outside of water. Many of our niche businesses however, are more optimistic about their chances of land survival, sometimes at their peril. The strategies of the hippopotamus are about knowing our 'rivers' of supremacy and not seeking to overextend into the 'grasslands' where we are vulnerable.

And the interesting social habit – the way a hippo shows respect to those higher in the social order is to stand, in water, at right angles to the superior beast and defecate slowly whilst rapidly moving its small tail from side to side. This effects a spraying motion where the waste matter is flicked into the superior's face as a sign of respect. Perhaps social climbing in hippo society is less advantageous than in other species.

The message from the hippopotamus to modern business is to know your niche, understand the nuances and variables of your niche and make a deliberate choice not to venture from it. Venturing from the niche can be tempting but is fraught with danger. It is a message which some authors have brought us in the recent past – Hamel and Prahalad's work on core competence, Tom Peters' advice to 'stick to the knitting' or Zook's 'profit from the core'. The knowledge of the elephant is still needed to fully appreciate your USP (unique selling proposition), fully comprehend your niche, totally grasp your competitive mapping and issues of importance (i.o.i.s), and then to deepen your exploitation of your niche. Dangers of niche strategies include the possibility of becoming myopic and failing to look beyond the niche towards future areas of competition. For example, I forsee a future where the PC monitor is an irrelevance. We will all have large flatscreens similar to current flatscreen televisions available in the domestic market and small handheld screens – large and small together replacing the medium sized 19" or 23" screens currently dominant. However, I also forsee a future where all domestic televisions will be redundant as projecting images onto walls is becoming increasingly common. For the flatscreen manufacturer to focus and market to the television niche, if my view of the future is right, will be short lived. If, instead, he is able to be attractive to the current PC market there is a brighter future. The niche here is not about the end use of the product but about that provision of high quality flatscreen technology for any end use.

The hippopotamus knows its niche, understands its environment and seeks to fully exploit its river superiority whilst minimising its exposure to vulnerable areas such as the land where it is forced to compete with others who are better able to survive in that environment. Knowing its disadvantages, the hippopotamus decides to spend as much time as possible in the water where he is king of the river niche and his advantages of thick fat layers, buoyancy and specific gravity make him ideally suited.

In chapter 2 we briefly outlined how Mercedes had abandoned its hippopotamus strategies, no longer seeking niche dominance, but favouring an all embracing 'something for everyone' strategy. I think it would be better to maintain, develop and reinforce the niches outlined in chapter 2 rather than abandon the very niche rivers which have generated success over the decades. The management are clearly of the opposite opinion and only time will tell which of us is right. It is my opinion that Mercedes are partially repeating the errors made by General Motors in the last century. Their opinion is that the 'strategies of the wildebeest' are the most appropriate to follow for their future success.

General Motors was founded by William Durant in 1904 and rapidly acquired a number of vehicle manufacturers as this fledgling industry developed. By 1918 he owned 18 car companies including Chevrolet, Buick, Cadillac and Oldsmobile. 1918 was also the year Alfred Sloan, from GM investors du Pont, joined the company as Vice President. Sloan famously described the inheritance as an "irrational product line" with no overall strategy for the business and with ranges of vehicles competing against each other. Price points were seemingly random and most brands were making losses. In 1921 the price points were:

Buick	$1,795–$3,295
Cadillac	$3,790–$5,690
Chevrolet	$795–$2,075
Oakland	$1,395–$2,050
Oldsmobile	$1,445–$3,295
Scripps Booth	$1,545–$2,295
Sheridan	$1695

Sloan initiated the strategies of the hippopotamus. He sought to understand the various niches of the car market and sought to treat them separately. By generating a combination of parallel strategies each aimed at separate 'rivers' within the market he embarked on a policy of multiple niche market dominance by specific niche targeted brands. Price was not the only factor for niche strategies but under Sloan's new strategies the price profile changed to:

Chevrolet	$450–$600
Pontiac	$600–$900
Buick	$900–$1,700
Oldsmobile	$1,700–$2,500
Cadillac	$2,500–$3,500

➡

→

These five brands developed, the specific targeting reduced cannibalisation where they were competing with each other and the combination of brands stretching from $450 to $3,500 captured in excess of 50% of the US car market.

Success was transient. In the late 1950's Frederic Donner became CEO and embarked on 'badge engineering' which sought to reduce costs through using interchangeable parts. The difference between this and the similar strategy currently being implemented within the Volkswagen group is that GM applied it to all aspects of the vehicle including the exterior. The GM range started to lose individuality and the concept of each brand mastering a niche was lost. By the early 1980's the range had returned to its chaotic pricing points and vehicles again competed with each other.

Chevrolet	$13,995–$21,360
Pontiac	$16,295–$32,415
Buick	$26,095–$37,490
Oldsmobile	$18,620–$35,315
Cadillac	$31,295–$48,045

In August 1983 *Fortune* magazine ran an article on GM which included a photograph of a Chevrolet, an Oldsmobile, a Buick and a Pontiac – they all looked the same! By this time market share had fallen from a peak of 57% to a mere 28%. Jack Trout estimates this fall to be worth $90bn.

An example of successful hippopotamus strategies is that of Apple's iPod. Apple have become the leaders of a growing and envious niche within the portable music playing market. Many years ago the Sony Walkman started the niche of portable music in the old fashioned days of tape cassettes. A few variants have developed over the years as CD's replaced cassettes as the dominant recording format but now Apple have utilised cutting edge technology to update this niche and become undisputed leaders. Niche technology and niche appeal is not new to Apple. Their iMac has become an icon and successfully filled the niche of the computer of choice for those in the creative design functions. However, Apple initially fell into strategies of the hippopotamus by default. The company history could have been very different.

A number of industry commentators believe that Apple could have generated the insurmountable dominance exhibited by Microsoft in the late 20th and early 21st century if it had taken a number of different decisions. The core of the issue is that Apple refused to licence its operating system to other computer manufacturers seeking to control and exploit the niche. Meanwhile, Microsoft realised that this was not a mere niche of a hippopotamus river – it was vast expanse of Serengeti where the giraffe, wildebeest and zebra strategies would dominate. A hippopotamus approach to the vast grassland plain was suicidal. Apple perpetuated with hippopotamus strategies whilst Microsoft ruled the plain with the successful strategies of these major grazers. The rest is history – Apple were relegated to a comparatively minor player and Microsoft took over the world of the 1990's and 2000's. Fortunately for Apple, the later success of their niche strategies propelled the iPod far beyond a mere niche and into mainstream. They then overtook Microsoft in May 2010 by the measure of market capitalisation.

Having initially been ousted from the main areas of the business I.T. Serengeti, Apple applied its operating system to function best for these specific users, such as designers. Continual reinvention and perpetual tailoring to the needs of this specific user has given Apple an enviable depth of experience in using strategies to enhance, develop and protect their niche. These are the skills they used with the iPod and then the iPhone. Whilst the products of iMac, iPod and iPhone are vastly different, the strategies are broadly similar.

The 1G (1st generation) iPod was launched in October 2001. 5Gb of memory, huge for its time, enabled users to have 1,000 music tracks at their disposal. Priced, in the UK at £329 the product appealed to the 'early adopters' and became a high fashion item. Early adopters usually have low price sensitivity and will seek strongly differentiated products. With a large take-up boosting revenues, Apple sought to develop the niche to become king of this particular river. Strategies to prevent newcomers gaining ground included perpetual reinvention, aggressive product improvement and active price reduction. The 2G 10Gb and 20Gb versions were launched in July 2002 with the 10Gb version priced at £329 – the same as the 5Gb 1G. This instantly made the 1G and any imitations of it by competitors redundant technology or redundant fashion. By ensuring there was no price difference between 1G and 2G Apple did the equivalent of the hippo surrounding itself with the safety of water. It did not allow predator competitors a chance to attack, and reinvented the niche by instantly collapsing the 1G market. More traditional mainstream strategies of the 1950's with life cycle curves and antiquated Boston box mentality would have suggested pricing the 2G higher to allow the 1G to retire gracefully whilst still 'milking' the 1G 'cash cow'. Simultaneously the higher revenues from the 2G could be derived and in due course the 2G could reduce price as the 1G exited. Apple, however, with its years of experience in a niche market did not listen to this traditional pricing approach. Apple now understood niche strategies.

3G arrived in August 2003 with 30Gb of memory and a price point of £399. This was an interesting move, and created a price split in the market –

£329 for 2G or £399 for 3G. The modest price difference for increased functionality indicated that perhaps the functionality difference was not as great as Apple had stated. Confusion was generated amongst consumers as the products were then able to compete against each other. Apple had uncharacteristically abandoned the river and moved to the grassland plain – 2G and 3G could co-exist in a complete reversal of the successful 1G to 2G strategy. I believe this was a mistake. It allowed the possibility for the 'river' to be inhabited by others and to dilute Apple's dominance. The strategies of the hippopotamus do not involve competing in the same niche with different products. If there are different products they must be for separate and distinct market niches – as Alfred Sloan drove General Motors to. I may not be alone in thinking of this as a mistake because the stock price fell. In the 3 months to September 2003 Apple shipped 6.5m iPods – some 2G and some 3G. The markets greeted this news in October 2003 by downgrading the share price by over 10% – they were expecting in excess of 8m to be shipped. The higher price point was a strategy of differential building and not a strategy of niche building. Such a strategy could only be maintained if new entrants were able to be excluded and the brand enthusiast buyers persuaded to re-purchase. Apple were very quick to bring out a further market offering. In January 2004, a mere 5 months after the 3G launch, the iPod mini was released as a lower price, lower capacity machine to open up the price points which would appeal to almost everyone, and critically, to children. Previously, the iPod was essentially for the adult and generally the affluent. The mini opened up a low price tributary to the iPod river whilst simultaneously cutting off any ability of a competitor producing a lower cost version for mass market attraction.

July 2004 saw the 4G, including the 40Gb iPod priced at £299 – cheaper than the original 1G 5Gb which had been launched less that 3 years previously. In one swift move Apple had recovered from the mistake of the 3G, created a huge barrier to future market entrants and built its strategies within the niche strategies options of the hippopotamus. In doing so it had furthered the successful strategic direction made with the 1G and 2G. Diagram 'hippo 1' shows the products on the differentiation and price sensitivity axes developed in the chapter 'strategies of the elephant'. The 1G–2G–4G direction is driving Apple towards the niche strategies resultant from the analysis and the incongruent placing of the 3G emphasises how the 3G was a departure from the niche strategies of perpetuating competitive differential yet forcing down price to appeal to a wider range of consumers – i.e. moving upward to the right.

Apple have understood niche marketing long enough to know that they cannot stand still. Their future success will depend on how far upward and to the right they are able to take the product range. The main iPod product (1G – 2G – 4G) had by now been supplemented by the mini. In October

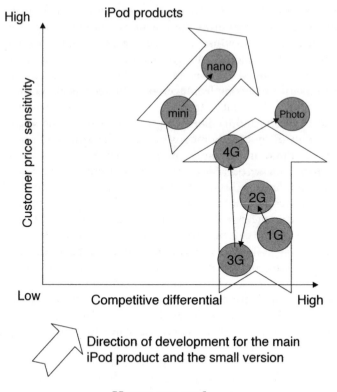

HIPPOPOTAMUS 1

2004 the photo iPod was launched in 20Gb and 60Gb versions with an even lower price point of £270 for the top of the range 60Gb version – further up and to the right increasing differential and making the product cheaper to appeal to more and more price sensitive consumers.

In September 2005 the Nano replaced the mini at a price point of £180. The strategic moves of the small version are therefore moving in harmony with that of the mainstream product – upward and to the right – classic niche/hippo strategies. This is further enhanced by the iPod Shuffle at £85.

Further hippopotamus strategies are in place with the development and marketing of peripherals for the iPod. A vast range of peripherals is now available and the effect of them is to enhance the differentiation between the iPod and imitation products. The decision regarding compatibility is critical. If Apple believe that they are going to gain sufficient niche strength by driving into the top right of the differentiation/price sensitivity graph to dominate the niche and gain overwhelming market share, the tactic of making the peripherals compatible only with the iPod will enhance differentiation – i.e. assist in driving the product to the right of the graph. If however, like the operating system some decades ago, they make the non-compatibility decision but fail to dominate the niche, they open themselves to history repeating itself. If Apple do not believe they can overwhelmingly dominate the niche, the peripherals should be compatible with all iPod imitations. Buyers of imitation products will therefore be able to purchase Apple peripherals and thereby generate some income for Apple. This is why an intimate understanding of the niche is vital and why no text book will always give the 'right' answer. If Apple choose not to be compatible and then fail to dominate the niche they will have made a tactical blunder. If Apple choose compatibility and then find that they have dominated the niche they have a wasted opportunity of maximising differentials within the niche and thereby reinforcing their position. This is partly a decision based on niche knowledge and market judgement and partly a decision based on bravery. The easier, lower risk option is to risk missing the opportunity, the tougher, braver decision is to make a 'winner takes all' dash for niche dominance obliterating the competition whenever they emerge.

Further danger for Apple will come when the niche ceases to expand and they will have the choice to settle for mastery of a river where they reign, as they do with the iMac, or to attempt to spread themselves, emerging from their river and seek to colonise other areas of their business Serengeti – as

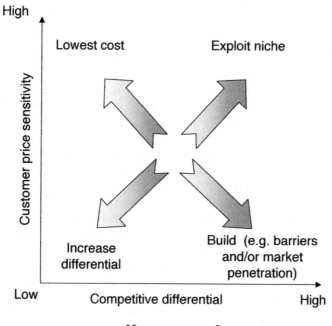

HIPPOPOTAMUS 2

would be the case were they to seek to challenge mainstream PC's with iMac. My hope is that they have learnt from their previous failure with their former operating system strategies and learnt further from their current successes with niche strategies to seek to deepen the niche rather than try to expand it and risk having to emerge from the water where their competitive advantage is evident.

The world markets are littered with the carcasses of organisations who have emerged from their niches seeking continual expansion only to find that they are like a hippopotamus on the grasslands. The established parent company survives but the venture onto the grasslands is, at best, sold, or at worst tarnishes the parent. In either case the losses are usually significant. Marks & Spencer sought to expand its very British offering into Continental Europe and had to make a hasty retreat; British Airways jumped on the low cost airline bandwagon by forming GO and also made an ignominious exit; Carrefour brought their successful French approach to the UK and departed; Lego had a fleeting venture into television; Norwich Union stretched beyond financial services with estate agency; clothing retailer Matalan tried to sell wine.

One incentive for many to move out of the water and abandon the very environment which has generated their success is regrettably the approach many companies have to take in order to seek to fulfil the desires of city shareholders. Shareholders generally require progression, increased profits and strategies for steady expansion. The focus is on consistency of profitability and dividend payments. Unlike investors in Amazon, most investors do not tolerate a lack of dividends or large start up losses beyond the first year or two. Once a growth pattern is established, the investment analysts like to draw nice straight lines of growth in order to recommend the stock to their customers. I am of the opinion that the need to demonstrate smooth, low risk profit growth to investors is probably the greatest hindrance to running a niche focused business. Many analysts also generate a short-termism within executives by their constant focus on year end, half year results and quarterly results. Much of the City expects executives to run businesses on 26 or 13 week cycles with steady year on year growth by quarter. This short-termism is the enemy of success and the demand of investors.

Niche strategy companies, more than any others, are unlikely to be able to fulfil these destructive demands for consistency. A niche will expand and contract not necessarily in line with the traditional established life cycle curve. It may undulate; it may have sudden peaks or troughs. Niche strategies deal with the development of opportunities and with developing niche extensions through appropriate risk. The very nature of these strategies do not lend the corporate emulators of the highly successful hippopotamus to consistent performance. It may even be that it is more difficult for companies exhibiting the strategies of the hippopotamus to entertain the possibilities of public ownership and of a presence of the global stock markets.

In the UK Bernard Matthews turkeys started in the 1950's with 1 man, 20 turkey eggs and a second hand incubator. It is now a global company with £400m turnover and 7,000 employees. The organisation floated on the London Stock Market in 1971 and the cash injection fuelled greater expansion. The city investors demanded continual steady, straight line growth and strategies to implement this desire. However, a drive for perpetually increasing expansion may not be appropriate for a company occupying a specialist niche such as Bernard Matthew's turkeys. In order to expand further the niche may be compromised and the company could lose the very advantages which have brought it success. In 2001 the company was purchased by the Matthews family and has remained in family hands ever since. It can therefore remain as the niche champion in turkey meats without the pressure to leave the 'river' it occupies so successfully in order to chase numbers to make its balance sheet look attractive to investors.

Sir Richard Branson's Virgin Group had a brief flirtation with the stock market with a floatation of 35% of the business in 1986 and a further partial listing on the New York NASDAQ in the following year. Branson did not enjoy the relationship with city investors and particularly with investment analysts whom he said misunderstood his business. The demand for information, accountability and transparent profitability was more than Sir Richard wanted to expose and so, after the stock market crash of October 1987 he took the opportunity to spend in the region of £200m to buy the company back into private hands. In March 1998, in a letter to the *Economist* Richard Branson stated *"the approach to running a group of private companies is fundamentally different to that of running public companies. Short term taxable profits with good dividends are a pre-requisite of public life. Avoiding short-term taxable profits and seeking long term capital growth is the best approach to growing private companies"*. I do not necessarily agree that this is the best approach for all private companies, but I do wholeheartedly agree with Sir Richard that this is the most effective approach for companies who are seeking to develop their niche and emulate the strategies of the hippopotamus – as many, if not most, of the Virgin group companies are doing. Niche trading and consistency may be mutually exclusive. If this is the case it may follow that niche trading and public listing may be incompatible. In order to be effective in the stock market a company will need to develop greater consistency and perpetual growth. They may then be forced into a choice of abandoning their niche and moving either downwards, to the left or both downwards and to the left on the differential/price sensitivity graph. If a niche trading company is considering floatation, I would therefore expect to see active, well constructed strategies to develop lower price sensitivity amongst the customers or to move actively to the left by making the product more mainstream. Failure to do this will result in inevitable conflict between City expectations and company performance as the niche becomes saturated.

In 1998 Richard Branson had come under criticism in the press. On 21st February 1998 the *Economist* produced the feature to which Sir Richard was responding, entitled *'Behind Branson'* it sought to question the nature of the losses and raise the issue of the complex formation of the group and intercompany loan activities. With a veiled comparison to the earlier Maxwell empire it raised some suspicions but made them sufficiently covert to avoid challenges of libel and defamation. On the same day the *Independent* newspaper published an article entitled *'Is Branson's honeymoon over?'* with a similar theme. The *Financial Times* fuelled such rumour on 13 August 1998 with *'The future for Virgin'*. So far, the Virgin empire remains buoyant, trading in the Branson mould rather than the City mould. It is true that losses are being incurred in many Virgin ventures. However it is also true that profits are being made elsewhere. Virgin Blue, the Australian airline has now given Sir Richard a return to the stockmarket where he has sold 75% of the business. His 25% stake was valued at A$800m. Virgin Mobile is also stuttering towards floatation on the London stock market, over two decades since the buy back and since the public debate about the differences between running private and public companies. My opinion is that these isolated companies within the Virgin Group have reached the point where the niche strategies are no longer appropriate and they may no longer be seeking a top right positioning on the competitive differential/price sensitivity graph. In short, they may be looking elsewhere in the Serengeti for their new strategies rather than to the hippopotamus's river. The vast majority of Virgin companies are still utilising the hippopotamus's strategies because they are still in the niche river. For some that may be their permanent domain, for others, in due course they may enact a metamorphosis and abandon their niches.

Abandoning a niche which has made a company successful is a bold move. We have discussed Mercedes current attempt to do this. We have seen Marks & Spencer, British Airways and Lego all fail to do so. One of the greatest disasters of niche abandonment was that of Levi Strauss.

Levi Strauss arrived in New York from Bavaria in 1847. With his half brothers he opened and ran a dry goods store. In 1853 he left his brothers to move West and set up his own dry goods store in San Fransisco to serve the rapidly growing market formed by opportunist

→

→

gold miners. A fortunate encounter with a Nevada tailor called Jacob Davis changed his life and changed world fashion. Davis was experimenting with riveting cloth rather than stitching it and in 1873 Davis and Strauss patented the riveting technology for men's trousers (US pants) at a cost of $68. One of the problems of gold panning was the propensity for the panning action to wear through the gold miner's trousers and Levi Strauss, ever innovative, purchased some canvas at an auction and made a number of canvas trousers using the new riveting technology. The canvas was lot number 501 at the auction – and a name was born. These 'waist-high overalls' became popular with miners and farmers and an industry was born. Strauss moved from canvas to denim, chose to dye them blue and the hardy trousers became the staple clothing of the working man – gold miners, farmers, oil workers, railway workers, road makers, lumberjacks, cowboys and the iconic American, Marlboro man. By the 1920's–1930's every working man wore Levi's. By the early 1950's, these denim trousers, or jeans, became the standard uniform of American youth. James Dean wore them and hundreds of thousands copied. A twofold niche was born, developed and filled – working men and youth.

From a strategy perspective, Levi's then had some choices to make. Up until the 1950's the company had been following the strategies of the hippopotamus – knowing their niche and filling it. Gradually expanding the niche from gold miners to all manual workers to all American youth, and ensuring that they were unique. The target markets were not affluent and so low price and high differential were strong parts of the strategy. The decision Levi's made was to expand beyond the niche and to expand internationally. These are two expansions which take the company from being a niche player and start on the rocky route to mass market commercialism. In Serengeti terms, these were the first stage of emerging from the river and inhabiting the plains. This is wholly feasible if the company then changes its overall strategies and, as Microsoft did, implements the strategies of the successful plains dwellers – the giraffe, the zebra and the wildebeest. It is likely to be a disaster if any company uses the niche river strategies of the hippopotamus on the vast grassland plains. There is no guarantee that even with grassland animal strategies, a product and company who have grown up in a niche river will have the product, the management, the ability and the change of operating style to succeed on the plains. This is an organisational metamorphosis for which most are unprepared, and which none will ever find easy. Perhaps the most important lesson to learn from the ungainly hippo is that harbouring an ambition

→

→

to inhabit the grassland plains courts disaster. Harbouring an ambition to retain supremacy within your organisational chosen domain, may not be sufficiently expansive for conventional investors, but may be the most astute strategy of all.

In 1959 Levi's started exporting to Europe, again as a niche company and with hippopotamus strategies. This is wholly advisable provided that the organisation recognises the river of 'Europe' is an entirely different river to that of the USA. Some US companies have the perception that because a product or an approach works in the US, it will work in Europe. Alas, unless there is the recognition that the markets are vastly different they are doomed to failure. Levi's were successful. The 1960's pro-Americanism in Europe and the radical social changes of the time created a rich environment for a second series of niche hippopotamus strategies. Jeans became the European uniform of the youth as they had in the US.

In the early 1960's Levi's started making women's clothes. Hitherto the product had been almost exclusively male – although most family farms used all available family members and clothed each member in the practical hardwearing denim workwear. This was the start of a departure from the niche which had made the company so successful.

The 1970's started disastrously and became worse. 1971 saw a major injection of cash from a public floatation on the New York Stock Exchange, and to generate the financial growth demands of the City, new strategies were formulated. The company decided that it was not a niche creator of jeans but instead was a clothing manufacturer. Brand extensions developed such as Levi's swimwear, footwear, rainwear and headgear. These are the mass coverage strategies of the wildebeest, not the specific, tailored strategies of the hippopotamus. Simultaneously Levi Strauss was successfully prosecuted in California under anti-trust legislation and the relentless rise of the company in public perception started to crumble. Market penetration and financial performance continued to climb and sales peaked at 502m pairs of jeans in the US in 1981.

The financial success did not continue. In 1980–1984 company profitability fell by 80%. The organisation shut 25% of its manufacturing sites and cut the workforce by over 30%. The company could not exhibit the financial or strategic requirements of City investors and like Virgin and Bernard Matthews, the company was bought out to return to private family ownership in 1985. However, the damage had been done. A series of non-niche, non-hippo, grassland plains strategies with

→

➜

varying successes were attempted including the development of Dockers pants in 1986, retail stores from 1991 and Slates from 1996. By 1989 sales of jeans in the US had fallen by almost 23% from the 1981 peak to 387m pairs.

The market ceased to recognise Levi's as a differentiated product – it was just one of many jeans manufacturers. The market share statistics make sad reading:

	1990	*1998*
Levi's	48%	25%
Wrangler's & Lee's	27%	31%
Other jeans brands	22%	23%
Private label jeans	3%	21%
	100%	100%

Whilst there had been modest gains for Wrangler's, Lee's and the other branded manufacturers, the major gains were from the private labels at the lower end of the market. Jeans had moved from the niche to being a commodity product with negligible perceived difference between the brands. Diagram hippo 3 charts the history of the jeans market.

The majority are competing on the basis of a price focussed undifferentiated product, but there are a minority of designer labels such as Hilfiger, Diesel and Calvin Klein who have now managed to split the market by appealing to the less price sensitive fashion preference buyers. The designer jeans have the competitive advantage of imputed image and what was once the apparel of the manual worker has now made it into designer label fashion.

The current Levis strategy seems to be a mixture of continuing with brand extensions plus seeking to position itself alongside the designer brands in addition to doing what should have been done in the first place – position itself as the original, the unique and the unchallengeable. This is seeking to add some differentiation and reduce the reliance on the price sensitive commodity purchasers. The arrow showing the intended direction of this present collection of strategies is illustrating that the strategies are seeking to take the brand to the right, more differentiated side, of the designer brands yet position with them on price. Ironically, an extrapolation of this direction would take Levi's to the very place they occupied in the 1870's – the only clothing which could do the job and the virtually compulsory purchase of the gold miner.

➜

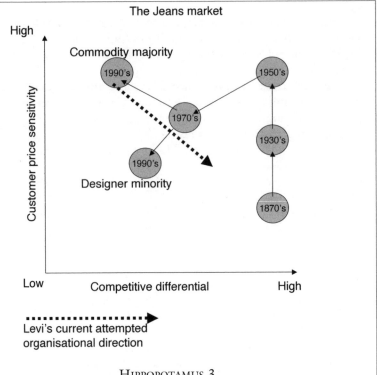

HIPPOPOTAMUS 3

With the benefit of hindsight we can analyse where Levis' went wrong and where they lost their niche dominance turning themselves into an 'also ran' brand amongst a range of commodity brands. Levi's left their niche. Levi's followed the mantra of the 1970's and 1980's that a stock exchange listing was the natural progression for a success-ful company. Levi's allowed the niche to be invaded by a range of competitors and failed to challenge them appropriately.

Strategies of the hippopotamus would have guided them into not leaving the niche. Regardless of the relative success of Dockers, it is a movement from the niche and positions Levi's as mere clothing manu-facturers rather than the specialist manufacturers of jeans for the work-ing man and the young. Levi's stopped being specialists and started to be generalists. Their move to Europe with the implementation of niche strategies was wholly compatible with its 'river' positioning, but the peripheral brand extensions were not and the move into women's clothing, whilst debateable, was probably not.

→

Levi's also failed to defend the niche. The hippopotamus is an aggressive territorial animal who will defend territory with all of its 3 tonnes of bulk. In Africa, hippos generate more human fatalities than elephants, crocodiles or snakes – they take their territory seriously and no-one may trespass. Levi's were the first, the original, but their marketing of this fact has been negligible. They make weak statements to that effect but not with the verve, the pride or the aggression which would make the statement compelling.

Were Levi's able to inject the perception that Levi's were 'proper jeans' and everything else was a poor imitation, their entire corporate history may have been different – and we'd still be wearing Levi's. Some others have attempted this approach. Coca Cola promote the strap line *'the real thing'* with the inference that every other cola is, by definition, not the real thing. Hertz, the initiators of the rental car market use the strapline *'There's Hertz, and not exactly'* – again, the message is that the others, the imitators, aren't in the same league – they miss the standards of Hertz.

Where do Levi's go from here? The niche is now mainstream and so a return to wholly hippo strategies regrettably may not impossible. They have chosen not to compete with the commodity jeans suppliers with denim at low prices (increasingly further up and to the left on the graph). They have chosen to extend the brand and add a multi-brand approach with Dockers and Slates. Levi's jeans, Dockers and Slates need different niche strategies as they are in different 'rivers'.

For all the products, but particularly the jeans I would suggest that they revisit the parallel niches which they once ruled. For the US, they were the first jeans. A strapline such as "The jeans that built America" would link into patriotic history. They missed the chance to tie this in with the catchy music of the film the *Gangs of New York* – "the hands that built America" by supergroup U2 (2002) and have Liam Nielson, Leonardo Di Caprio, Daniel Day-Lewis and Cameron Diaz all wearing Levi's – because no other jeans would do. The emphasis would be on the fact that they were the only jeans that built the US railroads and highways; the only jeans that drilled for oil and panned for gold; the only jeans that turned the mid-West into farmland. Here they would be returning to their working class roots in an idealised setting under the guise of patriotism. Why would anyone buy any other imitation brand? The US is a gigantic market for Levi's and such a niche strategy would be in keeping with the strategies of the hippopotamus.

For outside the US, the river is different, the niche needs different marketing. The building of America would be a non-issue internationally

➜
but the original, the first, the unique would be a positive statement. To
compete at high differentiation level with mid price sensitivity we need
to see high profile aspirational individuals wearing Levi's. 2005 examples could be David Beckham, Prince William and Michael Schumacher
(for the Germans). Alternatively, Levi's could have linked with super-
model Kate Moss who had been dropped by numerous customers and
agencies due to her highly reported drugs issue in 2005, not to
condone drug use but to be rebellious and go against the flow standing by someone who others were dropping – as Sir Phillip Green did
so successfully. The link of Kate Moss and Sir Phillip Green lasted until
2010, spanned the release of 14 clothing collections and made Ms
Moss at least £3m. The 1950's teenage jeans wearing was about rebel-
lion – return to the river. The emphasis on being the original could still
be advantageous even though this should have been done 30 years ago.
Everything else being a copy could work in the same way that many of
us buy Budvar (Czech republic) rather than Budweiser (US imitation)
if we get a chance.

Much of these recommendations are the current Nike strategies –
align with celebrities (sportsmen in the example of Nike) who
exemplify the image you want to project. Levi's could learn from Nike.

The one business crime greater, in the eyes of the hippopotamus, than
departing your niche, would be to seek to enter someone else's for which
you are ill prepared. A wide range of niches have developed over the years
with varying levels of short and long term success – on the UK High Street
we saw examples such as Body Shop, Tie Rack, Sock Shop, Superdrug, Prêt
a Manger and even the 'adult products' shop Ann Summers. Ann Summers
has a particular market niche of retailing lingerie and the more socially
acceptable products of the sex industry. They have emerged from the 'Avon
and Tupperware' direct marketing approach of single sex home parties into
having a presence on UK High Streets. This in itself is a stunning example
of creating, developing and sustaining a specialist niche. Having become the
niche leaders, their success was noted by others – particularly the chemist
chain Boots and their competitor Superdrug. The former has a traditional
reputation as the sort of place your grandmother would shop. Superdrug is
seen as being lower in the market and providing over the counter drugs at
the cheapest possible price. On the differential/price sensitivity graph,
Superdrug would be top left, Boots further right and Ann Summers yet
further right and slightly lower as in diagram Hippo 4.

Both Boots and Superdrug viewed certain Ann Summers products which
were aimed at the female market with interest and considered launching their

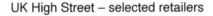

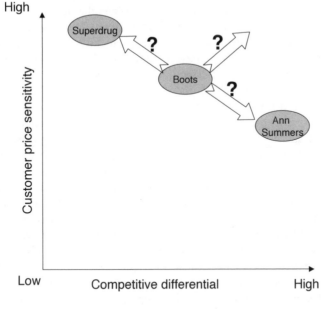

HIPPOPOTAMUS 4

own versions. For Superdrug this should not present a strategic problem provided that they are able to perpetuate the low price strategies used with their pharmacy products. Social acceptability of certain products in this industry have altered over the years and putting some products onto the shelves, presumably those out of reach of children, is now possible whereas a mere 10 years ago, when Ann Summers was wedded to the 'direct marketing' approach and before they had transformed the UK's attitudes and acceptability, this would have been impossible. Superdrug, by focusing on low price and maximising availability by stocking with mainstream goods, can present a viable competitor to Ann Summers – for the most socially acceptable end of the spectrum only!

Boots, however, as seen in diagram Hippo 4 are in a position where their strategy is unclear. In order to compete with Ann Summers for this limited range of specialist products they will have to make a strategic move – in one of the directions indicated. They could move to the low differentiated end and compete on cost as Superdrug do. This would run contrary to the remainder of their product offerings and potentially compromise their market positioning. They could seek to increase their differentiation and compete directly with Ann Summers – this would remove the traditional, acceptable, conservative parts of their differential and so would not be viable in the context of the remainder of their market offering. The only alternative is to increase differential and drive down costs to inhabit the top right of the diagram. This loses on both counts. The most elementary reading of a Competitive Mapping chart for Boots would include 'stability', 'tradition', 'health', 'safety' for example. These attributes are the opposite of those one would expect for a retailer who includes sex products.

The proposed invasion of the Ann Summers niche by Boots and Superdrug is a good example of how the combination of the graph (Hippo 4) and the Competitive Mapping (see strategies of the Elephant) demonstrate where success will occur. Ann Summers have a strong differential and will remain dominant in the niche. Superdrug are able to add on minor elements of the product range in direct competition with Ann Summers provided that they retain their core focus of price minimisation and do not stray too far into borderline social acceptability. Boots is a non-starter. Sex products do not fit with their differentiation and any movement to make them fit would jeopardise the differentiation the company presently has. The only people who thought this potential launch was a good ideas must have been the Boots management because, once the UK press found out about the possibilities of Boots selling 'sex toys' it became headline news. The clash of traditional and avant guard was seized upon, the reputation of Boots was tarnished and the management had to make an embarrassing withdrawal of plans to make such a launch. Had they viewed the strategies of the hippopotamus, and probably the strategies of the elephant, the possibility would never have been developed and the humiliating climbdown and decision not to launch would never have tarnished the brand or the management.

Later in 2005 UK grocers Tesco and Sainsbury also approached this market. As they both have a variety of positions on the model for different products, they are able to place the sex products amongst their 'family planning' sections and utilise the strategies near to Superdrug on the graph. Boots, seeing the entry of the grocers re-reversed their decision and decided to re-enter the market yet without addressing any of the positioning mentioned above. After market research they re-re-reversed their decision and did not launch – wisely.

The strategies of the hippopotamus are therefore those of a Serengeti resident who has a clear perspective of where they have a competitive advantage and where they do not. The hippopotamus plays to its strengths and stays within the domain where he is overwhelmingly strong. He ventures onto land reluctantly, at night and in a state of full alert as being on land means danger for the king of the river due to the strengths he has in water becoming weaknesses on land. The hippopotamus has no intention of straying beyond its domain for long. Whilst in some circles this can be seen as having a lack of ambition, it is a strategy which has ensured survival for hundreds of years. The hippopotamus is ill suited to the grassland plains and so does not aspire to inhabit them – regardless of the success it may observe from others inhabiting them – the giraffe, wildebeest and zebra for example. The hippopotamus is also one of the most aggressive defenders of territory on the Serengeti – if anyone seeks to enter its domain it will attack with up to 3 tonnes of bulk and extremely powerful jaws.

It may not be fashionable to stay within one's business domain, it may not fulfil the perpetual growth requirements of investors, but for the hippopotamus it is an effective strategy ensuring longevity, low levels of loss or attrition and a strategy of maximising strengths to dominate a market. The hippopotamus's focus on its area of competitive advantage and its refusal to stray beyond this area has ensured that it has survived longer and more fruitfully than most of our businesses, and certainly than almost all of our niche businesses who have chosen to ignore the lessons of the 'river horse' and elected to stray from their niche.

Chapter summary

- The characteristics of the hippopotamus make it the master of the river, strong, graceful in the water and perfectly adapted for a life in the river.
- On land the hippopotamus is cumbersome, slow and at its most vulnerable.
- The hippopotamus, like many niche market companies, has a tendency to emerge from its river niche and stray onto the land where it is disadvantaged. For the hippopotamus this is in search of food – for companies it is often in search of expansion beyond their niche.
- If the hippopotamus were to evolve to eat river food it would be content in its niche and never need to leave the security of the river.
- A danger of a niche strategy is corporate myopia where we fail to look beyond the niche and are then surprised by an event which impacts on the niche.
- Multi-branding can run niches in parallel, just like inhabiting parallel rivers – as Alfred Sloan led General Motors to do.
- The strategies of the hippopotamus do not involve filling the market space with competing products, but rather one product, or range of related products, per river niche.
- Niches need to be maintained, developed and re-inforced.
- The hippopotamus fiercely defends territory – as should any niche market company.
- Hippopotamus strategies involve driving price down and constant innovation to create market entry barriers – upwards and to the right of the differential/price sensitivity graph.

➔

→
- Niche market companies may have more difficulty satisfying the consistency requirements of the stock exchanges and may therefore be wise to consider carefully whether stock exchange listing is the best move for them – like Virgin, Bernard Matthews and arguably Levi's.
- Short termism is the enemy of success and the demand of investors.
- Niche companies do not usually follow the 1950's wisdom of conventional life cycle curves and Boston boxes.

CHAPTER 7

Strategies of the cheetah – getting there first

The distinctive long-legged, swift-running cat of the Serengeti (*Acinonyx jubatus*) is famed as the fastest land animal over short distances. It has tawny, black-spotted short fur, distinctive 'tear marks' extending from the inner corner of each eye, specialist non-retractile claws and is thought to be able to run for short distances at up to 120 kilometres (75 miles) per hour although the fastest verified speed from a captive cheetah is 112 kph measured by K.Sprevin. The cheetah is undoubtedly a sprinter and will not entertain middle distance running as a cheetah sprint will very rarely be over 200m and almost never over 300m.

The name is derived from the Hindi '*chiti*', meaning 'spotted one', and the wild cat was once widespread throughout Africa, India and into Asia Minor but due to the invasion of man, the only significant populations of cheetahs remaining are now in the African game reserves of South Africa and the Serengeti. One consequence of this numeric and geographic reduction is a greatly reduced gene pool which makes the animal vulnerable to disease and possible negative genetic variations. Most species, including humans tend to share approximately 80% of the same genes. Cheetahs share almost 99% due to inbreeding. A single virus may have a significant effect on, for example the leopard population, but would probably not cause irreversible leopard decline due to the genetic diversity of this nocturnal tree climbing cat – there is sufficient genetic variety to ward off most diseases. The diurnal land based cheetah however, is not so lucky. One virus could affect a particular genetic framework and as the number of frameworks are so limited within the cheetah population, one single virus could be catastrophic. The inbreeding caused by lower numbers has other effects. Poor sperm quality is common within inbred communities and this exacerbates the problem by generating a high infant mortality – with up to 90% of cubs dying before reaching 6 months of age. Low survival rates are due largely to predation, but lack of genetic diversity adds to the survival disadvantages of the lean speed machine.

The cheetah poses no threat to humans and is unfairly hunted as a perceived enemy of domestic cattle. They are superbly adapted hunters, but cattle are usually too large for them and much of the human fear of cheetahs is irrational. Cheetahs have had a positive relationship with mankind in the past where they have been trained and used as hunting animals by several ancient civilisations including the Sumerians over 5,000 years ago and the Egyptians about a millennia later from their third dynasty. A leashed cheetah was the official seal of the Sumerian royalty and the Mafdet cat-goddess was revered as a royal symbol in ancient Egypt. More latterly William the Conqueror used the cheetah's skills in the 11th century and the Western Crusaders saw cheetahs used to hunt gazelles in the 12th century. In the 14th–16th centuries hunting was the primary sport of European kings and the cheetah was a frequent piece of sporting equipment for them. The 16th century Indian Mogol Emperor Akbar is said to have retained a stable of 1,000 hunting cheetahs.

Cheetah fact file:

Height	Up 75cm
Mass	approximately 45kg
Life expectancy	8–12 years in captivity, but in the wild up to 90% may die before reaching 6 months of age
Diet	Small to medium sized hoofed animals, particularly antelope or gazelle
Reproduction	95 day gestation producing 4–5 cubs

The cheetah has only one strategy – speed. Everything within its body is honed to perfect this one strategy. The list of speed enabling modifications is awe inspiring – a deep chest and large lungs for fuller breathing, comparatively longer legs than all other cats, an oversized liver, wide strong arteries and an enlarged heart for blood efficiency, a flexible and elongated spine, wide nostrils, enlarged bronchi and a larger nasal aperture for increased oxygen intake, exposed claws for greater traction, adapted metacarpal pads enabling swift changes of direction or braking, prominent dew claws, flexible pivots on the hip and shoulder skeletal girdle and to the rear, a long tail to assist balance at high speed. Speed is of such critical importance that almost all else is sacrificed in order to maximise this competitive advantage. Cheetahs have small jaws and weak teeth – because they are lighter. They are slight and do not have sufficient bulk to effect a robust defence. Consequently, a cheetah kill is often stolen by others, particularly lions and hyenas – the cheetah is powerless to intervene and is forced to retire sheepishly from any conflict with the more muscular carnivores.

To counterbalance the disadvantages, the cheetah is diurnal – a daytime hunter – whereas its carnivore competitors are primarily nocturnal. The cheetah then has a chance of making a kill, eating sufficiently and then moving on before the heavyweights muscle in on the cheetah's spoils. Daytime hunting tips the balance towards the defending animal as they have the additional advantage of better line of sight as a form of defence. The cheetah counters this with large high set eyes, closely positioned in a small head to maximise binocular vision, which effectively pinpoints the prey with the accuracy of a sniper. The cheetah will then creep through whatever grass cover is available close to its prey, very low to the ground, downwind, silently and seek to get within 50 metres, sometimes as close as 10 metres, before unleashing its lethal acceleration. Accelerating from 0 to 40mph in three strides, the cheetah can rival a performance car. F = MA (force = mass × acceleration) and so the low body mass propelled by enormous force yields spectacular acceleration. The stride length then increases and at three strides a second, each of 7–8 metres; this drives the cat towards full speed. In full flow the cheetah is awe inspiring. The ultra-flexible spine means that the combination of concave bending when the legs are at the compact point in the stride and convex bending when the animal is at full stretch increases stride length by an estimated 25%. By the time the targeted impala, waterbuck or gazelle becomes conscious of the cheetah, the cat is closing down the distance between them at the rate of up to 70 miles per hour. For the targeted animal, only one strategy works – try to escape. Using zebra strategies of 'flock' reduces the risk to any individual animal, but the cheetah will target one specific animal, even in a crowd, and for that animal the only chance is to run, change direction, run amongst others and seek to confuse the cheetah. The target animal cannot outrun, cannot outmanoeuvre and cannot fight off the cheetah. The only chances of survival are to confuse the attacker and to seek to make the chase go on long enough that the cheetah, the sprinter of the plains, gives up. As about 50% of cheetah chases result in success for the predator, the odds for the prey are not good. According to Schaller (1972) chases of gazelles resulted in a 70% success ratio.

As the cheetah accelerates and closes down its prey, the bodily advantages combine to maximum effect. The wide nostrils, enlarged nasal aperture, deep chest and enlarged bronchi enable greater oxygen intake to fuel the muscles of the sprinter. Respiration will increase from about 60 breaths per minute to 150. The prey will make changes of direction to seek to outmanoeuvre the cheetah but the cat is uniquely adapted to change direction rapidly with claws and pads built for sharp cornering. The exposed claws act like sprinter's shoe spikes granting additional grip. The hard pointed digital and metacarpal pads also give grip but are thought to have a greater effect in enhancing braking – feline ABS. The palmar pads have a pair of longitudinal ridges instead of the slight depressions in other felines. These provide the same functionality as tyre (US – tire) treads with friction for grip and simultaneously act as anti-skid devices. The long tail also acts as a balancing aid to enable the cheetah to turn at sharp angles and at a speed which would be impossible for any other land mammal – a combination of a rudder, stabiliser and weight counterbalance. With these advantages the chase usually lasts about 20 seconds, occasionally up to a minute, but rarely beyond. The cheetah is unable to maintain this effort beyond the short term as heat builds up rapidly during the sprint and the cheetah has not evolved a mode of evaporative heat release as have many other animals – including their favourite prey, the gazelle. If a gazelle can jink, change, confuse and shift sufficiently to elongate the chase beyond 60 seconds, the cheetah tends to give up exhausted and overheated.

For the 50%–70% of chases which are successful, the cheetah gets close enough to the prey to trip it up using the prominent feline dew claws as hooks. The prey stumbles, falls and the cheetah's ABS brings it almost instantaneously to a halt upon the prey. The cheetah then bites the throat of the prone, and now doomed, animal to kill it. The bite is not to puncture the throat but to suffocate the prey by removing its ability to breath. The chase and death are quick. The same physical features which enable oxygen intake during the chase now enable oxygen intake maximization to facilitate rapid recovery. The cheetah is at its most vulnerable immediately after the chase as it is exhausted and hot to the extent that it would be unable to defend itself if attacked. Once the kill is complete and the respiration rate reduces to normal, the meal is as quick as possible before the stronger carnivores converge to steal the carcass. With a high chase-kill ratio, the cheetah is not unduly concerned about the loss of its kill provided that it has had some nourishment from its efforts and, even in areas without the more muscular rivals, cheetahs never return to a kill after having departed. In the Namibian ranchlands, where the cheetah's rivals are absent, the cats stay at the kill longer than they do in the Serengeti but once they depart, they do not return. The cheetah's strategy is 'chase – kill – eat – go'.

The cheetah in business

Whilst there are many aspects of the cheetah we have not mentioned – such as the fascinating chirping and hissing noises they make, their social and mating habits, the care of their young, and their territorial behaviour – the strategy of the cheetah is all about speed. The cheetah uses pure speed to get to its destination first. It has honed the ingrained ability to make effortless changes of direction at high speed and in order to achieve this, the cheetah sacrifices everything else for speed, including generating some consequent weaknesses. The strategies of the cheetah are therefore about innovating, then getting to the market first, gaining first mover advantage and building the ability to make swift directional changes when the market moves. Being able to get there first and change direction at speed is our twofold business lesson from the majestic feline. We need to build businesses which get to the market first, outsprinting all others and also which have the ability to react to market directional changes more rapidly than anyone else. However, there is a tertiary lesson. Getting there first does generate an advantage but in order to maintain that advantage other animal strategies will be required. The cheetah gets there first, eats and moves on. In our modern business world this is insufficient for perpetual business success. It lacks longevity unless we were perpetually inventing new successes. The business which seeks to emulate the cheetah needs to be simultaneously considering, once they have made their market inroads and achieved cheetah success, which would be the most beneficial animal to follow subsequently as cheetah strategies are short term strategies. Vital, but short term. Stay with the cheetah too long and your business gains will be stolen by the hyenas or lions as are the gains of the cheetah.

Getting there first – the entrepreneur

First mover advantage – getting into the market before anyone else – is the specialism of the entrepreneur. The entrepreneur can be fleet of foot, passionate about their dream and have the drive to develop the theme to completion. Numerically most business are small, most start with the passion of the initiator. Jill Barker was a mother who was passionate about the environment – hence she started Green Baby which sells chemical free nappies (US diapers) and rose to achieve sales of £3m per year. Darren Richards started the internet dating agency Dating Direct because he did not want to remain single. The company value peaked at about £35m – and his second date through the site was the answer of his dreams. Trisha Mason started renovating an old mill in France and discovered that she could assist others to buy properties abroad. Her company VEF progressed to £8m sales and 30 offices in France. Other chapters in this book have traced the entrepreneurial steps by the founders of Coca Cola, Pepsi Cola, Levi Strauss and Harley Davidson to name just a few. The key for all of them is seeing a gap in the market and mobilising their resources and energies to fill the gap. Entrepreneurial activity generally commences for one of a number of reasons:

- Frustration with the inability to buy what someone wants – and so they form a company which will do it – such as Green Baby or Dating Direct.
- Frustration with a format or distribution channel which could be improved; such as EvaluationStore.com which used centuries old thinking to produce a range of business team and personal evaluations, but make them available on-line rather than on paper.
- The acquisition of a skill followed by the vision to see the opportunity to use it beyond an immediate network of friends – such as VEF.
- Seeing a problem which could be solved – such as Dyson whose domestic vacuum cleaner suffered reduced suction; or my current favourite – the Cocoa Processing Company of Ghana – who have launched a brand of chocolate called Golden Tree. It claims to have solved the problem of chocolate melting in African heat. Golden Tree is allegedly non-melting chocolate.
- Creating something which was previously unknown – such as a strategy book which is not dry and academic!
- Considering something which is already being utilised – but in a new way – such as Betfair.

Betfair was the original brainchild of Andrew Black (known as 'Bert' ever since school days – we were in the same year at the same school). In the 1990's Andrew moved around a variety of IT roles within London without huge success.

In the late 1990's as the IT industry growth was becoming less exciting and recruitment was suffering, Andrew devoted himself full time to his major past time – gambling – mostly on horses. This was an exciting time in the wider gambling market. Companies such as 888.com launched an on-line casino in 1996 and Partygaming started

→

➜

on-line poker in 1997. As a professional gambler with an IT background Andrew started to mull the idea of a betting exchange where gamblers could set their own odds for horses and thus bet against each other rather than perpetually betting against a bookmaker. Andrew met financier Edward Wray and in 1999 the idea began to take shape. Andrew and Edward formed their company in August 1999 and spent almost a year developing the proposition. The first market for which they offered the betting exchange facility was the Oaks horse race on 9 June 2000. 27 people bet. The idea worked, and most importantly, had public appeal.

The business relies on taking a small margin from a large number of punters and so volume generation is key. By April 2001 the company had generated £480,000 of turnover but with low margins and high costs of setting up made a loss of approximately £2m. In order to implement the strategies of the cheetah, Betfair had to generate market penetration seeking higher awareness amongst the betting public – and achieve this rapidly before other entrants to the market swallowed potential users and before the established companies added horse racing to their portfolios. Web sites, like shops, have a degree of habitual usage but moving from one to another, as Amazon's Jeff Bezos pointed out, is easier on the web. Betfair therefore had to seek to get new customers and customers of other on-line gaming sites to try the Betfair experience. They then set a standard of site ease of use by which other sites can be judged. Andrew was aware that just having a betting exchange was insufficient to have a major impact on the betting industry, with his IT experience he realised, as Amazon's Jeff Bezos had done before, that ease of use was to become a major source of competitive advantage. However, having the most user-friendly site is futile unless people are aware of it and so awareness generation was another key to Betfair's success.

Whilst honing the functionality of the proprietary technology, a variety of methods of gaining awareness were used including conventional advertising – the first advert was placed in October 2000 and also by maximising press publicity through traditional articles and ancillary opportunities such as winning the Ernst & Young Emerging Entrepreneurs Award in October 2002 and the Queens Award for Enterprise in 2003. July 2002 saw sponsoring of Fulham Football Club to generate visibility on television. In 2005 exceptional television advertising was achieved due to high profile sponsorship of 'the Ashes' – the England versus Australia cricket series which is usually won by Australia but in 2005 had a number of the most exciting finishes to

➜

➔
cricket matches ever seen and culminated in an England win. No-one could watch the Ashes and be unaware of Betfair's presence – either from the advertisement breaks, the pitch-side hoardings or the TV 'blimp' balloon hovering above each venue.

The strategy of maximum publicity worked. By April 2002, almost two years after the first market offered, Betfair had struggled to 10,000 users. By 2003 it was 35,000. 2004 saw 65,000 and April 2005, before the Ashes cricket series, the number of users was marginally short of 95,000. In the year to April 2005 the company turned over in excess of £100m and made profits of £20m. It now offers in excess of 1 million markets, has over 100,000 people betting each month, makes 3 million betting transactions a day and at the peak services 12,000 bets per minute. UK horseracing is still its most important market, but a wide variety of non-UK markets are now being developed in multifarious languages.

One lesson from entrepreneurs is that very few sit around seeking to dream up a new idea. For most they implement a plan to create a market from something they are already doing or to solve a problem they are encountering – the non-drip toddler cup (Anywayup Cup) was invented by Mandy Haberman who was fed up with her toddler's drink spilling over the carpet. Sally Preston couldn't find convenient but healthy baby food – so she formed Babylicious by copying what parents have been doing at home for years, yet no-one had previously thought of making a business from it by making it available to others. Babylicious now sells in excess of £4m. The strategies of the cheetah are not necessarily about having the idea – many mothers made healthy food before Sally Preston did – but they are about chasing the idea through with speed to bring it to the market before anyone else does. The best entrepreneurial ideas are often about doing something which is already being done, but in a simpler, better or cheaper way – whether it is vacuuming, feeding a child, choosing a present or having a bet.

Friends Reunited started as an idea in the summer of 1999 when Julie Pankhurst was pregnant with her first child and wondering about the situation of some of her old schoolfriends – did they have children? Were they married? Divorced? Where did they live? The idea developed slowly with Julie, husband Steve and business partner Jason Porter and was eventually launched in July 2000. By December 2000, 3,000 people had registered on the site. In 2001 the site featured as 'web site
➔

of the day' on BBC Radio 2. 3,000 more people registered that week. By February 2001 there were 19,000 registered members. Maintaining the site was now becoming a time consuming activity and so if it were to involve leaving employment, Friends Reunited would have to generate an income. A decision was therefore taken to make a small annual charge. By May 2001 there were 96,000 members and the 'snowball' had started to roll. It then spread through conversation and personal recommendation. By August the 1m barrier was breached. This brought some substantial problems. 5 million site hits a day required 15 servers to cope with the technology of the time.

2002 saw membership double from 4m to 8m. Brand extensions developed to link former work places, teams, clubs, associations and several overseas sites were developed. In 2003 Genes Reunited sought to assist in the development of family trees and Friends Reunited Dating extended the brand further. By 2005 there were 12m registered members, a global presence and an extensive brand.

Friends Reunited is a tremendous entrepreneurial example of a simple idea, well executed and then given a little 'luck' being featured on a popular radio programme. The product was sufficiently user friendly and interesting to maximise usage and the concept of finding out about school friends was sufficiently interesting to be part of pub conversation. In terms of the strategies of the cheetah, it was all about speed – maximising registrations and critical mass before an imitation product could reach the market. The radio was an enormous help at the right time but the continued success after that was more attributable to having an interesting idea, ease of use and very low charges. May 2001 to August 2001 increased the site from under 100,000 members to 1m and thereafter exceptional growth continued until 2002 when the 8m barrier was breached. Subsequent growth was slower and the point of saturation reached with approximately half of UK homes with internet capacity having registered. In December 2005, Friends Reunited was sold to television company ITV and declined into virtual oblivion, but it was the first of many relationship based web sites who have forged web 2.0.

The cheetah strategies were successful up until 2002 – after that it was time for alternatives. After the strategies of speed, the cheetah then needs to rest. This is when the cat is at its most vulnerable. The same is true of entrepreneurial companies. Having reached a success plateau, vulnerability can set in. It all depends on where they look for the next phase of strategies. Friends Reunited could have chosen to learn from the hippo and maximise its niche development – low pricing and

➜
emphasising differential between itself and competitor products or media. They could have looked to the wildebeest by seeing themselves as 'information providers' rather than 'people reuniters' and develop a 'something for everyone' strategy maximising the types of information they provide. Alternatively they could have imitated the lion and maximised co-operation with other sites and information providers to be a part of a much larger whole. The cheetah's job was done, the next choice was critical and was never fully made.

Whilst individual entrepreneurs rightly feature most prominently in the strategies of the cheetah, the feline's strategies can be used by existing organisations to make major transformations of their markets. The essence of the strategy is the same – see the market gap, find the way of filling the gap and get there first. Once there the cheetah will have to look wider for other strategies to maintain its place before the hyenas or lions deprive him of his just deserts but getting there first can lead to initial success.

Getting there first – the company

Most cheetah strategies for established companies are about doing something in their existing market in a new, innovative, easier or cheaper way. The entrepreneur is frequently creating a new market, the established company is usually using strategies of the cheetah in their existing market. It is these markets which they know the best and are therefore best placed to understand the problems which need overcoming. Regrettably most of us find that we fall into the trap of accepting our market is how it is without thinking of how to change it. Supermarkets used to pay a small fortune in handling cash. Many customers paid by cash which made the cashiers slow. To keep queues low more cashiers had to be employed than would be the case with other faster payment methods. More cashiers meant more tills which had a capital investment cost and an opportunity cost of space being utilised which could alternatively be used to display stock. The cash was then taken from the tills to the 'cash room' where it was counted – that is someone being paid a salary. Cash is always double counted – that is two salaries. The cash is then packed and collected by a security company – they charge a small fortune for such labour intensive activity. The security company deliver the cash to the bank who also count it and charge the supermarket for the activity. The cashier, the two people in the cash room, the security guard and the bank cashier all get involved with the cash and all cost money. In addition to this, there is the ever present risk of theft at any point in the chain, plus the insurance payments required to support staff who handle cash and therefore put themselves at risk of robbery. Accepting cash is therefore a costly activity for any supermarket. One day, one person looked at this ludicrous state of affairs and made a suggestion – give the cash away! If a customer pays by a more sensible method – credit card or debit card – the supermarket will be charged a small handling fee – typically 1–1½%. This is a lot cheaper than all those cash handling charges. So when someone pays by such a method, why not ask them whether they would like to increase the charge to their card and have some cash? Everyone wins – the supermarket saves a small fortune in salaries and cash handling charges and the customer doesn't have to make a separate visit to the bank – which has antiquated inconvenient opening hours, absurd queues at peak hours and the ability to ensure that you are always in the queue behind the person who seems to be seeking a Guinness book of records listing for taking as much time as possible to undertake the simplest of transactions. Cashback was someone's very smart idea about saving money for supermarkets. The fact that they promoted it as an idea for greater customer service was a work of pure genius. Two excellent ideas from someone looking at an inconvenience and a cost and not accepting that this was the way things had to be. Two excellent ideas borne from dissatisfaction with the status quo – the first sign of progress and the catalyst for cheetah strategies. Acceptance of the status quo is the first stage towards fossilisation. Perpetual challenging of the status quo is the first step of the entrepreneur – even an entrepreneurial spirit in a large established company like Tesco! It was such a good idea that every supermarket now does it as do most outlets who bank large sums of cash – from retailers to pubs.

Reduction of cash is not the only impact of cheetah strategies on the unventilated atmosphere of the banking world. One transformational cheetah strategy came from within – from what was then called Midland Bank, now part of HSBC. Midland formed First Direct who proceeded to transform domestic personal banking. In addition to the attributes listed above, the industry was traditional, antiquated and lacked dynamism in its competition. First Direct changed that. Their concept was so innovative and such a departure from the norm that for the first time, people were talking about their bank amongst friends. In its pre-internet formative years, satisfied customers started recommending the telephone banking system to others – recommending a bank was unheard of – previously they were all the same and with low customer satisfaction ratings!

First Direct started a 24/7 telephone banking system on Sunday 1st October 1989. The first 24 hours resulted in 1,000 calls. The concept was simple – banking without branches. Everything could be achieved

➔

→

over the telephone and First Direct ensured that callers spoke to a real person and not a machine. Having answered some security questions individuals could make bill payments, enquire of balances, request loans, order currency – in fact anything that could be achieved in a bank branch could be achieved from the comfort of your own home via the telephone.

It was revolutionary at the time. I was a relatively 'early adopter' of this product as this entrepreneurial thinking solved the very problem I was encountering of not working near a bank and requiring a special journey to undertake any banking transaction. However, I was not in the first 100,000 customers – that landmark was reached in May 1991 – I joined shortly afterwards. From this point the number of customers doubled by 1993, and doubled again by 1995. The bank became profitable in 1995 and has returned a profit every subsequent year.

Their approach to personnel recruitment was different. First Direct realised that communication skills were the most important skills to possess above all others. They therefore recruited primarily on communication skills and a customer friendly attitude with the knowledge that banking skills could be learnt later. The reaction to a customer, just the right amount of conversation, and sometimes banter, is something which is very difficult to learn. Every First Direct call I have made has been answered by someone who is able to meet this difficult balance of friendliness, professionalism and matching to the customer absolutely perfectly. In almost 20 years, I have never had a bad call to First Direct. The key learning that we could recruit for attitude and train for skills later is a lesson which many, if not all of our recruiters would be well advised to follow.

By 1997 the internet was emerging as a safe and rapidly expanding vehicle. The cheetah company would look for a medium in its infancy with great potential and seek to master it before others did – which is what First Direct did. The extension from telephone banking to internet banking was a natural progression of cheetah strategies. PC banking (as it was then called) was trialled from July 1997 and fully launched in April 1998. Again, First Direct successfully employed the strategies of the cheetah using the skills and competitive advantages honed in the telephone banking initiative to achieve primacy in the PC banking world, and in due course the internet banking market. The organisation is now well positioned in both the internet banking and telephone banking markets. 750,000 of First Direct's customers use internet banking and almost 500,000

→

→
use telephone banking and so the older technology is still a large part of the business. First Direct receives 13,000 telephone calls a day (40% of its total) outside traditional banking hours – they correctly identified 24/7 banking as prey for the cheetah to stalk. For each of the last 20 years polls by MORI and NOP have shown First Direct to be the most recommended bank and the bank with the highest customer satisfaction. 36% of customers join because they were given personal recommendations – that is the result of entrepreneurial thinking in a supposedly stuffy market.

Banking innovation and 'getting there first' did not stop with First Direct. Virgin Direct is a financial services joint venture with Norwich Union and the Virgin Group which was formed in 1995. A number of products were launched with varying success until in 1997, teaming up with Royal Bank of Scotland and replicating an Australian idea 'Virgin One' was launched. This is where an individual's mortgage, cheque and savings accounts are pooled so that they are charged interest only on the outstanding balance of the net. Instead of paying a comparatively high rate of interest on a mortgage, receiving nothing for the surplus funds on the cheque account and receiving a negligible rate of interest on the savings account, all funds are pooled. The 1997 pilot was successful and full roll out was achieved in 1998. Looking at a person's whole financial arrangements rather than segmenting mortgage, cheque and savings was entrepreneurial thinking and Virgin One got there first. The thinking was so good that even the original banking 'cheetah' First Direct replicated it and now offer an 'offset mortgage'.

Cheetah strategies need not be about creating something new – they could involve appropriate brand extensions. Here I observe a cultural difference between the US and Europe. My observation of the US is that a business is likely to pursue half a dozen brand extension ideas knowing that most will fail but hoping that one or two will succeed. They perceive value in trying something new and less attention is paid to the consequences of failure.

My observation of the Europeans is that we tend to be more analytical, consider a potential brand extension more carefully, including the reputational risk to the core brand and make brand extensions with less haste. The US approach runs the risks discussed in the chapter 'strategies of the hippopotamus' where the niche player seeks to leave the niche and ends with either disaster or a humiliating return to the original river having abandoned the initiative. The European approach runs the risk of being too cautious, too slow and analytical and of allowing others to get to the market first – an inability to apply cheetah strategies due to pontification and procrastination when taking a measured risk may be a more appropriate action.

The cheetah probably has something to teach both those who are more aligned to the US trait and those who exhibit the European trait. The cat moves carefully, silently, stealthily as close as possible to its target and chases for a very short time – cheetahs do not peruse prey for long. After 1 minute the cat gives up and moves on to an easier meal. This should lead those of the US persuasion to consider their entrepreneurial attempts more carefully. Perhaps they could get closer before launching into a chase. Perhaps they should set specific short term success parameters and immediately give up a chase when the parameters are not met rather than pouring money after a lost cause. Perhaps they should look at the cheetah's success rate and emulate it rather than being content with a lower percentage of successful innovations, range developments or brand extensions.

The cheetah will try to get very close – sometimes up to 10 metres – before striking. However, he will sometimes have to break cover and run from further than 50 metres relying on his instinct, skills and speed for a successful kill. A chase of up to 300m is possible. If the cheetah were to lie low and wait for the antelope to always be within 10 metres for a short, low risk chase he will probably go hungry. Those of the European persuasion may have to look at the cheetah and observe that sometimes he has to make the attack before he is as close as he would ideally like. The acceptance that there will be a 30%–50% failure rate is not strongly entrenched within European culture and this is one reason why we Europeans find it such a difficult animal to emulate in business. Accepting a longer distance chase than ideal and accepting a possibility of failure would be something we Europeans can learn. Even accepting that there is a chase to be made and that the prey will not fall into your lap may also be a lesson for some Europeans in applying the cheetah's strategies. We generally do not view failure as having any positives. *Financial Times* journalist Fiona Harvey interviewed John Lundgren, CEO of Stanley Works in 2004. He stated "failure is extremely important" and went on to say that "any manager ... who hasn't failed is either terribly risk averse or hasn't pushed enough to challenge himself, his organisation or the people around him". This is a refreshing view for a European as we generally accept failure in principle only. Perhaps we have something to learn from the Americans.

Of all the Europeans, the British are past masters of failing to apply the strategies of the cheetah. These strategies are not about innovation – not about having the idea or creating the new product. They are about getting first to the market. Having the idea is innovation, bringing it to the market successfully is entrepreneurship. Capitalising on the idea, being the entrepreneur, is the strategy of the cheetah. Previous British innovations and discoveries which have failed to achieve their potential include:

- Food canning – patented by Peter Durand in 1810 but he was hampered in maximising the potential of the invention as the can opener was not invented until 1858.
- Powered flight – not by the Wright brothers in 1903 at Kittyhawk, North Carolina but by John Stringfellow in Chard, Somerset in 1843. He achieved a flight of 10 yards but failed to capitalise on his innovation. Fellow Brit Percy Pilcher furthered this with a powered triplane in September 1899 but again failed to bring it to the market adequately as he regrettably died in a flying accident. He was gliding his 'Hawk' aeroplane on 30 September 1899 immediately before fitting the engine, when structural failure caused a catastrophic fall from which Pilcher died 2 days later.
- Pedal cycle – produced by Kirkpatrick MacMillan in 1839 but, as he failed to patent it, others pedalled into the market, into wealth and into history.
- The motor car – Karl Benz gets the credit for the invention in 1889, but Christopher Holtum was demonstrating his horseless carriage in Covent Garden, London in 1711.
- Photography – not Frenchman Louis Daguerre in 1838, but by Thomas Wedgewood and Humphrey Davey who published their ideas in 1802 but failed to take advantage and sprint into market development. Daguerre furthered their work.
- America – possibly not Columbus in 1492, but perhaps Welsh prince Madog ab Owain Gwynedd in 1170. The memorial tablet at Mobile Bay, Alabama records the discovery. Regrettably his descendents (known as Mandans) failed to diversify throughout the country, remained in their fort based settlements and were wiped out by smallpox in 1837. Had they moved from cheetah to other strategies as recommended, the history of America may have been very different and the official language may have been Welsh!

We could add to the list the computer (Charles Babbage 1791–1879), an affordable home computer (Clive Sinclair's ZX80), the guillotine (apologies to all French royalty, but it was invented and used in Halifax UK in 1286), the world wide web (Tim Berners-Lee – but development and popularisation was achieved in the US), electric light bulb (Joseph Swan in Newcastle UK, 10 months before Thomas Eddison), plus the submarine, lawnmower, crossword puzzles, viagra, toilet paper, vacuum cleaner, television, sewing machine and hundreds of others. In fact, over the last 50 years 40% of worldwide patents have been filed by Brits. Our inability to utilise the strategies of the cheetah have meant that we have had great ideas but not brought them to the market. Historically and traditionally we Brits are the innovators not the entrepreneurs – here is a brief A–Z of a few inventions by Brits:

Aircraft carrier, adjustable spanner and anemometer
Balloons (as a toy – Michael Faraday)
Corkscrews (funny for a nation that has only recently embraced proper wine drinking)
Disc brakes and depth charges
Electric motor and electromagnet
Fax machine and the flushing lavatory
Gas masks and golf
Holograph, hovercraft and hygrometer
Internal combustion engine, immunisation and the iPod (Jonathan Ive at Apple Inc)
Jet engine, jubilee clip and jellied eels
Kelvin scale and Kendal mint cake
Locomotive and lawnmower
Mousetrap and magnifying glass
Nuclear physics and the nature reserve (Charles Waterton)
Odometer (maritime version)
Periscopes, police forces and modern parliaments (although the Greeks created democracy)
Quintessentially English high tea at 4pm
Rubber bands, radio (David Hughes, 50 years before Marconi) and radar
Scuba gear, sewing machines, steel production and sparkling wine (Robert Mansell 1630)
Television, telephone and thermos flasks
Umbrella and underground railways
Vacuum cleaner, vertical take-off aircraft and Viagra
World wide web and waterproof fabric (Charles Macintosh)
X perhaps I can find an X for the 3rd edition!
YMCA (in London 1844)
Zebra pedestrian road crossing.

In many cases it has taken others to implement the ideas and bring them, cheetah style, to market.

Changing direction

The cheetah's strategy is one of getting to the prey rapidly and is ably facilitated by a combination of physical features. These are twofold – those enhancing speed and those enhancing the ability to change direction at speed. They work in harmony enabling the cat to move rapidly in response to the directional efforts of the antelope which is trying to avoid being caught for lunch.

What learning can we develop to ensure that our great ideas impact on the market? This book, in the major chapters – giraffe, elephant and zebra – has developed some new ideas and revisited some older ones. Many, if not all, are appropriate at some point in taking a good idea and getting it to market. If I could choose only one to assist in taking a good idea and making it a marketable idea it would be Competitive Mapping. This looks at the entrepreneurial proposition from the perspective of the market – not from the perspective of the entrepreneur, the product, or the bank.

As an illustration I will use the non-work (and non-animal) example of WWII military tanks. Whilst this is obviously neither modern, nor business, the factors it illuminates are part of the difference between being an innovator and being an entrepreneur.

Some of the key players were:

- The American Sherman
- The German Panzers (especially Mark III and Mark IV) plus the Mark V (Panther), Tiger and King Tiger
- The Russian T34

Whilst there were others such as the Cromwell, Churchill, Matilda, Lee and Grant, simplicity suggests we focus on a more limited range.

The essential first step in creating the Competitive Mapping is to generate the most appropriate issues of importance (i.o.i.s) from the market perspective and then, secondly to rank them in the order of their impact on the market. This ranking will always be a debate and one reason why I am choosing to use the WWII tank example is that the Russians and Americans seemed to have a broadly similar i.o.i. ranking but the Germans had a markedly different ranking believing different issues to be of greater importance. In business we would rightly tend to focus on the factors at the top of our ranked i.o.i. list – which is what both the American/Russian view and German view did. The fact that their views contrasted so radically had an outcome on the Second World War in Europe and consequent late 20th century history. Using the Mark V Panzer, or Panther as a representative German tank, and acknowledging that there were many variants on each model, the bare statistics of the weapons were:

	US Sherman	Russian T34	Panther
Crew numbers	5	4	5
Date introduced	1942	1939	1943
Top speed	39kph	55kph	46kph
Weight	30.7 tonnes	26 tonnes	45.5 tonnes
Gun size	75mm	76mm	75mm
Armour (max)	85mm	45mm	110mm
Manoeuvrability	Good	Excellent	Good
Transportability	Excellent	Excellent	Good
Design complexity	Medium	Simple	Complex
Fuel consumption	OK	Good	Poor
Speed to build	Quick	Very quick	OK

The Russians prized manoeuvrability, the ability to transport the tank to the battlefield by train if necessary, exceptional speed and the simplicity of construction which enabled vast quantities of tanks to be produced rapidly. The Americans were not identical but broadly similar sacrificing speed for additional armour thickness. They also made the decision to power the tank with a petrol engine as petrol was much more widely available to them than diesel. Petrol is highly flammable whereas diesel is not. A vulnerability of the Sherman was its propensity to burst into flames with the slightest hit which earned it the nickname 'Tommy cooker' during the North Africa campaign. It was however, sufficiently light to be transported en masse by ship or rail and sufficiently simple for rapid mass manufacture.

The German tanks valued thick armour, a big gun and sacrificed other attributes in order to gain these – in the same way that the cheetah sacrifices everything for speed which would be at the top of his ranked i.o.i. list.

The two parties will therefore have two different views on the ranking of Competitive Mapping.

The battle of Kursk in July 1943 was the greatest tank battle of all time and the Germans were eventually repelled. Whilst it is not true that the battle was merely T34 versus the Panzer, both were actively involved and the Germans saw the effectiveness of the Russian tank. They realised that they would need to make improvements to their tanks for the future and so, with their Competitive Mapping perspective, the Germans continued developing tanks maximising what they thought to be the critical i.o.i.s. 13,500 Panzer III's were made during the war and 8,500 Panzer IV's. The Tiger did appear before the battle of Kursk, but of the 200 which served in that battle only 40 were still in operation after the first day due to mechanical failures in their complex cooling systems. After the Tiger came our earlier

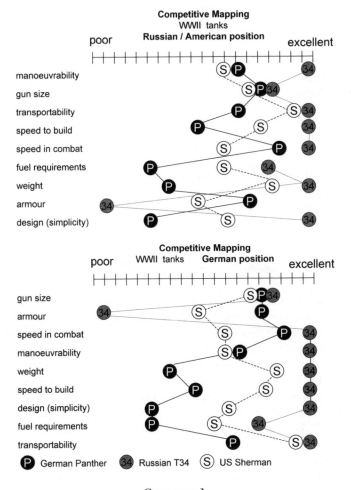

Competitive Mapping
WWII tanks
Russian / American position
poor   excellent

manoeuvrability
gun size
transportability
speed to build
speed in combat
fuel requirements
weight
armour
design (simplicity)

Competitive Mapping
WWII tanks   **German position**
poor   excellent

gun size
armour
speed in combat
manoeuvrability
weight
speed to build
design (simplicity)
fuel requirements
transportability

P German Panther   **34** Russian T34   **S** US Sherman

CHEETAH 1

benchmark, the Panzer V or Panther, and after this came the feared Tiger II, more often referred to as the King Tiger. The Competitive Mapping of the development of these tanks is seen in diagram cheetah 2 from both the German and the Russian/American perspective. The King Tiger, the ultimate WWII tank from the German viewpoint, was indeed one of the most feared weapons of the war. It arrived very late – in 1944 and was virtually impervious to Allied attacks. The massive 88mm gun was such that it could knock out allied tanks before they were even within the range they required for them to open fire and its mere arrival on the battlefield, as a virtually undefeatable champion was sufficient to create severe angst amongst the allies.

	Panzer III	Panzer IV	Tiger	Panther (Panzer mkV)	King Tiger
Crew numbers	5	5	5	5	5
Date introduced	1939	1941	1942	1943	June 1944
Top speed	40kph	40kph	38kph	46kph	35kph
Weight	19.8 tonnes	23.6 tonnes	56 tonnes	45.5 tonnes	69.8 tonnes
Gun size	50mm	75mm	88mm	75mm	88mm
Armour (max)	30mm	50mm	100mm	110mm	180mm
Manoeuvrability	Excellent	Excellent	OK	Good	Poor
Transportability	Excellent	Excellent	OK	Good	Poor
Design complexity	Simple	Medium	Complex	Complex	Very complex
Fuel consumption	Good	Good	Poor	Poor	Abysmal
Speed to build	Quick	Quick	Slow	OK	Very slow

As the Germans developed the tank with the Tiger, Panther, and the King Tiger they were pushing the boundaries of their Competitive Mapping by accentuating their highest i.o.i.s – exactly as we should do. The Tiger was certainly an improvement on the Panzer III by either i.o.i. ranking, and the Panther was similarly an improvement on the Tiger albeit with smaller fire-power. In 1944 by direct orders from Hitler one of his pet projects, origi-nally launched in 1939, the super-heavy tank was rekindled. The result was the focus on the top two i.o.i.s from a German perspective to the detriment of all others. The gun size and armour was to be maximised regardless of consequences elsewhere. From the American/Russian perspective, the i.o.i.s were different and as the progression towards the King Tiger was evolving, the higher i.o.i.s were reducing in compensation for the German focus on developing their armour and gun size. The Germans thought they were producing a better tank, the Americans and Russians, whilst admiring its technical excellence and almost indestructibility saw the evolution as a nega-tive step producing a less battle-able weapon. By their Competitive Mapping the development was overall making a weaker tank.

From the viewpoint of the allied Competitive Mapping the King Tiger was vulnerable and had some severe disadvantages:

- It could not fit onto a railway transporter without its tracks being removed.
- Many roads and bridges were unable to support its weight.
- Cross country speed was a maximum of 17kph.
- It was prone to mechanical failure due to complexity.

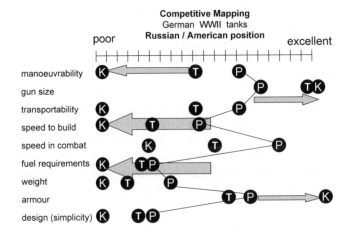

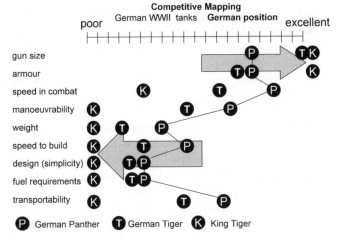

CHEETAH 2

- The interlocking wheels were awkward to repair.
- It was too big to manoeuvre quickly.
- Internal space was so limited that it could only carry 16 rounds of ammunition.
- Its fuel consumption meant that it could only work for a maximum of 80km.

In the battle of the Ardennes, where it caused such fear, more were abandoned due to lack of fuel than were put out of action by allied firepower.

The Germans therefore did the opposite of the cheetah. They produced a leviathan which was all the things the cheetah wasn't and ultimately, despite its technical brilliance and superiority over all other previous tanks in many ways, it was of negligible use due to its disadvantages and poor availability. The availability was partially a function of its complex construction and partially a function of the British Royal Air Force ensuring that the factories were never able to operate well – only 489 were ever produced.

Being sufficiently swift to change direction is a strategy of the cheetah. Being a slow moving leviathan is the strategy of the German King Tiger. The cheetah has proven effectiveness, the King Tiger had negligible impact on WWII. One key learning for us from this example of WWII tanks is to ensure that the cheetah's speed advantage is maintained and encouraged in our businesses. In the words of Harvey Golub, CEO American Express, as quoted in *Fortune* magazine 2005,

> To succeed I believe an organisation has to change and adjust before it is forced to do so by external forces. It must reinvent itself and become the very company that could put it out of business before someone else does.
>
> Harvey Golub

Another key learning for us from the tank example is to ensure that in our analysis we have the i.o.i.s in the correct ranking. By the American/Russian ranking the King Tiger was a mistake. By the German ranking the King Tiger was the ultimate of focus on the top i.o.i.s. The consequences of getting the order wrong can be catastrophic.

One challenge for any organisation could be to revisit the ladder in the 'strategies of the giraffe' chapter and consider the two ladder uprights solely from the perspective of the ability to change direction. The left upright, the external factors, could be enhanced by the competitive mapping as illustrated above and the right upright, the internal factors, should use the culture diagram as expounded in that chapter (see diagram cheetah 3). The left upright would then give an indication of how important it was to be able to change direction and exhibit the trait of being nimble. The right upright would examine the values and beliefs, behaviours, written statements, surface level observations and organisational structure to establish which of these are aids to the ability to make rapid directional changes and which are hindrances. The organisation, provided that the external side shows that the cheetahs strategies of rapid directional change are required, can then view the elements of the culture model to establish what it needs to do to become more nimble.

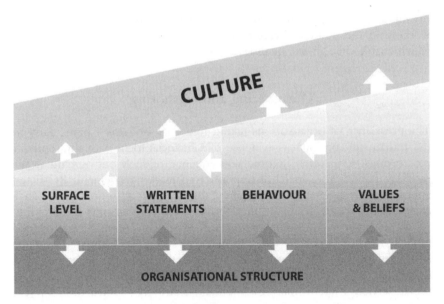

CHEETAH 3

A rapid change of direction created an American legend – the Marlboro man. Marlboros were initially marketed in the 1950's as a woman's cigarette, complete with red filter tip to ensure that lipstick would not be visible. The less than stunning strapline 'mild as May' may have contributed to its utter failure to grab market share and so Philip Morris invoked the strategies of the cheetah. With enviable rapidity they switched from a woman's cigarette to being the staple smoke of the macho frontiermen cowboys. Riding gallantly through Marlboro country, Marlboro Man encouraged millions to switch brands and smoke the brand into corporate celebrity status with a current brand value in excess of $20bn.

The organisational structure, if cumbersome and hierarchical will not assist the fleetness of foot required by the cheetah. However, autonomous groups or subsidiaries could. A behaviour of top down control will not assist the strategies of the cheetah, a more empowered behaviour would. For the surface issues, what are the stories told of heroes and villains? Do they encourage and facilitate the ability to change direction or do they inject paralysis? I would suggest revisiting this model line by line, revisit each constituent factor and enquire of the effect on the ability it gives the organisation to be a cheetah. Action can then be taken to reduce those not working in the desired direction, remove others and to accentuate those which enable cheetah-like qualities.

Outsourcing and offshoring

The prevalence of organisations taking functions overseas – particularly to the Indian sub-continent is evidence of a financial focus with the resultant cost savings. One often ignored consequence of such outsourcing is the resultant reduction in speed of response to a market movement. Restricted contractual arrangements are required for effective outsourcing, but in a changing market environment, these can become cumbersome and limiting. Whilst an estimated £500bn of outsourced service contracts were signed globally in 2008, some are realising that cost saving has hampered strategic swiftness. Realising the advantages of the cheetah, some companies are now insourcing. For example, Prudential brought previously outsourced data centre services back in house in 2005 and Sainsbury's ended their 10 year outsourcing contract with Accenture, the world's largest recipient of outsourced work, with 3 years remaining.

Moving from innovator to entrepreneur

The innovator has the great ideas. The entrepreneur gets them to the market. Clive Sinclair was both. With his home computers and calculators he was both. With the C5, he was exceptionally innovative but hopelessly non-entrepreneurial.

The innovator views his or her product – its features, benefits, aesthetics. The view is mostly introspective. The entrepreneur views the market – all the aspects of Competitive Mapping. The learning from the WWII tanks example is that merely completing and acting on a Competitive Mapping is not enough. Your view of the market's desires may not be the same as others in the market. I recall launching a teambuilding product which I thought highly innovative, creative, had strong appeal to a certain sector of the business population and, in my opinion, would have a probability of success. The product did not generate sufficient workstreams to justify success – it was simply perceived as too dangerous by potential customers. All the insurance cover in the world is inadequate if you think you are putting yourself in real danger. My attitude to novelty, physical risk and 'macho-management' profiles was not matched by customers in the market. I had made a Competitive Mapping and accentuated the issues I though important, but the people whose opinions actually were important – the potential customers would have a different prioritisation to the i.o.i.s – just like with the WWII tanks. There are many important aspects of moving from innovator to entrepreneur – such as an understanding of finance, marketing approach, customer communication etc. From the discipline of this book – business strategy – the critical appreciation is to know the market's Competitive Mapping, have the markets i.o.i.s and have them in the right prioritisation. Rush this stage, or pay inadequate attention to it and you could be left in the Ardennes with no fuel and a crippled super-weapon.

> Peter Durand, the inventor of the process of food canning, was a great innovator. If he'd invented the can opener too, he'd have been a wealthy entrepreneur.

How others have 'got there first'

Innovation – creating something previously unknown – like Dr Pemberton's 1886 brain tonic which included ingredients from the South American coca plant and African cola nuts, or Colonel Sanders making a highly flavoured coating for chicken which became "finger lickin' good".

Transforming the existing – Easy Jet was started by Stelios Haji-Ioannou, the son of a Greek shipping magnate, in 1995, allegedly after an idea by Stelios whilst in the back of a taxi on the way to a Scottish airport. Stelios transformed an industry by doing something no-one else was doing – he took an industry with an established modus operandi, and re-invented it. Reuben Mattus did the same with ice cream in 1961 when he formed Haagen-Dazs which transformed the children's treat of ice cream into an adult indulgence.

Developing a process – such as the one for an on-line auction which became e-Bay, a process to connect members of the betting public in Betfair or a process to find long lost friends which was Friends Reunited.

Reinvention of the company – like a Finnish forestry company focussing on paper manufacturing with ancillary business connections in rubber and cabling. It entered telecommunications and consumer electronics with a few mergers and progressed into information technology whilst still engaging in its original industries – including the rubber company making brightly coloured rubber boots! Since the 1990's it has divested most of its operations focussing on its core telecommunications business. We know the company as Nokia.

Rapid decision making – after the terrible events of 9/11 it was clear that trans-Atlantic traffic was going to plummet. Virgin Atlantic Airways and First Choice Holidays were both very quick to react with vast cost saving initiatives and huge scale redundancies to cut the staff cost base. Some staff even took unpaid leave and headcount plummeted as their market had. Due to such rapid action, both companies not only survived, but when the market upturn happened, were not as cash depleted as their rivals and subsequently able to maximise upturn gain. Many others dithered.

Pace, pace pace – sheer speed at everything – development, market penetration, innovation, new markets, alliances – everything which makes Amazon what it is.

Maintaining the lead

The cheetah gets to the market first and makes a commercial success. The cheetah is entrepreneurial. In order to do this, a cheetah company must have:

- a strong perspective of the market i.o.i.s.
- the ability to monitor market changes.
- a structure and series of processes which aid rapid decision making.
- decentralised decision making.
- pre-set risk parameters and empowerment to clear and agreed levels.
- the ability to make a mistake and the acceptance that 30%–40% of cheetah chases are unsuccessful.

Once the cheetah chase is successful, its problems really start. The competitive situations outlined in the strategies of the elephant chapter will be important, as will the vision of the giraffe and the threat responses of the zebra. The speed and rapid directional change ability of the cheetah give an organisation first mover advantage. Maintaining that market advantage is not the expertise of the cheetah – once the entrepreneurial phase is over an organisation can still use fleetness of foot as a competitive advantage for attack, like the cheetah or for defence, as does the zebra, but relying on this alone would lead to vulnerability, chance, risk and the probability of an unsustainable business. The organisation should then look beyond the cheetah as, having made the chase, the cat lies prone adjacent to its kill, breathing heavily as it seeks to recover from its exertions. This is the time of greatest vulnerability for the cheetah – when the entrepreneurial phase is complete, the antelope lies dead and the cheetah lies next to its meal – exhausted, unable to defend itself or its lunch. The next kernel of learning we can gain from the cat is that the strategies of the entrepreneurial phase can become the vulnerabilities of the sustainability phase. Our great advantage is that, unlike the cheetah, we are able to follow another's strategic example.

Chapter summary

- Speed is everything for the cheetah – multiple variations to enhance speed and multiple consequent weaknesses have to be tolerated
- The cheetah only operates over short distances, with a 60%–70% success rate (depending on which prey) and is vulnerable when exhausted after a chase
- Innovation is not entrepreneurship
- Dissatisfaction with the status quo is the starting block of progress
- The US and Europeans appear to have slightly different attitudes to risk and cheetah strategies – both could probably learn from each other
- Being nimble in the market, with the ability to change direction can be a competitive advantage
- Organisations need to ensure that the i.o.i.s of their Competitive Mapping is right – and not merely their own internal perspective of the market
- Once the chase is complete, the cheetah's problems start as it is not built to defend its gain. For our organisations, the strategies which bring entrepreneurial success may not be the ones required for a more stable market penetrative future.

CHAPTER 8

Strategies of the warthog – protecting vulnerabilities

The warthog is the jester of the Serengeti. Its bizarre looks, curious behaviour and habit of running with its tail erect, like a flag on the rear of a bike, make it a fascinating addition to the Serengeti. An African wild pig with close relations to the European wild boar and the domesticated pig, the warthog (*phacochoerus aethiopicus*) is not famed for its good looks. So much so that the ugliest flying machine ever to be invented – the American A-10 tank-buster – is nicknamed 'the warthog'. The Serengeti animal warthog has two sharp tusks protruding from a seemingly overlarge head and a number of facial wart-like growths from whence its name is derived. These protrusions are not actually warts, but the poor hog is fixed with the name. His face is flattened and the snout elongated. Eyes sit relatively high on the head maximizing their utilisation as a defence mechanism although the actual quality of this is not overly useful as the warthog has fairly poor sight. This positioning of the eyes means that the hog can graze safely whilst simultaneously keeping a wary eye on the surroundings in case of predators – particularly lions and leopards, but also frequently hyenas. The wart-like protective pads appear on both sides of the head with two further large pairs of 'warts' below the eyes, yet more between the eyes and the tusks, and a very small pair is found near the jaw in most males. To compensate for the poor eyesight, the warthog has good hearing and an excellent sense of smell.

Warthog fact file:

Height	Up to 80cm at the shoulder
Mass	up to 90kg
Life expectancy	approximately 10 years in the wild, up to 15 years in captivity
Diet	grass and roots
Reproduction	gestation 175 days, with litters usually limited to 4 offspring

---

They are the only hogs globally who are able to go without water for several months of the year if they need to. Their tactic for this feat is to endure a body temperature higher than other pigs and thereby conserve moisture which would otherwise be used for cooling. It is a tactic not dissimilar to that used by desert camels.

The warthog's tusks are unique. The upper ones emerge from each side of the snout growing to form a semicircle. The lower tusks form at the base of the uppers and are worn to an exceptionally sharp cutting edge. This hog is no easy touch for predators – the combination of semi-circular tusks with the ability to puncture thick hide and the supremely sharp lower tusks mean that a frontal assault on a warthog is more likely to result in serious injury for the attacker than it is to result in a successful pork dinner – even for a lion.

Warthogs are sparsely haired with a long and bristly mane down the neck to the middle of the back. Their skin is dark, usually grey or brown, and exceptionally thick which is a useful defensive property frequently allowing escape from serious injury if attacked. The skin is frequently discoloured by mud as, like the hippo, the elephant and the domestic pig, the warthog enjoys a good wallow. This wallowing fulfils a similar function to the others who enjoy the practice – a mud bath to deal with parasites and a degree of sun damage prevention in the same way that we use lotion.

The legs are longer than most pigs but with comparatively small hooves, each with four toes. These longer legs give an impressive turn of speed as the warthog can use speed to evade attack. Its run is part prance, part gait and the high held tail adds to the comic nature of the beast. One thought about the erect tail is that, as the younger warthogs run in single file, it may fulfil a similar function to the tourist guide's umbrella by indicating the whereabouts of the group leader. The warthog's comic appeal is furthered by the thought that we believe they may have very short memories. It is not infrequent for the warthog to avoid a predator, then to stop 50 metres later seemingly forgetting what he was running from. Further amusing habits would include kneeling to graze and then rising, hind legs first before prancing away. I recall at one safari lodge in Kenya my wife, myself and our fellow tourists were most ably entertained by a young female warthog who spent about 20 minutes in close proximity to our lodge. The mixture of comic actions and alertness toward potential threat had us all enthralled.

Gregarious in nature, the hogs tend to live in family groups, known as clans or 'sounders', and tend to share territory between several families. The clans usually consist of 4–6 animals and are female led. These females form friendship bonds that last many years. Whilst 4–6 is the norm, it is reasonably common for sounders to congregate – a group of 40 warthogs has been observed in Tanzania. Male warthogs are more solitary and aggressive. They reach maturity at about 18 months but tend not to breed until they are about 4 years old. They earn the right to breed by physical prowess and warthog feuds can be bloody affairs. Feuding tends to involve charging at each other head on and clashing heads with mouths firmly shut. Whilst this will have a similar neurological effect to that experienced by human boxers, it does ensure survival as they knock each other senseless rather than use their fearsome tusk armoury. The wart-like protrusions give a degree of protection from this head butting and the fights then progress to head to head pushing matches. On rare occasions the fights may escalate and the tusks come into play but generally the tusks are reserved for predators.

Warthogs live in burrows, but rarely dig them themselves. Despite having an ability to excavate, they prefer to move into borrows made by others such as aardvarks. The hogs proceed to line the burrows with grass for insulation. It is common for a warthog clan to have a number of burrows, perhaps up to 10, within their territory. The preponderance of available burrows is vital to the specific strategy of the warthog which we will outline as our analogy for business. The warthog does not like to stray far from the burrow as this is integral to her defence. If her keen sense of smell or hearing establishes the proximity of a predator the first line of defence is speed – like the 'flight' strategy of the zebra. However, rather than seeking to outrun the predator, as the zebra does, the warthog will run to her nearest burrow. The smaller warthogs in the clan will run headfirst into the hole but the largest, dominant hog will reverse in so that any predator foolish enough to put their face in the burrow will encounter two large semi-circular puncturing tusks and two exceptionally sharp lower tusks, any combination of which would damage the most determined predator.

The predators' only hope of success is to attack in sufficient numbers to be able to neutralise the effect of the tusks and to attack the vulnerable hind quarters. The warthog is a feisty opponent and will not submit to becoming lunch lightly. This combination of a combatative attitude, sharp tusks, speed and use of her defensive burrows mean that the warthog is not on any list of endangered animals. Their biggest enemy, as with many of the Serengeti animals, is man because the warthog carries ASF (African Swine Fever) which can be transferred to domestic pigs, and also because they host the tsetse fly which causes trypanosomiasis (sleeping sickness) in both humans and animals. Sleeping sickness is caused by a parasite named Trypanosoma brucei rhodesiense which the tsetse fly hosts. The painful bite of the tsetse fly will develop into a red sore followed by fever, severe headaches, irritability, extreme fatigue, swollen lymph nodes, and aching muscles and joints. Progressive confusion, personality changes, slurred speech, seizures, and difficulty in walking and talking occur when infection has invaded the central nervous system. If left untreated, infection becomes worse and death will occur within several weeks or months.

The aesthetically challenged Serengeti comedian is also therefore a danger to the Serengeti invader – man. However, her approach to defence is admirable and able to be replicated in business. She protects her vulnerabilities, has a pugnacious attitude even when heavily outnumbered and if threatened has sharp offensive weapons on display and ready for use. The strategy of the warthog we will focus on is the strategy of protecting our corporate vulnerabilities.

Corporate vulnerabilities

The warthog is well aware of her weaknesses – the unprotected hind quarters – and so when threatened she returns rapidly to the nearest of her burrows, reversing in so that the hind quarters are protected and the outward facing part is the less than venerable face complete with menacing tusks. I observed an encounter between a warthog and three hyenas. Out in the open this would be a mismatch – the hyena's jaw strength is exceptional and with three present they would be able to surround and overpower the hapless warthog. Such a fight would not last long despite the warthog's legendary truculent defence. In this instance, the warthog outran the hyenas for a short distance utilising her speed and deft changes of direction to seek sanctuary in her burrow. She achieved this with nothing more than a few minor scratches to her hind quarters as the hyenas sought and failed to grasp her. She reversed into the burrow and for the next ten minutes the hyenas attempted to assail but acted most cautiously as they were aware of her defensive tusks. Each offensive initiative resulted in a series of yelps and a hasty retreat with the consequences of a warthog tusk sometimes even visible. After about ten minutes the hyenas retreated defeated. The significance of the ten minutes is that the hyena can be a very patient and persistent foe, but in this instance they quickly realised that their cause was hopeless.

Our corporate vulnerabilities can be from any direction illustrated on the performance ladder outlined in the strategies of the giraffe chapter. We can experience vulnerability to the left upright – the external perception of the organisation, the brand and the reputation in the marketplace. On the internal side, the right upright of the ladder, the employees, processes, lack of financial resources, lack of management ability or experience, or even intellectual property protection can all create corporate vulnerabilities. All are within our control, but generally the factors of the right upright are easier to control than the factors on the left upright. If the threat is positioned on the S.W.O.T. as outlined in the strategies of the zebra chapter, the right upright issues therefore tend to be more towards the centre of the S.W.O.T. model than the left ladder upright issues.

As part of the aim of this book is to present a range of different approaches in different chapters, the strategies of the warthog will consist of a number of examples where organisations have either dealt with or failed to deal with corporate vulnerabilities. Each of the examples chosen are included with the intention that they ask the reader to consider the specific vulnerability and further vulnerabilities in surrounding issues – so please consider each carefully with reference to your own organisation – where is your warthog backside? Where are the burrows you seek to protect it with? What are the tusks you could employ? To what extent do you feel you have the sparky attitude of the threatened warthog? Are you alert to the current threats to that weakness?

A number of British companies were finding that their origin was a hindrance to internationalisation. The fact that they included the word 'British' in their title was seen as restrictive abroad – British Gas, British Airways, British Petroleum, British Telecom. A vulnerability had been created and needed to be overcome. The solution was to change names to BG, BA, BP and BT. Three of the four made this transition seamlessly. British Airways didn't. As part of the strategy to promote internationalisation and to appreciate that 60% of its customers were non-British, the distinctive red white and blue of the aeroplane tailfins

➜

➜

were replaced in 1997 with a variety of international designs reflecting destinations served by BA. The industry was in the midst of some aggressive competitive activity and the accusation of being ashamed to be called British emerged. The press jumped on the issue and then boss Bob Ayling was vilified. Further to that, the UK had a former Prime Minister called Baroness Margaret Thatcher. On a televised visit to British Airways she saw a model of a plane with a non-British tail fin, expressed her displeasure, withdrew a handkerchief from her handbag and covered the fin. In one televised action, one little old lady had undone the strategy and the £60m rebranding investment of seeking to be marketed as 'International' rather than 'British'. The vulnerability was the exposure to the press and of failing to ensure that all key players could see and agree with the internationalisation strategy. These key players included one press-wise old lady. Rod Ellington, Bob Ayling's successor reversed the strategy and focussed on the 'Britishness' of the product arguing that BMW's 'German-ness' is a considerable asset to the brand. The tail fins are now red, white and blue again.

Lego was founded by Danish carpenter Ole Kirk Christiansen after he had been made redundant in the 1930's recession. Starting from his home in Billund, Jutland, Western Denmark, Ole started using his skills to build wooden animals, cars and other toys. His best selling item was a 'pull-along duck'. The name under which he traded – Lego – was a combination of the Danish words *Leg godt* meaning 'play well' and the fact that one Latin translation could be 'I am joining together' is apparently purely coincidental as the name was in use before the famous bricks were developed. In the 1940's Ole's son Gotfred travelled to England and a business encounter resulted in him considering building bricks as a play medium. At first the bricks were wooden and then developed into the plastic versions we all know. The original launch was in Denmark in 1955.

Lego's unique patented technology was the stud and tube connection methodology. The patent brought protection from imitation and business progressed well. The company sought innovative diversification for a variety of reasons. It would reduce reliance on a solitary technology, it would keep the product up to date and it would further the concept of the construction play format. The diversification took the form of product enhancement such as the introduction of wheels in 1968 and the development of Lego technical sets with the ability to produce working models in 1977. Also in 1968 the first Legoland opened in Billund. This included a model village, a Lego museum and a variety of other attractions. The extension into theme park type attractions was working well and so further Legolands were opened in

Windsor (west of London) UK, California US and in Gunzberg (between Stuttgart and Munich) in southern Germany.

Until the late 1990's Lego had developed well. The company protected vulnerabilities and prospered. The patent prevented replication. The theme parks enhanced the brand and provided a supplementary income stream. Brand extensions in areas such as clothing, bags, books, watches and trading cards further spread the sole income risk whilst continuing to enhance the core the brand.

Construction play competitors had always existed – such as Meccano. Meccano predated Lego as Frank Hornby developed a nuts and bolts play system in Liverpool UK in 1898. The concept was patented as 'Mechanics made easy' in 1901 and renamed Meccano in 1907. Production started in Germany in 1912 and France in 1920, but it was France and her colonies where the product became exceptionally popular. Using the same concept of constructive play but with nuts and bolts rather than Lego's stud and tube, Meccano also developed with a large manufacturing facility outside Paris in the 1930's and in Calais in 1951. Until this point, Meccano had ruled the construction play market, but now Lego entered. Meccano was utterly unprepared for this challenge and failed to adapt appropriately. The stud and tube binding system was much easier than the nut and bolt mechanism of Meccano and the plastic construction of Lego gave it a cost advantage over Meccano's metal. Meccano did not deal with the competitive threat of Lego and saw the market split by age – Lego for the easier construction younger market and Meccano for the older market. This was fatal. The advent of television, mass consumerism and electronic products meant than the older child moved on from construction toys. Meccano had failed to protect their market, tamely acquiesced into seeking to segment it by age and then lost out when the age they were targeting lost interest in building models. Meccano were unable to adapt to the competitive threat and negligible changes were made to the market offering until the 1970's when some modifications were developed. By this time it was too late – Lego was ruling the world.

In 1950 Meccano had passed into French hands and then in the late 1970's became American owned having been bought by General Mills. In 1985 General Mills sold the brand and a reorganisation and refocus included the development of plastic components to supplement the metal basic product. In 1999 the company was taken over by Nikko of Japan and so this cosmopolitan British, then French, then American, then Japanese firm has suffered a lack of focus, a failure to protect its market and a consequent decline. Current production is in France and China and the vital question is whether the decline is terminal.

Another longstanding US construction toy is Lincoln logs. In 1917 architect John Lloyd Wright replicated the interlocking building system used to construct Tokyo's Imperial Hotel, designed by his father, Frank Lloyd Wright. The construction sets were named after Abraham Lincoln in celebration of the 50th anniversary of the end of the American Civil War and are focussed on simple building system, friendly styling, and using real wood logs. The major vulnerability for this product is its inextricable association with America. It does not appear to have had success in, or even put much effort into, international expansion. This reliance on the US as its single market creates a vulnerability which any newcomer such as Lego could exploit. Single market reliance is usually a high risk strategy and for a market with multiple offerings, it is unlikely to be able to see off new entrants perpetually.

A more recent competitor is K'nex which started as an idea at a wedding reception in 1989 by Joel Glickman when he put a plastic straw over a fork prong and considered a whole new way to make connections. Joel's family business made plastic components and he started research the next day. The toy had little interest from the toy industry companies – as brother Robert stated "We got letters back from Hasbro and Mattel that are framed in our foyer that said, 'Sorry, you're off-strategy,'". However, showing the perseverance required for the strategies of the rhinoceros, Joel finally managed to get an interview with a buyer from Toys "R" Us in December 1991. In Robert's words "The man looked at it for about 20 seconds and said, 'How much does it cost and where can I get one?'" K'Nex Industries Inc. was a multimillion-dollar company by 1992 with Joel as chairman.

Lego should therefore be accustomed to competition and the fierceness of the market. They have endured and outlived competitors. They have seen newcomers and mostly seen them off. Meccano made some strategic errors which benefited Lego, Lincoln Logs are essentially a US product, and K'Nex has, as yet, not fulfilled its potential. Lego should control the market. They have sought to drive the product range with knights and dragons, dinosaurs and Vikings. They have undertaken some licensed products, particularly Star Wars and Bob the Builder. They have developed and marketed Bionicle. Lego have also overambitiously sought ventures into television and even attempted to create their own licensed intellectual property product. The strategies are expansive, sometimes aggressive and ambitious, but they are building on the product and seeking extensions. However, all this has paled into insignificance by comparison with a warthog leaving its hind quarters exposed. The Lego patent for the stud and tube connection technology expired and Lego did little, if anything, to make further protection of the property. The result is the exposure of a vulnerability and expansion by a Canadian company called Megabloks who are using exactly the same, now non-patent and unprotected technology to develop products which are eating up Lego's market share. Being Canadian, Megabloks are better positioned to develop in the large US market and being new they are more able to employ the fast moving strategies of the cheetah to outmanoeuvre Lego when in direct competition.

Lego made its first ever loss in 1999 (€48.5m) and a further €134m loss in 2000. Factories were closed in Hungary and Switzerland and in 2005 30% of the theme parks business was sold to generate cash. Rather than ruling the construction play market, Lego is now just one of many toy production companies – mostly down to allowing the exposure of a vulnerability. The fragmentation of the market will be of assistance to the smaller and less well established brands and I expect to see a repeat of the lessons of Levi Strauss in the jeans market (see the chapter 'strategies of the hippopotamus'). If these lessons are repeated, Lego will be under pressure from cheaper but compatible imitations such as Megabloks, there will be comparably priced competitive products such as K'nex and Geomax and there will be the development of premium priced competitors such as specialist architect beech wood construction blocks, the aggressively named Mechamo and the Easy Brick construction sets with real bricks and non-toxic mortar. There may even be the possibility of a resurrection of Meccano!

Challenge for action

- Consider the details of the construction play market and construct a Competitive Mapping position for the buyers of such toys (see 'strategies of the elephant' for the model)
- Plot the various players on the model
- Use the model to consider possible broad strategic actions if you were the executive team of one (or more) of the players in the market (or if multiple groups, take different companies and conduct this for each)
- Conduct a S.W.O.T. (see 'strategies of the zebra' for the use of S.W.O.T.) for the construction play company you have chosen
- Explore how the two tools, Competitive Mapping and S.W.O.T., can be used to leverage each other to generate a series of strategic priorities

---

The protection of the vulnerabilities of ownership are illustrated by the English football team Manchester United. They embraced public ownership with a stock exchange floatation in 1991. In 2005 American tycoon Malcolm Glazer gained control of the club against the wishes of a large number of faithful Manchester United football fans who view the club more akin with religion than business. The vulnerability was the lack of protection in share ownership. By contrast, in 2004 lowly

→

➜

English team Bristol Rovers started a shareholding scheme where the supporters club are substantial shareholders and have seats on the board. No major decisions and no major ownership changes are therefore possible without the agreement of the supporter's club. It is refreshing to see a 'minnow' in the game implementing protection strategies which could have been a lesson for the multi-millionaire Manchester United. It is not unknown for companies to insert 'poison pill' clauses into ownership documents to prevent takeover. This is a bona fide strategy of the warthog.

This ownership strategy is not unusual in football – Rovers west Country rivals Exeter City are supporter owned, and 2010 has seen large press coverage of Scottish club Stirling Albion becoming supporter owned. More critically, Spanish giants Real Madrid and Barcelona are supporter owned. By enacting this ownership strategy they will not see the trauma of conflict between supporters and owners as experienced by Manchester United.

Business names are important. They can be tremendous assets or potential vulnerabilities. When Price Waterhouse and Coopers & Lybrand accountancy firms merged they were highly innovative in their merged name – PriceWaterhouseCoopers. They later decided to rebrand their consulting arm to seek to make a more distinct separation between consulting and audit. This is evidence of seeking to address a vulnerability, namely the accusation of too much cross-over between the two with the auditing arm selling the consultancy arm to clients. They chose to call the consultancy 'Monday', the idea of consultancy Wolff Olins, apparently conjuring up notions of 'fresh coffee and fresh thinking'. I would suggest that the name is more likely to conjure up the idea of 'I don't want to get out of bed and go to work'! Less than two months and allegedly £75 million later, the Monday name was abandoned and the consultancy returned to PwC.

The accountancy world also provided Accenture – supposedly combining 'accent' and 'future' – when the consultancy and accounting parts of the late Arthur Andersen separated. The inclusion of curious ungrammatical marks added to the mirth in the branding consultancies, but over time, it has become accepted, less laughed at and continual establishment of the name has removed the laughable liability. Were I at Accenture, I would have been tempted to abandon the name. Accenture stuck with it, put effort into establishing it and removed the vulnerability.

The same cannot be said for the British Royal Mail who rebranded with the name Consignia in January 2002 – the name coming from the verb 'to consign'. It was a public relations disaster. The original name 'Royal Mail' was established and easier to remember. Assisted by disaffected employees, the press became aware of the cost of the rebranding and after fifteen months the name was consigned to the bin.

Australian construction company Lend Lease provides real estate management, project management, construction and investment management. The name sounds like a finance company. In the UK it has protected that vulnerability by trading as Bovis Lend Lease using the well known and respected construction brand.

Vulnerability to a narrow market can be addressed by diversification. Campbell's the soup company has in its diversified portfolio Prego pasta sauces, Pace traditional sauces, V8 beverages and Godiva chocolates. The 1970's–1990's saw diversification taken to extremes by what were originally known as conglomerates and then diversified industrials. At its heights Tomkins had companies in bread, cakes, coffee, belt buckles, lawnmowers, automotive components and firearms. The market started to move away from cross industry diversification in the mid 1990's and the very strength which Tomkins had cultivated became a vulnerability. Tomkins addressed this by deciding on its core activities and divesting profitably of all non core businesses. It now markets itself as a global engineering group with approximately 75% of turnover and profits from the industrial and automotive sector with the remaining 25% from the building products division.

In 1831 John Cadbury started making cocoa products in Birmingham UK and a legendary confectionery company started. A deeply religious man, he sought, as many Victorian industrialists did, to benefit his workers rather than use them. His creation of the settlement of Bourneville is testament to this. The Cadbury product range started with cocoa and drinking chocolate but rapidly expanded into a variety of chocolate confectionery including, from 1897, chocolate for eating. The early chocolate was of fairly poor quality and was not likely to rival the Swiss, Belgian and French manufacturers. Under the leadership of George Cadbury Jnr, a project was launched to manufacture chocolate of the highest quality. In 1905 Cadbury's Dairy Milk was the result. By 1913 it was the company's best selling product and the market leader in the UK – and has remained so ever since.

Over the next 90 years the company expanded by organic growth, by acquisition and by merger to offer a plethora of confectionery and drinks products. Focussing on the chocolate products, the origin of the company, the extensive brand range had wandered relatively unplanned into a 'something for everyone' strategy of the wildebeest. There was a vast range including household name brands such as Caramel, Crème egg (launched 1971), Crunchie (1929), Flake (1920, and dipped flake 2003), Picnic (launched 1958 and relaunched 1999), Roses (a brand worth £56m alone), Turkish Delight (produced under the name Fry's – merger 1919), Wispa and others. Separate marketing support of such a vast array of consumer choice is an expensive activity as the washing powder users of wildebeest strategies, Procter & Gamble and Unilever will testify. In 2003 Cadbury took the bold step of umbrella branding their chocolate confectionery products under the overall title of their strongest, longest lasting and most durable brand – Cadbury's Dairy Milk (CDM). Some umbrella branded products had a name change – chocolate bars such as Fruit & Nut became Dairy Milk Fruit & Nut and Caramel became Dairy Milk Caramel. Others retained their original name but had the addition of gratuitous use of the Cadbury name, logo and the patented shade of purple. The yellow of Flake remained but with a strong purple patch from CDM. The blue of Picnic and the lighter purple of Turkish delight were similarly adorned.

Cadbury were taking the strength of their brands and seeking to mould them under the CDM umbrella. This was, on one side, a dangerous strategy as it took the primary brand, CDM, and ran the risk of diluting it by such blatant association with ancillary products. On the other hand it was a superb strategy of the warthog by protecting the vulnerability of brand multiplicity. Each brand alone was fairly strong, but the combined umbrella brand developed mutual fortification. In addition to the strength in combination is the obvious knock on effect that advertising support for CDM will have a subsidiary minor support for the ancillary umbrella branded products – a financial effect which has undoubtedly not gone unnoticed!

In 2010 Kraft completed a take-over of Cadbury's which catapulted the group to being the market leader by volume (14.8% of the global market) with Mars close behind at 14.6%, followed by Nestle at 7.8%, Hershey 4.6% and Ferrero 4.5% (Top 5 have 46.3% of the market). Kraft/Cadbury appear to be better established in the emerging markets and so have immediate growth potential. However, Mars and Nestle will not remain idle and will undoubtedly seek to capitalise on the trauma of takeover which Kraft/Cadbury will inevitably suffer. The first half of the decade could be an interesting one to watch in the confectionery market with some vulnerabilities to be protected and some aggressive moves to make by all parties.

Whilst Cadbury's moved to protect the vulnerability by umbrella branding, other organisations have moved in an alternative direction. I have already commented on Mercedes failing to protect their brand, in my opinion, by developing a series of low entry point products such as the 'A' class. Only time will tell if they have adequately protected the core brand with these low price offshoots but initial signs are not promising. Another example of the motor industry failing to protect something adequately would be with Chevrolet when it introduced the Monza (1975–1980). The vulnerability was built in to the design as the entire engine needed to be removed in order to change the spark plugs thus multiplying servicing complexity and costs. Chevrolet are not alone in creating vulnerabilities through design. The original design of the Ford Pinto were such that the pipe from the petrol cap to the tank would tear loose in a rear end collision. The tank would be shunted forward against the hot rear axle metal and spillage would result. If a spark was generated from either loose wiring or scraping metal in the shunt, an explosion could occur. It is estimated that at least 500 people died as a result of this design vulnerability, and it took Ford 8 years to correct the fault.

However, the prize for the most expensive design vulnerability goes to the US Mariner space programme. $18m was spent in order to get a look at the planet Venus. The craft was meticulously designed and manufactured and the launch was perfect – for a few minutes. The unmanned craft then inexplicably veered right and crashed into the Atlantic ocean. It did exactly as it was programmed to. The design vulnerability was allegedly that a programmer had omitted a minus sign on a set of electronic directions and there was no checking procedure to verify this part of the programme.

Protected exits are a trait of the warthog. In the televised example of the warthog eluding and successfully defending herself from 3 hyenas, she beat a hasty but well enacted retreat. Carrefour have beat hasty but well executed retreats in several countries due to their strategy, not dissimilar to that of GE under Jack Welch, of either being in the top 3 in any country or exiting. The entrance and rapid exit in the UK market in the 1970's was probably an expensive mistake, but great learning. Then CEO, Jose Luis Duran continued the strategy with exits in Mexico (27 stores) and Japan (7 hypermarkets) in 2004, in both cases selling to indigenous companies. In 2005, Carrefour were still only 8th in the Czech Republic and exited by selling 11 stores to UK giant Tesco, together with 4 Slovakian stores. Tesco, in turn has sold 6 stores and 2 shopping centres in Taiwan to Carrefour to boost the French retailer's position there, adding £57.5m in cash to make up the difference. Carrefour have protected their vulnerabilities of overextension and disproportionate focus by replicating the successful GE strategy. This is not a retrenchment or retreat as they still operate in 3 times as many countries as Wal-Mart. It is a protection of financial and reputational aspects of the business – a strategy of the warthog.

When disaster strikes

It is inevitable that business will never progress along a perpetually smooth path – disasters will happen. The utilisations of the strategies of the warthog in these instances are about protecting vulnerabilities and minimising loss during a disaster. In 1999 Coca Cola suffered contamination of its product in Belgium with a number of people suffering ill effects after drinking the popular brand. Coca Cola's response to the situation was weak – it withdrew approximately 2.5m bottles 2 days after the issue came to light. It did nothing else. Coca Cola did not give immediate useful information to the public, nor the authorities, it did not take a proactive stance and manage the situation, but it just allowed events to drift. Rather than taking action to protect its vulnerabilities, it chose inaction. Events spiralled beyond Coca Cola's control as Belgian Health Minister, Luc Van den Bossche, urged Belgians not to drink Coca-Cola. Later The Belgian Government banned the sale of all Coca-Cola drinks. Other European countries – France, the Netherlands and Luxembourg – started taking Coca-Cola soft drinks off their shelves and 2 states in Germany considered conducting spot tests on Coca-Cola products. French authorities then suspended the sale of all canned drinks manufactured by the Coca-Cola company as the French Junior Commerce Minister, Marylise Lebranchu, said France was not satisfied with Coca-Cola's explanations for the health scare and illnesses in Belgium. Coca Cola's inaction led to a reputational damage to the world's largest brand and even Philippe Lenfant, Director General of bottling at Coca Cola Enterprises Belgium admitted "we perhaps lost control of the situation". When CEO Douglas Ivester eventually communicated with the public via a newspaper advert he said "my apologies ... I should have spoken [to the public] earlier".

The world's previously best known bottled water, Perrier, equally mishandled their crisis of 1990 when carcinogenic benzene was found in the product. They asserted that the problem was localised in France, only for it to be found in North America. The market makers lost confidence in the company and its management, the share price plummeted 40% and the Swiss giant Nestle pounced to takeover the business at such a deflated bargain price.

Conversely, in 1999 when KFC discovered that some of its chicken, also from Belgium, was contaminated with dioxins it acted swiftly, decisively and publicly. All Belgian produce was instantly withdrawn and a PR offensive was instigated. The rapid response still brought bad publicity – there was still contamination, but the speed, effectiveness and publicity of the response reassured consumers.

The difficulty CEO's often face is the legal advice to say little and admit nothing for fear of lawsuits. In the cases of Coca Cola and Perrier above, this was disastrous advice. When disaster strikes, the vulnerability of the brand must be protected and actively managed. The warthog does not delay in getting that vulnerable rear protected when the disaster of marauding hyenas approaches. Nor should we. Our organisations should operate with rapid crisis management responses to protect the brand. For many, their crisis management plans are weak, or non-existent.

Recession planning

Another area of inadequate protection of a vulnerability is that of planning for a downturn in organisational performance. Without it, responses are either too slow, too shallow or poorly thought out. These then have to be revisited and phase 2, then 3, then 4 of an organisational 'death by 1,000 cuts' lumbers onwards. I am of the opinion that every organisation should have a recession plan where it takes a range of pessimistic scenarios and assesses what it would do were these events to become reality. By spending the time doing this it can save effort and angst compared to having to make a rushed and partially thought through plan in the event of a recession actually happening. A rushed plan can be a fatal plan. A carefully thought through plan, shelved and then taken off the shelf in time of need can mean rapid saving action when all competitors are flapping and panicking about what they should do.

Developing a recession plan is not as simple as merely asking what would be done if sales dried up. It should:

- Consider how previous recessions have affected the specific industry
- Add opinions which would mean that a future recession would have a different effect from a past recession
- Do the numbers – set a recession barometer with three depressingly deeper levels of recession
- Set 'traffic light' indicators for each level – when they turn 'red' the plan gets implemented that day
- Work backwards for each level on the barometer to determine the cost base which can be afforded yet ensure survival
- Plan that cost base in detail – the more specific the better. Rather than stating that the executive board is reduced from 7 to 4 people, decide in advance who are the 3 to go. Certainty will benefit all, including the 3, and curtail unhelpful male lion territorial behaviour or irrelevant ostrich strategy posturing
- I would also advise starting at the top – make executive pay cuts, executive bonus abandonment, executive redundancies and executive benefit restraints deeper, tougher and quicker than any other – lead by example

The plan can then sit on the shelf hopefully never to emerge, but with the reassurance that rapid action can result if the lights do turn red. The traffic lights do not have to be observed by all – they just need a guardian or custodian who will alert all when any one turns amber and at that point they need to be observed by the whole board regularly.

Warthog vulnerabilities

The list of potential vulnerabilities for the warthog companies to protect could be almost endless – we have discussed examples of:

- Origin – BA, BP, BG, BT
- Market positioning and unique offering – Lego and Meccano
- New competition – K'Nex and Megabloks
- Ownership – Manchester United
- Name – PwC/Lend Lease/Royal Mail
- Exposure through limited diversification – Campbell's
- Brand overdiversification – Cadbury's
- Brand character – Mercedes, BMW, Porche
- Design vulnerabilities – Chevrolet's Monza and Ford's Pinto
- Image and successful market exits – Carrefour
- Recession – and the need to plan for the worst but hope for the best

There could be dozens more – such as:

- The supply chain – two 2005 examples, Land Rover struggled to obtain petrol engines for their Freelander after the demise of Rover and British Airways had to offer a depleted service due to a dispute within its caterer Gate Gourmet.
- Shareholder reputation – see the various financial scandals which heralded in the cumbersome Sarbanes-Oxley requirements in the US or the Higgs recommendations in the UK.
- Public reputation – see British Airways after the 'dirty tricks' campaign and lawsuit with Virgin Atlantic or the collapse and near collapse of various financial organisations 2008–9.
- Control systems – financial companies such as Lehman Brothers, or more recently Mizuho Securities (Japan's second largest bank) with the laughably termed 'fat finger' syndrome where millions of pounds/dollars/yen are lost when a stock market dealer keys an error – £132m in Mizuho's case, £30bn in Lehman's.
- Inability to adapt – see the French wine industry's inability to change with the world market and the consequential erosion of its previous

dominance by the Australians, Californians and now Chileans, Argentineans, and even the Italian and Spanish!

For any company perhaps the best test is to revisit the Competitive Mapping outlined in the strategies of the elephant chapter and seek to evaluate the vulnerabilities of the elements (or i.o.i.s) which give the company its unique selling proposition (USP) or give the customer the reason to buy from them rather than anyone else (my competitive advantage definition). Once identified, active warthog strategies for their protection could be developed and the successes of some of our examples – Cadbury's, Campbell's, Carrefour, could be emulated. Fail to do so and the failures of some of our other examples could be your corporate inheritance.

Chapter summary

- The warthog has sharp tusks and a truculent nature, but vulnerable hindquarters.
- Reversing into one of several burrows in her domain protects the vulnerable quarters and presents an aggressor with the sharp tusks to contend with.
- Organisational vulnerabilities need protecting. They can come in a wide variety of forms but summarise to:
  - What gives a company its USP?
  - What causes a customer to choose you rather than someone else?
- Failure to actively protect the vulnerable butt will more than likely result not in a sharp kick but in extinction.

CHAPTER 9

Strategies of the lion – co-ordinating resources

The lion is unique amongst cats in that it is the only known social cat. Undoubtedly Africa's greatest land predator with a low build but powerful, heavy and fearsome, the lion is the most abundant of the Serengeti cats. Samuel Johnson in his 1755 'D*ictionary of the English Language*' described the lion as "the fiercest and most magnanimous of all four legged beasts". Even today, few would disagree with him. They spend most of the day, up to 20 hours, resting and become active in their search for food in the late afternoon when the day starts cooling. Despite that, it is not unusual to observe them hunting at other times in the day and frequently at night. The dominant male controls a pride of several females and lives from their hunting successes.

Male lions are the only cats to have their distinctive manes. It is thought that the mane offers protection when fighting and is a long distance indicator of gender but is also an indication of breeding potential because mane development is spurred by testosterone. Another unique, but less useful feature exhibited by this powerful feline is that both male and females have tufted tails although there appears to be no practical reason for this. The females are the hunters working with precision and co-ordination to great effect. In many cases the females are observed as specialists in the team hunting effort – some chasing the prey towards others who specialise in the kill. Some groups have also been observed taking different roles depending on the prey being sought. This makes the lion the undisputed expert in co-ordinating their efforts and resources in co-operative hunting, simultaneously using each lioness' skills to achieve the objective of species survival.

Lion fact file:

Height	Up 1.3 metres at the shoulder
Mass	up to 250kg (male) 180kg (female)
Life expectancy	up to 16 years (male), 18 years (female), up to 20 years in captivity
Diet	Prey generally consists of wildebeest, zebra, giraffes, buffalo and gazelles but occasionally, lions may hunt young elephants, rhinoceros or hippopotamus provided that the heavyweight parent is absent. They also sometimes scavenge food, chasing away hyenas, cheetahs, leopards and other carnivores from their kills.
Reproduction	Gestation of 120 days can lead to as many as 6 cubs although 3–4 is most common. Approximately 50% of cubs survive the first year.

The lion's name derives originally from '*leon*' which is of Greek origin and the Latin species name '*panthera leo*' refers to all 36 species of lion. These majestic carnivores once lived throughout Southern Europe, almost all of Africa and several parts of Asia. Their habitat tolerance is broad, with only desert and tropical rainforest being unfavourable. Savannah grass plains, thick or light scrub bush and open woodlands are all acceptable domains. It is ironic that they are sometimes colloquially referred to as 'the king of the jungle' as they are not found in tropical rainforest jungles! Today they are mostly confined to the protected reserves, including those on the Serengeti, although a few still reside elsewhere such as the Gir forest of India.

A group of lions is termed a 'pride' and pride size in the Serengeti and else-where correlates to the availability of prey. Lean times will generate smaller prides and the arid regions of South Africa's Kalahari Gemsbok National Park have an average pride size of 2.2. In the Serengeti, prey is more abundant and pride size is significantly larger with the largest prides being observed near the Ngorongoro crater where the seasonal migration generates abundance. Here prides of 20 females can frequently exist. The pride is a social unit but can subdivide. These subdivisions can result in many lions spending long periods of time alone, although the pride will regroup and subsequently subdivide again to spread out over the vast areas of their territory.

The early 1990's saw a number of new studies on lion behaviour and Stander (1992) found a complex division of labour in hunting. He noted that some lionesses always acted as 'wings' who would chase the prey and some, usually the larger, heavier ones, operated as 'centres' who would deliver the final kill. Joubert (1993) went a stage further and noted some lionesses switching roles for different prey with consistency. For example, a lioness may take the lead when hunting a warthog but act as a chasing 'wing' or 'flanker' when chasing wildebeest. Joubert also observed that these roles were often consistent but many were not rigidly fixed. Many lionesses could switch roles if required. This specialisation, role alteration and co-operative behaviour is not unique in the animal kingdom as chimpanzees are also observed using similar strategies; however, the lion is the only co-ordinated hunter in the Serengeti. McBride (1990) and Mills and Biggs (1993) observed that prides had different prey selection, different hunt techniques and even different killing techniques. This indicates an ability to learn and maybe experiment rather than a genetic programming of hunting behaviour.

Whilst the females provide the food for the pride, the males focus their energies on protecting their tenure of the pride and rarely participate in hunts. Standler's 1992 study, albeit in Namibia rather than the Serengeti, observed that males only participated in 18 of 461 hunting forays (4%). Despite this, the larger, stronger male makes his way to the carcass and eats first. This male lifestyle may not be quite the utopian existence it seems as average pride tenure is in the region of 2.5 years. A new challenger will enter the territory, fight the existing dominant male and if successful eject the male from the region. He will then systematically kill all the cubs of the ousted male. This infanticide appears repugnant to us and an obstacle to species survival but the females will soon become ready to mate once their young are killed and the new ruler of the pride will them generate his own offspring. For the first 3 months after the pride tenure has changed, most females remain infertile. After this time, tenure has stabilised and females become synchronically fertile so that a further 6 months later, the pride will again become a nursery. One consequence of this synchronicity is that the young can be cared for by the collective pride thus freeing some mothers for hunting rather than each having permanent protective duties and thus being unproductive as hunters. The care of the young is sufficiently communal for young to feed from any lactating female, not just their mother. Shared nurseries are another example of the lion's social co-ordinated behaviour.

The co-ordinated hunting and social behaviour yield a number of advantages for the lion:

- Shared kills reduce the possibility of no food for any one individual.
- Defence of the young in 'nurseries' allows mothers to hunt and provide meat which would have been impossible if they were babysitting.
- The alternative of leaving their young defenceless whilst they seek food, as the giraffe does, is also avoided.
- A larger pride enables a larger territory to be defended and reaps the benefits of greater potential from a greater area.
- Any individual injury and consequent inability to hunt may not lead to starvation as it would in a solitary existence.
- Larger numbers enhance the ability to scavenge, or steal other predators kills – such as hyenas or cheetahs.

The male lion in business

The primary concern of the male lion is maintaining his tenure of the pride. He is on the constant look-out for other males who may threaten his position, and when they are encountered his entire focus is on the eradication of their threat. This can be achieved without severe bloodshed as posturing and mild skirmishing may see off the less determined opponent. For our business analogy there is a positive and a negative aspect relating to executive behaviour. The difference between what makes it positive or negative is one of focus. If the male lion's focus on using his attributes is primarily external to the organisation it is likely to be positive, if the focus is essentially internal within his organisation it is likely to have a negative effect. First, the positive.

Emulate the male lion

The male is removed from the day to day activity of survival. His participation in hunting is negligible and his contribution to rearing the young is primarily protective. In some ways he is a model C.E.O. for the pride. If a C.E.O. is getting drawn into the operational activities of hunting and rearing the young, he or she is failing as a C.E.O. assuming the role of the lioness rather than the lion. The male lion's decisions are about pride survival, hunting grounds, where and when to move. The male lion assumes the role of the strategist. He is not concerned with what prey the lionesses attack or how to attack it – he is merely concerned with ensuring that they are in the right place to generate sufficient meat to ensure the pride achieves its corporate objectives – survival. He also has the added weight to be a supreme defender of the pride were any other animal to threaten it.

Were the male lion to be more active in hunting he may be insufficiently removed from the operational aspects to make effective strategic decisions. If drawn into hunting, he may not see a threat until it is too late. From this perspective, the male lion therefore deserves the first share of any kill due to the benefit he brings to the pride which, without him, would wander directionless and have depreciated survival prospects.

Another positive of the male lion is when lions scavenge. Lions and hyenas, and other predators, regularly steal each other's kills. Hyenas will be able to stand up to a lioness or small number of lionesses provided that they have a reasonable numeric advantage. When a male lion is on the scene, his additional strength and consequent ability to see off larger numbers of hyenas tips the balance significantly. In business, the male lion executive may be able to scavenge good ideas from others and implement them well, where a less robust animal may not. Examples of this sort of male lion behaviour in the retail industry could be Primark implementing some of Monsoon's good ideas or the way in which Matalan was started when John Hargreaves was inspired by the US store Target and implemented many of their ideas. The toy industry is awash with imitation: observe the number of toys built around original ideas such as Jenga, Connect 4, Hungry Hippos or even Ker-Plunk. The difficulty is that a slight name variation and a modest adjustment to function will often render a copyright redundant and hence the lion can legitimately come in and steal a share of the spoils.

Furtherance of this strategy would be to have the ability to spot the good ideas of others and, not just imitate them, but to implement them more thoroughly and more forcefully than the originator. Ultimately, in the fiercely competitive savannah of modern business, it is often not the originator who will achieve success but rather the imitator who is able to start from the originator's finished research without the costly and timely efforts of development. In new business creation the survival record of the second entrant to a market is statistically superior to the survival record of the first entrant. First mover advantage can indeed be a significant advantage, but with strategies of the lion, where there is a good idea it can be imitated, improved, possibly have some disadvantages removed and more importantly made cheaper – then the lion can tear away at the market despite the original entrant remaining in it. If the original entrant does not react to this better, often cheaper, maybe better marketed imitator, they in turn may have to vacate the business plain and retire, hyena-like with the tail between the legs and watch from the sidelines as the lion picks the carcass clean.

Survival based on the efforts of others is achieved by the lion's unchallenged physical superiority amongst Serengeti land carnivores – a bona fide strategy to emulate.

Do not emulate the male lion

Conversely, the male lion analogy could be one for senior executives to avoid. One could argue that he is solely focussed on internal issues, and mostly on his own internal agenda of maintaining pride tenure. Other lions are seen as a threat and when the 'workers' or lionesses provide a kill, he greedily makes his way to it and takes first share – the lion's share. Here we have the issue of internal business politics. Every organisation has internal politics. For some they create an unhelpful, obsessive culture which impedes progress and where those who have climbed to the top are the best politicians rather than the best business people. All of the aspects in the culture model explored in the strategies of the giraffe chapter can work positively or negatively. They can facilitate progress or inhibit it. The values, behaviours, written statements and surface level issues determine the culture, supported by the organisational structure. These sometimes regrettably have a large focus on individuals gaining and retaining tenure.

I recall one example where someone I knew was the regional C.E.O. of the largest and most important region in an organisation. The company had a leadership battle where it was clear that one of two men was to become the new overall C.E.O. People throughout the organisation, in a manner reminiscent of politician's leadership battles, sought to align themselves with the person whom they thought would win this battle. The person I knew made the wrong choice. He openly backed the losing candidate. Shortly afterwards he therefore found himself reporting to the winning candidate and an unpleasant relationship built on school playground grudges and inevitable mistrust developed.

The winning C.E.O. had focussed on his tenure and, as male lions do when they secure tenure, he systematically removed the cubs of the previous dominant male. One of the early changes made by the new overall C.E.O. was to move from a regional structure to a divisional structure based on product and function rather than on geography. The former regional C.E.O. of the most prestigious region was, despite his previous success, relegated to running a backwater internal service division. A few years ticked away and he took early retirement at the first opportunity – the lion's victory was complete.

Despite praising the male lion's scavenging ability and suggesting emulation, there is also a negative aspect to it. The male lion does not merely take the industry of other carnivores – he assumes the right to take first share of the hard won prey of his own lionesses. Pushing them aside and snarling threateningly if they object, the male lion bullies his way to ensuring that he is the primary beneficiary of others hard work. One of the habits of management most irritating to lower management is senior people taking the glory and benefit of the achievements of those lower down the corporate scale. I have seen this in a variety of guises but nowhere is this more evident than in the allocation of corporate bonuses where a higher proportion of a higher salary sometimes creates an inequity which is difficult to defend.

The lioness – aligning the diversified

The ability of the hunting members of the pride to co-ordinate their activities and to achieve their corporate objectives of feeding the whole pride is enviable. We can learn from their co-ordinating ability in a number of areas including:

- Optimising the success of multi-disciplined teams – such as most company executive boards.
- Internal co-ordination of business aims and objectives.
- Co-ordination of departments within any one business.
- Multiple business co-ordination.
- Alliance co-ordination.
- National culture co-ordination.
- National Government.

Multi-disciplined teams

Most businesses operate some form of multi-disciplined team – whether it is the executive board or an operational team. Whilst, as is often quoted, there is no 'I' in team, as the character David Brent, in the British comedy '*The Office*' commented "if you look hard enough there's a ME". For any team to function adequately, let alone optimally, there needs to be a full appreciation of what each member brings.

As a young teenager I was in the Marine cadets – the teenagers attached to the British Royal Marine Commando. We had a number of tremendous activities, but several involved weekend competitions with various tests – from 30 mile route marches, to speed marches, assault courses, fieldcraft and the like. I was fit and was in the unit's top team for these competitions at the tender age of 14. I recall on one 30 mile march we came through some woods and down a hill to see an 'incident' a few hundred yards ahead of us. The existence of a road traffic accident, with a military landrover and a number of groaning bodies may have been offputting, but the presence of Royal Marines with clipboards doing nothing gave away that this was an exercise for assessment rather than a real accident. As the first aid expert in the team, regardless of my youth and lack of rank, I was in command, and the others did as I instructed. We passed the assessment well and were about to progress on our march when a Royal Marine officer pulled me aside and asked my name. He then gave assurances that there was nothing to worry about and that he had been impressed. Later, in the debrief the following day, it transpired that what had impressed him was the fact that a group of 16 and 17 year old cadet Corporals and cadet Sergeants had the team ethos that they would do whatever a young 14 year old mere cadet Marine asked of them.

As a 14 year old I did not have the stamina nor strength of the rest of the team, and whether it was on this same event or another I cannot recall, but there was a time when I simply could not run any more on a 5 mile speed march. Four of the team carried my backback between them – running carrying a corner each and the team leader ran, still carrying all his equipment, at what must have been a very awkward angle for him, grabbing my combat jacket and giving me enough support to finish the course. I have absolutely no doubt that, had I not even been able to run with his support, they would have used my backpack as a stretcher to carry both it and me at full running speed. That team leader was an inspirational man who later went on to serve in the Royal Marine Commandos and the Special Boat Squadron. We were a multi-disciplined team and mutually supportive – no egos, no 'I', not even a 'me', but a team. Maybe there was just a hint of the lioness with that team.

The male lion may look powerful and impressive, but there is little room for the negative aspects of his attitude in our multi-disciplined teams. A successful team will be the team exhibiting the strategies of the lioness. The requirements of this are simple to write but difficult to put into practice – merely the overwhelming trust and commitment required for every team member to put the team before themselves. There are a variety of available models and team structures in use to assist teams – from Tuckman to Katzenbach – but all are merely tools for consideration. The entire battle for a successful multi-disciplined team is a battle for the alignment of individual attitudes. Many management team building processes and exercises fail to deliver the results as all participants know in theory that they should ensure that their personal agendas are subordinate to the team agenda, but in practice the 'ME' in team tends to rear its head with depressing regularity.

Internal co-ordination of business aims and objectives

I recall some interesting consequences to the non-alignment of overall company goals and divisional goals from my own experience. Following are a few examples, without naming the companies, for obvious reasons.

One major organisation with a large property portfolio. The organisational aspiration for the property was a modest income to supplement trading income at negligible risk and certainly no adverse publicity. The internal property professionals' aspirations were more about using their profit making skills as property developers. Some projects were therefore started which would have been outside the risk parameters of the parent organisation, but by emphasising the positive sides and being economical with comment on risk; corporate approval was granted. The division therefore initiated something for its own agenda which was not aligned to the corporate agenda – certainly not the co-ordination of the lioness.

In a different organisation, a press release was made by the parent company which made a number of points to reinforce the corporate story being given to the market. One point was playing down the reliance on one company within a major division. The corporate story was of a low risk, wide spreading, safety in multiple markets strategy of the wildebeest. This was contrary to the subsidiary's message of dominance in their area of operation. For a moment there were two stories in the market: one from the parent company and one from the subsidiary. A heated exchange resulted and eventually the mess of mixed communication in the public domain was reduced. Reduced, not eliminated. The parent was not aware of the subsidiary marketing strategies and the subsidiary was not aware of the corporate investor strategies. This was not lioness co-ordination.

Perhaps the most common failure to use the co-ordination ability of the lioness is witnessed within corporate performance management programmes. If managed well, performance management processes can provide direction, motivation and personal development for the individuals. It can also harness internal talent to drive towards the corporate objectives. However, it often goes wrong in practice. One reason is that the performance management (PM) cascade is often truncated. If the CEO's PM cascades to the board, and theirs cascade to their departmental heads direct reports and these cascade further and further into the organisation there is a degree of co-ordinated effort. The most common error I witness in PM is the Board, for some reason which always eludes me, thinking that they should have a different PM method or system to the rest of the company. If theirs is different there cannot be a cascade and there will not be internal co-ordination.

Co-ordination of departments within any one business

Interdepartmental rivalry is seldom beneficial. It results in confrontation, non-value adding debate, mistrust, posturing (see the strategies of the ostrich), and is ultimately a failure of managers to run a business effectively. The usual culprits for destructive confrontation and mutual mistrust are the finance/marketing departments and the finance/HR departments. The more astute may note that there is a common thread in those conflicts and as a former financier I have probably been responsible for more than my fair share of uncoordinated activity! In the retail business many working at High Street stores, where every other weekend and several evenings are working times, have a negative impression of those working in the services or Head Office functions who get every weekend off and go home at 5pm. In production oriented businesses those making the product frequently feel as if their productive activity supports the 'support staff' functions rather than the other way around. In consultancy based organisations it is little different – the fee earning staff and the non-fee earning staff do not always co-exist harmoniously with the former reminding the latter that their activity pays for salaries. The message is the same as that to the multi-disciplined team because a business is made up of departments, each of which are specialists – in essence the business is made up of multi-disciplined teams. The issue of debate is not the need for co-ordination, that should be self-evident, but how best to do it.

Learning from the strategies of the giraffe, the cascade of vision to action can be fully implemented within a departmental framework. The overarching corporate direction is at the foot of the ladder illustrated in the giraffe chapter and one of the roles of the executive is to establish the two upright parts of the ladder. Each department can develop is own ladder with the bottom rung (or two) and the uprights common throughout every department. Synchronicity of departmental performance ladders will be an invaluable aid to interdepartmental co-ordination.

I would also add that positive personal relationships of members of a department with members of another department are probably of greater significance than a whole raft of processes and procedures for inter-departmental harmony. Of all these, the department heads are the ones who can make the greatest impact and for whom the responsibility to work harmoniously is therefore the largest. Top team mutual activity is, in my belief, essential for the smooth running of a company.

The ability to see ourselves as one team rather than rival teams is obviously also enhanced by non-work activity. I recall in one company, I →

→

refereed a football match between two shifts of the same manufacturing business. Other people from various support departments watched the match and a great time was had by all. On another occasion when with a different company, there was a company-wide darts competition and despite lack of prowess, every department entered a team. Most of the 250 people present decided that as the company accountant I should be banned from any scoring as my figures were usually suspect! Great banter, great relationship building and great reinforcement of building a multi-departmental business to work to the same ends. If the people get on, the business will become aligned, if the people do not get on, the business will not become aligned regardless of the processes, rules and procedures which aim to generate alignment. Departments are comprised of people. People interact with other people, not other departments.

Multiple business co-ordination

I have worked in multi-divisional organisations, both within divisions and at the corporate apex. Working well with a mutual big picture focus, the inter-divisional rivalry and subsequent competition can be a great spur to performance. Working badly it becomes a little more of a nuisance than the metaphorical thorn in the lion's paw.

Working in a diverse division of an even more diverse group, I once had a very good Divisional CFO. One of the many things he was good at was bringing new people into the various businesses in the division, with new ideas, from elsewhere in the organisation. I usually comment that 'contact men' are all con and no tact. This CFO was the exception. If we discussed an issue, he invariably knew someone somewhere within the organisation who had experienced something similar either within the company or in one of their former companies. He made it his business to know what working experiences and issues many people had, well beyond his own division. He also had the ability to persuade subsidiary CEO's to release senior staff for, say a 3 month secondment to advise and work with another company, maybe even in another division, about an issue. This was multiple business co-ordination of diverse skills and experience through the exceptional knowledge, skills and relationships of one man. We lost contact after he retired, but he remains one of my major business influences.

In a multi-division construction company I encountered the opposite. Some divisions were winning more work than their staff could cope with, others had surplus staff. The obvious thing would be to make short term transfers from the lax to the busy divisions. Alas this did not happen as the divisional CEO's of the lax divisions would not let the staff go because they feared not being able to get them back in the event of success in outstanding tenders. They would then have a staff shortage and would have probably sent their best people to other divisions. Also in this company, the bonuses were divisionally based so a CEO would want to retain his best people and only let other divisions have his second or third tier in staff transfers. If the basis of the bonuses was different and if the executive board generated a more co-ordinated culture, perhaps the strategies of the lioness would have generated the advantages experienced under my former CFO, overall profitability would have been higher and even overall bonuses may have risen. The myopic divisional directors prevented this.

Alliance co-ordination

Examples of alliances have already been explored in the strategies of the zebra chapter (zebra strategy 3 – 'flock'). The essence of success will always be the same – team over individual. In alliances, mergers or joint ventures, co-ordination is enhanced if the new or joint entity is a new identity. For example, the MOD contracts mentioned in the strategy of the zebra chapter necessitated companies combining to be able to fulfil the needs of the customer. In each case a new entity was formed and each partner seconded people to the joint entity. In all cases which I observed these employees deliberately referred to themselves as employees of the merged entity rather than of their original employers. It is not the terminology which is important but the attitude. The same is true in the BP/Bovis Lend Lease Alliance. When I did a piece of work for a team from this alliance, everyone referred to themselves as 'Alliance' rather than from their original company and I genuinely do not know which company many of them originally came from. I don't need to, it is an irrelevance, they work for the 'Alliance'.

The converse is true when I was discussing some of the issues raised with a merged accountancy based consultancy. As they need to project the image of professionalism and competence to their customers, and would therefore be highly likely to be litigatious if I tell their story in depth, let us say that consultancy X merged with consultancy Y to make consultancy XY. Still years later, they had not established whether they should structure themselves on a geographical basis as X had done or on a product/service basis as Y had done. Still years later, only the new recruits referred to themselves as consultants with XY, whilst the older partners still saw themselves as X or Y. Compounded by the complex partnership structure of such large consultancies, they worked separately, they socialised separately, they were not a co-ordinated merger at all. They knew a lot about the lion, but little about the lioness.

National culture co-ordination

Prof. Geert Hofstede conducted perhaps the most comprehensive study of how the workplace is influenced by national culture. He analysed data from over 40 countries collected whilst he worked as a psychologist at IBM between 1967 and 1973 but further studies on multi-national management have been developed since his groundbreaking conclusions, for example Hofstede 1980; ILO 1991; Frenkel 1994; Garsten 1994. These studies reach different conclusions about how cultural factors influence local management and employees in multinational companies. Some claim that local cultural is crucial in shaping employees' attitudes towards working life (Hofstede 1980). Others claim that the corporate culture in a multinational group overrides the indigenous culture of local employees (Garsten 1994). With such inconclusive results the problem facing multi-national organisations is how to co-ordinate themselves most effectively when working across boundaries. The boundaries may not be merely political – Canada is one country but has an element of US based English speaking culture and another of French speaking culture. Belgium is similarly bi-lingual and Switzerland has 4 official languages (German 66%, French 20%, Italian 10%, Romansch 1%) and still uses English in much of business.

Space does not permit extensive exploration of the topic and it is one of the areas which has had to be truncated in order to maintain a book of a manageable size. In short, the multi-national organisation can follow one of four cultural concepts – colonialism, culture blend, localisation or the development of a non-national corporate culture.

Colonialism is probably the poorest option. Here it imposes the national culture of the parent company or the Head Office on all other areas of the business. A French Head Office will then demand that wherever the company is in the world, it entertains the French culture. Many years ago that would have been the stance of French defence giant Thales or most Japanese banks operating in Europe. Most large users of this tactic, including Thales and most banks, have now moved on from this nineteenth century approach.

Culture blend is where the company seeks to incorporate a multiplicity of national cultures within its own. It accepts that none are superior to others but that there may be aspects of advantage from any culture for the corporate whole. These aspects could be emphasised differently in different areas of the world. For example they may seek the clinical efficiency of the Germans and the discursive ability of the Greeks but will have a stronger emphasis on efficiency in Germany and discursive nature in Greece. One of the most amusing jobs I have ever had was helping a multinational team become more effective – there were Greeks, Turks, Germans, Spaniards, an

Italian and a Frenchman. Once we managed to start appreciating each other's approach rather than arguing over whose is the most effective, real progress was made.

Localisation is where the cliché 'think global, act local' emerges from. Each region tailors itself to its national market and there is no need for a co-ordinated culture. I have seen this work very effectively in a European/Middle East media based company where the directness of the Germans would have been offensive to the Saudis, or the focus of the Brits would have been seen as rude and narrow minded by the Egyptians. Coca Cola operate this strategy most effectively.

Non-national corporate culture is where a company seeks to create its own culture for all geographic regions. This culture is not, per se, to be American, Japanese or Australian, nor is it necessarily a pick and mix blend of any of them. Its aim is to be the same corporate culture wherever it operates. The aim is for the organisation to be more dominant than any country, although obviously the interface with each national culture will generate slight variations. Exponents of this strategy would be most high technology companies such as Microsoft, IBM, Hewlett Packard et cetera.

National Government co-ordination

National Governments have to deal with such diverse aspects of life – from road-building to pensions; from defence to taxation; from legislation to education. They are making prioritisations which affect millions of people's lives on a daily basis. Here, perhaps more than anywhere else we need to see the strategies of the lioness in action. One good friend of mine was recruited to a senior role in the British Civil Service after a career in commerce. Early on in the new career a piece of advice was passed on by an old experienced campaigner who had spent a lifetime in the workings of Government. He said that some politicians are genuinely seeking to do good and to make life better for the population and the nation. Others seem to have become politicians merely to serve their own ego and personal agendas. He went on to give examples of both, in his opinion, at very high levels within the British Government – the lionesses and the lions.

One spectacular example of failure to employ the strategies of the lion is from the British Government's procurement of certain military equipment according to articles from periodicals Aviation Week and

➡

→
Space Technology. The naval aircraft the Sea Harrier sank into oblivion in 2006 and was due to be replaced by the vertical or short take off and landing (VTOL) F35. This is not planned to become operational until 2014. During the period 2006–2014, the British Navy will apparently be using the RAF Harrier GR7 instead. The calamity does not apparently cease there. The new F35 is too heavy for VTOL in direct replacement for the Harrier, as the new plane could not take of vertically with a full payload, so a weight saving programme was initiated and the weight of the plane was reduced by 20%. This meant less fuel and fewer weapons could be carried, thereby reducing capability and range. Further to this, the new aircraft carriers are due for completion in 2012. Presumably they will be fitted out for Harriers for 2 years before having an expensive refit for F35's. These ships were running into cost barriers and so changes were made to save money on ship manufacture. This apparently has reduced the military capability of the ship. This spectacular combination of uncoordinated events, according to these periodicals, shows a lack of ability to employ the strategies of the lion, the cost of which will run into more millions of pounds than most of our companies ever spend.

The French Government has better examples of being part of a co-ordinated strategy when it employs its protectionist policies to its farmers and industrialists. In 2005 US company Pepsico were rumoured to be about to make a hostile takeover bid for French food company Danone. Danone brands include a wide range of biscuits, dairy products and bottled water including Volvic and Evian, the top selling global water brand by volume. Free market forces would probably yield benefit from such a merger with Danone benefiting from Pepsico's global exposure, distribution links and experience. However, the likelihood is that a merged company would have a lesser tendency to manufacture in France and so would mean fewer French jobs. The management of Danone were understandably against such a merger, as it would have probably cost most of them their jobs, and so, despite any shareholder benefit, they mobilised the French Government in support of their protectionist anti-take-over cause. French Prime Minister Dominique de Villepin voiced his support for Danone and BBC News reported that French President Jacques Chirac said "France's priority is to defend its industrial competitiveness and the strength of its businesses" as he publicly stood against any possible take-over. Leaving aside the fact that competitiveness and protectionism are rarely synonymous, the co-ordination of industry and Government to achieve an objective is a fair lion strategy. French Finance Minister Thierry Breton commented on RTL radio that "[the Government would] deploy all its efforts to establish a vigorous and solid industrial base in our country". With its fragmented shareholder base and strong compatibility with Pepsico, there is strong business logic in such a merger but rather than take on the French Government, Pepsico wisely chose the 'freeze' strategy of the zebra to wait until the political dust has settled and perhaps until the Danone share price reduces. I would expect Pepsico to switch to a stealth and ambush strategy of the crocodile if they wish to pursue the prey, but for the immediate future, the co-ordination of Danone and Government in a lion strategy has bought more time for Danone.

A successful team building event

As so much of the lioness is about working as a co-ordinated team, and as so many team building events seem to fail in their objectives, it seems wise to share my experience of good team building.

Return to the culture model outlined in the strategy of the giraffe chapter.

The team need a structure to support them, but more importantly they need the values, behaviours, written statements and surface level issues to support them. The further the focus of the team build is to the right in the

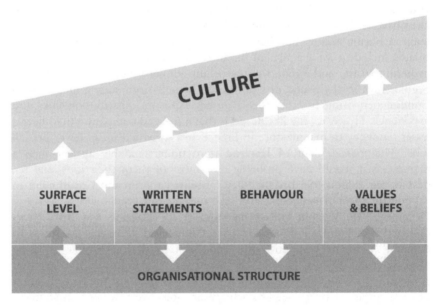

LION 1

diagram, the greater the influence on the team culture. Team building focussed on surface level issues is very unlikely to have any effect the following day. Team building events focussed primarily on behaviours is likely to have a longer lasting effect, but without perpetual reinforcement will die within weeks or months. Values focus stand a chance of longevity.

I suggest making team building events two day exercises. Day 1 will deal with the following issues in the following order:

- What does this team exist to do?
- What are the deliverables of that purpose?
- What are the behaviours that will enable this?
- What are the behaviours that will inhibit this?
- What are the underpinning values that support the enablers?
- Develop a behavioural contract – 'this is how we will act'

By ensuring that the values are sought to underpin the behaviours, the behaviours have a context, a purpose, some drivers and have a greater chance of becoming real.

Day 2 is then putting that behavioural contract to the test, probably in an unfamiliar setting. It does not matter whether it is a series of exercises in a conference centre, running a company scenario, swinging through the trees, or crewing yachts – provided that it has strong levels of interaction, mutual interdependence and the ability to stop at several points to review how the team is doing against the contract. Usually they do pretty poorly at first and then have an exponential improvement second time around. I have heard of supposed team building events where people are doing go-karting, archery, quad biking and the like. There is a place for fun, it is important, but don't pretend that fun is teambuilding. Without interaction, interdependence and regular review of performance to the behavioural contract, it is not teambuilding.

Chapter summary

- Lions exhibit social, co-ordinated behaviour in many areas of life – from hunting to rearing their young – unique amongst cats
- The male lion primarily seeks to secure his tenure of the pride. He rarely hunts, yet is given the 'lion's share' of any kill.
- Females hunt co-operatively, often with consistent specialist roles – using their skills and resources for the common benefit
- The male lion is separate from most operational aspects of the pride
- The male lion's strength enables the pride to benefit from the hard won kills of other predators →

→
- When focussed internally, the attributes of the male lion become detrimental to the business
- Co-ordination of disparate teams, activities or businesses is critical for success
- Co-ordination requires a team ethos to override any personal agenda
- Team building needs to address the deeper issues of culture to be successful

CHAPTER 10

Strategies of the rhinoceros – keep on going

This intelligent and affectionate, albeit also bad tempered, armour-plated giant is thought to have existed on earth for over 60 million years. One species of rhino (*baluchitherum grangeri*) was the largest land mammal yet found being 27 feet (8 metres) long and 18 feet (5½ metres) at the shoulder. Fossil evidence has been found in Mongolia and the animal was estimated to have weighted 23 tonnes. The facial horn is thought to have been the root of stories of unicorns and Venetian explorer Marco Polo is said to have described Sumatran rhinoceroses when stating "there are wild elephants in this country and numerous unicorns which are almost as big". Today there are only 5 species of rhino remaining on earth, and only 2 of these are in Africa – the white rhino and the black rhino. Both are endangered and have man as their only predator. Numerically both African species have been drastically reduced by human hunters and in several areas are now protected by armed wildlife guards. This is a hazardous occupation as poachers can fetch a high price for rhino horns and so are able to afford sophisticated weaponry and transport. The cause of this absurd hunting to the point of extinction is twofold – the Far East and the Arab world. In the Far East rhino horn is used in medicines and in the Arab world, particularly Yemen, the horns are decorative dagger handles for the fashionable elite.

Rhinoceros fact file:	
Height	Up to 5 feet (over 1½ metres) at the shoulder
Mass	Black rhinos are up to 4,000 pounds, 1,800kg. White rhinos can be up to 15% larger
Life expectancy	up to 40 years
Diet	grasses and a wide variety of small plants
Reproduction	16 month gestation producing a single calf

The Serengeti has previously been home to over 1,000 black rhino who ranged from Ngorongoro to the Maasai Mara and as late as 1970 there were an estimated 65,000 black rhinos throughout sub-Saharan Africa. However, extensive poaching in the 1970's and 1980's led to the drastic position where only 2 remained within the Serengeti National Park boundaries. These 2 females, situated in the West of the Serengeti had a male imported from the Serengeti but outside the park boundaries, near Ngorongoro, in 1994. In the next 5 years, 4 calves resulted giving 7 animals in that region. There are 25–30 black rhinos in the Kenya/Tanzania borderlands, 13 in the Moru region and a few isolated and protected small pockets elsewhere – or rather 'crashes' the seemingly appropriate collective noun for rhinoceroses! Together with crashes outside the Serengeti it is estimated that there are presently about 2,000 throughout Africa.

The difference between the white and black rhino is not colour – they are not white nor black – but their lips. The white rhino's name is derived from the Dutch '*weit*' meaning wide and their wide square mouth is ideal for grazing. The black rhino has a more hooked, triangular lip suited to grasping plants. They therefore prefer more wooded environments where their varied plant diet of leaves, buds, shoots and bushes abound.

Rhinoceroses are creatures of habit and will use the same waterhole if it is available – often at a similar time of day. This habit makes them easy to ambush and more vulnerable to human interference.

The horn which has hastened their demise is comprised of millions of closely packed hair fibres and can reach 50cm (20 inches). Both black and white rhino also have a second shorter horn. In some places conservation officials have tranquilised rhinos and removed their horns to give the poachers no reason to kill them although the effects of this action on the rhino are currently unsubstantiated. It may be that there is an effect on breeding ability due to a hornless rhino having difficulty locating a mate. Horn removal certainly impairs self defence as the sharp hard horn is a key weapon for a mother to defend her calf from various predator cats.

Rhinos live in territories, termed 'ranges' which are quite limited and sometimes overlap without quarrels. The black rhino is more solitary and the white rhino more social staying with family groups. Their most famous behaviour is the charge. Being ill tempered and short sighted, the rhino is an uncomfortable companion. They will seemingly charge for no reason when disturbed and unlike the charge of an elephant, they are usually not bluffing. This charge can be at up to 30 miles per hour and will usually result in either a barging or goring. Being barged by up to 4 tonne of rhino is usually about as fatal as being gored by half a metre of rock hard spiked horn. Even a Land Rover is an inadequate defence.

Once the rhino has decided to charge, only the rhino can decide to stop. Even at their colossal size and weight they are surprisingly agile and able to negotiate sharp turns and changes of direction if the object of their attention is sensibly seeking to preserve their life by moving rapidly away. It is this habit which we will allude to in the behaviour of the strategies of the rhinoceros – the ability to charge and not stop. In business there are multifarious factors which cause us to stop a given strategy. It may be the view of the market, financial limitation, deprivation of a required resource, lack of focus, loss of momentum or even loss of enthusiasm which cause us to stop our strategic initiatives and give up. The rhino pays negligible attention to these external factors and only gives up when they choose to do so. The strategy of the rhino is the strategy of keeping going – charging on when others would have stopped. As outlined in other chapters, notably the strategies of the elephant and of the zebra, this will not always be an appropriate strategy and its use should be employed carefully and sparingly. However if it was not used, James Dyson would not have brought his dual cyclone cleaning technology to the market, John Pemberton would have deprived us of the ability to drink 'the real thing' and Colonel Sanders would not have graced us with his 'finger licking good' Kentucky Fried Chicken.

Pre-requisites for a charge

The strategy of the rhino charge in business, the strategy of keeping going and not permitting anything to stop you is the strategy of legends. I will

RHINOCEROS 1

recount some of the success stories of people who kept going, even when there was no-one else backing them. However, there is also a cautionary tale. For every successful 'charge' strategy there may be several unsuccessful 'charge' strategies of people who have kept going when they should have given up. I will also recount some of these tales in the hope that they prove as salutary as the successful ones.

In order for any business to function adequately it has to meet its requirements in the building blocks of business as illustrated in diagram Rhino 1. At different stages in a business life, and for different industries the requirements and relative importance of each building block may vary, but provided that every block has its requirements appropriately fulfilled, the strategies of the rhino remain a possibility. If, for any reason, one building block is incomplete, the construction of a successful business is in jeopardy and the continuance of 'keep on going' may need to be revisited.

Product – there is no point in a 'charge' strategy and pressing on if the product is not fundamentally meeting a market need. Sir Clive Sinclair could have pumped millions of pounds behind the C5, but despite its technical excellence for its time, the market had no desire for it. There was a need to be met in affordable, environmentally friendly transport, perhaps without the effort required to ride a bike, but the C5 was not the answer.

The fact that a product was once right does not make the rhino charge perpetually feasible. In the times of rising stock markets many of us provided for our mortgage repayments by utilising endowment mortgages. Lip service was paid to the possibility that the markets may retreat at some time in the future and consequently hundreds of thousands of policies were mis-sold. As global stock markets retreated in the early part of the 21st century, the endowment was probably no longer an appropriate way to fund a mortgage. It relied on growth and stability. Stagnation and downward risk are not part of the equation from which the product is derived. That realisation would signal the time for the rhino to halt its charge.

One reasonable, but not foolproof, suggestion for entrepreneurs is to consider circumstantial evidence. An entrepreneur is wildly enthusiastic about their product, but if colleagues, the bank, business awards and market research do not support this enthusiasm it may be time to question the business decisions which would result in a blind charge rather than a sighted charge. A blind charge is one of charging on regardless of taking into account external factors and influences. It often has more to do with bloody-mindedness than business strategy. A sighted charge is where the organisation considers the external feedback it is receiving and weighs it appropriately, then deciding to press on with a charge. This is not foolproof as many – Joanna Rowling, James Dyson, John Caudwell for example – did not have the circumstantial evidence but fortunately for each of them, they charged on regardless. One of the problems we business people have in common with the rhino is that we are often equally short-sighted and have a tendency to make charges at poorly thought through targets – be it a business idea or a landrover full of camera clicking tourists.

> Many managers knee-jerk from one crisis to another. The ability to think properly and consistently is a rare commodity.

People are the only aspect of a business which will yield success. We hear the trumpeted cliché of people being any organisation's greatest asset, and then this asset is the first to be cast off in times of crisis. Along with those cast off, those remaining have investment in training and development curtailed. Whilst this is frequently a pre-requisite of meeting short term investor demands, the further consequences are often not considered whilst under pressure from institutional financial driving myopic shareholders. Considering the culture model from the chapter on the strategies of the elephant, a financially driven programme of redundancies, training cuts and consequent middle management restructuring impinge on every element of the culture model except the written statements. Short term financial decisions therefore reach far beyond the mere numbers into the very cultural fabric of the business. I am not advocating failing to meet shareholder demands, that would be equally myopic, but rather that the full consideration to the cultural impact is planned for and managed rather than seeing the issue as purely financial. Culture should be proactively managed and developed not left as a consequential result of financial decisions.

Another consequential effect of short term financial strategies is in workforce motivation, which will in turn impact on behaviour, and therefore both on performance and culture.

One traditional 4 box diagram, which is used in a variety of guises for organisational performance management purposes is the challenge/support variant as shown in diagram rhino 2. As with most 4 box models, the consultants seek to encourage each of us to the top right, in this case with high challenge and high support. Our working lives, for most of us, are more interesting and more fulfilling if there is challenge, new hurdles, innovation, variety and new tasks. Too little of this and we get bored, demotivated and develop mentally lethargy. Too much of this and we move into the stress zone. In both cases performance is sub-optimal and both the organisation and the individual suffer.

My personal preference is to make a slight adjustment to the traditional 4 box graph and illustrate 'boredom' where challenge is low, regardless of the

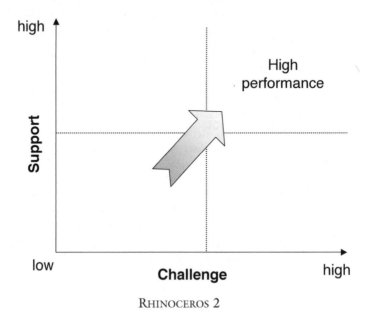

RHINOCEROS 2

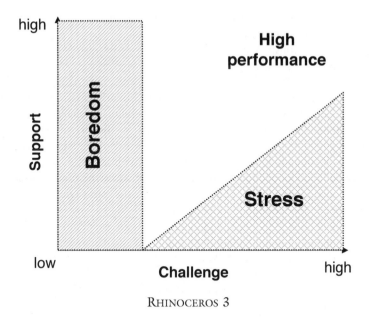

RHINOCEROS 3

level of support, plus a line defining the stress zone rising as challenge increases. These adaptations are illustrated in diagram rhino 3.

The advantage of this adaptation is that it still shows the ideal scenario of high challenge with high support but illustrates increased need for additional support as challenge continues to rise.

By reducing staff numbers and thereby increasing the workload of those who remain we move to the right on the graph. By simultaneously decreasing training and various other supports, usually HR related and consequently difficult to show a financial return, we move lower in the graph. Whilst that may result in a beneficial positioning, it may also push too far towards, or into, the stress zone and be detrimental. My observation is that it is frequently 'assumed' that managers will 'rise to the challenge' without providing them the support to do so, and in many cases even reducing the level of support. The graph indicates that if 'challenge' increases, 'support' should usually rise accordingly

From the angle of creating a tick list to consider the strategies of the rhino, the tick in the box is achieved in the 'people' section if the workforce feel that they are correctly positioned on this graph. If they do not, there is a cause for considering halting the rhino charge.

Finance is the primary reason most businesses fail – the funds run out and the rhino charge grinds to a painful halt. A managed halt is always preferable

to the rhino halting due to running out of energy resources, and similarly a
halt initiated by barren coffers is usually terminal.

In order to establish whether the financial pre-requisites are in place to
permit a rhino charge strategy, good planning is essential. Most companies
operate strategic and financial business plans. Some even manage to co-ordinate them to tell the same story! What is frequently missing is the cold,
calculated numeric awareness to provide the ability to charge. A frequent
pattern is that the enthusiast will sell an idea to the board, the financier
expresses caution, the idea is launched, fails to meet objectives, more money
is thrown at it, objectives are still not met and the board then become reluctant to cease the charge due to the amount of investment which has been
forced into the project. The Mattel example in the 'strategies of the zebra'
chapter, where the company initiated a rapid 'flight' when the learning
related project failed to meet expectations is an excellent example of a
company setting financial parameters and then not throwing more money
after the project when it failed. Many, maybe even most, companies would
have found it very tempting to charge on regardless committing greater
financial resources to the failing project in the vain hope that the additional
resources will facilitate a turn of fortune. Mattel was wise enough not to
launch such an inappropriate rhino charge.

Finance as a pre-requisite to permitting a rhino charge strategy of continuance catches us in a cleft stick. On the one hand we seek not to throw good
money after bad by further investment in a failing project. We would therefore, at inception, agree a sum of money to be spent, financial sales parameters and a deadline. The spend is not increased and if the agreed revenue is
not derived the charge ceases in a controlled manner. On the other hand we
are aware of the military mantra than 'no plan survives contact with the
enemy'. The plan is out of date as soon as it is written.

The largest danger is probably that of intuition versus analysis. In May
2002 international executive search company Christian & Timbers revealed
their research that 45% of executives rely more on 'gut feel' than on facts and
figures in running their businesses. May 2003 *Harvard Business Review* article 'Don't trust your gut' by Eric Bonabeau quoted from Gary Klein's book
'*Intuition at work*' where he asserted that intuition is "at the center (sic) of
the decision making process" and that analysis is merely "a supporting tool
for making intuitive decisions". Our desire for believing in intuition is fuelled
by the success stories of rhino strategy adherents who have succeeded – they
kept trusting their intuition and did not give up. I would suggest that there
is little more dangerous in business than an intuitively driven rhino charge
strategy. Bonabeau's article reminds us of our selective memories by stating
"we remember the examples of hunches that pay off but conveniently forget
all the ones that turn out badly. FedEx's Fred Smith also launched Zap-Mail
... that bombed, Michael Eisner (who turned the TV game show 'Who

Wants To Be A Millionaire' into a multi-million pound success) was responsible for the debacle of EuroDisney ... George Soros lost a fortune speculating in Russian securities in the late 1990's and then promptly lost another one betting on tech stocks in 2000".

Whilst I disagree with much of Eric Bonabeau's comment on intuition versus analysis, I fully support what I consider to be his best quote:

> The more complex the situation, the more misleading intuition becomes.

I would therefore suggest that for a rhino strategy to be effective and for continuance beyond the point where others would have given up, the finances need to be sound. Chasing losses is not a valid reason for the charge of a rhino.

Processes within an organisation can fall behind the more dynamic and loud drive for sales or product development. However, the greatest product can fail due to inadequate processes. I recall an issue of an on-line business where organisations registered to partake and were then charged an annual fee. The organisational processes were such that not all invoices were generated. Over the years of the existence of the company a large sum of potential income was forgone as the process of companies registering was not connected to the financial invoicing process.

Another frequent finance process which fails is that of raising credit notes. I was recently discussing an issue in a company where a debt which was approximately 4 years outstanding remains so because the minimal credit note required to eradicate the dispute has never been raised.

The list can be almost endless – considering the processes for sales data alone – perhaps inadequate information management could fail to connect relevant pieces of information, such as products purchased and ancillary products available; maybe the logging of buying habits could indicate an absence of a regular purchase and enable it to be chased; perhaps the processes of recording products purchased do not adequately inform other sales areas and thus prevent cross-sale potential. Today I have received 2 telephone calls showing good processes from suppliers. My supplier of printing toner called noticing that I had not made a purchase for 4 months and my accountant called to check that I had paid my tax to the Revenue because any delay would result in a fine. Both were pro-active responses from having good information processes.

Processes are not limited to the information and the electronic world. I recall working in a plastics factory where plastic was extruded, then stored.

It was extracted from the stores to be printed, then stored. It was taken out of the stores again to be converted into plastic bags – then stored for dispatch. Many hours and many pounds of non-value added activity were saved when we sought to make the route extrusion to print to conversion to despatch stores without the intermediate storage requirements. This was not 'rocket science' but had curiously been previously thought too difficult to co-ordinate.

A UK food manufacturing company where I worked was a purpose built manufacturing palace. The previous site had been outgrown and had become a mess of part manufacturing and multiple unnecessary handling of the product. The new site was designed so that it was a 'C' shape. The raw materials went in at one end of the 'C' and the various manufacturing processes progressed until the finished goods came out of the other end of the 'C'. Almost all intermediate handling was automated and part process inputs and outputs – such as packaging or waste – went in or out of the 'C' along the concave side. It was a masterstroke of design where the building was totally designed around the manufacturing process.

One high technology organisation with whom I work had a multifarious series of computer system driven initiatives. As their internal processes treated each initiative as a separate item, they developed in parallel without gaining benefit from each other. As an example of the chaos caused, there were 13 separate servers whereas for a significant cheaper price, 2 massive servers would have coped with the workload of all 13 smaller ones. This is an example of processes failing to allow 'joined up thinking' (excuse the cliché). Everyone involved knew that 2 large servers would be the better solution, it was just that the cumbersome organisational processes prevented the ability to achieve this.

One of my favourite examples of good process is seen worldwide in McDonalds. When training Finance Directors, I recommend that they all visit McDonalds, buy a coffee, and sit to observe the process of how raw material is transformed into finished goods and then transferred to the customer with unequalled rapidity. Not only should their business be imitating Big Mac's, their financial reporting should too. Far too many have cumbersome 'multi-handling' of data with built-in tardiness and opportunity for error.

Technology drives business effectiveness. The critical word is 'appropriate'. Many organisations fail to understand 'appropriate' and seek a high tech solution where a cheaper low tech solution would suffice. Conversely, many seek the lowest cost solution where a higher cost higher tech solution would generate greater benefit. For the rhino charge to be an appropriate strategy, the level of technology must be appropriate – neither too high, nor too low. I feel that some technological advancement can drive inefficiencies. Reliance on palmtop devices for mobile e-mails can be good, but I have seen it lead to a reliance on the last minute and a failure to plan properly. I still steadfastly refuse 24/7 communication and my world hasn't ended as a result.

Marketing is the organisational interface with potential customers. The chapter on the 'strategies of the elephant' deal with market based and competitive based intelligence, but without either of these the marketing effort is at best a combination of dice throws, and at worst money poured down the drain. With the advent of accountants having ever larger levels of controls in companies, marketing is measured in terms of money spent. This is because it is easy – invoices can be counted. However, it is a totally meaningless method of measuring marketing effectiveness. I feel that the most sensible way of measuring marketing is taking the principles of capital expenditure and aligning them to areas of marketing spend. Time precludes detailed expansion of the point but both have a "spend now and gain benefit later" aspect. Both make assumptions about the future impact of their expenditure which, because we cannot predict the future, will be imperfect. The DCF, NPV and IRR of marketing spend can be treated identically to the DCF, NPV and IRR of capital expenditure. Marketing spend is therefore more tightly controlled, more accountable and more transparent. The fact that it is a revenue spend and we are using capital spend techniques for its regulation is wholly irrelevant. Marketing teams having to consider the DCF, NPV and IRR of their marketing decisions also improves their commercial awareness and simplifies budgetary control. Before the marketing team dread added bureaucracy, a capital appraisal spreadsheet would take about 1 minute to fill out and pre-set parameters would mean that they would be aware of any shortfall in the marketing spend appraisal and could seek to alleviate this before committing to a process of wasting money on an ineffective marketing activity. Some of the marketing estimations will come true, others will not. As a Finance Director I would be very interested to know who was consistently estimating well and who was not as evidence of their understanding of their market.

Such an approach works, even the production of this book has been subject to it. It ensures added value for any marketing spend, allows actual results to be tracked to the original spend justification and saves plenty of non-value added time of CFO's trying to understand what happened to the marketing budget! For the building blocks of business to be adequate, the marketing effort must have the insight from the elephant and the analytical thoroughness of the rhino.

However, there are caveats. Not all marketing expenditure has a single financial aim to generate greater sales, or margin. It may be about strategic repositioning, or market awareness. The first two are easily quantifiable in the financial terms, the latter two are not. The entire marketing effort can be multifocused but the constituent parts must be strongly targeted. It can have many activities, but each must be with definite aims. Untargeted bland and broad marketing efforts are unlikely to achieve anything except the denudation of the organisational cash reserves.

One structure which I find useful to focus each part of the marketing effort is the 'marketing funnel'. Each part of the funnel seeks to achieve an organisational objective and aim to pass as many customers or potential customers as possible through to the next stage of the funnel. Many will not pass through successive stages of the funnel and it may take a considerable time and many 'touches' of the customer before some do progress. However, each individual part of the organisational marketing activity should be able to clearly demonstrate which segment of the funnel it is seeking to influence and what it is trying to do within that segment.

Awareness: where the aim of the marketing is to ensure that those in the target market group who are unaware of the organisational offering become aware of its existence.

Consideration: the next phase is generating the possibility of purchase in the mind of the potential customer. Often the aim is to be seen as having parity with a market leader or with a successful market player.

Purchase: effort aimed at encouraging the actual buying of the product/service for the first time. Many start here without having paid appropriate attention to the previous stages and then wonder why their efforts do not achieve their desires.

Repurchase: aiming for repeat purchase, not necessarily habitual purchase at this phase, just repeat and maybe regular purchase.

Loyalty: here the customer is a preference buyer (using the terminology of the structure used in the strategies of the elephant chapter) who is probably a regular, if not habitual, purchaser. Marketing strategies in this segment seek to turn repurchase into regular purchase and turn a category buyer to a preference buyer (see elephant chapter).

Advocacy: efforts here seek to develop customer loyalty to the point where they actively recommend the product/service to others and activity here should also facilitate the ability to do so. This is the territory of First Direct (Cheetah chapter) and Harley Davidson (Elephant chapter).

Organisations with the ability of the rhino to 'charge on' regardless of what is in their way, require marketing which is robust in its thinking, targeted in its objectives and, where possible, measurable in financial terms.

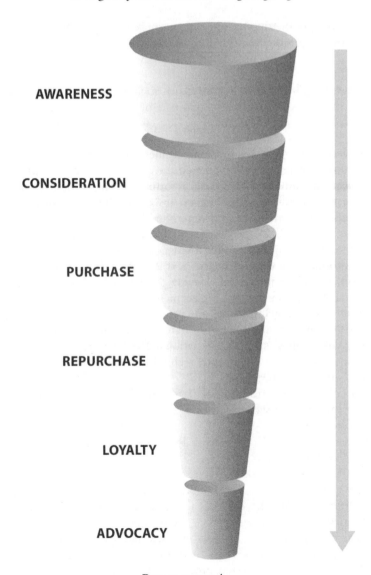

AWARENESS

CONSIDERATION

PURCHASE

REPURCHASE

LOYALTY

ADVOCACY

RHINOCEROS 4

Strategy aims to connect all of these building blocks of business and combine them, co-ordinate them and cajole them into driving the business in the direction it seeks to go. The other building blocks are the foundational tools, the ammunition, the modus operandi by which the organisational strategy seeks to make strides towards its intended destination. Strategy which does not encompass all of these building blocks is a strategy with a strong possibility of tripping up, and certainly not the strategy of the rhino who keeps going when the building blocks are in place and adequate.

Some examples – rhino strategies – some successful, some not

James Dyson

Famously fed up with his vacuum cleaner's inability to retain adequate suction, inventor James Dyson created the centrifugal action of the machine which bears his name and has made his fortune. Without the strategies of the rhino he would still be scribbling on his design board making inventions such as his ball wheelbarrow and waterfilled lawn roller.

Dyson created 5,127 prototypes in a little over 5 years from his first attempt in 1978. Eventually, after 5 years of pressing on in a rhino charge he had his product. He then spent the next 2 years seeking to find a manufacturer who would be interested. Having toured throughout Europe he was unsuccessful. The fact that the replacement bag market was worth in excess of £100m p.a. in the UK alone was probably a contributory factor, and as the Dyson.com web site gloatingly states "… Hoover's Vice President for Europe, Mike Rutter, said on UK national TV: "I do regret that Hoover as a company did not take the product technology off Dyson; it would have lain on the shelf and not been used" … "

After complete rejection, James Dyson decided to press on and manufacture the product himself and within 2 years it was the UK's best selling vacuum cleaner.

The use of a Dyson in the sitcom Friends sent US sales soaring with just short of 900,000 units in 2004 – a 350% increase on 2003. Dyson captured about 20% of the US market, despite selling the machine for almost 3 times the price of rival products. The Dyson became the 'must have' of US homes – and all from a man who couldn't find anyone to manufacture his product and decided to press on regardless – the strategies of the rhino.

Of the building blocks, 'Product' was strong. None of the others initially existed. Dyson was therefore wise to seek others to manufacture and distribute – his marketing, technology, processes and finance did not permit him to do it. Only after so many rejections did he have to seek to forge them himself. One by one Dyson collected his building blocks, grew each steadily, and cleaned up the market.

John Pemberton

In 1886 pharmacist Dr Pemberton created the soft drink sensation combining the leaf of the coca plant of South America and the seeds of the cola plant of Africa with caramel, phosphoric acid and a secret combination of 'seven natural flavours'. Coca-Cola, as Pemberton's book-keeper named it, was born. Initially Pemberton produced the syrup in a three legged pot in his back yard and from 8th May 1886 sold the concoction for 5cents per glass at Jacobs Pharmacy in downtown Atlanta, Georgia, US.

This new drink, advertised as 'delicious and refreshing', did not sell well. In the first 8 months an average of 13 glasses a day were sold. In the next 4 months sales picked up, even exceeding 20 glasses a day and first year sales totalled $50. With materials costs in that year of $74, this was not the business start up Pemberton had dreamed of.

John Pemberton did not follow the strategies of the rhino. Instead of continuing, he sold 2 friends 1/3 of the company each for $1,220. At least he had made a profit from the venture. In 1888 he sold his remaining 1/3 of the company and its rights to Asa G. Candler for $500. Regrettably John Pemberton died 4 months later and never saw his creation soar to the heights where today almost 1bn Cokes are sold every day worldwide.

The rhino of the Coke story was Asa Candler. He bought up the other rights to the business, gained complete control and went on an aggressive advertising offensive. He gave away thousands of coupons for free drinks and initiated large promotions with calendars, clocks and a wide range of other novelty giveaways.

Inspired by the sales in his shop, Joseph Biedenharn installed bottling machinery in his store in Vicksburg Mississippi and imported the concentrated syrup from Candler in Atlanta. Biedenharn then diluted the syrup and serviced local lumber camps. Within 30 years, Candler and his son Howard had grown the process of bottling under licence in the US to 1,000 bottling plants. Howard went on holiday to London with a jug of syrup. Within a week there was an order for a 5 gallon drum.

The Candlers pressed on and were succeeded by fellow 'rhino' Robert Winship who saw the vision of internationalisation. He set up an overseas sales department in 1926, and global domination had started.

When the Apollo 11 astronauts returned to Earth after their successful landing on the moon in July 1969, they were greeted by a banner in New York's Times Square which read 'Welcome back to Earth, home of Coca-Cola'.

Whereas Dyson's 'charge' was product led, Candler's was marketing led. The 'Product' section was a beverage with the ability to be concentrated and diluted. This added a 'Process', 'Finance' and 'Strategy' advantage as the cost and headache of transporting comparatively heavy but inexpensive liquid over long distances was curtailed. Candler worked the marketing funnel heavily – strategies aimed at awareness, purchase, repurchase and loyalty running concurrently. The high margins drove the 'Finance' block of the rhino diagram, as did the strategy of licensing rather than self-manufacture. An admirable and heavyweight rhino performance.

'Colonel' Sanders

Born in 1890, Harland Sanders suffered the misfortune of his father dying in 1896. His mother needed to work to support the family of Harland, his 3 year old brother and his baby sister and so Harland assumed the role of family cook. By the age of 7 he was a very proficient exponent of culinary skills. He held a series of jobs – a farmworker, streetcar conductor, soldier, fireman, lawyer, insurance salesman, steamboat ferry operator, tyre salesman and roadside service station operator, but his real love was cooking. Aged 40 he ran a service station in Corbyn Kentucky and served food on his dining room table to travellers. Soon people were travelling as much for the food as for the petrol, so he purchased a 142 seat restaurant and cooked happily for 20 years. In the early 1950's a bypass transferred the restaurant from the main thoroughfare to being on a disused backtrack. In 1952, with trade having dwindled to unsustainable levels, Harland sold everything he had, cleared his debts and was left with little other than his $105 Social Security cheque. Aged 62 most would have stopped and retired. Harland followed the strategies of the rhinoceros. He visited restaurants and cooked his famous mixture of 11 herbs and spices for them. If they liked it, they could buy the mix from him and produce chicken which was 'finger lickin' good'. In 12 years he had acquired 600 restaurant outlets – good but not outstanding. This was enough to attract the attention of investors and he sold his interest in the company for $2m. Harland stayed with the new owners who promoted and expanded the business professionally and the 1986 sale from Nabisco to Pepsico valued the business at $840m.

Even aged 62, virtually penniless, he had a product, a strategy and a marketing plan which enabled him to press on when others would have given up. Harland died of Leukaemia in 1980 but his face is still on almost every High Street of the U.S.A. and the U.K. and is well known in a further 100 countries – a true rhino!

Driving on 'Product', 'Marketing, 'Process' and 'Strategy', Harland saw his dream come to fruition.

Joanna Rowling

The idea of a story about a wizard arrived in Joanna's head on a train from Manchester to London in 1990. The train was apparently delayed by 4 hours giving her sufficient time to think through many aspects of the story which were to develop later. She spent the next 5 years writing a book – partly in Manchester, partly in Portugal and famously partly in Edinburgh where she would sit in a local café completing her manuscript with sleeping daughter Jessica in the pushchair beside her. Life as an unemployed single mother with a violent estranged husband searching for her almost inevitably led to depression – but Joanna pressed on.

This commitment to 5 years of writing within those circumstances is enviable enough to be included in the 'just press on' strategies of the rhino hall of fame, but pressing on did not stop there. Sending the first part of the manuscript to a literary agent, she recounts that it was immediately returned, rejected, within a couple of days. Fortunately the second agent was interested and at last, Joanna had a partner to pursue the rhino strategies. 12 major publishers were contacted and 12 major publishers rejected her story of wizards, spells, outlandish creatures and a curious aerial broomstick game of quidditch. Author and literary agent charged on. After about a year, in August 1996 Bloomsbury offered to publish for a meagre advance of £1,500 (I received more than that for the Korean edition of this book alone!), thus demonstrating that they were not confident of success.

The strategies of the rhino were successful, the books succeeded and the US rights were secured by Scholastic for a bid of $100,000 – an unheard of amount for a children's book. Despite their lack of confidence, Joanna Rowling's writings boosted Bloomsbury and some have speculated that they may not have even survived without the revenue she gave them.

The 'Finance' and 'Marketing' building blocks dictated that for her book a large publisher would be preferable, and so the options were limited. The publisher then takes responsibility for the 'technology' and the sales interface in 'People', plus the marketing impetus. Joanna's huge advantage was that the industry has the building blocks in place for an author – she provides the product into a pre-built industry building blocks structure. The 'Process' of book publishing is designed to eliminate titles unlikely to succeed. Here, the process missed one of the biggest successes of the century and Rowling simply refused to give up. She believed in her product, few others did, but once Bloomsbury brought her into their 'building blocks' the rhino charge was unstoppable.

John Caudwell

The entrepreneur behind Phones 4 U bought his first consignment of 26 mobile phones from Motorola in 1986. They were priced at £1,400 each. After 8 months of hard work and persuasion he had managed to sell them at a retail price of £2,500 each. Most people would have viewed 8 months to sell 26 units as a failure and moved on to another enterprise. With this level of take up the product was obviously flawed, had even less market appeal than Sir Clive's C5 and was pricing most people out of the purchasing arena. The 'strategies of the rhino' are about charging on. John Caudwell chose the rhino. Persistence paid off – at is peak, the Caudwell Group sold more than 26 phones every minute and had sales of £1.85bn.

One reason why I particularly like this example is that the 'building blocks of business' approach would probably have voted against Caudwell continuing.

The analytical approach would have probably said that the rhino was the wrong animal to emulate. The product was cumbersome, the marketing clearly inadequate from the first 8 months experience and the technology was in its infancy. It took a brave man to even buy the first 26! Business is an art not a science. Whilst still believing in the earlier comments about intuition verses analysis, sometimes something just works. The fact that a diagnostic, a model or an approach indicates success or failure is not a guarantee of success or failure. Like the 'strategies of the cheetah' chapter example of WWII battle tanks, the model could be applied differently, in that case with different priorities, or as in this case with 'building blocks', sometimes the diagnostic fails to predict success. Caudwell was in the right place at the right time having doggedly continued. As the market grew he switched to the niche strategies of the hippopotamus and soared on the advancing sales curves of the mobile phone industry.

French wine industry

The French wine industry does not embrace change readily. The very essence of the industry is a reliance on tradition as illustrated by the observation that the formal hierarchy of the 21 appellations from the famous Bordeaux region has had only one minor alteration in its glorious history. Despite £213m of subsidies from The European Union for the industry out of the £6.75bn allocated to prop up French agriculture (2002 figures) the industry is in decline and not adapting to the challenges of good wines from the New World of California, Australia and New Zealand. Further competition is now developing as South American wines are increasing in standard at an alarming rate. The South Africans have long been experts and the Spanish and Italians have at last mastered the dark arts of marketing. The French industry meanwhile presses on in broadly the same fashion as it has for centuries – they have adopted the strategies of the rhino. For the strategy to have a chance of success the pre-requisites – product, people, finance, process, technology, marketing, strategy – must be met. The product is an 'old world' product, and whilst it is often to my taste, it is less so to that of a wider range of consumers. The French growers have resisted the calls to change their product to reflect the changes in consumer taste which are benefiting the New World. French wine growing people are amongst the most knowledgeable in the world but amongst the least flexible. Finance gains a tick in the box as The European Union seems to be a bottomless pit of support. Process and Technology are ancient and traditional. Marketing emphasises the ancient and traditional. Strategy to cope with competition seems unprepared. So, with a few notable exceptions, the French wine industry is wholly unsuited to pursuing the strategies of the rhinoceros, yet it continues to charge onwards. In 2005 the EU provided £100m to turn 670m bottles of wine into industrial alcohol to help reduce a surplus of unsold wine. In the same year 45,000 acres of vines were dug up. The 2004 share of the global market was 20%, I would suggest that with inappropriate rhino strategies this will suffer inevitable decline.

Index retail stores

In April 2005 Littlewoods decided to shut the 126 catalogue based retail outlets marketed as 'Index'. 3,200 jobs were reportedly cut although some were saved as GUS bought some of the stores to convert them to their catalogue outlet Argos. In its press release Littlewoods stated that Index had accumulated in excess of £100m of losses over 2 decades. David Boardman of Littlewoods told the BBC "Index has not made a profit in 18 of its 20 years". I would venture to suggest that only 2 years of profit in 20 does not fit the financial requirements for a strategy of the rhinoceros and the continuation was a salutary error. Index should never have followed the rhinoceros, and were it to have given up the charge based on the rational, objective aspects discussed under the part of this chapter on financial pre-requisites, much of that £100m could have been saved.

Chapter summary

- The rhino's strategy is one of charging, and not stopping. Nothing stops 4 tonne of rhino when it has decided to charge.
- The rhino doesn't bluff. Unlike the elephant, the charge is direct and will result in impact.
- This strategy in business is the stuff of legends – Dyson, Sanders, Rowling, Caudwell and the like.
- It is also a strategy of high risk – many attempted rhino strategies fail, we are less competent at remembering them as they do not inspire the heart as much as the successes.
- In order for a charge strategy to be possible the building blocks of business need to be appropriately in place – product, people, finance, process, technology, marketing and strategy. A failure or shortfall in any one of these could render the rhinoceros charge an inappropriate choice of business strategy.

CHAPTER 11

Strategies of the wildebeest – safety in numbers

The wildebeest is an ungainly aesthetically challenged type of large antelope with a broad head, bearded throat, deep chest, short neck, high shoulders, a long tufted tail, thin legs and heavy buffalo-like horns. African mythology says that God made the wildebeest using parts left over after he had compiled the remainder of the earth's population, although I think that this description could equally fit the camel, the duck billed platypus or the occasional work colleague. They are a vital part of the delicate Serengeti ecosystem providing huge quantities of meat for carnivores and equally huge quantities of dung to assist grass growth for the herbivores – and of course to be the object of delight for our dung beetle of the prologue to this book. They are non-aggressive and presumably rather dim as even when running to escape a predator they will stop, turn around and look again at whatever was causing them to run.

Wildebeest fact file:

Height	Up to 1.3m at the shoulder
Mass	up to 250kg
Life expectancy	up to 20 years
Diet	grasses – preferably short grasses
Reproduction	250 day gestation producing a single calf

Wildebeest, originally from an obsolete old Afrikaans Dutch dialect meaning, unsurprisingly, 'wild beast', have a keen sense of smell and good hearing but not particularly good eyesight. They are very efficient grazers and, in common with the zebra, can rapidly clip knee-high grass to less than 2cm but leave the roots to allow for future growth. Each wildebeest eats approximately 4kg of grass each day and as there can be in excess of two million on the move at any time, this can create several tonnes of dung a day.

They are timid animals and feel safer when crowded together. Being in the midst of a large herd lessens any individual's chance of being attacked whilst exposure creates vulnerability. However, their docile nature and abundance means that their numbers are perpetually whittled away by lions, hyenas, wild dogs, crocodiles, cheetahs and leopards. Wildebeest are the staple diet of the main predators. In order to survive they must therefore instigate a strategy of numeric replacement. This they do admirably with synchronised births – the only member of the antelope family to do so. In the birthing season as many as 24,000 calves are born each day. With such vast numbers in such a short time span, they again rely on the safety of numbers for survival – there are so many calves that even after predators have attacked, there are tens or even hundreds of thousands of survivors. Calves are often on their feet within 3 minutes of birth and able to run within 20 minutes of birth. For this vulnerable 20 minutes they are in the midst of a huge dark cloud of animals stretching almost immeasurably across the Serengeti plain. Birth is also co-ordinated to occur in the morning thus avoiding the nocturnal predators and allowing the calves to gain strength during daylight.

Migratory all year round, the wildebeest travel in superherds sometimes containing over a million animals. These herds are usually accompanied by other grazers including other antelopes and zebras. Within each herd there are huge numbers of small family herds each ruled by a territorial bull who shepherds his cows and young in a rolling territory through which other males are forbidden to pass. Despite this, there is constant poaching of females by other males and if not adequately corralled the cows can move from one harem herd to another. The synchronicity of birth determines the need for a synchronicity of conception and accordingly the cows come into season for only one day. If the male has not adequately protected his harem and females have escaped, he will reduce his ability to pass his genes to the subsequent generation.

The wildebeest always starts the year in the South East of the Serengeti where good grazing is plentiful. February is the peak month for wildebeest births and throughout the March and April rains the animals are comparatively dispersed throughout the short-grass southern plains. In May and June the water becomes scarcer and the animals move westward near the Grumeti river, towards Lake Victoria. This is where the superherds form although they never follow precisely the same route, the general direction of the migration is identical year after year. In June they cross the Grumeti with many drowning and thus ensuring the future survival of crocodiles. Again, the strategy for river crossing is safety in numbers. By thousands crossing simultaneously, the herds can afford to lose a few hundred animals without any significant consequences for the overall population. The safety in numbers strategy does have its disadvantages as well as its ability to ensure the survival of the overwhelming majority. As animals start to accumulate on the riverbanks, many more arrive and there is a consequential pushing where new arrivals join the crowd. Pushing from the back eventually leads to those at the front being forced into the river and the mass crossings begin. Being at the front increases exposure and consequent vulnerability to crocodiles. It also means that the exit point is not clearly identified and the front animals need to locate one before being swept away by the river, becoming exhausted and drowning. However, being in the middle or at the back is not safe either. The front animals find an exit from the river and the procession route becomes defined. As more animals cross, density at river entrance points can result in some animals being forced wide after entering the river and therefore becoming easier for crocodiles to pick off. After a while the exit points become muddy and slippery. This too is a danger as it causes a bottleneck with fallen and stumbling animals obstructing the exit. An exit queue results and a strong stream can then carry queuing animals past the exit point. Here some are crushed to death or forced underwater by the sheer weight of others at the exit, some swept away to find alternative exits, some swept away and drown and some become isolated and easier for crocodiles to target. It is estimated that herd losses in a major river crossing never reach as much as 1%. Whilst the numbers lost may look large, the statistics of mass movement mean that with over 99% surviving a crossing the strategy is effective.

Having crossed the river, the wildebeest head north through northern Tanzania and into Kenya by September; fording rivers, feeding predators, cutting the grass and depositing fertilizer throughout. By November they turn south, arriving in December and the cycle repeats endlessly. They may be ugly, they may be dim, but they are a critical part of the ecosystem feeding carnivores directly and herbivores indirectly throughout the plains. Despite their role in the maintenance of carnivore populations their major enemy is not a predator. Despite the river crossing losses, drowning affects a mere fraction of the population. Their biggest enemy is disease which kills many more wildebeest than predators and rivers combined, particularly rinderpest which is a highly contagious disease of ungulates (cloven hooved animals) registered as a class 'A' disease by the Parisian based Office International des Epizooties (OIE). The wildebeest's desire for proximity enables the disease to spread rapidly through herds with fatality the usual consequence 6–10 days after being contracted.

The safety in numbers strategy, together with its synchronised birthing, has ensured survival, prosperity and numeric advantage for centuries. However, as with many strategies, the very aspects which generate success also expose vulnerabilities – in the case of the wildebeest at river crossings and through the spreading of disease. Fortunately for the wildebeest and the countless animals who rely on them for their own survival, the advantages have always outweighed the disadvantages.

The wildebeest in business

There are two main reasons for businesses to use wildebeest strategies: risk reduction and dominance. In both cases the company seeks to ensure that the Serengeti grassland of their chosen market is intensely populated with their products. In the risk reduction aspect of the strategy, one product can fail and the organisation will still survive by the success of other products. Consistency of performance is achieved as overall variability is reduced by minimising reliance on one product, one market or one set of circumstances. For the dominance element of the wildebeest strategy it is an attempt to crowd the market with its products. This can be achieved in a variety of ways: for example, Procter & Gamble having such a range of laundry brands that the consumer is often choosing between several brands of the same company, or McDonalds so heavily populating the fast food market by physical location that one is never further than a few hundred metres from a Big Mac in any city. In both the P&G and McDonalds examples their wildebeest strategies have achieved dominance, although by different tactics.

Companies will opt for the strategy of 'safety in numbers' for either of these reasons, risk or dominance, and in some cases both. Risk based strategies are about diluting risk through numeric advantage. It could be market

risk, product risk or probability risk – all are equally valid reasons for replicating the strategies of the most ungainly gnu. Probability risk could be
'upside' or 'downside'. An upside risk-spreading is to ensure that there are
sufficient 'irons in the fire' that at least one may succeed. Downside risk is
to ensure that in the event of a fall by one aspect of the business, others will
ensure organisational survival. Examples to be used include drug companies, First Choice Holidays, Conglomerates (or diversified industrial
companies) and the Volkswagen Group. Dominance driven wildebeest
strategies are about creating such a numeric advantage in market offering
that the competition cannot penetrate – the plain is full of wildebeest and is
dominated by the sheer numbers of the species – such as McDonalds,
Microsoft or Intel.

Risk – industrial

The heydays of the conglomerates were the 1970's and 1980's and the
undisputed champion of the sector was Hanson plc. Driven by James
Hanson and Gordon White, subsequently Lord Hanson and Lord White, the
giant organisation incorporated industries as varied as gold mining, electric-
ity, chemicals, food supplements, cigarettes, cranes, batteries, timber and
toys. The strategy was simple – risk dilution. Some sectors would gain benefit to compensate for others who were struggling. The safe, secure and reliable results of some companies would enable mild risk to be taken in others
which would not be possible in a stand-alone company.

Other organisations who have used the wildebeest strategies of spreading
industrial risk by expanding across multiple industry borders at various times
would include Mitsibishi of Japan (plastics, paper, oil, life insurance, beer,
aluminium, glass and chemicals), Nokia of Finland (timber, telecommunications, rubber, cables, information technology) General Electric of the US
(finance, energy, healthcare, insurance and nuclear fuel) and Tomkins of the
UK (lawnmowers, belt buckles, cakes, coffee, food ingredients, firearms).

The economic position of the 1970's and 1980's created markets which
rose and fell rapidly meaning that acquisitions could frequently be made at
knockdown prices. The legacy of 1960's asset based industries also meant
that there was often hidden value for the conglomerate predator to extract.
Consequently the conglomerate seemed to be an unstoppable force in the
1980's when Hanson and Tomkins were buying everything in their path.
However, after the early 1990's minor recession, investor trends turned
away from the arguably overdiversified giants and they were forced to shed
industrial sectors more like reptiles shedding skin than like wildebeest dominating their savannah. The investor demands were then for single sector
companies.

The strategies of the wildebeest can still be applied within single sectors as demonstrated most ably by UK holiday company First Choice. The holiday company employs over 14,000 people in 17 countries and 8m customers go on holiday with them each year.

The holiday industry can be fickle. If we, the consumers, feel well off, we will engage in luxurious holidays but if we feel the tightness of economic downturn we will compensate by taking cheaper holidays. Whereas a few decades ago the position was different, now an annual holiday or two is seen as a necessity rather than a luxury by the majority of the population of the UK. The variability is not whether we go on holiday but where we go on holiday. Our response to economic circumstances is to downgrade or upgrade our annual overseas pilgrimage.

First Choice was the 1993 rebrand of Owners Abroad which had floated on the stock market in 1982. The rebrand co-incided with the appointment, as CEO, of the highly respected Peter Long. From the late 1990's onwards a strategy of perpetual acquisition has been pursued which has led to the position of the group having a foothold in almost every holiday market. These acquisitions included Hayes & Jarvis, Bakers Dolphin and Intatravel in 1998; Meon and Sunsail in 1999; Royal Caribbean Cruises, Barcelo Travel, Holiday Hypermarket, Crown Travel and Stardust Yachts in 2000; Virgin Sun, Sunrise (Netherlands), Tourinter (France) and I Viaggi Del Turchese (Italy) in 2001; Exodus, Waymark and Connoisseur in 2002; Trek America in 2003 and others. From this partial list the blistering pace is obvious with multiple acquisitions each year.

It is not merely the consistent pace of acquisition which was impressive. The coverage of holiday types is unrivalled. For almost a decade First Choice relentlessly acquired, in addition to its mainstream holiday businesses, a vast range of specialist holiday companies such as Sovereign (high value holidays 4*+ accommodation), Sunsail (specialist sailing holidays), Platinum Crewed (luxury yacht charter), First Choice Ski, Flexiski, Hayes (self-compiled holidays), Meon Villas, Citalia (Italian specialists), Crown Blue (European Inland waterways), Exodus (adventure holidays), Caradonna (Scuba diving holidays), Lets Trek Aus&NZ, Island Cruises, Studentcity, Holiday Hypermarket (holiday retailer) and many more.

Under Peter Long's leadership, the group has risen from its knees to become very impressive market leaders due to its diversification strategy. The accumulation of a vast range of offerings to the market has meant that whatever you want from a holiday, whatever your price bracket and destination requirements, the First Choice Group has something to offer you. Drawing the various small companies together limits the extinction risk for any individual small company and enhances the financial consistency of the wider organisation. Further issues of economies of scale, buying power and cross fertilisation of ideas adds further benefit to this wildebeest strategy of having a wide variety of holiday organisations encompassing the entire gamut of possible vacations. The consequences for First Choice was a 'textbook' financial performance 2003–2004–2005 with sales, earnings per share and margin all having gentle upward sloping graphs – just like the City analysts love.

However, despite investors' demands for single industry diversification rather than the cross-industry diversification of the 1970's and 1980's, as always, there is one company swimming against the tide. As it often is, that company is the maverick Virgin Group who, as previously documented, no longer have to dance to the tune of City financial fashion. With 6 divisions – travel, entertainment, mobile communications, lifestyle, motoring and finance – the group comprises consumer offerings as diverse as flights, holidays, train travel, phones, cosmetics, mortgages, wine, weddings, books, jewellery, insurance and Virgin Galactic which signs people up for space travel when the technology makes it more publicly affordable!

Risk – product

Procter & Gamble have a degree of industrial risk diversification as they use the strategies of the wildebeest to cover the industries of personal care, homecare, baby products and pet products. The similarity in range with one of their key rivals, Unilever, is obvious as the latter operates by the safety in numbers strategy in markets of personal care, homecare and foods. Within each of the industrial sectors through which they have diversified, they are each further spread across the market with a vast range of brands to give a product risk mitigation within each industrial category. P&G's homecare laundry range shows extreme wildebeest coverage of as many aspects of the market as possible, even to the extent of the various brands competing against each other in some circumstances. P&G's laundry range includes Ace, Ariel, Bold, Bounce, Daz, Dreft, Era, Fairy, Febreze, and Lenor. It would be impossible to seek something in the home laundry sector for which a P&G product, or more than one, will not do the job. Whilst competing against Unilever's Comfort, Persil, Radiant and Surf, the P&G brands present such a strong presence on the supermarket shelves that they achieve both dominance and risk reduction within the home laundry market. The consumer perceives a degree of choice from the large range of brands on display, yet in reality the choice is between a number of P&G products and a smaller number of Unilever products. Both companies, but P&G *in extremis*, have populated their business Serengeti with a range aimed at achieving market dominance by sheer numbers – precisely the same as the grassland dominance by sheer numbers which ensures wildebeest species survival.

The UK's Arcadia High Street clothing retail group collected a variety of brands by acquisition including the high fashion Top Shop and Top Man brands, the young teenage girls Miss Selfridge, Evans for larger sizes, Burtons for older men and Dorothy Perkins for older women. The idea was to acquire a series of brands to cover a very wide range of the clothing market and hence whichever part of the market was in ascendancy, the company would have representation and therefore be able to take advantage of the trend. In 2002 Arcadia joined the Philip Green empire which consisted of over 2,300 retail outlets. Whilst Philip Green's acquisition strategy is a series of textbook examples of the stealth and ambush strategies of the crocodile, his strategy for ongoing business is now that of the wildebeest. Arcadia originally entered wildebeest strategy to mitigate fashion industry risk, but now within the Philip Green empire, Arcadia finds itself in both the risk minimisation and High Street dominance aspects of wildebeest strategy. Philip Green now has approximately 12% of the UK clothing retail sector and is second only to Marks & Spencer.

The Volkswagen Group have now incorporated the single industry version of the wildebeest strategy as they have expanded over the last decade. The Group currently includes VW, Audi, Lamborghini, Bentley, Bugatti, SEAT and Skoda in the domestic vehicle market. The Group also operates very effectively in the commercial vehicles market.

The VW brand was suffering in the mid 1990's with a loss in 1993, a return to profit in 1994 but with slim margins in the following years. 1994 also saw VW introduce a 4 day working week which is an indication of the problems it was facing. The European family car market was where VW achieved 75% of its sales, yet this market was one of the slowest growing in the vehicle industry. It was also a market where competition had intensified due to the unstoppable onslaught of the Japanese giants. Margins were plummeting. Further pressure was being exerted by Japanese manufacturing efficiencies and the combination of these factors meant that from the early-mid 1990's the direction of the group was unsustainable.

The position today is somewhat different. The luxury car market is served variously by the Bentley, Lamborghini and Bugatti brands. In the high quality executive arena Audi can compete with fellow German BMW. The VW brand provides the mass central market positioning and both SEAT and Skoda provide a strong presence in the value driven part of the market (i.e. low price, high price sensitivity). The adoption of the wildebeest strategies has taken VW Group from the brink of disaster in the early-mid 1990's to being a strong force throughout the whole range of the domestic vehicle market where it has manufactured and sold approximately 5m vehicles in each year of the early 21st century. This volume creates a global market share of between 11.5% and 12.4% for each year 2000–2004.

Using the same wildebeest strategies as First Choice Holidays applied in their market, VW created the position where the group offers something at each level of the market and if an individual chooses to upgrade or down-grade in choice of vehicle, there is another group member waiting with a product.

Risk – probability

The probability of a lottery win is miniscule – yet many try. The probability is increased with multiple ticket purchase. If you hold enough tickets, one might win. Wildebeest strategies in the uncertain markets of business are about ensuring that sufficient tickets are held to ensure success.

Research in the pharmaceutical industry is an activity of high cost, vast numbers and of success percentages. It takes an average of 13.2 years from the discovery of a drug to it gaining approval for use by members of the public and only after this point can a pharmaceutical business seek to gain financial recompense from its years of development, testing, perfecting and making the drug safe for use. With high litigation possibilities, high barriers of proof of effectiveness and stringent safety legislation, this is not a market for the short term focus. The average cost of bringing a pharmaceutical product to the market place is $800m – and many will not become financial successes. According to research by Grabowski and Vernon published in 1994, 7/10 drugs made available on the market do not recoup their research and development costs. A further 1/10 just break even. This means that only 2/10 have a positive financial impact with post-tax profits exceeding research and development costs. If these odds were replicated throughout the phar-maceutical industry the average commercial success rate would be 2/10, or 20%. So for 10 drugs each costing the average $800m to bring to the market, a pharmaceutical company is investing $8bn. The 7/10 failures can be expected to bring in under $2bn for their $5.6bn (7 × $800m) of invest-ment. 1/10 will generate the break even $800m and so the remaining 2 drugs must generate in excess of $5.2bn between them just for the company to break even. Mere break even is inadequate for corporate survival and so these 2 successful drugs would need to bring in greater revenue to ensure ongoing success. The figures are large, the percentages small and the stakes high.

Presently there are approximately 900 medicines in the process of devel-opment worldwide for countering the various effects of ageing. These include 146 products targeting heart disease or strokes and 399 targeting various cancers. There are also 82 medicines in development for HIV/AIDS, 27 for Alzheimer's, 20 for osteoporosis and 17 for Parkinson's disease (*source* Pharmaceutical Research and Manufacturers of America – PhaRMA – December 2005). The overwhelming majority of these products will never make it to market. They will either fail to prove their effectiveness or become redundant, superseded by another before launch. In this market the probability of success is negligible and the large drug companies engage in the strategies of the wildebeest to ensure overall success from the small percentage of products which do make it.

Pfizer claims to be the largest research based pharmaceutical company in the world. In 2005 it spent $7.4m on research and development – the largest amount in the pharmaceutical industry. Pfizer has hundreds of projects covering many areas of medicinal development with over 200 drugs in active development stages – either being developed, tested or made safe. With a medicine library of approximately 3m drugable compounds, over 140 new molecular entities in their research pipeline and almost 400 new compounds at their disposal, Pfizer are at the forefront of pharmaceutical research. For any research project, from millions of tested compounds, perhaps a dozen candidates reach measurement stage. From these, their hope is that one will make it to the market as a pharmaceutical product. In these business areas of weak probability, mass is critical. If a company, such as Pfizer, can continue a pipeline with perhaps 10 or a dozen drugs emerging annually and sufficient pipeline investment to bring others through their average 13.2 years of development they can generate success over time. If they were to abandon the critical mass of numbers so ably demonstrated by the wildebeest and focus on just a few products, mathematically they would seem certain to fail.

This is not a case of having a strategy with a back up plan 'B'. It is a case of leveraging the process and committing the perpetual annual expenditure to continue whilst knowing that 7/10 projects will fail financially. For the pharmaceutical industry to survive and generate cures for the presently incurable, the 2/10 successes must be remunerative and compensate for the 7/10.

The wildebeest does everything it can to ensure survival by numbers including synchronising morning births to increase the probability of calves surviving nocturnal predators. The famed river crossings accept a failure rate, either from crocodiles or drowning. The lions and hyenas take their share. Meanwhile the wildebeest continues with its honed safety in numbers strategy by producing more offspring than the combined predators can consume and hence ensuring survival of the species, and survival of the awesome sight of the annual migration.

Dominance – blanket coverage

One is never far away from a McDonalds outlet. As I climb the steps from various London underground stations, each step has a message alerting me how far and in which direction the nearest McDonalds lies. In a city one can also never be more than yards away from the opportunity to purchase a can of Coca-Cola. Seldom are we far from either product or the message of their advertising. McDonalds and Coca-Cola are expert exponents of the wildebeest strategy of dominance by coverage.

It is an expensive option as vast sums of money need to be available to ensure the product is visible at every turn. Naturally one would expect the world's number 1 and number 6 brands to have the financial ability to generate global blanket coverage every week of the year. However, most are not in such a favourable position. A cheaper variant of the coverage strategy is that of 'blitz advertising' where the company seeks to be everywhere in view for the period of the advertising campaign but realises that they do not have the resources to commit to being everywhere permanently as Coca-Cola and McDonalds do. Blitz is the opposite of the 'drip drip drip' approach of perpetually reinforcing a message in a smaller way over a long period of time. Honda takes the 'drip drip drip' approach with, for example the continual reinforcement of the brand on Channel 4 documentaries. Toy companies Hasbro and Mattel take the blitz option with incessant presence in late October and throughout November. They will blitz television and magazines to maximise exposure at the time when we are considering Christmas presents. The UK market in children's toys and games is worth in excess of £2bn per annum with Christmas presents slightly outweighing birthday presents to give over half of this sum being spent in the 6 weeks leading up to Christmas. The blitz aims to start a few weeks before the spending frenzy and continues until the late December to early January follow up blitz seeks to advise children how to spend any monetary gifts received over the festive period. Whilst it is intensely frustrating for me to watch the television with my children for 40 minutes and see the same advertisement 4 times – the strategy works – the children will talk about the frequently advertised 'blitz' strategy product. The sheer concentrated volume of advertising gives a short term blanket coverage which is very difficult to ignore – the sheer volume of wildebeest on the plain are testament to the success of their strategies.

For the toy companies it is an obvious annual strategy. Others who readily take this approach are the film industry. Just prior to a film launch and in its earliest weeks the blitz is perpetuated with television, posters, toys given away by fast food outlets, clothing and any possible peripherals for the film. These too are big budget, large scale blitzes. For others with a more meagre budget there is no reason why a blitz blanket coverage approach cannot be undertaken by co-ordinating marketing media – perhaps television, newspapers, billboards, bus sides and even the ambush marketing strategies outlined in the chapter on the strategies of the crocodile. The perpetually reinforced 'blitz' for a short time period can be just as effective as Honda's 'drip drip drip', even many months after the 'blitz' has come and gone.

Dominance – volume usage

For evidence of the effectiveness of dominance by sheer volume, try finding an office or a home which does not contain the products of IT wildebeests Microsoft or Intel. Whereas the dominance by blanket coverage is all about visibility and presence at every purchasing opportunity, Microsoft and Intel products are not visible – yet are everywhere. Their advertising is less obtrusive, but the product is with us wherever we turn. The strength of the strategy lies in the ability to secure the supply chain so that no alternative supplier is able to penetrate. Without the loud advertising noises of the blanket coverage exponents of wildebeest dominance strategies, they will, nevertheless, seep into every area of their market and dominate by volume – there is no widely available alternative to them as the supply chain is secure and the market saturated.

Greyhound buses in the US operate such a vast fleet that their volume creates a difficulty for any potential entrant. Were an entrant to challenge them, the new business would not be able to compete with the sheer scale of Greyhound and thus be unable to invoke wildebeest strategies of volume generation. They would be forced into niche strategies offering certain routes only, and Greyhound could respond, due to their vast coverage by competitively pricing them out of the market in those niches. The remaining routes would temporarily bolster the discounted competitive route until the competitor was removed.

It is a similar strategy to a leading brand of coffee shop. This brand will apparently assess the number of viable outlets an area can sustain. Regardless of the competition existing in the area it will open more than the viable number operating at a loss, but also forcing any competitor to take losses. When the competitor ceases trading, the dominant brand can reduce its number of outlets to what it considered viable and trade profitably – a superb example of using wildebeest dominance strategies to take new ground.

It would be a false assumption that once a market has been dominated by volume, that it is safe, uncompetitive, exorbitantly profitable and the dominating organisation can regress to the 1950's bovine member of the Boston menagerie – the cash cow. As previously mentioned, I do not believe that the theories and models of the relatively stable world of the 1950's are particularly relevant in the faster, dynamic business Serengeti's of the 21st century. An example of companies which used wildebeest strategies to generate global dominance, but now have to reconsider would be the vehicle tyre market (US – tire). They used to operate wildebeest strategies with dominance from the big players – Goodyear, Bridgestone, Michelin, Continental and Dunlop. There were always cheap alternatives but these 5 brands covered the market well. However, their dominance has not lasted. The exhaustive globalisation of the market, the consumer's drive away from premium brands and their positioning of a multibrand strategy now means that there are about 150 tyre brands to choose from. Some competitors in the market choose premium brand strategies such as Italy's Pirelli, but most seek the mass mid-market and Yokohama, Cooper, Toyo, Kumho, Hankook, Ohtsu and others have increasingly eroded the market dominance of the big players. The formerly volume dominant companies were unable to prevent new entrants and were unable to maintain sufficient alliances with manufacturers to perpetuate their wildebeest successes. The end of the 20th century, and certainly the start of the 21st century have seen this market change to the extent that the strategies which brought earlier success are no longer the strategies for future success. It is inevitable in the business world in which we operate that at some point this will also be the case for the current dominant wildebeests of Microsoft and Intel, McDonalds and Coca-Cola. Their dominance will become eroded and they will have to alter their strategies to deal with the changes in the market. For those who have achieved the numeric dominance of the wildebeest, perhaps the most important series of strategies to consider is not the maintenance of wildebeest strategies, but to become well acquainted with the responses to threat as exhibited by the zebra, as one day the threat to dominance will inevitably arrive.

Chapter summary

- The wildebeest survives by a strategy of sheer numbers.
- Numeric superiority strategies are for risk reduction, dominance or both.
- Risk strategies are about diversification to reduce downside or sufficient size to take advantage of upside.
- If you hold enough tickets, one might win.   →

→
- Dominance strategies are about being seen to be everywhere in the chosen market.
- Blitz strategies give the appearance of being everywhere for a short period of time without the long term cost of perpetual blanket coverage.
- Dominance is not the end – the market will still need ongoing populating and a keen series of threat response strategies.

CHAPTER 12

Strategies of the hyena – benefiting from others

Possibly one of the most maligned and least admired animals of the Serengeti, the hyena has clearly employed the wrong PR consultant. Caricatured as a sniggering wimpering scavenger, the hyena has an image problem which is mostly unfounded. As the most common carnivore in Africa, the misunderstood dog-like creature is a survival success and is far from any endangered list. Africa has 3 main species – the spotted, the rare striped and the brown. Spotted and striped are found on the plains of the Serengeti. Hyenas probably have the most powerful jaws in proportion to their size of any land animal on the planet. The river dwelling crocodile can 'out-crush' them possessing jaws with 13 tonnes of force but the hyenas jaw strength is still approximately 3 times that of the much larger lion. Far from being scavengers and cowards, their collective hunting is sufficiently sophisticated to bring down an adult zebra and, if they attack in numbers, they are able to chase a small pride of lions from a carcass – beating the male lion at his own game!

Not every piece of hyena folklore is false. They do have cannibalistic tendencies, particularly males eating their own young, and the young themselves are competitive seeking to gain suckling dominance, depriving siblings of nourishment to the point where the smaller or weaker cubs starve to death. In addition to gaining feeding primacy, the precocious young will fight using their sharp baby teeth and employing the same techniques as adults in hunting, namely grabbing the opponent by the neck and shaking violently. In such a pugnacious rearing, clearly the larger firstborn has an advantage. As there is seldom any maternal intervention to this bullying, it is estimated that sibling rivalry accounts for about 25% of mortality amongst infants.

Hyena fact file:

Height	up to 90cm
Mass	up to 70kg
Life expectancy	up to 25 years in captivity, nearer a 20 year maximum in the wild
Diet	Carnivorous – carrion and own killed prey
Reproduction	105 day gestation averaging 2 cubs

The '*crocuta crocuta*' (the common spotted hyena) and '*hyaena hyaena*' (striped) spend most of the daytime in holes or rocky dens emerging to hunt mostly at night. They are dangerous predators able to attack large animals and, if the opportunity arises, humans. Although the situation was two way in ancient Egypt where hyenas were domesticated, fattened and eaten as a delicacy.

Physically comical, the strong jaws are counterbalanced by short and weak hind legs. Whilst strong and stocky, the hind quarters stoop and this front to rear imbalance means that they are not particularly fast runners. Male and female share similar physical characteristics and so it is very difficult to distinguish the sexes, even at close range as the female labial swellings are not strikingly dissimilar from the male's testes. This led to the myth that hyenas could change sex.

Some of their most distinctive features are the vocal cries and bloodcurdling howls. The famed 'laugh' is the sound they make when attacked, when they are running from a larger predator or when they feel threatened and is therefore when they are at their most dangerous. In all they make 11 separate and distinct calls from the low groans exchanged in greetings to the closed mouth grunting which accompanies aggressive behaviour and the cackling laugh when they are being chased. They have a staccato vibration growl as a threat and a fast whooping sound made in the excitement of a kill.

Hyenas are social animals organised in clans and they will defend clan territory against invasion by other clans. The social epicentre of the clan is the den which is usually situated on high ground and usually fairly central within their territory. Communication is through a variety of calls, postures and signals with the tail playing a major role in indicating intention. For example, a straight tail indicates an imminent aggressive act, a tail carried high over the back is an indication of excitement or frivolity, a limp hanging tail is the usual position of leisure and a tail tucked away between the hind legs, as with domesticated dogs, is a sign of submission or retreat. Social interaction is, however, limited as there is no male input to rearing the young and no cross-suckling, as observed by lions, even amongst very close relatives. The clan appears to be a loose collection of family members who hunt together and protect each other yet who also compete more and co-operate less than most social carnivores.

Hyenas can be skilful hunters but will invariably seek the easiest meal. Carrion is taken if available which yields the hyena its scavenging reputation but even fresh carrion will be ignored if there is an abundance of easy food such as young relatively poorly defended wildebeest calves, or old, sick or crippled animals. Some observers state that hyenas are pack hunters, like lions but without their sophisticated role definitions, but most feel that hyenas tend to attack alone but are then joined by any other clan members within earshot in a chaotic cacophony of chasing and killing prey. Killing is fairly gruesome as hyenas use their jaw strength to tear an animal apart. The severing of major arteries in the neck and disembowelling are the most common approaches taken by hyenas to tackle live prey.

Following a kill, the hyenas will invariably squabble and the resultant noise will alert all nearby of the presence of fresh meat. Other members of the clan will join in the squabble and occasionally, if the kill is near a territory border, another clan may be alerted. The consequence is then more squabbling even when a more co-operative approach would yield sufficient food for all. This lack of co-operation and perpetual competition, whilst repeated in many board rooms, does place a limitation and survival disadvantage on the hyena, and on the occupants of the board room. Lions may also be alerted by the noise and despite popular perception to the contrary, lions steal more hyena kills than the other way around. The lion-hyena dominance of a kill is usually down to sheer numbers and down to the experience of the lion. A young or inexperienced lion may back away from just a few aggressive hyenas, yet the hyena would not dare get close to an adult male lion in any circumstance and in any numbers, even in times of extreme hunger, as this would be tantamount to suicide.

The disadvantages of failing to co-operate are the antithesis of the co-ordinated approach of the lion. The business lessons from aspects relating to this behaviour are therefore dealt with in the chapter on the lion's strategies. It is true that hyenas will readily eat carrion, even after it has been abandoned by the original owner – lion, leopard or cheetah – and it is also true that they will force the owner of a kill to abandon it before it would have ideally wanted to do so. Although there are some estimates which indicate that carrion may be as little as 5% of a hyena's diet. The central feature of the hyena which we will focus on is their ability to make use of what others would not. Whilst there is an element of truth that the crocodile acts similarly, the hyena is the land-based master of using what others would not. With their strong jaws and highly acidic stomach the hyena can digest material beyond the ability of other animals. Meat, carrion, bones, skin, vegetable matter and even other animals droppings are all readily taken. The highly effective jaws make short work of pulping bones and the equally effective digestive tract is able to extract nutrients from every part of an animal except horns, hooves, teeth and hair. These 'inedible' parts are still devoured avidly and later regurgitated in the form of pellets. This led to another hyena myth – that they regurgitate food for their young as birds do. The truth is that hyenas do not bring food back to the den and the young eat from carrion and kills near the den as early as 5 months. At 1 year old the cubs hunt with the adults. Bones form such a large part of hyenas' diets that their faeces are often white.

The ability to survive on skin, bones and droppings which are utterly useless to most other animals makes the hyena a survival master with some strategies worth emulating. Many animals chase the prime cuts of zebra or wildebeest, but only one can revisit what others have left behind as useless and incorporate them into its own very successful survival strategy. As the Serengeti's most abundant carnivore and as one not on any endangered species list, these strategies have been immensely successful for centuries if not longer thus demanding our attention and consideration for business.

We will explore and illustrate a number of hyena strategies such as organisations benefiting from the carnage of war, those benefiting by growing due to the efforts of a dominant customer and hyena strategies of aligning with fringe but growing consumer preferences. We will consider lucky breaks where a hyena strategy develops due to a fortunate situation instigated by someone else beyond the company's control. The hyena is an opportunistic feeder and so we will illustrate where some organisations have seized one issue to take advantage. The hyena is also persistent, and we will show where rejection by others can turn into a disguised blessing. Finally we will consider the hyena strategy of seeing value where others do not and developing that value to generate a business.

Wartime hyenas

Coca-Cola and Gillette were amongst the many companies who benefited from the two World Wars. Others, like Harley Davidson, provided the mechanisms of war and benefited from their use by the military. In addition, the returning GI's wanted to ride the high quality motorcycles they had been accustomed to during the conflict and so post war sales soared. Coca-Cola and Gillette were more astute. The Harley Davidson had a direct impact on the war – transporting people with messages rapidly, over harsh terrain, reliably. Coca-Cola and Gillette could hardly be seen as vital to the war effort – or could they? As the US entered WWI in 1917, it ordered 3.5m razors and 36m blades – the troops needed to be clean shaven. In WWII both Gillette razor blades and Coca-Cola were seen as essential for the correct functioning of GI's and so their inclusion on the list of items of front line necessity created a wartime bonanza at a time when other companies were feeling squeezed by the economic consequences of the war. Benefiting from others – a classic hyena strategy – in this case, a war.

At a national level the USA operated war hyena strategies. Whilst the country made an immense, if not belated contribution to both WWI and WWII, in both cases their main economic rivals were busy blowing up the infrastructure of each other's future economic prosperity. All nations involved lost many lives and spent huge sums of money but with no damage on US soil, its infrastructure was intact, maybe even enhanced by the manufacturing upsurge required for the war. Add to this the financing of the European wars by loans, the USA gained a post war income stream. It should be noted that admittedly not all national loans were repaid, but on 31 December 2006 Britain finally paid the last £43m of war debt to the USA. The USA ended WWII at a significant competitive advantage. It had manufacturing infrastructure and a huge income stream of loan repayments. Its former rivals in Europe had cities of rubble to rebuild and American loans to rebuild them with. Taking advantage of this competitive discrepancy due to war is a bona fide hyena strategy – benefiting from the actions of others.

Dependent supplier hyenas

The concept of choosing to become a dependent supplier is a hyena strategy where the supplier benefits from the actions of the customer. Here a supplier makes a deliberate choice to serve one, or a very limited number of customers. The supplier's future becomes dependent on the success of the customer and the customer's product offering is only as good as the offering of the supplier – the two become inextricably linked.

In the UK, the most frequent examples of this strategy are suppliers to Marks & Spencer (M&S). The strategy started in M&S in the 1920's where retailers usually had to approach manufacturers via 'middle-man' wholesalers. The wholesalers tended to operate warehouses and receive large quantities from manufacturers, then release smaller quantities to retailers on demand. Simon Marks sought to transform the manner of retail business by having his own warehouses thus bypassing the whole-salers, particularly in his key supplier area of textiles. The Wholesale Textile Association (WTA) resisted this move strongly and threatened to remove any manufacturer trading directly with M&S from its list of approved suppliers. This would have meant that the manufacturer had no other outlet for sale.

In 1926 textile manufacturer Corah suffered a severe slump in trade and felt compelled to take the gamble of siding with M&S. Corah was consequently removed from the list of WTA suppliers. However M&S was growing to the extent that between 1922 and 1938 its turnover increased to 35 times the 1922 level. Rather than seeing its sales struggle through exclusion from the WTA, Corah's sales rocketed as a result of it becoming a sole customer supplier to M&S. For M&S the success was that for stockings previously bought through the WTA at 9s6d a dozen (9 shillings and sixpence), the price direct from Corah was 8s6d. M&S used part of this saved shilling to keep prices low and worked with Corah to use another part to increase quality levels, thus improving its reputation with the consumer. M&S made some aggressive moves in the market to strengthen its position. For example, whole-salers would take 3–4 months to pay suppliers. M&S took the decision to pay much more promptly therefore giving manufacturers a financial incentive to side with them. By 1933 M&S was responsible for significant increases in workforce numbers at 42 of its key suppliers.

Corah operated the strategies of the hyena – growing as a result of the efforts of M&S. It is true that the majority of M&S suppliers see themselves as partners rather than mere suppliers but the concept of aligning with a dominant customer to 'ride the wave' as they grow is a bona fide strategy of the hyena in benefiting from others.

Vehicle retailers also actively use hyena strategies. Dealerships usually sell the vehicles from one manufacturer and so are tied in to that manufacturer's success. When Renault unveiled the revolutionary Espace, it was a great time to be a hyena benefiting from Renault's efforts. However, when Rover collapsed, Rover dealers were suddenly acutely aware of the inherent risks of a hyena-dependent supplier strategy.

Fringe preference hyenas

Another wave to ride is that of a consumer trend in its infancy, or even better, like Body Shop, create the wave. Started by Anita Roddick in Brighton on the UK South coast in 1976, the Body Shop sought to trade cosmetic products in an ethical and environmentally friendly way, and refused to deal with products which were tested on animals. The company values are:

- Against animal testing
- Support Community Trade
- Activate Self Esteem
- Defend Human Rights
- Protect Our Planet

The initial 25 products were handmixed and packaging was kept to a minimum. Customers were encouraged to bring back bottles to be refilled rather than embrace the disposable society. The Body Shop was the first business which blatantly stressed its ethics as a driving force and the consumers loved it. A stock market floatation ensued, although, in my opinion, all the ingredients for not listing on a stock market were present (hippopotamus chapter), and for a while the company was the darling of investors. Growth by global franchising mushroomed the Body Shop to over 2,000 stores in 50 countries. As with any initiative, predators gathered. In this case the mainstream retailers moved in, like the hyena benefiting from other's good ideas, and started selling similar natural herbal based products. The boom ended, the company fell out of favour with consumers and investors and Anita Roddick stood down as CEO in 1998.

The hyena strategy for Body Shop was not just to identify and focus on a short term fringe element with strong growth potential, but in their case it was to create the fringe preference growth almost single handed. The largest mistake was perhaps not to consider the competitive actions of the stores, not to complete the analysis from the strategies of the elephant and to ignore the inevitable presence of hyena strategies from others. With hindsight the company would probably have benefited if it had followed the example of Apple with iPod and seen itself as a niche player (hippopotamus chapter).

Other hyena strategies of short term benefit from following trends which, at the time, would be too small for others to be interested in would include the minor specialist retailers such as tie rack and sock shop which bloomed for a while, but, like the hyena, would inevitably not be able to hang on to their prey for ever. If they don't lose it to lions they lose it to other hyenas and a cacophonic squabble results – not unlike business takeovers. Their hyena strategy should be to take the opportunistic feeding of aligning with the short term trend but realise that it is a short term trend and whilst they will grow with it, they will shrink with it just as fast. Their business model should reflect this transient nature and potential volatility aiming to move from the opportunist to more consistent strategies over time.

A cautionary tale where thousands of people entertained bona fide hyena strategies, but with the mistaken belief that they would go on for ever, comes from 17th century Holland. Carolus Clusius was an aged botanist without whom the Netherlands would not have one of its core identities. In 1593 he planted a small number of bulbs from an obscure Turkish plant in a garden at the University of Leiden. It was the first tulip garden in Holland. The bulbs became fashionable, especially with the rich who used them as lavish, ostentatious displays of their wealth. By the early 1600's horticultural experimentation brought a vast array of varieties and the rich continued to flaunt their assets in floral form. Entrepreneurs sold their possessions and bought fields in which to grow tulips. The financiers were not far behind and a vast market in tulip futures developed with many people selling their houses to release funds for tulip investment. The futures market was such that vast sums were being invested on tulip fields before the bulbs were even planted. By 1630 some people were earning 70,000 Florins (approx US$ 50,000) per month from the bulbs and flowers. Demand continued to surge and the 1630's saw a new class of nouveau riche develop as a direct result. In 1637 the market collapsed. Tulip sellers were unable to get the inflated prices they had become accustomed to and panic selling of tulip shares sent stocks into terminal freefall. Fortunes were lost overnight. The phenomenon became known as tulipania, and was simply a hyena strategy of seeking to gain advantage from a consumer trend. The error was thinking that the trend would go on forever.

About 350 years later, in London, UK, Prêt a Manger identified a fringe preference and mobilised to take advantage of it. Meeting at the Polytechnic of Central London (now Westminster University) property undergraduates Sinclair Beecham and Julian Metcalfe were fed up with soggy sandwiches and sought, with a £17,000 loan, to create an alternative in London's Victoria heartland serving customers towards the lower half of the price sensitivity axis – professionals in a hurry for fast food but without the desire to clog up their arteries with saturated fats. Prêt a Manger produced high quality food, not cheaply, but with consistency and originality. They shunned food preservatives and genetically modified products, they sought ethically raised chickens and chemical free ingredients. Business progressed and 3 years later a second outlet was opened. Then the early 1990's saw a boom in a fashion for healthy eating. Spurred by increased awareness of junk food diets, the Prêt customers became an expanding market and the business took off. Prêt was in the right place at the right time and expanded aggressively to take advantage of this opportunity. They had not created the opportunity, they were just very well placed to take advantage of it, having spotted it as consumers in Westminster some years before it had really gathered pace. That is the essence of hyena fringe preference strategy – seeing a rising trend, positioning yourself to take advantage of it and feasting whilst the trend grows. For Prêt a Manger they have looked sufficiently widely to know that the hyena strategies will not be appropriate for long as either the trend will cease growing at some point or, learning from Body Shop, realise that other carnivores are coming. They therefore considered more long lasting strategic possibilities. They chose the strategies of the wildebeest with almost blanket coverage of London, then reaching beyond and abroad. They then also made a 'flock' strategy of the zebra alliance in 2001 with an unlikely partner – McDonalds – who have paid in the region of £25m (media estimates) for a 33% stake. Whilst the types of food seem diametrically opposed, Prêt is able to tap into McDonalds global presence, property portfolio, international experience and franchising ability for further development of the brand.

Lucky break hyenas

The hyena strategies are about benefiting from others and the lucky break is the dream ticket for most entrepreneurs. Every so often someone wins the lottery, and in business it is the hyena. Richard Branson started his empire like this. When he was 22, and already with his own mail order record company, Richard Branson decided to expand the business into making music and the Virgin Records music label was formed. One of the early recordings, in Virgin's first recording studio in an Oxfordshire barn, was Mike Oldfield's Tubular Bells which was released in 1973. No 1970's or 1980's record collection was complete without two albums – Pink Floyd's Dark side of the moon – also released in 1973 and the Virgin recorded Tubular Bells. Virgin Records was on the map with a sensational success in its first year. Richard Branson continued with the strategy of the hyena gambling on a band which no other record label would sign. The gamble was that the record labels' conservative attitude was at variance with the type of music the populous wanted – this was more of a fringe preference hyena approach, but he gambled well – the band was the Sex Pistols who heralded in the short term fad of Punk Rock – and millions of albums sold.

In the chapter on the strategies of the cheetah we considered Friends Reunited. They had a lucky break on their way to galloping into market penetration by being featured on the BBC Radio 2 web site of the week. They did not plan this, they did not even influence it, but as lucky break feeders benefiting from others, they were there to take full advantage of it – all credit to them.

Opportunistic hyenas

In this category, a situation arises which can have a beneficial knock on effect. The hyena is the master of seeing something useful which others do not see and so can derive personal benefit from the arising of an unrelated opportunity.

Shanghai Automotive Industry Corporation (SAIC) were in prolonged talks to take over beleaguered British car manufacturer Rover. In 2004 SAIC appeared to have taken control of the Rover marque for £67m together with the intellectual property (IP) behind the most advanced Rover cars the 75 and the 25. As the extent of Rover's perilous finances became clear in the first quarter of 2005, SAIC withdrew from takeover talks and Rover called in the administrators in April 2005. For a short time it looked as if SAIC had managed to acquire the Rover name and all relevant IP for a comparatively small price and without the encumbrances of an 'average' production plant, an expensive British workforce, Rover's excessive debts and a massive pension fund shortfall. That would have been a classic opportunistic hyena success story. However, all did not end well. The assets were eventually awarded to the little known Nanjing Auto, also of China, who outbid SAIC and secured the deal. It is also unlikely that this will end well. The situation was well summed up by Geoffrey Robinson, Labour MP for Coventry North West and former executive with Jaguar cars, who told BBC Radio 4's Today programme "We can only wish them luck but they are a very small company and they will face formidable difficulties." These hyenas look not to have succeeded, but their strategies were undoubtedly those of the Serengeti opportunist.

Another interesting example of opportunistic strategies is found on the British rail and London underground networks. Smoking is banned almost everywhere. There are two supporting factors, firstly the health aspect of smokers and secondary smokers and secondly the safety aspect as the catastrophic King's Cross underground fire in 1987, which killed 31 people, was probably caused by smokers' litter – either a discarded match or a discarded lit cigarette which ignited grease on the escalator and led to a disastrous inferno.

Smoking in public buildings has now been banned in many countries, but for the rail and underground network it was an opportunistic hyena strategy initiated many years before Government legislation on the matter. By using the issues of an unrelated situation not of their making, namely the King's Cross fire disaster, they used a hyena strategy of seizing a situation to further their own objectives. The safety factor is important, although many suggest that it may have been exaggerated in order to achieve the objective of banning smoking on public transport. By banning smoking on all trains and stations, the transport companies are saving thousands of pounds by not having to employ and pay cleaning staff. As the twin drivers of health and safety are undefeatable arguments, there can be negligible opposition to these cost savings – that is an astute strategy of the opportunistic hyena.

Smoking is forbidden even on railway platforms which are uncovered and so outside the legal ban on smoking. There is no safety argument. Negligible heath argument. However, the fact that the consequent litter does not have to be cleared up is a strong financial argument and a win for the hyena.

Persistent hyenas

The persistent hyenas are not usually directly benefiting from others, but take the habits of the hyena in generating value where other people do not see any. The lessons of persistence are better explored in the chapter on the strategies of the rhinoceros, but the essence is that some people see value and persist, others give up. For those who persist, one bi-product is that the painful rejection by others can indeed generate benefit beyond what would have been generated had their rejecters been more accepting. For example, Hoover saw no value in the Dyson dual cyclone vacuum machine forcing James Dyson to manufacture alone and become a multi-millionaire in the process. Mere royalties from Hoover would have made him wealthy, but not to the present extent. Similarly, had Mattel and Hasbro, the toy giants not rejected Joel Glickman's idea of K'Nex, he would not have had to develop it himself, make millions and in due course have it distributed by one of his former rejecters. Next time someone rejects your 'bag of bones' think like the hyena – benefit from their rejection and show how you are able to see value where they did not by turning the metaphorical bones into nutrients as the hyena does.

The rejection may even enhance the offering with a challenge. I was involved in the creation of EvaluationStore.com. The first draft of the product was robustly challenged and ultimately rejected. The persistent hyenas did what they do best and picked through the bones and skin to find the key essence of the value in the proposition. This was then enhanced, had ancillary development and the proposition re-offered. Non-hyenas would have given up after the initial rejection. By picking through what others had rejected, the team distilled the value and developed something much better than the original proposition.

Seeing value where others don't

The ability to survive by gaining nourishment from the skin, bones and even the droppings of others is another major lesson the hyena can teach us. Other predators ignore these elements perceiving them as useless. However, with the hyena's digestive tract, they are far from useless – they can mean the difference between survival and death, between business success and failure.

US military 'expert' George Eliot had plenty of information at his disposal but drew negligible value from it. In 1938 he pronounced "war between Japan and the United States is not within the realm of reasonable possibility ... A Japanese attack on Pearl Harbor (sic) is a strategic impossibility".

He managed to be equally incorrect in his expert assessment of the information at his disposal from the European theatre of warfare one year later when he commented "the chances of Germany making a quick job of overwhelming Poland are not good".

Peter Minuit was a man who saw value where others did not. He purchased the Island of Manhattan for $24 of trinkets. The Dutch Government of the time saw negligible value in this partial swampland and suggested that Mr Minuit had been overcharged.

To show that we British also fail to appreciate the value of certain things, we need look no further than George Washington's first victory over the British at Trenton, New Jersey. A loyalist spy tried to report Washington's plans but was refused access to the Colonel in command as he was playing cards and did not wish to be interrupted. In desperation, the spy sent a note into the card game, which the Colonel promptly put in his pocket, unopened. It was found, still unopened, still in his uniform pocket when the victors searched his dead body some hours later.

In the chapter strategies of the giraffe we explored the concept of being driven by vision. In the context of the hyena, we use the same word – vision – to appreciate that some people are myopic and some are visionary. Some people will look at a piece of information or a situation and see no value. Others can look at the same piece of information or situation and have the vision to generate value from it.

The inspirational Helen Keller commented "It is a terrible thing to see and have no vision". Unfortunately most of us are surrounded by a number issues and situations where we see little value. The strategy of the hyena is to have the vision to see value where others do not.

No-one saw value in adhesive which was too weak to use until 3M developed the Post-it note. 3M chemist Dr Spencer Silver had developed a weak adhesive which left no residue when removed but was struggling to see an application until co-worker Art Fry was looking for a bookmark for his church hymn book. His problem was that traditional bookmarks fell out when the book was moved and he would want to mark several pages simultaneously to facilitate a rapid move from one song to another without delays sifting through pages. Another requirement was that the hymn book should not be damaged by having the pages marked, as would happen if the corners were turned down or if traditional adhesive tape were used. Fry saw Spencer's adhesive and applied some to a small piece of paper and the first post-it note was born. Fry had the vision to understand that his 'bookmark' had other possible functions, but early consumer tests showed that the public did not share his vision. In 1977, after failed consumer tests the product was almost abandoned. However, 3M persisted and in 1979 launched with a huge consumer sampling strategy. It worked and the Post-it note has become an essential part of most offices possibly even more widely used than Norwegian Johan Vaaler's 1899 invention – the paper clip – possibly Norway's greatest invention.

> During the Nazi occupation of Norway in WWII, the Norwegians were banned from wearing any memorabilia or buttons encompassing their king, a crown or the royal crest. The Norwegians responded by each wearing a paperclip in their jackets as a protest and symbol of being Norwegian. The Nazis realised that this was a protest against occupation and thereafter it became an arrestable offence to have a paperclip on your jacket in Nazi occupied Norway. A hyena strategy. Something of no value to the Nazis became a powerful symbol of defiance to the Norwegians.

Joanne Kathleen Rowling had an idea for a fictional children's character whilst on a train from Manchester to London. After 5 years of writing she had assembled the material for the first book and, with her literary agent, she sought a publisher. No publisher saw any value in this little bespectacled wizard. J.K.Rowling however, did see value. Eventually Bloomsbury Press thought that they may take a modest gamble with the book and the rest is history. Harry Potter is single-handedly responsible for getting young boys to read for pleasure. For Bloomsbury Press it was the hyena strategy of seeing value where other publishers had failed to do so. For the hundreds of childrens' books now being published every month there is the hyena strategy of seeking to capitalise on a trend of reading becoming fashionable – gaining benefit from another's initiative and hard work.

The strategies of the hyena have taken us from 17th century Holland to Harry Potter. We have observed great companies such as Gillette and Coca-Cola imitating the unfashionable savannah dog. Body Shop, Prêt a Manger and Richard Branson have emulated the strong jawed carnivore. My hope is that we have managed to re-address the poor PR suffered by the unfortunate hyena and explored examples of some relevant strategies for modern businesses to emulate. Most importantly, they work; the abundance of the hyena proves this – on the Serengeti and in business.

Chapter summary

- Hyenas do scavenge but will also make their own kills.
- In scavenging they are benefiting from others.
- Benefiting from others in business can take several forms – adverse scenarios, dependent suppliers, siding with a fringe preference or just getting a lucky break.
- Opportunistic hyenas can take advantage of a situation not of their making and not directly connected with the issues of their business to gain an advantage.
- Hyenas see value where others do not – they can extract nutrients from skin, bones and droppings.
- Hyena strategies are short and sharp – they will not go on forever. Forgetting this warning could leave you with a handful of limp tulips.

CHAPTER 13

Strategies of the crocodile – stealth and ambush

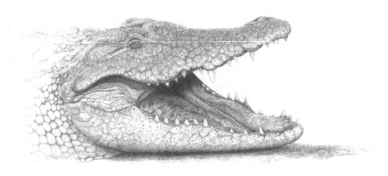

The fearsome large aquatic reptile '*crocodylus*' has 23 species worldwide of which 3 are in Africa but only 1 in the Serengeti – the large formidable and possibly the most dangerous of all 23 species, the Nile crocodile – '*crocodylus niloticus*'. With thick armour-plated skin, long tapering jaws, 66 sharp conical teeth, an expressionless face and immense strength, the crocodile has remained unchanged for thousands, possibly millions, of years. It is a survivor of the '*archosaria*', a group which included many well known dinosaurs, but this longevity should not imply simplicity. Crocodiles have a 4 chambered heart like mammals and unlike more modern reptiles. The hippo may well be king of the river but as a herbivore it is lower down the food chain and the top of the river food chain is one of the greatest and longest survival success stories – the crocodile.

The name '*crocodylus*' is derived from the Greek '*krokodeilos*' which literally means 'pebble worm' referring to the pebbled appearance of the skin and the fact that the crocodile has very short legs so that for most of its time on land the abdomen is in contact with the ground.

The Nile crocodile, also known as mamba, garwe and ngwenya, is found in most freshwater lakes, rivers, swamps and even smaller waterholes but is especially populous in rivers with dense vegetation on the banks – particularly the Mara and Grumeti rivers of the Serengeti. It is most at home in

Crocodile fact file:	
Length	Averaging 5m but unverified reports of 7m giants are commonplace
Mass	up to 1000lbs (450kg)
Life expectancy	approximately 45 years, 80 in captivity.
Diet	mostly (70%) fish, but are opportunist feeders and will take anything available – including humans
Reproduction	40–60 eggs laid and incubated for 70–100 days

water but is known to travel overland at night sometimes for many miles in search of new water.

Man is the only predator of the crocodile and as the skin is highly prized, crocodile populations have suffered. This could be catastrophic for the Serengeti ecosystem as the fish eating reptile helps maintain a balance within the food chain, particularly by limiting the numbers of barbel catfish. Were crocodile numbers to reduce further it seems probable that barbel numbers would increase. They in turn would then be free to consume larger numbers of other fish species, most of which are a food source for over 40 types of bird in the Serengeti. Further to this, if the birds then migrated elsewhere due to a lack of a suitable fish diet, there would be a decreased amount of bird droppings. These droppings provide food for a variety of fish and their absence would obviously reduce fish numbers further. Lack of fish would mean the barbel has lost its menu and so would reduce – and then turning full circle, the crocodile would have lost its main food source. Such is the delicate balance of this wonderous East African ecosystem that the removal of the reptile head of the river food chain could cause a negative spiral dramatically affecting birds, fish and reptile from which no reversal would seem possible.

Crocodiles, as reptiles, have no internal system for bodily temperature control and so spend much of their time seeking to maintain an appropriate temperature. They can be observed lying on the banks of rivers sunning themselves, often with mouths gaping to vent off heat. If the heat becomes too great they will return to their watery domain. Adults are dark green in colour with darker crossbands on the tail and this can be deceptively effective camouflage. The Nile crocodile has 3 or 4 rows of protective scales on the back of the neck, whereas most crocodilians have only 2. These merge with the remainder of the scales on the back and provide a hard exterior impenetrable to most conventional predators but not immune from being crushed by several tonne of hippo if the crocodile gets too close. The hippo will only attack the crocodile if it feels it is being threatened as the herbivore has no need for crocodile meat. I have handled baby crocodiles, and even at a young age this armour is exceptionally hard to touch. Sharp teethed predators can puncture this armour and so the young are vulnerable when not in the vicinity of the protective parent, although their little needle teeth meant that I kept my fingers well away. Male crocodiles are larger than females and generally more aggressive, although a female defending a nest of eggs should never be underestimated. Under the guidance of a ranger at a crocodile farm I placed a long staff near a female guarding a nest. With no warning and at lightning speed she swung her jaws around to snap them on the staff. Were that a limb, it would have been broken or severed, and it was the demonstration the ranger wanted to illustrate the sudden and aggressive reaction to an intruder. This poor female was unaware of the fact that the rangers had already removed the eggs and transferred them to incubators and that her protection was in vain.

At the onset of the breeding season, which varies in time from place to place, the normally solitary crocodiles group and the females construct nests on the riverbanks from plant matter. The Nile crocodile nests are about 50cm deep and several metres from the water. Fascinatingly, nest temperature determines the gender of the hatchlings. If the nest is perpetually below 85 degrees Farenheight, the hatchlings will be female, if the temperature is consistently above 95 degrees they will be male and if between 85 and 95 degrees both genders will hatch. The use of vegetable matter for nesting assists temperature maintenance as it composts and thus generates its own heat. Despite the fact that the Nile crocodile defends her nest less aggressively than probably all other crocodilians, over 50% of eggs survive the attentions of monitor lizards, hyenas and a variety of other predators including humans. Most nest raiding occurs when the female is forced to leave the nest temporarily in order to bask in the water to thermoregulate. Once the hatchlings start to emerge, both parents will assist them by using their immensely strong jaws to gently crack the eggs. The hatchlings are then scooped into the parent's mouths and transferred to the river, being deposited near to the comparative safety of underwater vegetation.

The young will start feeding on worms and small aquatic invertebrates but soon graduate to a diet of frogs, tadpoles and eventually fish. Adults will feed mostly on fish and co-operative behaviour is commonplace where groups of crocodiles will cordon off areas of a river and coral the fish into a killing zone in a controlled and patient manner before embarking on a chaotic shark-like feeding frenzy where it is every crocodile for itself. Lone crocodiles also use their long tails to coral fish into shallower waters where they then launch at the concentrated shoal with great sideways sweeping movements of their mouths scooping up several fish with each swipe. Adults may also venture several hundred metres inland at night in search of mammals dead or alive.

The most demonstrative of the adults feeding habits is when they take mammals from water – either when the mammals approach the river edge to drink or when, as in the great wildebeest migration, they seek to cross the river. The crocodile will lie just below the waterline with only eyes, ears and nose above the surface. Eyes, ears and nose are slightly raised and on the same horizontal plane facilitating the ability to have negligible presence above the water yet still be able to see, hear and smell. When they identify potential prey from this surface position they are able to calculate its position, dive below water and stalk the prospective victim. The ability to pinpoint the mammalian drinker is exceptional as the giant reptile moves slowly underwater to the point earlier identified. There is no rush as the crocodile can remain submerged for exceptional periods of time. Nostrils can close underwater and eyes have a third eyelid for submarine protection. He is therefore able to make his way to where the drinking mammals have been identified with extreme stealth, then lie in wait until the unfortunate animal steps just a fraction too far. At this point stealth turns to ambush. Using the immense power of legs and tail, the crocodile will lurch suddenly forward grabbing the hapless mammal before it has a chance even to comprehend what is happening. The speed of the ambush is in sharp contrast to the patient and unhurried stealth movement. Having grabbed the animal by whatever part available the crocodile will exert force with its jaws equivalent to up to 13 tonnes. He will then reverse into the water dragging the doomed mammal into the watery depths to drown. The animal's only hope is if the crocodile's grip is imperfect and if so, wriggling may facilitate escape. Crocodiles jaws are built for grabbing prey and they cannot chew or move their jaws from side to side. They therefore need to swallow great lumps of meat whole. In order to do this with a larger animal, groups of crocodiles will hold onto an animal carcass and, when they have a firm grip, twist their bodies violently tearing off portions of flesh. This mode of eating is known as the crocodile 'death roll'. The fact that several crocodiles are holding a carcass whilst others make the roll does not necessarily indicate further co-operative feeding behaviour. It may be that an individual chooses to roll whenever they feel that they have sufficient quantity of meat gripped and a sufficiently firm grip. Those holding may be doing so due to a reluctance to release, fearing that the presence of other crocodiles may not allow them to re-grip, rather than a desire to assist another with its feeding.

When no other crocodiles are available to hold the carcass the death roll diminishes in effectiveness. In these circumstances the reptile will push the carcass into underwater tree roots or even wedge it between riverbed boulders in order to hold it fast whilst it takes grip and rolls. This has led to the misunderstanding that the crocodile stores its food underwater and returns when the water has softened the flesh. With such forceful jaws there is no need for softening and for such an opportunistic feeder the time to eat is always in the present rather than the future. The digestion system also argues against delays in feeding. Crocodilian stomach acid is sufficiently strong and in such abundance that a steel bar would be digested if swallowed. Compared to this, slightly harder than ideal flesh is a negligible challenge.

The annual Serengeti migration provides a crocodilian feast captured innumerable times on the cameras of wildlife television programmes. Here wildebeest and zebra seek to cross the river. All the crocodiles have to do is lie in wait and advance upon an individual. This is not completely the equivalent of a meal on a plate for them as the confusion of so many crossing simultaneously and the activity of so many hooves splashing and swimming make it more akin to grabbing sushi from the moving conveyor belts of Japanese restaurants. There is a skill in doing so without the sushi falling embarrassingly to the floor or the wildebeest escaping and reaching the bank. In either case hunger is the result. The advantage humans have is that sushi belts tend to move slower than wildebeest and are not kicking out at the same time. The crocodile still uses its hunting technique of stealth and ambush. He identifies a victim, usually one marginally outside the main body of swimmers, advances underwater with stealth and accelerates to leap into the ambush grabbing whatever part of the victim he can and, in the same way as the drinking mammal is dragged deeper to drown, the fording mammal is taken away from the massed ranks of survivors. An abundance of crocodiles at these river crossings mean that there is a queue of willing assistants to anchor the meal for the death roll and share in the spoils themselves.

Incredible but true

On Wednesday 11 December 2002, BBC news reported the story 'Man bites crocodile'. Mac Bosco Chawinga, 43, was swimming in Lake Malawi to cool off after a days work when he was attacked by a crocodile. Both his arms were grabbed by crocodile's powerful jaws and were inside the reptile's mouth with immense pressure being exerted upon them as the teeth closed in. The crocodile started dragging Mr Chawinga into deeper waters when, despite the pain in his now helpless arms he fought back. He lunged at the crocodile's nose, one of the few soft parts on the body, and sank his teeth deep into the snout. The crocodile let go and retreated allowing Mr Chawinga to swim to the safety of the shore where fishermen found him and took him to hospital. Despite large blood loss from puncture wounds to his arms and legs, Mr Chawinga survived with a unique tale and a resolve to swim more carefully.

Stealth and ambush in business

In my opinion one of the greatest exponents of the crocodilian stealth and ambush strategies in modern business is Sir Philip Green. He is presently one of Britain's wealthiest men controlling in excess of 12% of the UK clothing retail market and with assets in excess of £3.6bn. Born in 1952, he set up his first enterprise as a teenager with the assistance of a £20,000 loan. He had been working for a shoe importer and travelled to Europe, the USA and the Far East. On these visits he developed the relationships and trade links to allow him to import jeans from the Far East and sell them to retailers in London. This was entrepreneurial activity, but he had not yet used the strategies of the crocodile. This changed in 1979 when a 27 year old Philip Green heard of a group of 10 designer clothing outlets going into receivership. These outlets included stock with a retail value of £35,000. The crocodile stalks with stealth, and then ambushes with extreme speed and power. The essence is often just being in the right place at the right time, waiting perhaps by a waterhole, and when the opportunity to ambush arrives, doing so with lightening speed. Philip Green didn't have time to inspect the stock. He was in the right place and sprung the ambush instantly. Purchasing the entire stock for a fraction of the book price, he dry-cleaned it, put it in polythene wrappers to make it look brand new, and rented a retail site in London from which to sell the items. His first ambush was a success.

His second ambush was much greater. In 1984 he heard of denim retailer Jean Jeannie considering how to close the business – by sale, receivership or any other method. The previously successful retailer had let itself go to the extent where an exit was inevitable. Time was pressing and the Jean Jeannie sale was to be achieved in 3 days. This set alarm bells ringing and a cursory inspection of the books showed £3.5m owing to the bank, £3.5m to suppliers and they were having difficulty paying staff. The company was about to collapse and was losing £70,000 each week. Green contacted the owner and was told that the asking price was £4m. Green, a strong negotiator, knowing the weak position of the company offered £65,000 with a further £435,000 if he turned the company around within 6 months. Jean Jeannie had no better offer and reluctantly accepted – the ambush had been sprung and the prey caught. By persuading the bank to freeze the debt for 6 months, then taking personal control of buying, stock management and the staff, Green started his revolution. Bringing in new personally chosen stock lines manufactured through his Far East contacts, Philip Green started to get customers through the doors again. Break even was achieved in 4 months. Early in the following year, 1985, Green was approached by Lee Cooper and sold the business to them for £7m. After clearing the remaining debts, he had a profit of £3m for less than a year's work.

Green's ambushes continued to increase in size and scope. In 1995, with Tom Hunter, he bought Olympus. 3 years later JJB sports bought the company from him for $550m, with Philip Green personally receiving $37m. The secret of the crocodile was being in the right place to pick up a tasty morsel and spring the purchase at its time of greatest vulnerability.

The crocodile can be an opportunist feeder, but other times it will lie, covertly, in wait for very long periods of time ready to spring the ambush. Philip Green lay in wait for the Sears Group. He watched them over a period of about 10 years. In 1999 the time was right and, backed by the Barclay brothers, he bought the group for approximately £550m. The break up of the group yielded £730m, of which £150m was Philip Green's.

His next ambush target was Marks & Spencer for whom he tabled a £7bn hostile bid in 1999. The ambush was fought off and Green turned his attentions to another weak and vulnerable creature by the water edge on whom most people had given up any hope of their survival – British Home Stores. With £50m of his own money and £150m of borrowed cash another ambush was sprung and the golden boy of retail turnarounds had his toughest task yet. Taking personal charge of almost every aspect of the business, the turnaround was completed and the previously dull brand has enjoyed a revival.

Increasing in size again, in 2002 Green purchased Arcadia for £850m – again £50m of his own money and the rest borrowed. Green paid back the loans within 2 years. By 2005 he had made sufficient improvement in the business to pay himself a dividend of £1.3bn.

2004 saw another attempted ambush of M&S at just over £9bn. This was again repelled but it must only be a matter of time before this ardent user of crocodile strategies manages a successful ambush on the prey he so clearly desires. One thing is for sure – he has not forgotten M&S. Like the crocodile, he will stalk its every move, proceed with stealth and wait until the time is perfect before driving with tail and legs to press immensely strong reptilian jaws around the prey.

Takeovers

One of the most obvious uses of stealth strategies are in hostile takeover bids. The predator builds up a war chest of financial reserves, produces and holds a communications strategy for the press and shareholders, builds an information reservoir on the intended prey and waits, like the crocodile, with just the eyes above the water's surface. When they deem the time appropriate they pounce into the ambush.

When septuagenarian Malcolm Glazer took control of Manchester United in 2005, then the richest football team in the world, there were all the signs of crocodile strategies. Whilst vilified in many sections of the UK press,

Malcolm Glazer is a hugely successful businessman who took control of his family business after the premature death of his father and turned it into an empire well in excess of $1bn. That empire includes excellent sporting interests including his 1995 purchase of the NFL Tampa Bay Buccaneers. Financial success has followed, as has sporting success with the Buccaneers winning the Super Bowl in 2003.

Approximately 23% of Manchester United shares were held by two Irishmen, J McManus and J Magnier. Glazer had gradually built up a holding from 2% in 2003, to 5%, then 14%, then to over 17%. If Glazer could persuade the Irishmen to sell to him he would have much more than the 30% required to launch a full takeover bid. This would be enough to launch a bid but not enough to launch a fatal ambush. Glazer chose stealth and waited. McManus and Magnier purchased more shares, raising their share to 29% – just below the 30% level where they would be required to declare takeover intentions. In doing so they maximised their usefulness to Glazer and put themselves in the most beneficial position to reap the rewards of any bid. They then waited.

Glazer continued to operate stealth strategies by continuing to buy shares throughout 2004 raising his stake to 28%. On 13 May 2005, both stealth strategies succeeded and Glazer bought the 29% of McManus and Magnier raising his stake to 57% and thus gaining control of the company. Had Glazer ambushed one year earlier when he only owned 14% and the Irish duo would have had 23%. The combined 37% would be enough to launch a takeover but would not be the fatal strike of the 2005 ambush with 57%. The crocodile's ambush is always spectacular, but preceding it are long periods of stealth. The key to crocodilian success is the timing of the ambush.

Stealth and ambush in a multiple market

The US tobacco industry saw an excellent example of stealth and ambush in 2003. On 2 April, Philip Morris slashed the price of its US tobacco brands by a huge 20%. Simultaneously they increased their US marketing expenditure. Rival company R.J.Reynolds were to some extent caught by surprise and had to use 'follow me' strategies copying the price cuts throughout the US. In due course R.J.Reynolds had to raise their short term advertising expenditure to deal with initial slow sales. Both companies suffered drastically reduced margins and the smokers of America rejoiced in the lowest prices for some years.

However, the price cut and marketing increase were not the ambush – they were part of a stealth strategy. R.J.Reynolds had depleted their cash reserves in keeping pace with Philip Morris. The latter had built up their financial coffers for this purpose and consequently did not suffer the denudation which Reynolds did. Then, with the rival weakened, Philip Morris sprung the ambush. The US market activity was the stealth activity of denuding Reynolds and weakening their financial ability to respond elsewhere. The real target for the ambush was Russia. Morris pushed $800m of investment into Russia and other former Eastern Block countries and with Reynolds unable to respond, Morris took a commanding lead in the race to secure brand dominance in the emerging Eastern European markets.

Crocodile strategies in marketing

Some of the greatest users of crocodile strategies are the marketing departments of several prestigious brands. They silently stalk a rival organisations marketing initiative, wait for exactly the right moment and then release a torrent of marketing activity which has the effect of neutralising the rivals efforts. The term has become known as 'ambush marketing'. The most common approach is in the sporting arena where one company will pay large sums to sponsor an event and a rival will ingeniously create the impression that they too are connected with the event, but without paying the sponsorship fee. The two rivals then share the benefit but one achieved it for free! Unsurprisingly the phenomenon is also known as 'parasitic marketing' but I think that does not do justice to the genius and creativity involved.

One of the earliest co-ordinated ambush marketing campaigns was by Kodak at the 1984 Olympics. Fuji were the official sponsor but Kodak sponsored the TV broadcasts and so achieved the effect of having their name mentioned in prominence to the trackside banners of Fuji. Kodak also sponsored the US athletics team and emblazoned their clothing with Kodak logos. The Fuji sponsored event therefore featured athletes running with 'Kodak' on their kit and commentated on by a TV presenter perpetually mentioning Kodak. Fuji learnt from the experience and managed to equalise by similar stealth and ambush techniques at the 1988 Seoul games where Kodak were an official sponsor.

At the 1992 Barcelona games Nike sponsored certain press conferences – despite Reebok being the official sponsor. Nike then ambushed Reebok again at the 1996 Atlanta Olympics by covering every available billboard in Atlanta with Nike posters. They also handed out banners for spectators to wave and built a temporary structure – the Nike Center (*sic*) – right next to the central Olympic stadium. Official sponsorship would have cost $50m. Nike paid nothing. Market research confirmed that a large majority of the public believed that Nike was an official sponsor to the Atlanta games. Nike also sponsored the US ice hockey team at the 2002 winter Olympics and thereby achieved considerable exposure despite not paying a penny to the Olympic Committee. The 2002 football world cup was another Nike success where bus-side billboards were the main offensive weapon.

Adidas produced a 12 part Olympic documentary featuring Adidas sponsored athletes to coincide with the Sydney 2000 games. The Adidas programme gained exceptionally heavy TV coverage for Adidas during the Olympic games despite them not being a sponsor. Another effective tactic used by both Adidas and Quantas in Sydney was to purchasing advertising time at each end of the competitor company's exposure.

However, my favourite was from Telecom New Zealand, also during Sydney 2000. The Olympic rings are a registered mark and using them would be illegal. However, writing the word 'ring' in different colours and in two rows – top row blue, black, red, bottom row yellow green – exactly as per the Olympic ring symbol was a stroke of creative genius. Add the phrase "with Telecom mobile you can take your own phone to the Olympics" and the association with the greatest sporting event on earth is complete – at no additional cost.

In his book '*Ambush marketing*' Frank Zimbo defines it as "the unauthorised association of a business or organisation with the marketing of a particular event". I accept the view that such tactics are potentially damaging to the economic interests of the sponsored event as there is no reason to pay exorbitant fees to be an official sponsor if the same effect can be achieved by crocodile strategies. With $700m being achieved as sponsorship revenue for the Sydney Olympics, the stakes are high and much has been written questioning the ethics of such approaches. The majority seems to look disparagingly down on such tactics from a morally high ivory tower. However, I admire the audacity, the creativity and the lateral thinking to achieve these ambushes and therefore endorse the approach. Provided that the law has not been broken, I feel that business, like nature, is 'red in tooth and claw' and that event organisers should stop whining about users of these strategies and be equally creative in countering them. For example, Nike would not have been able to buy billboard space if the International Olympic Committee has bought all the space before them! In 1997 the IOC stipulated that all billboard space in all future Olympic cities was to be secured by the host city for the duration of the games. This cost the Athens 2004 games in excess of $10m. That is just one avenue closed, many others remain and new ones will be created by marketing crocodiles each Olympics – personally I await the fruits of their creativity with alacrity with each World Cup or Olympics.

Probably my favourite ambush of all time was by the Dutch brewery 'Bavaria', the oldest brewer in Holland. They scored a tremendous success by providing orange lederhosen to Dutch football fans in the 2006 World Cup. Why lederhosen? – the world cup was in Germany and they are traditional German attire. Why orange? – the Dutch

➜

→

national colour. The lederhosen also each had a lion's tail. Two lions flank the Dutch coat of arms and so are intrinsic in Dutch identity, but it is deeper in football psyche than that. The Dutch sing a song from the 1950's:

Hup Holland Hup
Laat de leeuw niet in z'n hempie staan
Hup Holland Hup
Trek het beesie geen pantoffels aan
Hup Holland Hup
Laat je niet het veld uit slaan
Want een leeuw op voetbalschoenen
Durft de hele wereld aan

Which roughly translates as:

Hup Holland Hup
Do not embarrass the lion (implied: by playing football badly)
Hup Holland Hup
Put no slippers on this beast's claws (implied: making him power-less; you cannot play football in slippers!)
Hup Holland Hup
Do not let them intimidate you
For a football booted lion is a match for the world

I know it makes little sense, but the concept of the lion is rooted in Dutch football culture and Bavaria have identified with it. The fans were therefore pleased to wear the comical clothing.

However, as Budweiser was the 'official beer' of the world cup, the Germans were contractually obliged to ensure that no other beer was advertised within the stadia. The fans were therefore not permitted to enter the stadia wearing the lederhosen – and so the uninhibited Dutch promptly removed them, watching the matches in their underwear thus guaranteeing huge television coverage as it had to be mentioned by every commentator every time Holland played. This was a great ambush and the authorities contributed to the success and publicity through their farcical insistence on prohibiting the Bavaria logo being seen.

In the 2010 World Cup in South Africa, Bavaria attempted a more subtle ambush by having attractive female models wearing short skirts sporting small Bavaria logos. Cameras were drawn to these members of

→

> ➜
> the crowd and the Bavaria logo was briefly visible before South African
> authorities ejected the wearers from the stadia. This did not have the
> mass population appeal of the German ambush but was still sufficient
> for Bavarian beer to get media attention at negligible cost.

Marketing crocodile strategies can also have a slow patient build up. In 2010
American food giant Kraft purchased British confectioner Cadbury's. It is
fully expected that in due course they will extricate manufacture from the
United Kingdom and make the chocolate cheaper elsewhere, as they did with
the British firm Terry's after they acquired it in 1993. As the deal looked to
be closing Mars made a subtle but significant move. Mars, whilst American,
have a large British presence and manufacture West of London. They have
no intention of moving manufacture elsewhere. The subtle but significant
move was the addition of a small Union flag (the flag of the United
Kingdom) and the words 'Made in Slough, UK'. I make the assumption that
this is the first small step of stealth which will result in a huge nationalistic
ambush if and when Kraft to move Cadbury's manufacturing elsewhere.

A more innocent crocodile

Ambush marketing usually refers to sporting events and is a 'win–lose–lose'
position. The ambusher wins, the ambushed sponsor loses and the event
loses through decreased future revenue. One excellent exponent of these
strategies does so without anyone losing – Richard Branson. By devoting so
much time to crazy activities (allegedly 20% of his time) such as blue
ribband gaining trans-Atlantic powerboats or ballooning around the world,
he can maximise coverage through newspapers and television news channels, even reaching channels where there is no advertising such as the BBC.
The Virgin logo is emblazoned on all of his promotional activities and the
effect, for free, is probably greater than buying immense quantities of advertising space, much of which would be missed when I leave the room to
make a cup of tea. Even by supporting and sponsoring the record breaking
flight around the world in 2006 of former adventuring rival Steve Fossett
(now sadly deceased), Branson ensured that the Virgin logo was on every
television screen in every news broadcast. By taking off in the US he
acquired excessive US coverage, by landing in Britain he achieved tremendous UK coverage – brilliant. The only difference between this and conventional ambush marketing is that no-one was hurt, no-one disadvantaged and
no-one lost.

A less innocent crocodile

The crocodile strategy users of marketing departments of some food and drink companies were brought to the attention of the UK Government by the *Which?* Magazine report 'Health warning to Government, 2004. This was followed up by their 2005 report 'Shark Tales and Incredible Endorsements'. In 2006 *Which?* Made a further report 'Child catchers – the tricks used to push unhealthy food to your children'. Here they outlined an array of techniques used by companies to market direct to children, circumventing parental diet control. The tone of the *Which?* Reports has become increasingly critical whilst the inventiveness of the marketers has become increasingly creative and our children have become increasingly obese. I also congratulate them on their title – the child catcher in the children's film *Chitty Chitty Bang Bang* is still one of the scariest children's characters ever!

To illustrate a range of stealth strategies, below is a short list of some of the tactics and examples used in the report. The full report, available on the *Which?* Website, contains 40 marketing tactics aimed at children. The purpose of illustrating them here is to allow the reader to ponder whether variants of them could be successful within their own business – hopefully in creative marketing without the detrimental impact on our children. Please observe the creativity and the range of tactics and where appropriate, emulate responsibly.

- **Text 2 win competitions** – the Mobile Data Association estimates that 3.6m texts are sent every hour. Children and teenagers are major players in this market. A 2001 text 2 win competition by Cadbury drew major criticism. 65m confectionery products advertised £1m of prizes and chocolate sales soared. Flytxt.com, who developed the campaign stated that over 5m texts were received. In 2003 Coca-Cola initiated a promotion for Fanta where labels on Fanta contained a code to enter a competition. Although entry was not technically conditional on making a purchase, in practice, codes were obtained from a purchased can of Fanta which has 35g of sugar per 100g.
- **Voucher for equipment deals** – Cadbury's 2003 campaign had vouchers on confectionery to earn sports equipment. Walkers crisps used the same tactic. It would take a long time of using the exercise equipment to work off the calories gained by eating the confectionery or crisps. However, it was an effective way to persuade parents that there was a positive side to the purchase.
- **Internet games exposure** – in the Pepsi world game, a character has to race to feed a thirsty customer with Pepsi – at 36g of sugar per can.

- **On-line community style web sites** – Mars brand Starburst had a site which hosted an on-line magazine, celebrity gossip, competitions and games – and plenty of mentions of Starbursts.
- **On-line game sponsoring** – in 2005 Kellogg's Frosties (37g of sugar per 100g) were promoting links with *Star Wars II* including an on-line 'Jedi training programme' through the Kellogg's web site. Another game featured 'Tony the Tiger' (mascot of Frosties). Good innocent fun or gratuitous product reinforcement?
- **Toy invasion** – a McDonalds playset containing plastic burgers, chicken nuggets etc is on sale at Argos and Toys R Us.
- **Play invasion** – placing marketing messages on play equipment is not new. McDonalds, particularly in the US, have ensured good play equipment is available to facilitate children's visits. Scottish iconic drink Irn Bru (33g of sugar per can) sponsors the 'Irn Bru Fun Factory and Walk' in Falkirk Scotland – the children can also climb and slide through giant Irn Bru cans.
- **Film placement** – Burger King, Kellogg's and Pepsi all had their products positioned in the *Fantastic Four* film. Coca-Cola was positioned in *Madagascar*. This is an inventive method of gaining product exposure in the cinema or home, via the DVD. The product is featured subtly but positively. This is not limited to children. In the 2006 James bond film casino Royale, the product placement was gratuitous, blatant and excessive. I would suggest subtlety is less offensive.
- **Screen savers** – free screensavers with great features and perpetual product images.
- **Viral marketing** – internet based video clips sent by person to person. Many excellent ones have been developed, now they have invaded the children's marketing arena.
- **E-cards** – greetings cards to be e-mailed to friends with products on display. I have not seen this, but the *Which?* Report sites McDonalds as a user of this technique.
- **False focus** – Rowntree's Jelly Tots shout loud and large about 'now with real fruit juices', which is of course very healthy. Closer inspection reveals 6% fruit juice and 59% sugar. Mars Milky Way is 'rich in calcium, magnesium and vitamins', it also has 35g of fat and 56g of sugar per 100g.
- **Chatbots** – artificial intelligence software which monitors chat rooms, picks up on key words and steers the conversation in a pre-determined direction – often with brand data.
- **Blogs** – web based diaries – Dr Pepper launched a blog to promote its flavoured milk brand 'Raging Cow'.

Learning from this, I put a 'which animal are you?' mini-assessment on the Strategies of the Serengeti web site. It was reasonably interesting and informative and takes very little time to complete. I only ever intended it as a small awareness campaign but thousands of people have now assessed their business as using hippo or giraffe or dung beetle strategies. This is a wholly innocent and reasonable marketing activity to increase awareness of the book and conference speeches as no-one is detrimentally affected. What I was unprepared for was the number of businesses which contacted me to state that the assessment had alerted them to something within their business of which they were previously unaware.

Obsolescence, peripherals and refills

Another less than innocent stealth and ambush strategy is the gaining of customer tie in. Razors for male grooming are sold ridiculously cheaply so that refills of the blades can have higher margins due to the customer's reluctance to buy a different razor each time.

I am told that it is technically possible to have a light bulb which would probably never cease functioning. However, such an invention would kill a multi-million pound/dollar light bulb manufacturing market. Recent legislation emphasises long-life light bulbs, but still not indefinite bulbs. This is a similar strategy to that of Hoover, and others, which Dyson partially collapsed. Millions of vacuum cleaner bags were sold to customers tied in to a particular model. Without the bags, the vacuum cleaner would not work and so the market was captive. Lower margins on the machines could be offset by higher margins on the bags.

Computer printer manufacturers use refill ambush strategies. Each printer has a captive market from its unique ink cartridge and the printer is programmed to cease functioning when the toner is near empty. Regrettably there is no way to over-ride this programming and so we all throw away a small amount of expensive toner each time the printer dictates that it is 'almost empty' and demands a new cartridge.

Incredible but true
One US company was concerned with some of the risks attached to European operations. One of their concerns stemmed from a somewhat outdated impression of Italy, fuelled more by the American history on the 1930's than modern Italy. As a result they issued a dictate that their European operations were not permitted to undertake business south of Rome. The European board were aware that there were several opportunities south of Rome and that this arbitrary geographical line made no business sense, but challenges to it were unsuccessful.

→

→

A great business opportunity arose in Italy, on the Eastern coast but several miles south of Rome (which is near the Western coast). Being involved in this opportunity was forbidden by the US parent. The cunning European board engaged in an incredibly simple but superbly effective strategy to ambush the US parent. Every time they made presentations, they skewed the map of Europe so that North was at 45 degrees – in the 'North West' position. After keeping this up for a number of meetings they drew the US attention to the Italian opportunity and showed that it was above a horizontal line drawn "Eastwards" from Rome – actually the line was North West – South East, but being horizontal it looked 'West–East'. The US board therefore believed that because the town in question was above a horizontal line, it must be North of Rome. The project was sanctioned and was a success by all measures. I understand that even now, several years later, the stealth was so effective that there is no suspicion in the US that the project was South of Rome.

(details are vague and anonymous to protect
the careers of those involved)

Product launch ambush

I recall once being part of such an ambush but will again be vague to protect the guilty. The company for which I worked held approximately 30% of our market. Another company held approximately 40% and the remaining 30% was distributed between a variety of smaller players, the largest holding 8% – almost a classic duopoly position. Our major rival company had recently spent a small fortune on a manufacturing plant and were therefore at their most vulnerable. 30% of their output from this plant was one product.

We undertook a variety of espionage techniques – including myself having a meal with an outgoing disgruntled senior accountant of the rival. The meal was arranged by a recruitment consultant with whom I had a very good relationship. Combining our intelligence we determined how to best ambush them and prevent them maximising the benefits of utilising their pristine plant. With a large sum of cash having been spent on the premises and with new depreciation charges to absorb, they were likely to be financially vulnerable. We deliberately launched a version of one of our products to compete directly with their dominant product, and did so at unsustainably low profit levels. This forced them into price cutting and inevitable loss making in their early months of new premises operation. Having focused their minds on their financial position we invested heavily in new products, which in that industry have about a 2–3 month design to availability lag and a life cycle of anywhere from 6 months to a few decades. This stealth and ambush strategy was reasonably successful but not a killer blow as of the 6 or 7 products we launched, none were stunningly successful, and none lasted more than a year. In fact, the least successful held our record for the shortest period of time from launch to withdrawal – 23 weeks. Had all of them been successful our respective market shares may even have reversed with us having the 40% and them the 30%, but alas, our product launches were not good enough to maximise the effects of our ambush strategy.

A product launch ambush was achieved by UK grocer, the US Wal Mart owned ASDA in the Spring of 2006. The England football team were to play in the European finals in June 2006 and a new kit was designed for the team. Large numbers of supporters would want the new kit and so a lucrative market would exist. Kit manufacturer Umbro, according to ASDA, had declined to supply ASDA with the shirts and so ASDA cleverly purchased a large number of shirts which were surplus stock from European distributors – the so called 'grey market'. To compound the ambush and achieve maximum marketing coverage, 5,000 of the shirts were put on sale in 42 ASDA stores slightly before the official launch of the kit. A further 22,000 were added to sales on the day of the launch. By making a pre-emptive launch another achievement of ASDA is to set a pricing level which was communicated throughout the media. Competitors and customers would be well aware of ASDA's price and so any aspirations of higher prices by competitors were instantly wiped out – with 4 days notice – so competitor margins, estimates and budgets would have been thrown in turmoil. I see this as a brilliant ambush, where the two winners are the customer and the ambush perpetrator.

Sometimes stealth can go wrong

There is a tale of woe from the American brewing industry where the stealth of product re-engineering probably resulted in the near elimination of a once famous brand. I say 'probably' because some of the issues are debatable with no clear objective truth.

The brand was Schlitz beer. The Joseph Schlitz Brewing Company was formed by German immigrant Joseph who had come to America from Mainz in 1850. It rose to become the beer of the working class American and rejoiced in the strapline 'the beer that made Milwaukee famous'. In every year from 1960 to 1976 Schlitz was the second best selling brewer, by volume, in the US – second, of course to Anheuser-Busch. At its peak, in 1976, it held 16% of the market compared with Anheuser-Busch's 19%.

Beer margins were becoming strained and managers sought methods of cost reduction. In the early 1970's Schlitz sought to save money by manufacturing in North Carolina and shipping the beer to New York. This resulted in the closure of the Brooklyn brewery in 1973 and consequent adverse publicity. Schlitz made further cost savings by the introduction of high temperature fermentation and by gradually increasing the content of cheap malt in its product. Margins were boosted but the combination of several 'stealth cuts' were seen as quality cuts. Unfortunately this also coincided with a regrettable incident where the company image was tarnished due to it having to dump 10m bottles and cans of its Memphis and Tampa beer due to an unrelated quality issue. The image problem was exacerbated as drinkers claimed that the brewery closure, new brewing techniques and new ingredients were a callous abuse of the consumer by cheapening the product but retaining the original price. This was the stealth strategy which went wrong. Many other companies, including brewers, have also engaged in 'value engineering' to reduce costs and increase margins but Schlitz were unlucky that these unannounced and gradual changes (stealth) were forced into the open by the other issues of the brewery closure and the quality issue.

2 years later the situation worsened. Sales had slipped and 1978 market share was 12%. This was still reasonable but Schlitz was now a poor third place in the US domestic market with Anheuser-Busch at 25% and Miller at 19%. At this point the Federal Grand Jury brought over 700 indictments against the company for anti-competitive behaviour. Although the company eventually escaped with only a small fine, the damage to the already injured reputation was terminal. By 1980 market share had fallen to 8%. The final blow was probably the 1981 strike of workers at the Milwaukee brewery. The brewing process was unsustainably inefficient and operation was well below capacity. The Directors decided to close the Milwaukee brewery, the workers took strike action, the reputation suffered further and market share fell further. By June 1982, with market share of 5.6%, the Stroh Brewing Company of Detroit bought Schlitz for a knock down price of $500m. Whilst the brand has been kept alive, the company ceased to exist.

The popular conception is that this was a quality issue due to 'stealth cuts' of process, plant and ingredients but my opinion is that, whilst those aspects were certainly significant contributory factors, the other issues illustrated made an unfortunate and unsurvivable cocktail. However, the salutary lesson is clear – stealth quality cuts can seriously damage a product's survival chances.

Some learning from the military

Almost all British military units have a motto, unique to them. My favourite is probably that of the Black Watch '*nemo me impone lacessit*' – 'no-one attacks/provokes me with impunity' – a gentle Scottish way of saying 'if you annoy me, it will be the last thing you ever do'. This historic regiment wore kilts into battle – including the 2nd battle of Ypres 24th April 1915 where the German enemy nicknamed them 'the ladies from hell'. The crocodile's impressive armour, teeth and jaw strength mean that they could equally claim '*nemo me impone lacessit*'. Perhaps his defensive strategies have something of the Black Watch about them. The crocodile's attacking strategies, however, come from somewhere else.

Despite growing up within the geographical hinterland of the Black Watch, my father did not join them. Instead, he served with the Royal Marine Commandos and with the Special Boat Squadron (SBS). The SBS motto is another favourite, 'Not by strength, but by guile'. The SBS will raid, unseen, and be gone before the enemy even knew they were there. The concept of winning by guile rather than strength is appropriate both to the crocodile and our businesses.

The crocodile has immense strength, but not the dexterity, flexibility and speed to maximise its use. Despite such great strength, his main weapon is guile. The crocodile will lie undetected, 99% submerged, waiting. When the prey comes to drink the crocodile will not leap into action – he is much more subtle and much more effective than that. A sudden splash and ambush at distance would invariably leave the crocodile hungry. Once the prey has been identified, the crocodile sinks and swims slowly to the ambush point – and again, he waits. The prey will drink in seemingly perfect safety. Yards away, the submerged crocodile waits. This use of guile takes the crocodile within a couple of feet of the prey. He inches forward, coming patiently closer and closer, unseen, unheard, and because he is now fully submerged even without rippling the water. Now even closer, the guile has created the opportunity for the perfect ambush. Perhaps the prey takes one step deeper into the water – and SNAP – the ambush is made.

The crocodile's defensive strategies may have something of the Black Watch about them but the strategies by which he gets into his attacking position are undoubtedly 'not by strength, but by guile'. The actual execution of the ambush harnesses his strength, but this would have been useless without the guile.

Whilst on the plains, observing crocodile behaviour, I have been stalked by crocodiles. Those who experience the Serengeti conference speeches will probably have seen the photographs. In one incident I show a series of photos. The first photo shows two crocodiles close to each other. I was on the bank. The next photo a few seconds later shows one of the crocodiles has disappeared. A second or two more his eyes appear just above the surface of the water much closer to me. What is most impressive is that there are no ripples when he pokes his eyes up to check on my location – it is a smooth, perfect use of guile. I retreated and he was unable to spring the ambush. In this event and all of these cases, the danger is not from the crocodiles which I can see, but from the ones I cannot. The switch from stealth to ambush comes very rapidly and I do not intend to be the victim of up to 13 tonnes of ambush jaw pressure. The same is true in business. Those using crocodile strategies against you are invisible until the ambush. You need to be alert as the greatest danger is from the stealth predator. Early identification and neutralisation strategies are essential. In my case that has involved a good exit route, having another observer at a different angle, not lingering at the water's edge and being in areas where the gradient of the riverbed is shallow thus preventing a very rapid exit from the water from our reptilian friend – he moves faster from deep banks. These mitigation strategies are all analogous to your possible business defence against the crocodile.

Conversely if you are using crocodile strategies, all the hard work is done in the stealth phase. Do not emerge too early and do not ambush too early.

Chapter summary

- The crocodile is a stealth and ambush predator.
- He is patient – and waits either partially or fully submerged to execute the perfect ambush.
- Takeovers are the obvious illustration of stealth and ambush strategies but they can be expanded well beyond this limited field.
- In our global markets stealth and ambush can be enacted in different geographies, different markets and the effect in one area may impact on another.
- Ambush marketing is now an immense part of many global organisation's strategies.
- Specifically targeted product launches can be effective stealth and ambush strategies.
- Stealth, the gradual incremental approach pending an ambush, may not always work.
- 'Not by strength, but by guile' – the hard work is in the stealth phase.

CHAPTER 14

Strategies of the ostrich – strategies of bluff

The ostrich is the largest of over 8,000 bird species currently on the planet and is able to adapt to live in a wide variety of habitats including deserts, temperate climates and the Serengeti. This has led to successful ostrich farming in a wide variety of countries and habitats. The myth that the ostrich hides its head in the sand originates from the Greek writer Pliny the Elder who thought he observed this behaviour and recorded it in his writing '*naturalis historia*'. When the ostrich does have its head to the ground it is either feeding or selecting and swallowing small stones which it retains in its stomach to assist the grinding of swallowed food.

The size, long neck and stark plumage of the bird make it distinctive with the male body being mostly black with white wing and tail feathers, whilst the females are more greyish brown. Ostriches are ratites, or flightless birds, a situation shared with the closely related emus and rheas. Their unique feature is that they only have 2 toes on each foot rather than the 3 of most ratites. The larger of the toes resembles a hoof and is thought to be an aid to running.

Ostrich fact file:

Height	Up to 2.6m (9 feet)
Mass	up to 140kg (300 pounds)
Life expectancy	up to 50 years or 70 years in captivity
Diet	seeds, plant matter, occasionally insects
Reproduction	lays eggs in a communal nest which can contain up to 60 eggs. Gestation is 35–45 days

---

Their eggs are the largest of any species weighing about 2.75 pounds and the volume being comparable with about 25 chicken eggs.

Struthio camelus – the ostrich – Greek for 'sparrow camel' – lives a nomadic existence in family groups of 5 – 50 birds. They often graze with other animals such as zebras or antelopes and their keen sense of smell and excellent eyesight assist their accompanying mammals by providing an early warning in the event of the arrival of a predator.

Mating behaviour varies between geographic regions but usually involves the male engaging in a lot of hissing and ostentatious displays of his wings. Males will fight for control of a harem of up to 5 hens but despite this multiple partner mating, the male will usually form a 1–1 pair bond with the dominant female. The mating season starts in March or April and consequent egg laying, in a communal pit 30–60cm deep, generates communal behaviour with females taking turns to incubate by day and the male rests on the eggs by night. One theory for this division of labour is that the black male is more difficult for predators to see at night than the predominantly brown females. Once the eggs hatch the male is usually the more active carer of the young. He is exceedingly territorial over this nesting month and will aggressively resist intruders – even those who would normally generate a flight response in non-nesting months. This territorial aggression continues as the hatchlings grow and then fades as the birds become more peripatetic later in the season.

Ostriches mainly feed on seeds and plant matter but willingly devour locusts and other insects. They will swallow sand and small pebbles which are retained in the gizzard and used as an aid to grinding food. This is an imaginative strategy to overcome the disadvantage of lacking teeth. Their diet incorporates matter with a high water content and so, if required, they can exist for extended periods of time without seeking water supplies. If water is available, however, they will drink regularly and even bathe in it.

The primary defence of the ostrich is its speed and its first instinct when frightened is to run, other than at nesting time. Stretching up to 25 feet per stride the ostrich can travel as fast as 50mph and it is not uncommon for the bird to maintain 30mph for up to 30 minutes. This puts the adult ostrich off the menu for most predators unless they use stealth strategies. Their strength and stamina also makes them a difficult meal for the sprinting cheetah.

Despite their speed, ostriches have a variety of other strategies. They can use defensive stealth strategies and are able to conceal themselves by lying flat with their neck outstretched along the ground. They can also enact 'fight' strategies using deceptively strong wings and strong kicking legs. These features have led to the ostrich being classified as a 'dangerous animal' in the USA, UK and Australia. There are several recorded incidents of ostriches attacking and killing humans, although this did not prevent my father-in-law riding one when given the opportunity whilst in South Africa.

From the perspective of this book there are many lessons we could learn from the ostrich such as their environmental adaptability or increased success rate through communal nesting. However, these have been explored with other animals and so the behaviour we are to concentrate on is the combination of their 'display' strategies. When threatened the ostrich can choose to draw himself up to full height, stamp his feet and spread his wings thus giving the appearance of a much larger and more powerful animal. The comparatively frail bird can then look inspiring and threatening being 9 foot in height and over 6 foot from the tip of one wing feather to the tip of the other wing. It would take a brave combatant to tackle a 9 foot by 6 foot, hissing, stamping, aggressively advancing opponent.

Taking strategy momentarily back to its military roots, the oft sited author of strategy, Sun Tsu stated that "all warfare is based on deception". The ostrich is a master of deception. Despite not having the full substance and bulk to back up its assertions, the ostrich will present itself as large and fierce when in reality it is a bird, hence light boned, and without the advantages of possessing teeth or even substantial claws unlike members of the dog or cat families.

The strategies of the ostrich for larger companies will therefore focus on aggressive ostentatious displays to achieve their objectives, and for smaller companies on the strategies employed to create the impression of greater size.

Ostrich strategies for larger companies

Spreading the wings, creating a hissing noise, stamping the feet and aggressive posturing including advancing towards the threat is the hostile action of the ostrich. When faced with a potential threat, some companies respond with ostrich-like direct, pugnacious, actions – like McDonalds and Microsoft. Their first instinct is to sue. The big, scary, successful, copiously resourced company seeks to scare off the threat using aggressive tactics, much of which are ostrich-like bluff and posturing. Were they to use the 'one on one' competitive analysis of the R.A.D.A.R. (see strategies of the elephant), they would conclude that their financial assets and their ability to have access to expensive legal wizardry could be utilised to their advantage and the opposition, being lighter and smaller in terms of financial assets or expertise would not be able to compete in this area. They are then able to posture, threaten, maybe initiate the legal proceedings but be fairly confident that the opposition will realise that they do not have the resources to complete and therefore choose to retreat before the financial assets they do possess are drained in legal costs or before the time they would have to divert from productive activity would be too costly to sidetrack in fighting off the corporate behemoth opponent.

We have previously discussed the McLibel case where McDonalds used ostrich strategies to scare away two individuals and failed abysmally. However, they have been using these strategies in other areas with varying degrees of success. Consider the age old battle between McDonalds and arch rivals Burger King.

Burger King merged with Pillsbury in 1967 after an unrealised ambition to float on the New York Stock Exchange. In the 1970's McDonalds forged ahead with an enormous expansion programme. Burger King responded with a campaign targeting McDonald's weaknesses of regimented inflexible burger making. The 'have it your way' campaign emphasised Burger King's ability to adapt the burger to customer demands with or without gherkins, lettuce or whatever. By the early 1980's the aggressiveness of Burger King's campaign stepped up the confrontation by attacking the McDonald's burger as fried rather than flame grilled. They emphasised the superiority of flame grilling, their superiority in blind taste tests and accentuated the fact that their burgers were bigger than McDonald's. This had now turned into an acrimonious burger battle. Burger King started to make winning inroads into the burger market. McDonald's, and the third competitor Wendy's, both reacted with ostrich strategies – they
→

→

postured aggressively, made a lot of noise and flapped their wings in legal action to seek to have certain Burger King advertisements banned. This is an example of inappropriate use of ostrich strategies as all it created was additional customer awareness for Burger King as news agencies reported the confrontation.

McDonald's successful ostrich strategy was then to focus not on the burgers of Burger King, but on the doughboy of Pillsbury, the parent company. The increase of lawsuits and open animosity was offensive to such a traditional mid-Western company and they steered Burger King into backing down from this aggressive advertising approach. McDonald's ostrich strategy had won – the direct legal approach had failed but the flapping of wings at the vulnerable, conflict averse parent company resulted in competitive retreat by Burger King. I would argue that for a number of reasons, 20 years later Burger King have still not recovered.

Microsoft is also a serial user of ostrich strategies. If Microsoft see any form of competition they will either buy it or make wing flapping posturing via the courts, or mostly the internal legal department. Even in the case of 17 year old Canadian Mike Rowe who registered his site Mike Rowe Soft .com. Microsoft lawyers e-mailed, subsequently made a derisory offer for the name and the naïve Mike Rowe fell into the obvious trap by offering to sell at a higher price. Early in 2004 a 25 page letter from Microsoft to Mike Rowe stating their case for infringement and violation and demanding release of the name. Mike Rowe alerted the press who will usually seize any anti-Microsoft story with alacrity and Microsoft temporarily backed down. Returning to the fight after a few days, once the publicity had subsided, Microsoft again spread its ostrich wings, flapped, postured, created threatening noises and agreed an out of court settlement which included some Microsoft goodies and a X-box!

I was once being escorted around Virgin Group's modest London headquarters and as we went through the first floor my corporate tour guide pointed out an internal legal team who, in his words, "spend all their time suing people who try to use the Virgin name" and therefore illegally infringe upon the group's legal identity. With a modicum of research I was not able to identify sufficient legal cases to justify such a team and therefore conclude that most infringements presumably cease with the use of the legal department's ostrich wings – flap, hiss, stamp, advance and scare the opponent away.

McDonalds, Microsoft and Virgin – all exceedingly successful organisations and all adept users of the ostrich strategy. They flap their wings, in these cases legal wings, create a noise and the opposition, realising the financial strength behind the ostrich strategy users usually relents and settles out of court perhaps in some cases, such as Mike Rowe, even for a fraction of what they could have achieved had they the resources to counter the legal wing flapping. In each case the score is usually one nil to the ostrich. McDonalds may have made some initial mistakes, but they won with the strategy eventually. Microsoft may have initially made a media blunder but recovered to achieve their objective with the site and win. However, all have a vast number of files stored which illustrate where they have previously used the strategies of the ostrich and won. Assuming my guide's comments to be true, I presume Virgin Group does too.

Stop flapping and run

The ostrich always has a secondary strategy. Aggressive posturing, flapping and hissing, stamping the feet and advancing threateningly may be enough to deter most threats – especially if you are 9 foot tall, or a global multinational quasi-monopoly. However, despite the weapons of strong kicking legs, the ostrich will not out-threaten a lion. Hyenas will prevail if in sufficient numbers, a leopard could win if sufficiently stealthy and even the lighter built cheetah will stand a sporting chance if the ostrich is static. The ostrich is perfectly aware of this, and like the zebra, is able to initiate a rapid market exit strategy. Exit strategies are dealt with when considering the strategies of the zebra, including when to make the choice to exit – too early or too late could court disaster. The issue for the ostrich is deciding when to switch from aggressive posturing strategies to flight strategies. There comes a point when the ostrich realises that its posturing is not working and that the opponent is now more threat than threatened. In this case there is usually a swift reversal from aggression to exit rather than the zebra's more considered movement from 'pause' or 'freeze' to 'flight'. The ostrich rapidly switches between extremes of strategy once plan 'A' (threat display) is deemed to have been unsuccessful and plan 'B' (exit) is instigated.

In March 2004 Microsoft Corporation was hit by record fine of 497 million euros ($600 million) by the European Union for abusing its dominant market position with Windows. According to Mario Monti, the European Competition Commissioner, Microsoft had abused its dominance of the operating systems market both by tying Windows Media Player to Windows and by failing to release information about Windows to competitors in the server market. The company was, in

➜

→

short, instructed to offer other manufacturers a version of Windows without Windows Media Player.

Microsoft responded with ostrich strategies – aggressive posturing, attacking the decision and launching an appeal which would take several years to complete. As part of this ostrich response Microsoft brought organisations such as The International Intellectual Property Institute, the Institute for Policy Innovation and the neo-liberal Progress & Freedom Foundation to add weight to its argument – in effect increasing the level of aggressive wing flapping. They supported Microsoft's appeal and attempted annulment of the judgement and the fine. In late December 2005 the Court of First Instance of the European Communities rejected the application of these organisations and thus materially weakened Microsoft's appeal.

In a subsequent news teleconference with International Journalists on 22 December 2005, Brad Smith, Senior Vice President and General Counsel of Microsoft made a carefully worded statement which included:

> *"We have an opportunity, as you know, to decide whether to appeal today's decision to the European Court of Justice. It's too early to know whether we will or we won't appeal. We will have to study today's decision and we'll have to make a decision. Even if we appeal, we obviously need to start moving forward with compliance, and so I think compliance is our first order of business today."*

Microsoft was keeping its ostrich strategy options open – continue the posturing and wing flapping but simultaneously starting on compliance with the 2004 ruling. This compliance enabled the possibility of the ostrich switching to its alternative strategy of running when it has met a more threatening opponent. A spokesman from the European Commission welcomed the order of the President of the Court of First Instance because it meant that the Commission's March 2004 Decision became effective immediately and thus forced Microsoft into compliance. At that point, Microsoft could continue their appeal, or switch to the ostrich's secondary strategy of running. This is interesting as Microsoft have been incredibly successful globally for over a decade with the primary strategy of posturing and threatening attack. They are not accustomed to the secondary strategy of running and therefore would be likely to be tempted to stay in the vicinity of the threat for too long. The timing of the decision to switch from wing to leg would be vital.

→

→ Microsoft chose to stay and posture by appealing against the decision. Microsoft lost the appeal in September 2007. Microsoft had persisted with the 'threat and bluff' strategy of the ostrich and had not taken the plan 'B' of rapid exit – in their case paying. July 2006 saw a further fine of Eu260m and non-compliance resulted in a further fine of Eu899m in February 2008 ($1.1bn). Competition Commissioner Neelie Kroes said *"Microsoft was the first company in 50 years of EU competition policy that the Commission has had to fine for failure to comply with an antitrust decision."* Consistent with its strategy, Microsoft appealed against this fine in may 2008 to *"seek clarity from the court"*. Both sides are fighting this battle aggressively. The judgement for Microsoft is whether to and when to make that shift from posturing to running away. The experienced ostrich makes the decision rapidly and implements it immediately. My opinion is that Microsoft are inexperienced at running away and so are likely to remain in the fray too long. Were this to happen Eu497m + Eu260m + Eu899m plus whatever new non-compliance fines are levied will become too high a prize for the European bureaucrats to let go. They will therefore press on. However, Microsoft should have little to fear as the precedent has already been set. In 1999 France illegally banned British beef and was fined Eu100,000 per day for doing so. The French Government simply refused to pay. If this example is followed, the courts will continue to levy ever increasing fines, but Microsoft will probably never have to open its cheque book!

Ostrich strategies for small companies

For smaller companies the strategies are not about the aggressive posturing of the ostrich but rather are about the spreading of wings to look bigger than they actually are. It is a strategy of bluff relating to size or capability. Before considering some of the possibilities I would like to make a challenge – sometimes big is not best. Sometimes it is good to look larger than you actually are, sometimes it is not. Many organisations make the assumption that they should seek growth. I would suggest that this is not necessarily always the wisest option.

Most customers do not look at size. Fred Reichheld's research at Bain & Co in 1996 identified the main reasons customers left supplier companies. 68% were due to 'perceived indifference'. I would suggest that the larger the company, the greater the chance of creating an image of indifference. It is not necessarily genuine indifference – just the customers perception of indifference. I believe the phrase 'perception is reality' was first used by Harvard Professor John Kotter, although the list of people using it, and claiming to be the origin is rather large. A small company is possibly better able to maintain a special and personal relationship than a larger one – or a small company seeking to look like a larger one. In her book '*Alpha Dogs: How Your Small Business Can Become a Leader of the Pack*' Donna Fenn remarks that customers are setting higher and higher standards for service. She continues "Customers want to be wooed and wowed at every turn". Sometimes this is the preserve of the small.

Another reason to question whether big is beautiful is to consider your motivation for being in business – why do you do the work that you do? One good friend emerged from the world of big business to start his own small company. It was successful and in due course had grown from a small company to a medium sized company. It then merged with a larger organisation and in turn the larger organisation merged with an even larger organisation. My friend then found that only 6 or 7 years after leaving the world of big business in order to enjoy his work more, he was back in the same position, albeit wealthier, but enjoyment and control of his own business destiny rather than remuneration were the drivers for his entrepreneurial activity. For him 'big' was cumbersome and restrictive, 'small' was liberating and beautiful. E.F. Schumacher produced the groundbreaking book '*Small Is Beautiful: Economics as if People Mattered*' back in 1973. Whilst the essence of this book was that of economics, the principle of 'small is beautiful' may be appropriate to some organisations. It may be that a review of the areas covered in the 'values' section of the strategies of the giraffe chapter may make some pointers regarding whether growth should be an aspiration or not. For many it will, for some it won't. In addition, the chapters about the strategies of the elephant, the warthog the hippopotamus and the cheetah can all give us lessons on where being small may be an advantage.

Lessons in being small – from the elephant

In the chapter of the strategies of the elephant we were concerned with corporate knowledge and developed some analytical tools to explore the competitive position of our organisations. It may seem paradoxical for the elephant to advise a company to stay small, but if on the R.A.D.A.R. analysis of an organisation there are strong comparative advantages in the areas of reputation (end user) and relationship (supply chain); and if these strengths are vested in certain individuals there is a case for ignoring the strategies of the ostrich which enable you to look larger than you actually are. The challenge of growing large is to do so and retain the reputation or relationship.

Another very good friend of over 20 years runs a hairdressing salon. He has no intention of franchising the business, no intention of expanding into multiple salons or developing new business in new neighbourhoods, and understands that when he retires he will not be able to sell the business for a fortune. Despite having negligible academic qualifications, he has a business acumen which would put many MBA graduates to shame. He is fully aware that he is the main draw for his customers – whether they actually have him or one of his other staff cutting the hair, without him the business loses the core reputational and relationship aspects. Overambitious plans to expand would not transfer to others the relationships which some customers have built up with him over 2 decades. Once he retires, there may be some customer loyalty to the location, but most is to him, his banter and the culture he instils within the salon.

I recall a conversation with one customer when forming a new company and seeking to transfer their business. As we found our table for lunch, I started with what I intended to be a brief summary of why we were forming the new company and was rapidly interrupted by the customer. "Do I still get you?" was the blunt question. "Yes" was the briefest of answers. "Then I don't need to know the details, that is absolutely fine by me – now where's the menu?". Reputation and relationship can be jeopardised by growth – even if it is the bluff of growth demonstrated by the ostrich.

Strategies of the elephant also outlined the analytical technique of Competitive Mapping. If the market positioning is that relationship with key individuals is deemed important, the ostrich may not be the animal whose strategies should be emulated. If specialist skills score high, consider expansion, or even looking big, with caution.

Lessons in being small – from the warthog

The chapter on the strategies of the warthog was about protecting vulnerabilities. Growth brings new vulnerabilities. I recall another group of successful friends who had started their own media business. They were (or rather are) superb at their jobs and work flooded in. This growth resulted in them having to undertake more and more co-ordination and organisational roles to enable the smooth running of the business – everything from recruitment to systems, from authorising payments to staff and suppliers to finding ever larger premises. This administrative activity was not their gifting and removed them from the clients. The choice was then whether to employ people to undertake the organisational aspects of the business or whether to employ people to undertake the customer relationship side. If they chose to bring in others to take on board the organisational side, they would be out of the office almost all the time and then not managing the business culture, identity and communications in the way they wanted. If they chose to employ people to engage in the customer relationship side they would have to transfer those personal relationship, reputation and loyalty. They wisely chose to retain their personal customer interfaces, recruit and then transfer the administrative and organisational aspects but then seek to move on all new customer contacts to other new recruits in the company. The influx of administrative, non-fee earning people make an immediate negative impression on profitability. Fortunately the freeing of their time overcame this with yet more work flowing in and profitability was back on track 6 months later, but in this example, the newly growth generated vulnerability, needed active management and strong protection. For many, the courage to hand over either the customer facing or administration aspects of their business constrain them to remaining small – and for many that is a good strategic decision – there is no need to look large.

Lessons in being small – from the hippopotamus

The lessons from the hippopotamus were all about being the champion of the niche and not seeking to stray outside it. The more specialist the market offering, the more likely that ostrich strategies would be inappropriate. For niche players, part of the competitive advantage is that you are experts in the niche. Growing from the niche, or creating the impression by ostrich strategies that you are too large will negate the customer perceived specialities of the niche. King of the river, but cumbersome on land, the challenge for those following the strategies of the hippopotamus is not whether to seek success on land and in due course seek to appear to have a wide market offering, but rather how to grow the river. Growth for the hippopotamus strategies is more about growing the market and letting the company ride the growth graph rather than seeking to grow the company per se.

Lessons in being small – from the cheetah

Strategies of the cheetah were about sacrificing everything for speed. The cheetah gets there first and has a number of inbuilt features which enable speed and also enable a rapid change of direction. The smaller and lighter an organisation is, the faster it can move and more particularly, the faster it can change direction. Huge research and development budgets can develop projects which get a product to market quickly. Huge marketing budgets can generate market penetration rapidly. Being quick, like the cheetah, is not the prerogative of the small. However, the ability to change direction rapidly in response to the movement of prey being chased is usually something larger organisations find most difficult. Small may not always be beautiful, but it is usually fleet of foot.

Lessons in being small – from the ostrich

Having considered the possible risks of looking large, having completed a R.A.D.A.R. analysis and a Competitive Mapping, having listened to the advice of the elephant, warthog, hippopotamus and cheetah, if looking big is still the desire how can it be achieved?

Many smaller companies feel intimidated by competing with larger ones. I recall my training company three times being down to the last two companies being considered by a prospective client for a job which we had the ability and resources to complete. On all three occasions in my mind, the large multi-national customer company chose the significantly larger competitors rather than us as they were more comfortable with a larger company, despite their offering of staff with, in the customers words, less gravitas, less experience and fewer relevant qualifications than us. Exploiting the perceived insecurity of choosing to work with a smaller supplier, as a sales pitch IBM used to use the tag line "No-one ever got sacked for choosing IBM" – there are times when big is beautiful.

So if you want to look big, to stretch out the wings and look 9 foot by 6 foot what could a small company do? Following is a fairly short list of suggestions and points for consideration. I could devote a whole book to the top 100 tips of ostrich bluffing – but here are a few:

- Pay enormous attention to your web site.
  - Pay extra to make a thoroughly professional job.
  - Make it as dynamic as possible – no-one reads dull text.
  - Avoid 'who we are' photos – it gives away that you only have a team of 10. Personal profiles run against the ostrich's bluff.
  - A displayed client list of only 20 shows that you only have 20 – especially if they are not all global household names – only use big customers' names.
  - Do your research – look at 20 relevant (possibly competitor) large company web sites – what do they have in common? How do they differ from yours? Don't necessarily copy, but learn lessons.
  - The 1990's habit of a visitor counter on the site deserves to stay in the 1990's – yet still I see them !
- Pay enormous attention to your branding.
  - Branding is more than a logo (see the chapter 'strategies of the giraffe'); it is a whole way of doing things.

- ○ What are the values of your brand? And does everything in the company re-inforce that? For example, a value of 'quality' is not helped by a slow response to an e-mail. The value of 'professionalism' is not helped by a voice mail message which is not changed daily (it takes 5 seconds) to reflect when the caller could expect you to call back, nor is failing to call back when that expectation is set.
- ○ Does your address fit with the brand? Use multiple occupation serviced offices with a suitable address – no-one will know that you only have 2 rooms in the complex! Similarly, on industrial sites, 'unit 6' is fine – no-one knows whether it is a small unit or a giant factory.
- Pay enormous attention to your communications.
  - ○ Written communication in 'comic sans' says "we're really small and mistakenly think that comic sans is a cool font".
  - ○ Use of off the shelf clip art is not for the ostrich.
  - ○ Do your newsletters appear to be derived from a very small number of authors? The ostrich would ensure that the impression of width is given by using different styles.
  - ○ Letters (on high gms, high quality paper), e-mails (with corporate logo and background), invoices (treat them with as much care as you would a letter), compliment slips (high gms, professional looking – no matter how irrelevant they are).
  - ○ Don't hand write envelopes.
  - ○ Don't have telephone and fax numbers which are the same.
  - ○ Don't include mobile numbers on anything except personal business cards.
  - ○ Personal E-mails sent at 10pm either show that you're working on another continent (if so, say so) or that you're catching up after the kids are in bed.
- Pay enormous attention to your customer contact.
  - ○ Avoid P.O. Boxes for your main mail address.
  - ○ If you are too small to have a receptionist, outsource it to a company so that the phone is answered in person by someone stating your company name. If the Managing Director answers the phone – it is clear that you are small.
  - ○ Think about what car you drive when you visit a customer – a Ferrari is undoubtedly not a corporate car! To look like a larger company you may have to be slightly duller – Jags and Mercedes. As a rule of thumb I suggest that small company Directors drive the same sort of car that their customer Managing Directors would drive – if your client base is SME's (Small to Medium sized Enterprises), a Jag or Merc may be too ostentatious.
- Pay enormous attention to getting your name in print, in the media and in people's minds.

- ○ Write articles and get them published in relevant journals.
- ○ Become a pundit for a T.V., radio or newspaper – start small and build up.
- ○ Be seen as an expert in your specialist field – someone people call – and give that advice for free if there is publicity attached.

The humble ostrich has lessons for the large and the small, but it is an animal whose strategies have a healthcare warning – beware. Looking aggressive, using the threat of litigation or otherwise may not be the image some large companies may want to portray. Looking larger than they are may also not be the image some smaller companies would find wise. However, the ostrich has been extremely successful in maximising their height and wingspan to appear large and threatening. Their aggressive behaviour amplifies their perceived bulk, and although all that lies behind the bluff are some soft feathers and tasty ostrich meat, their bluff has seen off countless predators to the extent that they are far from any endangered list. The strategies of the ostrich are a resounding success for this giant. But remember, the ostrich always has a second strategy available – rapid strategy reversal from bluff and aggressive advance to exceedingly rapid exit.

Chapter summary

- The ostrich is the largest bird on the planet and uses a variety of interesting strategies including communal nesting and lying low for concealment.
- When threatened, the first instinct is usually to run.
- The second option, often the first when protecting a nest, is one of bluff and deception.
- Appearing big, appearing frightening, appearing aggressive and intimidating are the strategies of the ostrich.
- For larger companies, the emphasis is on aggressive posturing.
- For smaller companies the emphasis is on looking big.
- In the case of both small and large, the ostrich strategies are not for everyone and careful consideration before use is imperative.

References

Berry, S.J. (1994) The dedicated supplier – strategic sense or marketing madness? Manchester Business School MBA project.

BBDO University (2001) *Understanding your Client's Business* Sitges (July).

Bonabeau, E (2003) Don't trust your gut *Harvard Business Review* (May) 116–124.

Bower, M. (1966) *The Will to Manage* McGraw Hill, New York.

Branson, R (1988) *Richard Branson the autobiography: losing my virginity* Virgin Publishing, London.

Ciulla, Joanne B (1999) The Importance of leadership in shaping business values *Long Range Planning* Vol 32 No.2 166

Collins, J.C. & Porras, J.I. (1994, 1997, 1998) *Built to Last* Century, London.

Cooley, A.R. (1995) The impact of culture on the implementation of strategic marketing planning: a participatory action research approach Loughborough University M.Phil

Corboy, M & O'Corrbui, D (1999) The seven deadly sins of strategy *Management Accounting* (November) 29–30

Crainer, S & Dearlove, D (2003) *The ultimate book of business brands insights from the worlds 50 greatest brands* Capstone, Oxford.

Dilts, R (1990). *Changing Belief Systems with NLP* Meta Publications, Capitola CA.

Dilts, R, Hallbom Smith (1990) *Beliefs: Pathways to Health & Well-*being Metamorphous Press, Portland, OR.

Fenn, D (2005) *Alpha Dogs: How Your Small Business Can Become a Leader of the Pack* Harper Collins, New York.

Grabowski H.G. & Vernon J.M.(1994) 'Returns to R&D on new drug introductions in the 1980's' *Jnl Health Econ* (December) 13(4) 383–406.

Herkstroter, C.A.J. (1997) *Introduction to statement of General Business Practices* Shell

Johnson, G and Scholes, K (1988) *Exploring Corporate Strategy* Prentice Hall, Hemel Hempstead.

Katcher, A & Pasternak, K (2002) *Managing Your Strengths* Xlibris.

Kim, W.C. & Mauborgne, R (2005) *Blue Ocean Strategy* Harvard Business School Press, Harvard CN.

MacGregor Burns, J (1977) *Leadership* Harper & Rowe, New York.

MacMillan, C, Putten A.B.Van, McGrath R.G. (2003) 'Global gamesmanship' *Harvard Business Review* (May) 63–70.

Nohira, N, Joyce, W, and Robertson, B (2003) 'What Really Works' *Harvard Business Review* (June) 43–52.

Pekar, P and Allio, R (1994) 'Making alliances work: guidelines for success' *Long Range Planning* Vol 27 No 4 54–65.

Pfizer journal (1999) vol 3 no 2 (Summer)

Rost, J. (1991) *Leadership for the twenty-first century* 102 Praegar, New York.

Saker, J and Speed, R (1992) 'Corporate culture: is it really a barrier to marketing planning?' *Journal of Marketing Management* 8(2), 177–181.

Schein, E.H. (1999) *The Corporate Culture Survival Guide* Jossey-Bass, San Francisco

Schumacher, E.F. (1973) *Small Is Beautiful: Economics As If People Mattered* Harper & Row, New York.

Sheshunoff, A (1991) ' Reality is here, are you ready?' *ABA Banking Journal* Vol 83(7) (July) 31–36.

Tabaksblat, M (1997) *Dialogue with society* Unilever

Trout, J (2001) *Big Brands Big Trouble: Lessons Learnt the Hard Way* John Wiley & Sons, New York.

Webley, S (1999) 'Sources of Corporate Values' *Long Range Planning* Vol 32 no.2 173–8

Welch, J & Byrne, J.A. (2001) *What I've learnt leading a great company and great people* Headline, London.

Which? (2006) Child Catchers, the tricks used to push unhealthy food to your children (January).

Zook, C (2001) *Profit from the core* Harvard Business School Press, Harvard CN.

Index of names

Index of companies/organisations

Do you want more?

Register on the **'Serengeti Business Network'** to hear further stories of the implementation of the strategies in this book. For details, see:

www.strategiesoftheserengeti.com

- **Keynote speaking** – on aspects of Strategies of the Serengeti and wider subject matter. For details, see:

  www.stephenberry.com

- A range of **training events** and **strategy development** events based on the Strategies of the Serengeti. For details, see:

  www.strategiesoftheserengeti.com

- Stephen Berry is a Director of Neos Learning. For a wider range of Neos Learning training and development in our innovative style, see:

  www.neoslearning.com

- **Artwork, posters and drawings** – the animal drawings featured in this book are available as a range of posters in various sizes and formats, with and without quotes from the book. For details, see:

  www.strategiesoftheserengeti.com